Crossing the Frontiers of Conflict
in
The North East
and
Jammu and Kashmir

Crossing the Frontiers of Conflict

in

The North East

and

Jammu and Kashmir

From Real Politik to Ideal Politik

Lt. Gen. V.K. Nayar, PVSM, SM (RETD.)

Under the auspices of
Centre for Policy Research, New Delhi

SHIPRA

The views expressed in the study are those of the author and not of the Centre for Policy Research.

(First Published in India in 2005)

Rs. 2000

ISBN: 978-81-7541-218-7

2027 PoD Impression

Crossing the Frontiers of Conflict in The North East and Jammu and Kashmir

Published by:
SHIPRA PUBLICATIONS
LG 18-19, Pankaj Central Market
I.P. Ext., Patparganj, Delhi 110092, India
+91 11 47322068; 9650028065, 9810522367
info@shiprapublication.com
www.shiprapublication.com

Foreword

The internal security environment in the country over the past decades has become more intense, volatile and complex. Conflicts are wide spread and terrorism and violence have become the main tools to resolve social, political, ethnic and religious differences and conflicts. The disturbed geopolitical environment in our neighbourhood and drugs and arms with its cross border nexus have facilitated ill designs of dissidents, extremists and their supporters' to escalate conflicts and perpetrate greater violence. The situation in the sensitive border states of the North East and Jammu and Kashmir is of special concern and poses the biggest challenge to the nation.

Terrorism, insurgency and extremism are the outcome of discontent and deprivation and thrives on denial, frustration, insensitivity and lack of response to just demands and aspirations, actual or perceived, resulting in a sense of alienation. The problems intrinsically rest on domestic roots, which are aggravated by the external factors. Recent trends in electoral politics of expediency and exploitation of diversities add to insecurity, divide societies and encourages religious fundamentalism and ethnic consciousness. This has resulted in diffusion of the state machinery and lack of governance. The state response has been primarily in the law and order field resulting in greater militarisation of the environment, without adequate response to the underlying fundamental causes of the turmoil.

With his vast experience in handling politico-social problems and those related to the law and order in the states of the North East and Jammu and Kashmir, Gen. Nayar is perhaps best placed to address the wide spectrum of issues in seeking a solution to these conflicts. He underlines the need for a policy shift and a holistic approach, with major initiatives in the political field by the national leadership.

I hope that this book by Gen. Nayar will be widely read and appropriate policy actions will be taken by the policy makers based on the constructive approach contained in this timely book.

Centre for Policy Research
New Delhi
30 July 2004

Dr. Charan Wadhva
President

Preface

Internal threats to India's security since independence have not only increased but in the last two decades these have grown in magnitude and complexity, giving rise to divisive and secessionist tendencies. The state has failed to respond adequately to these challenges, which is in sharp contrast to our effective response to external threats. In the years to come our inner weaknesses and instability will encourage external threats and pose a serious challenge to our security.

Each of our internal security problems have a historical, political and socio-economic content and in some cases these have also developed ethnic, religious and politico-strategic complexion. The problems of terrorism and insurgency in Punjab, Jammu & Kashmir and the North-East are different in their content, and their internal and external dimensions differ. Our major failure has been in identifying and recognising these, responses to the growing threat of terrorism and insurgency have been mainly confined to the law and order sphere and we have failed to deal with the situation in a holistic manner. Lack of a comprehensive and well formulated policy has resulted in event to event responses and disjointed functioning of the instruments of the Govt.

In our continental size country, there are diversities in the multiple areas of economy, social, ethnic and religious, between regions and within each region. Instead of resolving these or reducing their impact, in recent years these have been exploited for narrow parochial ends. The root cause of this is bad politics. In the last two decades, political will and perceptions have been primarily confined to electoral politics, which has led to political instability and subverted the state apparatus and institutions in most fields.

While political distortions, economic disparity and bad governance are common ingredients of the ferment in the entire society and the country as such but its effect in the disturbed areas of our interest are far more grave. It is therefore important to understand its implications.

Similarly, social, cultural, ethnic and religious factors and their inter play in each area are relevant as they are a part of the overall environment and impinge on security and handling of security related issues. Security involves and affects human beings and embraces all aspects of public life. It includes physical, economic, social, cultural and religious security. While physical security is the foundation on which actions in other fields are built to secure the environment but success can only be achieved by cohesive and coordinated efforts in all fields. This is the basis of conflict resolution.

To keep focus and due to the distinctive parameters of each area, the study is confined to the high priority areas of Jammu and Kashmir and the North-East on our frontiers . A separate chapter has been devoted to drugs and arms linkages; its cross border nexus and impact on internal security.

Acknowledgement

The idea of such a study was conceived during my tenure in Manipur and Nagaland in the 1990's which fructified at the Centre for Policy Research. I owe a special thanks to the then President Dr. V.A. Pai Panandiker, who helped in formulating the project and defining its contours. The continued support and help of his successor Dr. Charan D. Wadhva helped in completion of the project. My grateful thanks are also due to all the faculty members and staff of the Centre for Policy Research for their help and support. This apart, there are many acknowledgements due to my friends, supporters and people from all walks of life and professions in the North East, Jammu and Kashmir and in Delhi and other parts of India, who shared their experience and views with me. I shall ever remain grateful for their cooperation and consideration.

Lt. Gen. V.K. Nayar, PVSM, SM (RETD.)

Contents

Part I

The North-East Imbroglio

1

Geography and Historical Perspective

Geography

The North Eastern region has some common characteristics of its own, quite distinct from other parts of the country, whether from the point of view of geography, socio-economic conditions, political history and composition of people suffused with migration from outside. It occupies a strategic position, hills and forests cover 70 per cent of the region and cultivatable land is only 15.6 per cent as against the all India figure of 46 per cent. In Assam it is 34 per cent, Tripura 23.5 per cent, Meghayala 7.99 per cent, Nagaland 11 per cent, Manipur 6.3 per cent and Mizoram 3.7 per cent. Eighty per cent of the people depend on agriculture. 64.80 per cent of the scheduled tribes live in the hilly region, 12.83 per cent in plains and 22.38 per cent in the foot hills. The region is rich in forest produce, gas and hydro power potential. Communications in the region are underdeveloped and hazardous and are a handicap to economic development. Migration of outsiders and foreigners has put pressure on land and its resources.

The region is located in the North Eastern corner of India, between 22° and 29° North latitude and 89° – 4 and 97° – 51. East longitude covering an area of 255083 Sq.Km and is linked to rest of the country by the narrow Siliguri Corridor of 20 Kms width. The total population is 3,84,95,089 (2001 census). The North-East (NE) accounts for 7.7 per cent of country's land mass and 3.75 per cent of its population. It consists of three distinct regions of the Assam Valley, Purbanchal and Meghalaya Mikir Region. The Assam valley is demarcated by the Eastern Himalayas, Patkai Naga Hills and Garo, Khasi and Mikir Hills. The valley is 720 Kms long and 80 Kms wide and covers an area of 58274 Sq.Kms. Purbanchal covers an area of 94800 Sq.Kms. and includes Nagaland, Manipur, Tripura and Mizo and Chachar Hills. It borders China in the

North-East, Myanmar in the South East and Bangladesh in the South West. The Meghalaya Mikir Region includes the Garo, Khasi and Jaintia Hills and the extended Mikir Hills. The region extending from Dhansiri in the East to Singmari in the west is 400 Kms long and 40 Kms wide and covers an area of 35291 Sq. Kms. It comprises the state of Meghalaya and a portion of Karbi Anglong and North Chachar Hills (NC Hills) districts of Assam[1].

It is strategically located and has borders with China, Bhutan, Myanmar and Bangladesh in the North, East and South and militants have found sanctuaries in these countries. Bases in these countries provide easy access to areas in the North-East. The NE has approximately 4200 Kms of India's international boundary. The region has immense geopolitical significance. It is the eastern part of the region, which is dominated by the head waters of major rivers of Hwang HO, Yanktizekiang, Sikang, Irrawadi and the Brahmaputra. The topography is rough and fractured, with dense forests and poor accessibility.

The other area of great significance is the Patkai Range. This forms the water shed between India and Myanmar. This one hill range has influenced the history of the North-East and Assam the most. The Patkai Pass has proved as historic as the Khyberpass in North-West of India (Now in Pakistan). It is through this pass that Ahoms came to Kamrup and established their kingdom, which lasted for 600 years, the longest in Indian history. Again, Burmese entered through this pass in the early 19th century at the instance of Ahom King Chandra Kanta whose reign was plagued by internecine civil conflicts and bloodshed. The presence and overlordship of Burmans brought no relief to the Ahom Kingdom. In fact there was further deterioration which resulted in intervention by the East India company. The Anglo-Burman War ended in favour of the company and by virtue of the treaty of Yandaboo in 1826, the Ahom Kingdom virtually went into oblivion. During the second world war, it was again through the Patkai pass that the British built a metalled road connecting Assam valley to Hukawang Valley in Burma for movement of troops and equipment. Even today Naga insurgents and other North Eastern secessionist groups find shelter in Patkai Ranges.

Although Chittagong Hill Tracts (CHT) is a part of Bangladesh, the area influences to a great deal the security environment in the North-East. It forms an enclave between Mizoram in the East and Tripura in the west. CHT is home to twelve tribes, the largest being Chakmas and Marmas who are predominantly Budhists and Tripuris who are both Hindus and Christians as their counterparts across the border[2]. The partition of the subcontinent has shaped the events in this troubled area. As CHT has a population which was 97 per cent non muslim, it was logically assumed that it would become a part of India. But the Radcliffe Award did the Chakmas a great injustice by awarding it to Pakistan.

Chakmas had even raised the Indian Tricolour at Rangamati on 15 August, 1947 in anticipation of joining India. This has remained as an act of betrayal in the East Pakistani and now Bangladeshi psyche and the loyalty of these hill people will remain always suspect in their eyes, even after the birth of Bangladesh. The area of CHT has been a heaven for insurgents of the North-East and a distant home land of tribals of this area.

Communications

The surface communications to the North-East are tenuous, with only one road cum rail bridge over Brahamputra River, which was opened to traffic in 1963. The Kalia-Bhomara road bridge near Tezpur came up in 1987. The third road cum rail bridge at Jogighopa was commissioned in 1996. The fourth road cum rail bridge is planned to come up near Dibrugarh but its completion may take another decade. The railway line on the South bank of Brahmputra River was converted into broad gauge up to Guwahati in 1984 and up to Dibrugarh in 1997. The new South Bank extension across the Narnarayan Setu at Jogighopa will also be a broad gauge. Thus, with the commissioning of the Jogighopa bridge flood proof routing of the traffic into and out of Assam and along the South bank has become a reality. NH31 which connects the North-East is in bad state of maintenance.

The air services to the North-East are prone to disruption due to bad weather and climatic conditions. All the states are connected by air except Meghalaya and Mizoram as they have small size air strips which cannot take Boeing aircraft.The airfield at Umroi near Shillong and a new airport at Langpui in Mizoram are being developed to take bigger aircrafts. The Borjor airport in Assam is being upgraded to international standards. The region's location, isolation and inaccessibility continue to exert considerable influence on geopolitical perceptions and are a cause for socio-political instability and economic backwardness.

Mineral and Natural Resources

Assam produces 5.25 million tonnes of oil annually, which is 60 per cent of India's production. Of the three refineries in Assam, Digboi produces 0.58 million tonnes, Guwahati 0.77 million tonnes and Bongaigaon 0.46 million[3] tonnes per annum. The oil shale reserves are capable of sustaining crude oil production of 140 million tonnes annually for 100 years. The annual value of crude oil produced in Assam is approximately Rs.2000 crores. A new refinery is being set up at Numgligarh with a capacity of 3 million tonnes of crude oil.

Tea and jute are other major agricultural products which are exported from Assam. Assam was estimated to produce 402.9 million Kg of tea in 1993, almost 50 per cent of India's total production. The current estimated annual turnover is over rupees 3000 crores. This is a major foreign exchange earner[4]. In 1993/94 North-East produced 729000 tons of jute[5] but most of it goes to jute mills in Calcutta as Assam has only a few jute mills. The North-East has vast forest resources and a number of plywood factories and a variety of cottage industries based on forest produce have come up. Unplanned exploitation of forests has created ecological imbalances in many places. Assam also has large quantities of other mineral resources like coal, gas, lime stone and Mica. The region has 40 per cent of the water wealth of the country.

Anthropoligically, the North-East is inhabited by races of Mongoloid stock besides the Indo-Aryan groups. Barring the Khasis and Jantias who belong to Austric linguistic groups (or Mon Khmer cultural groups of Burma), almost all the other hill tribes belong to the Tibeto-Chinese and Tibeto Burman sub-family. There are over 200 ethnic groups and over 400 languages and dialects are spoken in the area. There is also vast cultural and religious diversity. There is high percentage of Scheduled Tribes (93 per cent in Mizoram, 84 per cent in Nagaland, 80 per cent in Meghalaya, 70 per cent in Arunachal Pradesh, 28 per cent in Tripura, 27 per cent in Manipur and 10 per cent in Assam)[6]. Political geography has imposed a high degree of isolation on the North-East. Absence of industrialisation worth the name has discouraged population movement not only between North-East and rest of India but amongst the political units of the North-East. Along with this vested interests in the North-East have been responsible for the cultivated ignorance. How else can one explain the opposition to entry of railways in certain areas of the North-East.[7]

On the Himalayan border, the British policy ensured that no foreign influence operated in Tibet. The weakness of the Imperial Chinese Govt. also resulted in Tibetan Govt. pursuing an independent policy. To ensure that Tibet did not follow too independent a policy, Lord Curzon sent a military mission under Colonel Sir Francis Young Husband to Tibet, resulting in the Treaty of Lhasa in 1904. Great Britain was given complete control of the foreign policy of Tibet. It envisaged that no part of the territory was to be given to any country and no concessions were to be extended to any other foreign power in the forms of roads, railways and telegraph. According to the treaty Chumbi valley was occupied by British troops till war indemnity was paid. British commercial agent was stationed at Gyantse and empowered to go to Lhasa when required. Trade marts were opened by the British at Yatung, Gyantse and Gartok. The treaty was some what modified by the home department as the British wished to maintain friendly relations with Russia, against whose activities it primarily aimed. The British followed a sort of Monroe doctrine to make this region of Asia as its exclusive sphere of influence. Tibet was so much influenced by the British that it played the British National Anthem as it had no national anthem of its own. While Burma and Malaya in East Asia were part of the British Empire, the Himalayan Kingdoms of Nepal, Sikkim and Bhutan were either directly under the control of British or within their sphere of influence. The foreign policy was totally controlled by the British.

On independence, India inherited a truncated country with fractured borders. In the East, we had international borders with two countries in three segments apart from the Northern border with China. There was border between West Bengal and East Pakistan (now Bangladesh), between Assam, Meghalaya, Tripura and Mizoram and East Pakistan and the third with Myanmar running along the hilly jungles of Mizoram, Manipur and Nagaland. The new borders did not have well defined features and in the west these passed through populated areas. It fractured centuries of relationship amongst people who were socially, culturally and economically interdependent. The net result was complex security problems due to immigration triggered by communal and ethnic tensions and economic pressure. This artificial division is prone to illegal activities, smuggling, infiltration and subversion.

The Northern borders with China are a source of tension due to continued Chinese claim of 32,300 Sq.Miles of territory in Arunachal Pradesh inspite of improvement of relations since 1962. Both Chinese potential and intentions need constant watch. China has extended its sphere of influence in our immediate periphery in the East, particularly in Myanmar and its influence in Bangladesh in collusion with activities of Inter Services Intelligence (ISI) is a source of worry, particularly in the internal security field. Our Northern and North-Eastern borders are inhabited by tribals, who have been living in isolation with traditional social, cultural and spiritual interaction with people across these borders due to physical proximity. The emergence of the border problems has put stress on the emotional integration of these people with the rest of India. Opening up of communications and the initiation of the process of modernisation has also created tensions as any change in traditional societies is bound to. However, it has broken their isolation and if we pursue policies of understanding and accommodation then the process of integration is bound to succeed even though it may take time.

Geostrategic Significance

Strategically, the NE is equally important as the North-West as was clearly brought out by the Chinese aggression in 1962. To day we are better prepared but our preoccupation with Pakistan tends to put it on the back burner. Assam's strategic location and its geo-military implications are obvious. It is the life-line to the entire North-East and all roads and rail communications to the area pass through Assam and Brahmputra River itself still continues to be a bottleneck to movement within Assam and to other States of the North-East. Peace and development of Assam is vital for development and progress of the entire North–East. Any turmoil in Assam is bound to affect all the North–Eastern States and its social and economic lives.

Assam is bounded by Bhutan and Arunachal Pradesh in the North, Arunachal Pradesh, Nagaland and Manipur in the East, Tripura, Bangladesh and Meghalaya in the South and West Bengal in the West. It provides access to Bhutan and Bangladesh and the states of North–East which were part of Assam earlier. All these areas are highly prone to infiltration by Bangladeshis and to some extent people of Nepali origin from Nepal through West Bengal and Bhutan. In addition, there has been infiltration of cheap Bihari labour into Assam like anywhere else in India.

Large scale military operations by China against India apart from the Northern Himalayas (Tibet) are a district possibility from Yunan via Northern Myanmar. This is the shortest and terrain wise easiest route from mainland China to India. The Northern routes across Himalayas through Tibet are longer and run over a more difficult terrain.

The above makes Assam prone to external threat from China and thereby a threat to the life of the entire North-East. The threat from Bangladesh directly is limited but threat to internal security is magnified due to the presence of the large number of immigrants from that area and their influx is continuing. This has not only resulted in pressure on the ethnic Assamese but also on the tribals, whose land is occupied by the migrants and Assamese both. At a time of crisis or conflict along the international border, whether in the East or West, India's frontiers and lines of communications will be exposed to grave danger by presence of so many foreigners.

We have had experience of it during the Chinese invasion in 1962, when illegal immigrants raised Pakistani flags welcoming Chinese in far-off distant places in the North. Utterances both by late Bhutto and Mujibur Rehman who had talked of special relationship with the non-Hindu population of Assam, need for land for expansion for the teeming millions of East Pakistan and need to incorporate natural resources of Assam to make Bangladesh, erstwhile East Pakistan, viable economically and financially strong are geopolitical and economic realities, which we cannot afford to ignore. Migration of Bangladeshis into Assam is an asset for their country as it lightens their economic burden and creates an area of influence at minimum cost. In spite of Indo-Bangladesh pact, neither have we tried to deport Bangladeshis nor has the Bangladesh Government acknowledged the presence of millions of her citizens in Assam. The above economic burden does not include the very sizeable Bengalee Hindu refugees in Assam. Today, the problem is only in Assam and Tripura where the original inhabitants have become a minority, soon it will invade the other North-Eastern States if permitted to continue. Today Assamese militants are talking of secession out of frustration, in not too distant future the immigrants will claim these areas, aided and abetted by our neighbour Bangladesh. The security implications are obvious.

Lastly, the economic implications of the security burden of the area will continue to increase as dissatisfaction, poverty and internal conflicts in the area grow. The threat to India's strategic and economic interests in Assam and the whole of the North-East is of a much higher magnitude than in Jammu and Kashmir.

Historical Perspective

The region as a whole always remained outside the central power structure. Tribals were the earlier inhabitants of the area before the Ahoms came to the region. Even the great Vashnavite Surge, Bhakti cult of Sankradev during the 15th and 16th century AD remained confined to the Brahmputra Valley, which the Manipur Kings integrated into the plains of the Imphal Valley. The Mughals could not annex the region beyond a portion of the lower Assam. East India Company on assumption of Dewani in 1765 could not extend its authority over the whole area. It is only after the Yandaboo Pact in 1826 that gradual annexation of the area without disturbing the customary social system of the tribals began. After 1858 British rule began to be firmly established in the Tribal areas but they did not want to bring them under regular administration. The Regulation X of 1822 set the pattern under which the commissioner of Assam combined in him the joint authority as collector, magistrate and judge[8]. It was only when there were occasional raids by the hill tribes on the neighbouring plains areas that punitive expeditions were led against them, otherwise tribals were left undisturbed to follow their traditional and customary life.

After the take over of the territories of the East India Company by the British Sovereign, a definite policy was adopted to extend and consolidate their power over the tribal areas. Separate legislation was enacted under the Govt. of India (GOI) Act 1870 for the back-ward tracts and areas and they were designated as excluded and partially excluded areas. When Assam was brought under a Chief Commissioner in 1874, the Scheduled District Act was passed. In a nutshell British annexation in the 19th century did not mean administrating the area, it was essentially to protect their interests in the plains. Inner Line Regulation of 1873, GOI Act 1919 and Excluded Area Act 1935 resulted in perpetuation of physical, social, political and economic isolation. The tribal or frontier policy followed by the British was designed to keep tribal people satisfied and immune from influences of the neighbouring countries and national movement from within the country. Failure of the national leadership to establish political and social contact with the hill people of the area and activities of the Christian missionaries through education and health services with the help of the British Govt. made them sympathetic towards the British and left no scope for Indianness. While there was occasional stiff resistance to the British imposition of administrative controls, their spirit of independence and traditional way of life continued unaltered.

The growth of Indian nationalism has to be viewed in the background of the British colonial interests, to protect which a highly centralised system of administration with an efficient and loyal bureaucracy on top, extension of surface communications, establishment of industry, introduction of money economy and a wide network of telecommunications brought India closer together. The aim was exploitation of resources for crown's requirements and administrative convenience. The Indian nationalism grew out of anti imperialist struggle against British rule, which was viewed as oppressive, exploitative and undemocratic. The interaction of the people of the North-East was confined to the bureaucratic officers, traders, money lenders and forest contractors, whose highhandedness and corrupt practices in the absence of other social and cultural contacts could hardly bring them closer to the broader Indian life.

The spirit of Indian nationalism left the underdeveloped areas of the North-East except Assam untouched. The capitalist money market gradually penetrated the hilly areas of the North-East, displacing the self sufficient rural economy and traditional economic system. Thus, although the North-East was exposed to the economic system of the rest of the country as well as the political and administrative system but its consciousness retained its regional experience.

The British territorial claims extended well beyond its system of Governance. It created a large stretch of no man's land frontier between India and China. In the North-East it let princely states of Manipur and Tripura coexisting within its orbit and compromised with traditional tribal structures in the hilly tribal areas. The policy was guided by cost benefits analysis rather than any respect for the traditional institutions with the result that neither territory nor tribal socio–economic structures of these areas were incorporated in the system of Governance. On independence, the task of territorial integration of the North-East and the people inhabiting these areas was a logical conclusion of the territorial integrity of the country.

Within two years, excluded and partially excluded areas were incorporated. The centralised system of Governance was already in place in Assam and princely states of Manippur and Tripura, both due to administrative convenience and perceived geopolitical considerations, integration through Assam, considered closer to the national mainstream, was effected by adding these areas to Assam. Arunachal Hills were brought under direct administration by creating North-East Frontier Agency (NEFA). Thus territorial incorporation and political and administrative integration preceded cultural and emotional integration. This process has been one of the major reasons for estrangement and resistance. The dilemma of Nagas is representative of the turmoil within the tribal societies, with variations based on their historical and traditional social and cultural experience. The choices varied from autonomy along with integration and complete independence. The first view was essentially of the moderates, the second of the extremists. The extremist views varied from a crown colony under British incorporating tribal areas of Naga Hills, North-East Frontier Agency, Tribal areas of Manipur and Burma, an independent State and to stay in India for a short period to establish relationship before independence. The dilema of Nagas for their future and the country's geopolitical interests in the area led to Hydari Agreement of 1947, which has been a bone of contention.

Contemporary Experience

Most people argue that the conflicts in the NE are to a large extent due to clash between the traditional culture and forces of change. The politicians point to the geographical isolation, long years of neglect and indifference of the nation to the suffering of the people of the North-East due to which they have developed a feeling of separation from rest of the country. Another area of agitations is the massive influx of foreigners. The fact is that historical, geographical, cultural as well as economic and political factors attracted people from different regions to the North-East for better opportunities. Marwaris for trade and commerce, Biharis and Oriyas for jobs in plantations, Bengalees for white collar jobs and Punjabis and many other from UP, Bihar for contracts and skilled and semi-skilled jobs. Even in the agricultural field Bengalee Muslim migrants outdid the natives. The presence of these migrants shook the foundation of the Assamese social structure and created solidarity amongst the Assamese, while generating cleavage between Assamese and Tribals. This assimilationist native sentiment and backlash separatist agitations resulted in massive conflict over language, education, employment policy and other political cleavages. The magnitude of the problem was very high, population wise Assam has been the fastest growing area between 1910 and 1980, that it has made North-East states particularly Assam linguistically and ethnically even more diversified[9].

In the post-independent period education spread rapidly. 1991 census per centage of literacy in North-East states except Meghalaya is much higher than all India figure of 52.11, (Assam 53.42 Manipur 60.96, Mizoram 81.23, Nagaland 61.30 Tripura 60.39 and Meghalaya 48.26)[10], educated youth out of colleges and universities found avenues for employment blocked. Young intelligentia instead of being guardian of their own interests fell prey to parochial interest groups. While the older generation of politicians will work out equations in a leisurely fashion, the younger generation would go for action. With vote bank politics coming in the forefront since the beginning 1980, each political party or even groups within each party have their own liberation groups or established links with some insurgent groups, thus resulting in patronage and resources being traded for political power. The ruling elite (including some in Delhi) instead of integrating tribals with non-tribals, hill people with plain people exploited and widened the diversities, thereby deepening the conflicts.

The process of political integration and economic development generated its own forces for raising ethnic sensibilities and added to insurgencies in the region. The process of incorporation of the North-Eastern region, particularly the Naga hills into the Indian Union started the process of current insurgencies in the region. As it has resulted in escalation of extra constitutional ethno-political movements, which seem to be achieving constitutional goals aided and abetted by the ruling elite in the North-East areas. But achievement of constitutional goals of statehood and autonomy has not solved the basic problem of sense of relative depravation of the smaller and peripheral ethnic groups and alienation of the people continue[11].

Modernity

Modernity, generally in the case of India has been a case of change without continuity, fission without fusion and differentiation without integration. Goals of modernity, universality and generality can be achieved in two ways–assimilation of parts in their fullest and then constructing it with all its vitalities, specificities and multifacedness. The other way is the abstract way by emphasising only those qualities of the various parts which are common with all parts, thus accentuating some and ignoring other qualities. The modern state is birth of the first process as concepts like nation state and nationality were unknown and therefore bear relationship to modernity[12]. The traditional identity in the case of individuals was distributed in different socio-cultural, politico-historical and territorial spheres. Modern national identity in the case of India not only consolidated earlier pluralistic identities but also tried to diffuse it. In the absence of a universal Indian identity the imposition of an abstract national identity generated violent resistance from the pluralist identities.

The other agenda of modernity is specialisation and standardisation of economic life based on freedom of individual in a society based on labour unrelated to birth and linkages. This remained elusive as the traditional social order still dictates social and economic mobility. The Mandal Commission has further legitimised it in the economic, political and social spheres of Indian life and polity[13].

Instability Parameters[14]

The inhabitants of the North-Eastern region have a long history of antagonism to established central authority. The nineteenth century political relation (under the British and Burmese) brought them under administrative control of major powers as a result of which they were politically divided and one or other set of inhabitants had frequently raised their banner of revolt. Provision of sanctuaries to adjoining groups in return for gains (gun running, drugs and so on) is the fall out in recent years. However the level of their activities has been curtailed due to the Counter Insurgency Operations in the region. Thus location, itself leads to socio-political instability and economic backwardness and isolation and economic backwardness influence their perceptions. The elements are in constant competition for opportunities, resources and participation, inspite of the known natural resources and have had experience of political, economic and social participation.

Separate social groups in separate areas, encouraged development of distinct perspectives and compatible political organisation led to demands for separate existence. This coupled with suspicion of extension of systematisation and extension of administration after independence which interfered with traditional political and consequently with economic and social structure. The response was revival of alternate (traditional) centres of power, which became the focal point of mobilisation. Efforts by the administration for modernisation and improvement of communication linkages and development highlighted the constraints in infrastructure development. Failure to achieve these confronted the state with new demands, aspirations and requirements. The response was purely political in granting autonomy or statehood but it did not overcome the inadequacies of the past 50 years, either in terms of minimising the differences within or develop alternative sources to overcome resource constraints and neither the locals nor the Govt. looked for an effective alternative.

Within this overall historical perspective, we should examine the historic back ground and contemporary perspective of each of the constituent areas/ethnic groups as these are not only different in their content but also bring out the varying perspectives of the people of each constituent area and community. Understating these is vital to finding a solution.

REFERENCES

1. V.K.Sarin, *India's North-East in Flames,* 1980, Delhi, also Survey of India Map, pp. 7-10.
2. Basic Statistics of NE Region 1995-Issued by North East Council, p. 68.
3. Prof Nilima Dutta "Let Statistic speak for Assam," Guwahati University – Printed at Roy Chowdhry Printer 1980 as quoted in Assam's Agony by Amiya Kumar Das, p. 228.
4. Basic Statistics, NE Region 1995 – NE Council, p. 88.
5. *Ibid*, p. 68.
6. *Ibid,* pp. 7-10 and Lecture by author 2 Aug, 1996, published in USI journal Oct–Dec, 1995.
7. Insurgency in North-East India, A Heretical view by S.K Chaube, published in *Insurgency in NE India* edited by B. Pahem – Omsons publications, New Delhi, 1997, p. 30.
8. Insurgency in North East India – Perspectives and Issues by P.C.Biswas —Published in *Insurgency in NE India* edited by B.Pahem – Published by Omsons Publications, New Delhi, p. 221.
9. *Sons of Soil-Migrational ethnic conflicts in India* – Myron Wiener.
10. Census 1991.
11. Understanding the insurgency phenomenon in India's North-East – An analytical frame work Gurudas Das. Published in "*Insurgency in NE India,* edited by B. Pahem – Omsons Publications, New Delhi, 1997, pp. 185, 186 and 193.
12. Kaviraj Sudita "Crisis of Nation State in India" Political Studies Vol XLII special issue, p. 115, 1994.
13. SC Dube, Indian Society, National Book Trust of India, 1990.
14. Instability Parameters in the North East – A National Internal Security Concern – R Gopala Krishnan – Published in *Insurgency in NE India,* pp. 101-15.

2

Mosaic of the North-East

Ahoms of Assam

The Sanskrit name Asom and its anglicized version Assam are not of distant origin. Asom, which means "unparalled or peerless", was used to describe the invincible might of the Ahoms, who marched into the country in the 13th century across the Patkoi ranges and "came, saw and conquered". Prior to Ahoms the country was known as Pragjyotishpura or the "city of eastern lights" as it enjoyed the reputation of the seat of eastern astrology and astronomy. The temple of Nabagraha or the "nine planets" served as an observatory for astronomical and astrological studies. In the Kalika Purana it is stated that "here Brahma first created stars" and hence the city is called Pragjyotishpura, a city equal to the city of "Indira or Sahra". Dr. B. Kahati gives the name a different interpretation, he connects it with Austro-Asiatic formation – Pagar-Juh (Jo)-tic (c-ch), which means land of great mountain heights, and according to him Pragjyotisha is a sanskritised word made of three non-aryan formations. The kingdom consisted of the present modern Assam and greater parts of northern and eastern Bengal at the time of Mahabharata from the times of Narakasura and Bhaga Dutta. The eastern boundaries were a series of hills reaching up to south China. It was a non-Aryan empire, with royalty of Mongoloid stock. They participated in Mahabharata as allies of Kauravas. There is reference to Pragjyotisha in Ramayana and Vishnu and other puranas. Bhagadutta was well versed in Vedic rites, rituals and religion – a torch bearer of Indo-Mongoloid culture and civilization. His army consisted of Kiratas and Cinas, Kiratas was the generic name given to all Mongoloid people, Tibeto-Burmans, Sino-Tibetans and Cinas particularly for Sino-Tibetans, possibly Bhutanese. There is reference to yellow or golden complexion of the soldiers in the epics. The reference to Amurtharaja in Ramayana, son of

Aryan king Kusha of Madhyadesa indicates penetration of Aryan way of life into ancient Pragjyotishpura. All his points to the fact that ancient Assam was predominantly Mongoloid but Aryan culture had made inroads into the Mongoloid kingdom.[1]

There is regular mention of different princes of ancient Assam with Asura or Danava tittles, followed by Naraka, the real founder of Pragjyotishpura, who met his death at the hands of Sri Krishna and his son Bhagadatta took over who was later killed by Arjuna during the battle of Kurukshetra. Similarly, there are innumerable legends and stories of Bana king of Sumitpura (Modern Tezpur), a Saivite, whose daughter's love story is connected with Anirudda grandson of Sri Krishna.[2] This led to fierce encounters between armies of Anirudda and Bana till Sri Krishna appeared on the battle ground. The romantic story is narrated in Bhagavatan and Harivamsam. Lord Shiva's participation on the side of Bana and encounter with Sri Krishna adds a religious motif to the story of love.

Ancient Pragjyotishpura came to be known as Kamarupa in the medieval times when Naraka established his suzerainty and put himself in charge of Kamakhya temple. The reference by the Chinese pilgrim Hiuen Tsang and Muslim historian Alberuni to Kamarupa are there but in different variations of the word as Kamru and Kamrut. This is also the basis of the authentic history of Assam during the reign of Bhaskar Varma in 643, the fourth king of the Varma dynasty. Hiuen Tsang described the kingdom as of almost 1700 miles in circuit, low lying but rich, with soft and temperate climate and inhabited by small statured people with yellow complexion. He said the king was a devoted disciple of Saivite Creed. The state religion was Brahmanical, in spite of animism prevailing amongst vast majority of the people. The kingdom of Bhaskar Varma, after his death in 650, fell to pieces in the hands of local chiefs and aboriginal rulers. Salastombha usurped the throne in 655 and ruled till 675 and established a new dynasty. Fifth in descent was Harshadeva (Harsh Varma) who ruled till the middle of the 8th century and his daughter Rajyamati was given in marriage to the Nepalese king; his rule is mentioned in the Pasupati inscriptions of Nepalese king Jayadeva II. This dynasty came to an end in the late 10th Century.

Palas dynasty succeeded and ruled till 12th century AD. They claimed their descent from Naraka, founder of the ancient kingdom of Pragjyotishpura. Ratanpala, the third king, built a number of Hindu temples and encouraged trade, commerce and Hindu religion. During his reign followed by Indrapala, Dharampala and Jayapala the kingdom extended over Assam and parts of Bengal. Palas were Hinduised Bodos who took interest in Hindu culture, religion and Sanskrit language. The

Pala dynasty was followed by Dev kings of whom Prithu was a very powerful king of Kamarupa and build Shiva temple at Jalpaiguri. He repulsed the first two Muslim invasions by Ibn-Bakhtiyar (1205-1206) and Sultan Giasuddin in 1227 AD. Western Assam and North Bengal formed into two separate entities under the same ruler and were known as the kingdom of Kamata before the Koch dynasty. King Durlabhanarayan was one of the most enlightened kings and ruled in first half of 14th century. He patronized Vaishnavite poets and scholars. History after the first-half of the 15th century following Indranarayan is lost in obscurity.

Khen dynasty under Niladhvaj was established in the 15th century. The third king Nilambar wrested parts of Bengal from the Muslims and built roads to all parts of the kingdom, the best from Kamatpur to Ghoraghat. Hussain Shah raided the kingdom in 1498 AD, Nilambar was overthrown and Kamata kingdom disintegrated till the Koch dynasty was founded by Biswa Singha in 1515 AD.

Biswa Singha was a devout Saivite but also worshipped Durga. He built the temple of Kamakhya on the Nilacha Hill overlooking the Brahmaputra and worship of Kamakhya came to the forefront. His capital was in Cooch Behar where he constructed a well laid-out town. He utilized the services of the influential Mech families by appointing ministers from among them; thus the aristocracy of Meches. He was an ally of Ahoms under Barpatra Gohain and pursued Muslims up to Karatoya. He reigned till 1533 and Koch and Ahom relationship amongst Mongoloid princes is a historical land mark. Biswa Singha was succeeded by his son Naranaryan, also known as Malladeva who was the most illustrious of the Koch kings. After subjugating local chieftains, the turned his attention to the Ahom kingdom. He captured the Ahom capital of Gargaon in eastern Assam and an agreement was signed with the Ahom king, who paid ransom and hostages. He then turned to the Muslim kingdom under Isa Khan in Bengal, where he was defeated and his brother Sukhadhvaja was taken prisoner. Naranaryan's troubles started when he invaded Pasha of Gaur's territories, which led to periodic incursions by Sulaiman Kararani who ruled Bengal from 1563 to 1572 AD. Naranarayan defeated Ahoms and Kacharis and kings of Manipur and Jaintia Hills paid him tribute. He was an ally of Akbar the Mogul Emperor and exchanged gifts and is recognised in the Ain-i-Akbari and Akbarnama by Abul Fazl. He died in 1584 AD. His son succeeded him, the kingdom was divided between his son Lakhinarayan and Raghu his nephew and finally fell to pieces in the 17th century. In 1613 Mohamedans occupied and annexed Kamrup. With the help of Ahoms, territories from the Mohamadans were recovered and Assam became a battle ground of a three cornered struggle between the Koches on the west and Ahoms in the east fighting each other and the Muslim Moghuls with both.

The advent of Ahoms, a Shan tribe belonging to the ancient kingdom of Mungman or Pong in upper Burma on the banks of Irrawady River in 1228 AD across the Patkoi ranges is a turning point in Assam's history. Sukapha a Shan prince denied of his throne wandered into Assam with his nobles and nine thousand men, women and children and after overcoming local resistance of Chutias and Kacharis in the North-East established his kingdom in eastern Assam. The Chutia and Kachari kingdoms flourished side by side, the tract lying beyond the Disang in eastern Assam was under the Chutias. The Kacharis were lower down the valley of Brahmaputra on the banks of Dhansiri. Sukapha found them as formidable opponents and settled amongst the Morans and Borahis of the easternmost tracts. He adopted a conciliatory approach and expanded his influence through social and political interaction on the basis of equality, resulting in a single Ahom race through interfusion and intermixture with indigenous races like Morans and Morahis, miscegenation of the great groups of Kirata people. The unending immigration across Patkoi Hills added to the strength of the Ahoms. The Kamata was subdued in the 14th century by the Ahoms. This was followed by war with Chutias and after a bitter fight, Ahom Singh Supempha was assassinated by Chutias during a regatta held in Safrai River to celebrate cessation of hostilities. The assassination led to renewal of hostilities and Chutias were finally routed in 1523 AD and Chutia territory was put under a Governor designated "Saidyakhowa Gohain", viceroy of Sadiya. Suhunnung in 1479 AD was a bold and resourceful ruler. He dispersed Chutia nobles and their followers throughout the valley and settled Ahoms in their place, thus consolidating the Ahoms hold in eastern Assam. He encouraged Vaishnavite religion and culture and Chutia artisans were imported and encouraged. Ahoms under him learnt about firearms from the Mohammedans and became experts in manufacture of fire arms and gun powder.

Kachari Kingdom was established in the 13the century with its capital at Dimapur as it extended up to Cachar, a name given to old Hidimba, a character in Mahabharata. Towards the end of 13th century Kachari kingdom east of Dikhan was occupied by Ahoms. In 1490 AD, Ahoms first came into conflict with Kacharis, a Bodo tribe and were defeated by them at Dikhan. Thirty years later Suhumung or Dihingia Raja defeated kacharis in 1536 and captured their capital at Dimapur. Kacharis shifted their capital to Maibong in North Cachar Hills. He died in 1539 AD. The contribution of the Kacharis to the composite culture of Assam in considerable.

The joginitantra describes the kingdom of Ahoms as octagonal in shape and the Ahom coinage system under Suklengmung (1539-1552 AD) had the same design and inscriptions in Ahom language and characters. Subsequently these were replaced by Sanskrit. The reign of Pratap Singha from 1603 to 1614 is remembered for the work done by him for the benefit of his people, he constructed roads, ponds and embankments to save people from floods. He controlled the oppression by the hill tribes like Daflas and Miris by appointing ambassadors (Katakis) in the hill states.

The Muslim invasions started in the 13th century, the Turks tried to ingress into Assam after subjugating Bengal in 1205. This was followed by Pathan and Afghan rulers of Delhi, most resulted in their being evicted. In spite of the fact that Moghul invaders achieved temporary success and reached as far east as Gargaon, the capital of Ahoms, they were driven out with heavy losses. The second Muslim invasion by General Turbak resulted in a similar disaster, a few who escaped death were settled and are the ancestors of Morias and Braziers. One of the most determined attacks by Muslims was launched in 1627 to avenge the intervention of Ahom kings on behalf of the Koch king Balitnarayan in 1614. They attacked simultaneously Balitnarayan and Ahoms with 10,000 foot soldiers and horsemen and 400 big boats. The attack, the 9th by Muslim invaders was repulsed and Balitnarayan was installed as the Koch king by the Ahom king Pratap Singha. Yet another attempt was repulsed in the battle of Kaliabar (Modern Nowgong) during the reign of Susenpha, this resulted in the incorporation of the Koch kingdom into Ahom territory and a viceroy (Borphukan) with his headquarters at Gauhati. A treaty was concluded between Moghuls and Ahoms in 1638. Koch kingdom remained confined to the west of river Sankosh, virtually as a vassal of the Moghuls. Taking advantage of the confusion after Shan Jehan's illness in 1658, Koch king Prannarayan attacked and defeated the Muslim Faujdar of Goalpara. The Kochs were in turn defeated by Ahom king Jayadhwaj Singha and whole of Brahmaputra valley fell to the Ahoms when they occupied Goalpara in 1658. Goalpara fell to the Moghuls in 1661 and remained outside the Ahom control till annexed by the British in 1765.

Nawab Mir Jumla, Governor of Dacca after defeating Prannarayan advanced against the Ahoms; he met initial success and captured Gargoan the eastern capital of Ahoms. But the Mughal army was defeated by the Ahoms aided by the monsoons. The Muslim historians accompanying Moghul armies have left detailed accounts of the period. Ahoms were acclaimed as valiant and fearless fighters and their military powers were acknowledged. The twelfth invasion by the Moghuls during Aurangzebs reign met similar fate and were routed at the battle of Saraighat by the legendary Ahom General Lachit Borphukan in 1670 and territories up to river Manah came under Ahom control. Yet another attack against Ahom was repulsed in the battle of Rangamati. Ahoms acted as a barrier against Muslim expansion into Assam and Burma. The last of the Moghul attack was during the reign of Godadhar Singha in 1662, where they met their waterloo in the battle of Itakhuli. He was succeeded by his son Rudra Singha, who ruled from 1691 to 1714. His reign was peaceful and free of foreign invasions and extended his territory to the Kacharis capital of Dimapur and later captured Maibang the new capital of Kacharis in the north Cachar Hills. He was a genius and built temples and tanks at Sibsagar the Ahom capital. The period also witnessed the ascendancy of Hinduism over the ancient religion of Ahoms. It was the golden period of Ahom rule. His successor Siva Singha was an ardent follower of Hinduism.

The reign of Rajeswar Singha was followed by Lakhi Singha (1769-1780), a weakling, who could not stand the uprisings of Moamarias, a sect of Vaishnavites and the Ahom umpire started crumbling. His successor Gaurinath Singha, indulged in mutilating the bodies of other royal princes, to render them ineligible for the throne as per Ahom state rules. As a sequel to Moamarias rebellion in April 1782, he ordered a general massacre of the Moamarias, wherein many thousands including women and children were put to death. The agitation went underground and subversive activities to sabotage the state machinery took its toll. Moamarias destroyed life and property and scorched and burnt villages. Having failed to quell the uprising Gaurinath Singha asked for British help in 1792. Kamaleshwar Singha during his reign of 15 years (1795-1810) was able to restore order. On his death, Buragohain nominated his brother Chandra Kanta to the throne. His reign was marked by religious and political fueds and Moamarias rebellions, which resulted in Badan Borphukan an Ahom ruler to invite Burmese in 1816, against the king. Borphukan gained power with Burmese help. Intrigues amongst the royals resulted in Chandra Kanta being deposed in 1818 AD and his fleeing to Rangpur. Badan Borphukan was assassinated and Purandar Singha was enthroned monarch. The Burmese, on hearing of Badan Borpukan's death, invaded Assam again. Chandra Kanta sided with the Burmese and was installed king again. The Burmese sovereignty lasted till 1820 when they came in conflict with the British in Cachar and suffered severe reverses. In Burma, the King of Ava ceased hostilities with the Ahoms. Ultimately Assam passed into the hands of the British by the Treaty of Yandaboo in 1826.

Ahoms, who had subjugated the whole of Brahmputra valley and brought it under their control and ruled over it for 600 years from the 13th century to the 19th century became a victim of internecine strife and turmoil due to conflicting religious forces of Saktaism and Vaishnavism. The anti-vaishnavite revolution was fuelled by Rajeshwar Singha's Queen openly persecuting the Vaishnavites for their religious professions and faith. This turmoil throughout the 18th century resulted in the Burmese invasion and decline of Ahom rule. The atrocities of Burmese under their General Mingi Maha Bandula put the bloodshed and ferocity of even Ghenghis Khan to shame.

The Ahom's system of administration was simple and effective. The king was the head, sovereign and enjoyed full power and could do no wrong. There was a council of three ministers called Gohains, regarded as pillars of the state. They dictated state policy and the king consulted them on all matters of war and peace. The king in his capacity as the sovereign gave effect to it or in other words executed it. Son succeeded the father to the throne, which was violated only in the later parts of Ahom rule because of rival claimants. The king was referred to as Swargadeo, a prince by blood without any scar or blemish on his body. The Ahom system of administration can be called "monarchical oligarchy". The king was selected from the royal families of Dihingia, Chungia, Tungkhungia, Namrupia, Chamuguria and Parvitia.

The Gohains or ministers represented the leading families of the aristocracy of the state. King's discretion in appointing ministers was restricted due to its being limited to a few noble families of the Gohains, the Bargohains, the Buragohain and Borpatra Gohain. The Bar-Baruas and Bor-Phukons were other aristocrat families, viceroys to the king who administered the districts. Similarly, the other offices of state were organised on a gradation and functional basis, which also determined their social status. There was an officer incharge of justice. (Nyaisodha-Phookan) and Deolia-Phookon was entrusted with religious affairs. Both military and civil posts carried authority and prestige, officials employed as arbitrators and superintendents of work, known as Kakatis and Katakis, were also ambassadors and messengers for diplomatic work with foreigners and hill tribes.

The entire population between 15 to 50 years could be commandeered for state service when required. The population was divided into the top privileged level and common men, known as Karis or shaftman or paiks or the foot soldier. Twenty paiks were commanded by a Bora, a hundred by a Saikia and a thousand by a Hazarika, three thousand by a Raj Khowa and six thousand by a Phookan. Each was granted land. Paik was granted three acres of land free of tax for his services to the state. In addition, he received land for his house and garden, for which he paid a tax of one rupee to the state treasury. Thus most nobles and officials had their own estates. Similarly, judicial system was organised under the three Gohains, who bore responsibility for the administration and legal matters.

The gift of Ahoms to Assam was primarily in their military organisation and their administration. Nothing so practical, eleborate and efficient appears to have existed not only in Assam but also in the whole of eastern India. The Ahoms were so powerful that the kingdom carved out for them came to be associated with their name as a nation. Ahom kings like Chakradhvaja Singha and Rudra Singha, statesman like Atan Buragohain and generals like Lachit Borpukan can adorn with pride and distinction any gallery of men in identical spheres.

The British Period

When Assam passed into the British hands after the treaty of Yandaboo in 1826, it was the first time that the Ahom (Assamese) heartland got incorporated into an Indian political formation. Earlier attempts of the mighty Moghuls having failed upon their defeat by the Ahom Army in 1682. However, it needs to be understood that apart from Ahom kingdom, there was the Koch kingdom, with Cooch Bihar (now in West Bengal) as its capital, its territory included Eastern Assam, parts of North Bengal (now in Bangladesh) and present West Bengal in the sixteenth century. The kingdom was split in 1581 into Koch Bihar consisting of districts of Koch Bihar and parts of Dinajpur, Jalpaiguri and Kamrup or Koch Hajo, which included all of Western Assam and much of Central Assam (Barpeta, Kamrup, Nalbari, Darang and parts of Sonitpur). Following the split western part of old kingdom Koch Bihar became a vassal of Moghuls. The eastern part (Kamrup or Koch Hajo) was annexed by the Moghuls in 1613, which became the frontier province of the Moghul empire bordering Ahom state but Moghuls could never effectively control eastern parts of Kamrup. Western part of Assam, the district of Golpara (now four distrcts) which then included Garo Hills region was part of Moghul province of Bengal and came under the East Indian Company on Moghul Emperors Firman of 12 August, 1765. It was formed as a Chief Commissioner's province in 1874 and its territorial jurisdiction included undivided districts of Golpara, Kamrup, Darang, Nowgong, Sibsagar, Lakhimpur, parts of Naga Hills and the district of Cachar and Garo Hills and eastern Duars, which were annexed by the British in 1866 from Bhutanese influence. Later Sylhet from East Bengal was included. The primary aim was administrative convenience, without major consideration to historical and cultural affirmity. The inclusion of Sylhet divided the Bengali speaking people astride Meghna River and was responsible for much of the antagonism between the valleys of Brahmaputra and Surma rivers. Later the annexed territories of Nagas (Lothas, Angamis and AOs) and Lushais were all incorporated in Assam by 1898.

A new expanded province of East Bengal was created in 1905 combining Assam with Eastern Bengal (Now Bangaldesh). The opposition came from Assmese but more effective opposition was from the British Tea Industry, as its tea was known from its province internationally (Assam Tea). This new entity was short lived and Assam reverted to its former status and name in 1912. It was upgraded to a Governor's province in 1921 under the GOI Act of 1919. Assam thus came to be expanded beyond the Ahom kingdom to include areas which were not historically, culturally and economically part of pre-colonial Assam purely for imperial administrative and strategic considerations.

The British policy driven by the needs of colonical economy, consolidation of its territorial jurisdiction and security considerations resulted in the breakdown of interconnectivity between different hill and plain communities; segregation, and immigration put serious constraints on the natural process of incorporation of different people and communities into the Indian civilisation, which has been its biggest asset and strength.

Historically it is beyond doubt that there were trade, commercial and political ties between the Ahoms and the Nagas. Nagas fought in Ahom armies and Nagas gave shelter to Ahom princes. There were also instances of land grants being given to Nagas in the plains. While Varrier Elwin believed that Ahom kings considered Nagas as subjects and took taxes from them in the form of slaves, elephant tusks, cloth and cotton (Elwin, 1961, p. 18), Edward Gait, the colonial historian, believed that Nagas were never subject of Ahoms (Gate 1990, p. 314). However, this is contradicted by the British officer Alexander Mackenzie, who acknowledged that Nagas occupying low hills in Sibsagar district, came down annually with gifts by way of tributes, whenever native kings were strong. The last Ahom king Purunder Singha asserted his right to share with the Nagas salt produced in the springs in the low hills. This relationship was well understood by the earlier British officers and they utilised this to establish relationship with the Nagas. Without going into the question of Naga-Assamese relationship in term of total independence or subjugation, there is no denying the fact they had economic and cultural relationship spread over a long period – probably Nagamese the common language between different Naga tribes and for interaction with people from the plain, its closeness to Assamese is the living proof of it.

However, realisation of this relationship underwent a change in perception to one of radical disconnection during the ten punitive expeditions for the pacification of the Naga areas from 1935 to 1951. The change is well illustrated over the period by varying accounts. William Robinson's Account of 1841 shows appreciation. He distinguished between Nagas who lived in lower mountains and closer to the plains and the Abor Nagas of the higher mountains. The Nagas in lower mountains always prevented contacts between Abor Nagas and the plains of Assam (Robinson – 1975, pp. 383, 384). This is in sharp contrast to the account of Lt. Gen. R G Woodenthrope of 1881, who maintained that there was virtually no interconnection between Nagas and Assamese. He challenged the authenticity of tribal names in Assamese on old colonial maps (Dup-duwar-ias, Paniduwaris and Hatigorias). (Minutes of the meeting of the Anthropological Institution of 9 March 1881-1969 pages 46-47 as quoted in India Against Itself - Sanjib Buruah, p. 34).

This change in perception in later years led to a policy of segregation of hills from the plains and regime of Scheduled Districts Act of 1874 and Frontier Tract Regulation of 1880 authorised these areas to be excluded from operation of civil and criminal code, rules for property registration and transfer and other laws considered unsuitable for these areas. Similarly, Bengal Eastern Frontier Regulation of 1873 empowered the Govt. to prescribe an "Inner Line". The line was drawn along the foot hills and people beyond the line were left to manage their own affairs, with only limited interference by the frontier officers to establish their influence among the chiefs and tribes (Makenzie 1977, p. 65). This policy also controlled undue expansion of British entrepreneurs into areas, which could have adverse effect. Generally this policy of segregating the plains from the hills was followed for the whole of Himalayas. This served the dual purpose of a boundary between hills and plains to consolidate their power in the plains and deprived the hill kingdoms the major source of revenue and access to markets and they became dependent on the British in the plains, (Rose 1977, p. 65). The inner line was later extended to all hills except the Khasi and Garo Hills and Karbi Anglong District of present Assam. The British administration was extended to all hill areas except the Himalaya Frontier Tracts (Arunachal Pradesh) and Naga Tribal Areas. The Govt. of India Act 1919 introduced another term "backward tracts". The Simon Commission of 1930, replaced the term backward with excluded and areas were divided further into "excluded" and "partially excluded". The governance of excluded areas was different from rest of the British India. While it was paternalistic but the British Administrator enjoyed enormous discretionary powers and limiting movement of people into the area was one such important power. The British believed that what the people needed was security of land tenure, freedom to pursue their traditional methods and to follow their customs and not self determination. Therefore the people of excluded areas did not require the system of representation as in other areas and political advancement would not satisfy them as much as protection from their neighbours, [Simon Commission Report, (34)]. The terms excluded area and partially excluded area applied to purely tribal and partially tribal areas where tribals lived along with the non-tribal population. Legally the main distinction was that while both types were excluded from the jurisdiction of the provincial and federal legislation. Governor could act on his own discretion in the case of excluded areas and in the case of partially excluded areas, the elected Govt. had some jurisdiction but Governor had a supervising and overriding power. The GOI Act of 1935 extended the territorial scope of these provisions of the Simon Commission.

Although the Assam Govt. had told the Simon Commission that artificial separation of the backward tracts from Assam was against the interest of both, but during the discussion in the British Parliament on the GOI Act of 1935, the defenders of the British policy argued that only British protection and control could save these areas from the "hell of civilisation". The same argument was used in the British attempt to hold onto these areas after their departure from rest of India – when British Civil Servants proposed a crown colony of the hill areas of Assam and Burma.

The policy of exclusion and control of access to outsiders led to isolation, a feeling of separation and suspicion. The British officers allowed Christian Missionaries to operate in these areas that were immensely successful. It resulted in a cultural change set in motion by material goods and ideas, which added to the tribal sense of separation and weakened the historical economic and social links with Assam. It was the different experience of colonial rule in the tribal areas which was so different from Assam and rest of India which laid the foundation of the sentiment of separation and, as we shall see later, after independence most of the situation of exclusion was retained in essence.

Tea, oil and forests were the precursors of Assam's economic boom of late nineteenth and twentieth century. The fact that there could be large scale commercial production of tea completely dominated Assam's economic future. It shook the London Stock exchange and there was scramble for tea shares and tea lands by financiers and speculators (Butler 1978). In late 1830's and 40's discovery of oil was closely followed by development of coal fields and felling of forests for timber and land for tea gardens. Decades of economic upsurge was followed by economic slide back in the later parts of twentieth century. Amalendu Guha, economic historian calls the late nineteenth century economic revolution "a big push without a take off. (A Guha, 1991, pp 186-205). Lack of interest in wage labour by the Assamese resulted in colonial machinery turning towards immigrants for labour. Redundant population of Bengal found it profitable to pour into Assam. In addition immigrants came to occupy middle class positions, which required new skills, and exploit trading opportunities. Large scale immigration was a major fall out of the economic boom, which resulted in outsiders forming one quarter to one third of the population of Assam in 1901 (A Guha 1991, p 195). This was accompanied by land grabbing by immigrant agriculturists. This was most prominent in the second decade of the twentieth century and continues even after the partition of the subcontinent.

During the Ahom period each Paik was allotted rent free two puras (about 2.66 acres) of wet land and piece of land for homestead and garden and in addition they were free to reclaim uncultivated lands and access to their surroundings for fish, fruits, vegetable and raw material. In addition peasants cultivated Charlands away from their home (Pan Basti) to carry on shifting cultivation of mustard, pulses and ahu rice (A Guha 1991, p. 13). The British land policy theoretically recognized precolonial property rights but it restructed the rights to parental occupation in his own village and not hereditary rights on land in other areas.

Major immigrant communities of Assam are Muslims of Bengali descent, Hindu Bengalis, Marwaris, Nepalis and the tea labour communities. The invasion of land hungry Bengali immigrants, mostly Muslims, from districts of Eastern Bengal (Mymensingh, Pabna, Bogra and Rangpur) started towards the end of the first decade, just before 1911, to the Charlands of Goalpara. By 1931 census the movement had attained alarming proportion as recorded by Superintendent of census G. S. Mullan. The Govt. Policy of encouraging immigrants was followed by a long period of privately driven immigration. Bengali Hindus staffed most of the colonial administration— Bengali being court language from 1837 to 1873. Apart from Govt. positions most professional positions were filled by the Bengalis. During the period 1905 to 1912 when Assam and Eastern Bengal was made into a province, migration was facilitated as it was deemed to be within the province. Similarly, as discussed earlier Bengalis from Sylhet were locals of the same province. Bengalis from Sylhet were appointed as Mouzdars (revenue officers) as Bengali was the language for all official work.

According to 1906 Govt. report Marwari merchants monopolised entire trade in Assam and played a major role in Assam's transition from a largely non-monetised economy to market economy. Although not a large group, but they dominate Fancy Bazar in Guwahati, the main market in the North-East, and are spread out in the entire North-East to the remotest corner of Arunachal Pradesh, Nagaland and other remote hill areas and trade with the border people in Myanmar. Being distinct in their socio-cultural identity, their trade centres and institutions are distinct and thereby vulnerable especially since 1970. Nepali migration had its roots in the Darjeeling district of Bengal and later into Sikkim in the tea gardens and by 1900 they were the majority community in both the places. Nepalis were allowed to settle in all excluded areas except NEFA. At the time of independence Nepalis were prominent in all the lower hill areas around Assam except NEFA and Tripura. A major source of Nepali immigrants was Nepalis recruited in the Assam Rifles, who settled in locations close to their units. Availabilty of grazing lands and growing business of milk supply in urban centres helped this. 1991 census recorded 433,000 (1.9%) Nepali speaking population in Assam, most of whom now speak Assamese.

Tea workers represent the oldest and largest modern day immigrants. Recruitment of tribal groups are Santhals, Mundas, Oraons, Kharias, Gonds, Khonds, Kisangs and Nagesias mostly from Bihar and Orissa. From individual private recruitment by Tea Companies from 1841 to 1859, a system of indentured labour recruitment under the Tea Planters Association functioned till 1926. However, even after this system was abolished recruitment from outside continued. But since late 60's, the situation has reversed due to surplus labour in tea gardens. Most of the contract labours settled around the tea gardens after retirement and till today meets the peak demand of casual labour during tea season.

Immigration into Assam began mainly as a result of colonial conquest. A land frontier which required more people to meet the demands of labour, trade, administration and for exploration of its rich forest and later oil resources. The tension due to immigrants has been simmering since 1930, when three of the Brahamputra valley Assamese out of nine members of the Line Committee wrote a dissenting note–highlighting that it is the sacred duty of the Govt. to protect the Assamese from the wave of East Bengal immigration. It is this sense of obligation which should be basis of Govt. policy and not the narrow consideration of development of the province "or consideration of the amount of land revenue that the Govt. can raise. The fundamental points of difference between the Assamese and the other majority members were "we look upon the Assam valley as home of the Assamese people, who have got a vested interest in the soil of these districts, which they successfully defended against hordes of invaders in the pre-British days. If they had the sovereign power today they would have still resisted the occupation of the lands here by outsiders against armed forces if necessary"[3]. Social peace and political stability in Assam to a large extent is a hostage to ethnic riots, political violence and innsurgencies is to large extent is due to the unaddressed problem of large scale immigration.

The British period saw the first organised demographic invasion of Assam. The first onslaught lasted from 1831 to 1875, when Assam was merged into the Bengal presidency and Bengali language was imposed on them. The second came when East Bengal and Assam were created as separate provinces and were separated from the province of Bengal in 1905. The province of Assam was later restored in 1912 and included the districts of Sylhet and Chachar due to Bengali protests. Tea cultivation started in 1839 and oil exploration in Digboi by the beginning of the century. The prime beneficiaries were Bengalees due to their western education some 140 years earlier than rest of the region. British policy of divide and rule resulted in political and social groups based on language and religion coming up. Congress boycott of the self rule in 1937, put Muslims in power and they grafted thousands of Muslims into Assam and in connivance with the British almost succeeded to include Assam in East Pakistan by placing Bengal and Assam in the same group but for the efforts of Gopinath Bardloi, the then Chief Minister, Mahatma Gandhi and Sardar Patel.

Post Independence

With the transfer of Sylhet District less Karimganj division to Pakistan in 1947, the North-East region was cut off from rest of India. It was linked through the Siliguri Carridor in 1950. During the Partition almost three lakh Hindus migrated to Assam from East Pakistan.

Mujibur Rehman in his book "East Pakistan and its Population and Economics" stated that East Pakistan must have sufficient land for its huge population and Assam with its abundant resources provided that scope. Even Zulfikar Ali Bhutto had advocated a policy of special relations with the non-Hindu population of Assam, untill the wrong can be righted. But for the events of 1971, both the leaders would have pursued these goals. During the 1962 Chinese aggression Muslim migrants displayed marked anti-India feelings. The problem of immigrants in 1960's and 70's was ignored by our leaders due to vote bank politics. The increase in Assamese population from 17 to 20 per cent per decade in the first half of the century jumped to 35 per cent for the decade 1971-1981, there was also a change in the demographic profile of the state. In 1971 Assam was estimated to have 10 million Hindus including indigenous displaced personnel and migrants and 4.25 Muslims including 2 million immigrants. The linguistic break up was 9 million Assamese speaking including 2 million immigrant Bengalis who had shown themselves as Assamese in 1961 census and 2.9 million Bengali speaking people including Hindus and Muslims and displaced personnel. In 1980, out of a total population of 20 million, 6 million were non Indians (including refugees), 7 million indigenous and rest immigrants. The indigenous Assamese population including assimilated migrants was just over 50 per cent.

Although the issue of illegal immigrants had been raised by the Assam leadership but the issue of illegal immigrants being listed in electoral rolls was first raised by the All Assam Students Union (AASU). The issue came to the forefront during the 1978 Assembly elections and AASU sent a sixteen point memorandum to the Central Govt. in July 1978. The same year during a conference of the electoral officers, Mr. S. L. Shakhdar, the CEO mentioned the abnormally high growth rate of 34.98 between 1961-71 due to influx of large number of persons from neighbouring countries. He also recorded the disturbing demand of migrants, who were not Indian citizens, to be included in the electoral rolls without verification. The spurt to the agitation was provided by the by election to the Mangaldoi Lok Sabha constituency. Because of the agitation CEO ordered the revision of electoral rolls, of the 70,000 objections raised in an electoral college of 6,00,000, the court sustained 45,000 all Bangladeshi immigrants. The by election could not be held and AASU launched the agitation in June, 1979. To make the agitation more broad based and gain support of regional parties, cultural and volunteer organisations and tribals AASU in its meeting at Dibrugarh in August 1979 formed the All Assam Gana Parishad (AAGSP) an umbrella organisation. The movement spread and demand for detection, deletion of names from electoral rolls and deportation of foreigners resulted in the fall of Golap Borbora's Janata Govt as Muslim MLAs irrespective of party affiliation withdrew support. Simultaneously, with the fall of Janata Govt. at the centre mid term polls for the Lok Sabha were ordered for January 1980. Inspite of mass protests, elections were not postponed, resulting in out of 14 parliamentary constituencies, no nominations were filed in 10 constituency and due to non-cooperation polling could not take place in 2 constituencies and elections could be held in only two contituencies in Chachar District. Thus 12 constituencies out of 14 remained unrepresented.

AASU President, Prafulla Mahanta wrote to Mrs. Gandhi and put forward a charter of eight demands and proposed that National Register of Citizenship 1951 and the electoral rolls of 1952 be used to identify Indian citizens and a zone clear of habitation and vegetation along the border be organised. During her visit to Assam on 12 April, 1980 Mrs. Gandhi suggested 25 March, 1971 when Bangladesh came into existence as the cut off date. AASU stuck to 1951 as the cut off year and quoted the Nehru-Liaqat Pact which permitted migrating people returning to their original homes up to December 1950. There was reaction in Chachar District, West Bangal and Tripura in the shape of Bengal bandh. All Assam Minorities Student Union (AAMSU) launched a counter agitation in Muslim dominated areas of Barpeta, Goalpara and Nowgong. In the agitation up to 1980, 2,30,000 persons were arrested, 3700 houses burnt of which 500 were Assamese. Army was called out in December 1980 to restore oil flow.

After a stint of President's rule a popular Govt. was established in December 1980 and strict measures were adopted to deal with the agitation. In june 1981, Anwara Taimur Govt. fell and President's rule was reimposed. In the meantime negotations and discussions centered around the cut off dates between 1961 and 1971 and migrants post-1971. In December, 1981, the opposition parties joined the talks and these became tripartite. In January 1982 the second Congress (I) Govt. under K. C. Gogoi was installed but due to continued agitation, violence and major acts of sabotage president's rule was reimposed in March. Simultaneously Govt., foreseeing elections started the process of detection of post - 1971 immigiants. AASU demanded the scrapping of the 1965 policy of granting refugee status to Hindus (9 lakhs) who came from East Pakistan and no elections without revision of electoral rolls. Mr. Ravinder Verma of Janata suggested 1951 National Register of Citizenship or the 1952 electoral rolls for determining the citizenship and deetion of all post-1961 citizens from the electoral rolls for the elections in March 1983. Elections were announced on 6 January 1983. AASU and AAGSP called for a boycott of the elections and all opposition parties and state Junior Officers Association lined up against the elections. AASU and AAGSP leaders were arrested. In the absence of leaders, the middle leadership indulged in violence resulting in Nellie massacre and counter violence by Bodos at Gohpur and other places. The Congress (I) received only 16 per cent of the votes of the total electorate, winning 90 of the 108 seats where polls could be held. The election riots completed the polarisation of the communities and discredited the Govt on going back on its promisses between 1980-82 for not holding the elections without revision of electoral rolls. The constitutional requirement of extending the President's rule beyond one year by a contitutional amendment for which support of all non-communist parties was assured. The issue of foreigners had not only been bypassed but indirectely supported by the Congress (I).

The new Chief Minister Hiteshwar Saikia's efforts to restart negotiations with the agitation leaders failed and his announcement of erection of a border fence drew reaction from Bangladesh. Similarly, his efforts to find judges for the tribunals from outside Assam also failed. The agitation was marred by violence and Saikia accused AASU for it. Muslim members of AASU met separately and accused RSS of infiltrating in AASU. AASU expelled Nurul Hasan and some Muslim members and the split was formalised in 1983. After Mrs. Gandhi's death and 1984 elections when Congress (I) won a land-slide victory Rajiv Gandhi, the new Prime Minister's efforts to resolve the issue finally met success and the agitating leaders came down on their demand of cut off year and agreed to debar immigrants of 1961-71 for ten years and the accord was signed on 15 August 1985. The deal envisaged fresh elections for the Assembly and Lok Sabha.

The elections were held in December, 1985 and the newly formed Assam Gana Parishad (AGP) won the elections and formed the Govt. The issues before the newly formed Govt. were the implementation of the accord, detection, deletion and deportation or dispersal of foreigners out of Assam, securing the Assam-Bangladesh border and safeguarding the interests of the people of Assam. The perception of the state and the centre on the basic issue of foreigners differed and amendment to the Citizens Act, raised further misgivings. United Minorities Front (UMF) called the accord anti-minorities. Government circular making Assamese as the third compulsory language drew reaction from All Assam Tribal Students Union (AATSU) and All Chachar and Karimganj Students Association. Eviction of tribals in Tamalpur and immigrants from the char areas of Brahmaputra further antagonised the tribals and immigrants. Plain Tribals Council of Assam (PTCA) raised the demand for separate state on behalf of the plains tribals, who had been denied the benefits of both the 5th and 6th schedule. Similar, dissatisfaction was fomenting in Karbi Anglong and North Chachar. Karbis were the only hill tribe who had not joined the All Party Hill Conference to break away from Assam. Most of the problems existed earlier but got accentuated during AGP's rule. To add to AGP's problems AASU was getting impatient with the slow implementation of the accord.

The centre provided encouragement to the PTCA in their demand for Udayachal and to the militant All Bodo Students Union (ABSU) for Bodoland. The centre-state rift widened when centre blaimed the state for non-implementation of the accord and refused to amend the IMDT Act to the effect that onus of proof lay on the individual and not with the Govt. AASU hardened its stand and launched a stir in February 1987, resulting in oil blockade and disruption of OIL and ONGC operations resulting in loss of Rs. 160,000 million. ABSU agitation followed the same pattern of bandhs, rasta roko and picketing of Govt. Offices but the level of riolence was much higher.

Autonomous State Demand committee (ASDC) and United Tribal National Liberation Front (UTNLF), a break away faction of the PTCA launched agitation in the hill districts of Karbi Anglong resulting in polarization of tribals of Assam against ethnic Assamese. AGP lost credibility when some ministers were charged with corruption and extravagant style of some others came under criticism. There was rift in the legislative party as some members asked corrupt ministers to resign. The State Govt's. difficulties mounted due to AASU-AGP rift, internal rift within the party and AASU's confrontalist attitude against the centre. Realising that the accord was on a dump heap, AGP joined the National Front in 1989. The ULFA activities increased, gunning down of Surinder Paul of Apee Jay Group in April 1990 was a clear indication that ULFA called the shots. The period from May to August 1990 saw Govt's. authority in tatters and with the central Govt. (Janata) having its own problems Assam received no help. With the fall of VP Singh Govt. in November 1990, the AGP Govt. was dismissed and President's rule was imposed on 28 November 1990 and state was declared a disturbed area.

The evacuation of Doom Dooma Staff provided a dramatic curtain raiser for President's rule. The Army moved into Assam but found ULFA camps deserted. ULFA re-emerged and caused serious damage to life and property. in just two months of President's rule 97 people were killed, mainly Congress (I) leaders and cadres. The new Janata Dal Govt. under Chander Shekhar resigned but before doing so extended the President's rule by 6 months beyond May 1991. The detailed account of AASU agitation, rise of ULFA and other militant groups is given in my book "Threat from Within".

The elections to the Assembly were held in June 1991 and a Congress (I) Govt. under Hiteshwar Saikia took over. Army was ordered to the barracks and general amnesty was granted to all detainees captured under operation "Bajrang". ULFA failed to honour its commitment and killed a number of hostages. Seeing the deteriorating situation operation "RHINO" was launched and a mumber of top and middle rung ULFA functionaries were captured. Talks were held between Prime Minister Narasimha Rao and top ULFA leaders in January, 1992 but Paresh Barua who was in Bangladesh was opposed to talks. Raj Khowa, Chetia and Gogoi returned to Bangladesh to talk to Paresh Barua but never to return.

After the death of Upen Brahma in 1990, the Bodo movemgnt passed into the hands of the extremists. After prolonged talks a bipartite agreement was signed on 20 February, 1993 and Bodo Autonomus Council (BAC) came into existence. Bodo Security Force (BSF) called it a sell out. There were communal riots in Bodo area. Final notification of 2750 villages to comprise BAC was made on 10 December 1993; this excluded the ten KM. belt along Bhutan border and Manas Reserve Forest and Games Sanctuary. The stalemate continued inspite of the formation of joint working group consisting of representatives of Central Govt., State Govt. and of Bodo organisations in October 1997.

Saikia took full advantage of the absence of senior ULFA leaders and managed the surrender of 4860 ULFA activists by 1993. However, violence continued and already suspected ULFA links with ISI were confirmed. With the change in political scenario in Bangladesh in 1996, ULFA established camps in Manas Reserve Forest and in the jungles of Southern Bhutan. This has become a serious security concern.

Death of Saikia before the 1996 elections resulted in AGP returning to power but violence increased as Mohanta vacillated and decission to get tough was forced on him by ULFA attacks on him resulting in hardening of stance and introduction of Unified Command system. The years 1997-98 saw increased ethnic and militant violence. With the installation of the BJP led coalition at the centre, its support to Mohanta cooled and his tenure finished at a new low and he lost the 2001 election and Congress returned to power. The situation in Assam is further confused and enviornmentally violence prone due to the emergence of a number of minority insurgent groups to safeguard their perceived community intrests.

In 1999 the AGP Govt. had suggested creation of Bodoland Territorial Council (BTC) by suitable amendements in the Sixth Sechedule of the constitution. The agreement was signed in February 2003 and finally BTC was created with four districts of Kokrajhar, Udalguri, Basha and Chirang. In the second week of December 2003, 2600 cadres of the Bodo Liberation Tigers (BLT) surrendered at Kokrajhar[4], which drew bandh calls by the 17 non-tribal organisations of lower Assam under the banner of Sammilita Agosthiya Sangram Samiti (SJSS). The BTC will have a 12 member interim council, 2 of which will be non Bodos. The agitation launched under the PTCA in 1966 for Udayachal is finally taking shape with Hagrama Mohilary Chairman of BLT taking over as the Chief Executive member of the BTC. NDFB opposed the BTC and vows to continue to fight for a sovreign Bodo state.

After seven years of dithering, the Royal Bhutan Govt. (RBG) fearing a long term threat to its internal security decided to take action against Assamese insurgent groups in Southern Assam. The crack down came after demnds by RBG to vacate its territory failed. The operations by the Royal Bhutan Army against ULFA, NDFB and Kamtapur Liberation Organisation (KLO) in the second weak of December 2003 resulted in over-running of all the 30 camps (ULFA 13, NDFB 12 and KLO 5) of the insurgents, a large number of casualties and capture of ULFA publicity secretary Mithinga Daimary, KLO Chief Joydeb Roy and a number of middle level cardres. The Indian army provided logistic support and sealed the Indo-Bhutan border. The ULFA cadres have shifted to Kachin province of Myanmar with its old ally NSCN(K).

THE NAGAS

The origin of the Naga people is mysterious and the meaning and interpretation of the word Naga are many. But the generally accepted version by the Nagas themselves is that the word Naga has its origin in the word "Nok" which means folk and as the Nagas used to live in groups, so they came to be known as Nagas.[5] There are numerous legends and stories of Naga tribes as to their origin, but the view which states that the Nagas belong to the Tibeto-Burma or Indo-Mongoloid race appears to be the generally accepted historical truth. Most scholars believe that originally the Naga people came from Central Asia and these people of Central Asia were known as the non-Chinese Chinang tribes. They first came to the North-West border of China many centuries before the Christian era and later spread to China, Indonesia, Philippines, Bhutan, Burma, other South Asian countries and the present Naga Hills land. This is borne out by the fact that they bear similarity to Dyaks (Indonesia) and Koyans (Indo-Chinese Countries) and their social customs and culture are similar. They belong to the same blood which is found in the people of Burma, Sikkim and Bhutan, Arunachal Pradesh and other hilly areas of the North-East.[6]

Nagas came to Naga Hills after crossing the Irrawadi and Chindwin rivers in Burma. While some of the allied tribes like Keren, Shan, Chin and Singpho settled in Burma, the Nagas came to North-Eastern India in the 10th century B.C. and remained confined to the present Naga inhabited areas. They established their sovereign village states in which customary laws and traditions fetermined their code of conduct.The Nagas in ancient times marked their territories with stones, rivers and mountains and followed both the Jhum (Shifting) and terrace system of cultivation.

These Greek city state-like village states contained a well organised political community. The base of their organisation was Republican – Sovereign or Aristocracy but they were never able to establish a united sovereign state combining these village states. The primitive Nagas must be appreciated for their local self govt. based on customary laws, though fights, head hunting, wars, rivalries and tribal feuds prevailed. They had very little contact with the outside world till the 12th century as even the

Mughal invasion of Assam failed to establish control over it. Contact with the outside world was established only after the rise of the Ahom Kingdom in Assam in the 13th century. Ahoms who were the original inhabitants of Burma came to North-East Assam through the Patkai Range and the present Arunachal Pradesh. Ahoms attacked Naga villages for food and the Nagas retaliated by raids on areas controlled by the Ahom Kings. The hostility and a war between the Nagas and Ahoms resulted in the Ahoms establishing control over some Naga tribes on the borders of Assam like Noctes, Konyaks and later on Lotha and AO Nagas. While these Naga tribes paid tribute to the Ahoms in the shape of Mithuns (local Buffalo), in return they were granted exemption from land tax and granted fishing rights. Nagas also joined the Ahom Army and Govt. Ahom control was confined to the Nagas within their area, which also weakened after the Burmese Invasion in 1728.

It was only after the conquest of Assam by the British and the treaty of Yandaboo in 1826 that the British contact with the Nagas began. During the Anglo-Burmese War, Capt. Neufr Ville crossed the Patkai Range to free the Naga slaves of Singhpos from the Burmese. The contact was mainly to protect the tea gardens of Assam against the raids by Angami Nagas. In 1832 Capt. Jenkins and Pemberton led an expedition of Manipuri troops into the Angami area and occupied Papoolongmai village after stiff resistance. But it was Lt.Briggs Ledan's expedition which resulted in friendly arrangements and in 1842, the Angami Nagas agreed to pay yearly tribute[7]. The British were also able to win over Semas by abolishing the Salt Tax.

Cecil Beadon, the Lt.Governor of Bengal in 1866 initiated a policy of slow but positive control over Naga territory and an outpost was opened at Shamaguting in 1866. The Inner Line established by the British in 1873 was gradually pushed inside to accommodate expanding tea gardens and to incorporate more areas into reserve forests. By 1978 forward posts were established at Wokha and Kohima and by 1881 the Naga Hill District was formed covering Lotha and Angami areas[8]. Beyond the administered area, the British created a zone of political control into the inner hills and AO area of Mokokchung was brought under British administration in 1890.

The political agent in Manipur (MC Cullock) and the Govt. of Bengal found it expedient to plant Kuki settlements as a barrier against Naga raids and boundaries were redrawn to accommodate these. The British desire was motivated by both commercial and political interests. The British Indian Govt. was concerned about the safety and security of Indian borders in the Himalayas from Tibet to Burma and the strategy demanded that the water shed South of Himalayas should be under their control.

Secondly to prevent Naga raids on the plains of Assam and gain direct access from Assam to Manipur for developing trade with the Manipuris and for protecting their commercial interests in upper Cachar, North Assam and Burma. A direct route to Manipur was possible only through the Naga areas. That is why Capt. Jenkin and Pemberton with 700 Manipuri soldiers and 800 coolies marched from Manipur to Assam in 1832. Lastly, King Gambhir Singh of Manipur had planned to permanently expand his influence in the Naga hills. To counter it the British were compelled to alter its policy of Naga hills. In the words of John Butler (Capt. John Butler, Principal Assistant of Nowgang, who visited Nagaland in 1845 and signed a non aggression pact with the Naga Chief in 1845), it was "one long sickening story of open insults, defiance, bold outrageous and cold blooded murders on one side and long suffering, forbearance, forgiveness, concession and outlook for favours on the other, varied now and again with tours, immovable deputation and expeditions."This expansion of the administration into the Hill district continued till 1927[9]. Agreements were signed by tribal chiefs from time to time, which upon death were not recognised by the latter chiefs.

While the process of bringing the whole of Naga areas under British jurisdiction was going on in the beginning of the 20th century, the British Govt. also contemplated carving out an area for hill tribes into their administrative system. While they made Naga hills district a part of Assam and declared it backward, it was placed under the Governor General by giving him special powers under the Govt. of India Act 1919. No interaction took place between the Nagas and the plainsmen, and the Nagas remained isolated from the nationalistic moment. When the Govt. of India Act, 1935 was enacted, the Naga hills District was declared an "Excluded Area". Sir Robert Reid, Governor of Assam, mentioned the Constitution Act of 1935 which said "Throughout the discussions previous to the framing of the new Act, the authorities concerned had no difficulty in agreeing that Naga hills ought to be kept out of the new Constitution. They were accordingly declared to be an "Excluded Area" under the Govt. of India (Excluded and partially excluded area) order, 1936 and were administered by the Governor in his discretion[10]. Robert Reid even made a proposal that after granting of Independence to India the Naga hills, NEFA and CHT of East Bengal (now Bangladesh) be retained as a Crown Colony. The British design to keep the area isolated from the national main stream is quite evident.

Nagas who returned from France at the end of the World War I after serving in the labour corps formed the Naga club in 1918 in Kohima and Mokokchung along with other Govt. servants. This started the articulation of the Naga identity and politics and when Simon Commission visited in 1929, they expressed their desire to be kept out of the proposed reforms. The plea was "You are the only people who have conquered us and when you go, we should be as we were". This was ignored and Govt. of India Act of 1935 came into effect on 1 May 1937, making Naga hills as backward and directly under the administration of the Governor[11]. Towards the end of the British period, the Coupland Plan to carve out a crown colony out of tribal areas of India and Burma was rejected by the Naga leaders and Phizo termed it as an extension of British Imperialism. In 1945, the Naga Hills District Tribal Council was reorganized to repair the damages of World War II and was converted into Nagaland National Council (NNC) in 1946, amalgamating the Naga club.

When Indian Independence became imminent in 1947 the then Governor of Assam Sir Akbar Hydairi signed an agreement with the Nagas giving a fair amount of autonomy to them. The agreement conceded to the NNC judicial processes based on Naga customary law, executive and legislative powers and control over the land and its resources. Clause 9 (j) of the agreement became a bone of contention. Although they had declared their independence a day prior to Indian Independence but no separate Government was formed. Administration of the area through the Ministry of Foreign Affairs gave the Nagas a wrong impression and credence to the secessionists. Although underground activities started in 1953 but it is only in 1955 that the Phizo announced the formation of the Naga Federal Government (NFG) and armed rebellion broke out. The army was inducted in 1956, Phizo was forced to flee to East Pakistan and then to London in 1957. With the onset of insurgency, people's hardships increased and moderates amongst the Nagas commenced a political movement under Naga Peoples Convention demanding maximum autonomy within the Indian Constitution, and not district autonomy within Assam. In a Naga peoples convention in August 1957, 1760 delegates representing all tribes in Naga Hills and Tuensang District of NEFA agreed on a single Naga Hills and Tuensang Administrative unit within the Indian Union. In December 1957, Naga Hills and Tuensang area (NHTA) was created as an Autonomous district directly under the Governor of Assam. After two more conventions, the sixteen point agreement with the Govt. of India was signed in 1960, under which NHTA was to become a state under the Ministry of External Affairs. Special provisions were made for financial grants to Nagaland.

The State of Nagaland was formed in December 1963 and the first general elections were held in 1964. This ushered in an era of comparative peace. To bring about complete normalcy in the State, a peace mission under late Jai Prakash Narayan, with late BP Chaliha, Chief Minister of

Assam and Rev. Michael Scott was formed. There were dissensions in the peace mission and Rev. Scott was not in agreement with the main purpose of the mission. The peace mission broke up when Rev. Scott was asked to leave the country. He even took up the cause of Naga independence with the Western press and UNO but failed. Failure of the peace mission again escalated the hostilities and underground activities spread to Ukhrul in Manipur. The ceasefire which had come into force in 1964 continued and the peace mission under Dr.Aram held talks with Gundevia, the foreign secretary. During the 4th round of talks peace mission suggested that "NFG" could on its own hold talks with the Govt. of India and the Govt. offered to consider the extent to which the aspirations of the people of Nagaland could be accommodated in the interest of peace. Indira Gandhi on becoming the Prime Minister continued the talks. In the meantime, Mowu Angami the Chief of Naga Federal Army (NFA) kept sending gangs to China, which was condemned by the Naga Nationalist Organisation (NNO), the ruling party. A section of the NFA under Kaito and Zuheto were in favour of giving up violence and finally surrendered in 1972. Mowu Angami with his gang on return from China was captured. After the third general elections, the Shillong Accord was signed in November 1975. However, some of the underground Nagas who were in China and had been under communist influence did not surrender and denounced the Accord. They established themselves in the North Burma Hills, under the leadership of Khaplang a Burmese Hemei Naga, Muivah (a Tangkhul Naga from Manipur) and Issac Swu a Sema. There was a vertical split in 1980 after intense infighting and the communist oriented hawks started calling themselves National Socialist Council of Nagaland (NSCN). Their professed aim was to establish a "Pan Mongoloid" state with a socialist structure. The other splinter group continued to call itself NFG.

Attempts by Rev.Longi AO and his Konyak associate for peace talks in 1985 failed due to the reported backing out of the Govt. of India. In 1988, the Government again sent word to Muviah for talks within the framework of the Indian Constitution but the offer was rejected. But rumour spread that Issac Swu and Muviah had sold out to the Govt. of India and planned to oust Khaplang (Vice President). A national assembly was called but in a pre-emptive attack on Muviah in April, 1988, 140 of his men were killed and many hid in the jungles. This resulted in a vertical split between Khaplang (Hemei Konyak) and Issac Swu-Muviah Group (Thangkhuls and Semas). The split led to bloody feuds between these groups with NSCN (IM) emerging as the stronger one but NSCN (K) having its own area of influence.

NSCN (I) over the years has spread its influence from the Ukhrul and Senapati districts of Manipur to the other hill areas of Manipur and in Kohima and surrounding Sema and Lotha areas in Wokha and Zunebthoto districts of Nagaland. Most important of all, they control Dimapur and NH 39 throghout Nagaland and Manipur except Kuki dominated areas in Chandal distt. near Moreh. The NSCN (K) has established itself in the Konyak area of Mon Distt. and the AO area of Mokokchung distt. in Nagaland. The period since the split is marked by factional fights to increase the area of influence and the elimination of potential rivals. Elimination of the Shaiza brothers, both Thangkuls, by NSCN (IM) is part of the same plan.

Rivalry between the NSCN factions provided the Naga politicians in Manipur and Nagaland the opportunity to exploit the same for furthering their political designs. The main motivation is power projection. The allegations of the then Chief Minister SC Jamir of Nagaland patronising NSCN (K) and Ex-chief Minister of Manipur Rishang Keishing patronising NSCN (IM) are well founded. It is a mutually convenient arrangement of trading patronage and Govt. resources for help in perpetuating power. Naga-Kuki conflict in Manipur and Nagaland is essentially an outcome of expansion of areas of influence by NSCN (IM) and ethnic exploitation by political players of the area.

NSCN (IM) while increasing its influence internally has simultaneously expanded its activities abroad. Its admission to the Unrepresented Nations and Peoples Organisations (UNPO), a Hague based NGO has provided them an opportunity to propagate its cause in international forums and open avenues for arms and ammunition in SE Asia, Europe and North America - a development which largely went uncontested by our diplomacy and the failure to send elected representatives and NGOs of the indigenous people.

The Naga underground movement is a three way divided house with their own areas of influence. NNC still has a faction of its remnants in UK under Phizo's daughter Adino, NNC (A), the other faction under Khado Yanthan is known as NNC (K). NNC has limited influence in the Angami and Chakasang areas. As discussed above NSCN (IM) have its areas of influence amongst Semas, Lothas, Phoms, and Angamis in Kohima and Dimapur areas in Nagaland and Thangkuls, Maos, Ziclionrnngs, in Manipur. NSCN (K) has influence in Konyak, AO and some lotha areas.

In response to the Govt. of India's initiative in 1997, negotiations with the NSCN (IM) were initiated and a cease fire effective from 1 August '97 that has been extended from time to time over the last six years, resulted in talks with the NSCN (IM) in January 2003. The talks ended in NSCN (IM) reiterating their position resulting in seventeen points being proposed for discussion. The main hurdle in implementation of the ceasefire and progress in the negotiations is the failure of the Naga militant groups to come to a common platform. The moving spirit behind the peace initiative has been the Naga Ho Ho. I for one would give all support to the peace initiatives and have full realisation of the desire for peace in Manipur and Nagaland but the dynamics of handling it so far leaves me unhappy and skeptical. Without making the people a party to it through the Naga Ho Ho and the Meitei and Kuki organisations, dealing only with the insurgent factions at the political level will result in the dynamics of internal Naga and inter community politics damaging its chances of success.

A Historical Review

The modern period of Naga history can be broadly divided into three, namely the British period from 1830 to 1947, the period after independence and upto the Shillong accord (1947 to 1975) and the post Shillong contemporary period from 1975 to date. Each of these periods has its indicators which have influenced the Naga perceptions. A broad analysis of these is therefore valid.

The British Period 1830-1947

The Nagas remained isolated from the outside world till the First World War, when some of them went to France as a part of the labour corps. The Second World War pitched Nagas and Manipuris in the midst of Indian and multinational opposing armies. The advent of Christianity gave them awareness, exposure to modern western culture and the modern concept of politics and governance, resulting in a demand for autonomy when the Simon Commission visited in 1929. But this was related to the experience of British with no Indianness as the Nagas were kept isolated from the mainstream struggle for independence. The Naga and other tribal areas being designated as excluded and partially excluded under the Govt. of India Act of 1935, implied that excluded areas were to be administered by the Governor himself in his discretion and partially excluded areas were to be the special responsibility of the Governor. The basic point in the Governance of these areas was that powers of the provincial legislature were not extended to these areas.

The aim was deliberately and determinedly to restrict administrative apparatus to the rock bottom minimum. The reasons for the slow process of bringing the Nagas under British administration were the absence of strong economic incentives and financial constraints on the administration. There were no geopolitical compulsions to impose control over the Nagas and finally though the Nagas posed a problem to the British but it posed no security threat to British India. Gradual annexation was only to prevent raids into the plains of British India. As long as colonial interests were maintained, the British did not interfere and native institutions were left undisturbed and administration was confined to law and order. With this background our retention of these provisions in the constitutional order of 1947 was a valid step.

While the British broke the splendid isolation of the Nagas and incorporated them in their system, it also resulted in greater coexistence amongst tribes and identifying themselves as Nagas. The formation of the Naga club in 1918 and NNC in 1946 gave them political exposure but kept them isolated from the rest of the area, which resulted in an inward looking ethnic group devoid of any socio-political fraternity even with the rest of the people of the North-East. The term excluded did not mean that they were outside India. Later, this coupled with different interpretation of the clause 9 of the Akbar Hydari Agreement of June 1947 combined with the administration of the area through MEA, gave the Nagas a wrong impression and credence to secessionists.

The ancient culture even though deep rooted could not remain totally unaffected due to its incompatibility with the norms of British administration. The practice of head hunting associated with the native belief of being a source of dynamism and productivity had no place under the British regime. Along with it, other social evils such as child marriage and human sacrifice were brought to an end. However, the British encouraged the preservation of other elements of the culture, in particular effort was to isolate the Nagas from Assam and rest of India. Because of this cultural isolationist policy, while the Nagas preserved their indigenous customs and culture, the limited avenue of interaction only with western colonial culture, education and spread of Christianity resulted in socio-cultural changes in the Naga society but it also perpetuated isolation[12].

The acceptance of Christianity made them more amenable to western culture, which also resulted in loyalty to the British, which is borne out by the fact that there was no resistance to colonisation. The American Christian missionaries made the greatest impact on Naga traditional culture and Naga Hills virtually became a colony of American Evengelism. It brought about immense socio-economic changes and political transformation. The gradual assimilation of alien culture inevitably led to erosion of Naga culture, for change and erosion were inseparable. Acceptance of the Gospel and discarding of animism accelerated the pace of change in the Naga society. This is inspite of the Govt.'s policy of cultural protectionism, which strove to maintain status quo, it tended to play a counter balancing role vis-à-vis both extremes. The spread of Christianity, while providing Nagas a sense of identity, also simultaneously promoted a sense of separateness from rest of the country.

In the economic field the colonial policy to exploit the natural resources did not succeed very much although attempts were made to exploit resources like tea, coffee, timber and coal. The main source of revenue in the district was house tax. The progress in the agricultural field was also minimal. Trade was the main activity, which was confined to the inter-village level and with border areas of Assam. The main constraint was the undeveloped barter system. The trade within the district was monopolised by non indigenous residents and Marwari and Muslim traders came in the wake of British expansion. Communications were improved to meet the requirements of the Administration.

Post Independence 1947 to 1975.

Most significant is the four point resolution passed by NNC on 19 June 1946, which inter-alia resolved "The Naga Hills should be constitutionally included in autonomous Assam in a free India with local autonomy and due safeguards for the interests of the Nagas" – The four point resolution formed part of the memorandum which was presented to the Cabinet Mission in June 1946 by T Sakhrie and M Sheshrmeren[13]. Sakhrie was the founder of the Naga movement. It is not very well known that Sakhrie differed with Phizo on the use of violence and had warned that the Nagas were ill prepared for such a clash. Although denied by Phizo, it is generally believed that Sakhrie was brutally tortured and murdered at the behest of Phizo.

Clause 9 of Akbar Hydari Agreement laying down that "the Governor of Assam as an agent of the Government of India, will have special responsibility for a period of ten years to ensure due observance of this agreement; at the end of this period the NNC will be asked whether they require this agreement to be extended for a further period or a new agreement regarding the future of Naga people be arrived at", was the most contentious. The Nagas interpreted this as acceptance of their right to selfdetermination, whereas the Govt. held the view that the agreement had been subsumed in the sixth schedule.

The harsh measures taken by the Army in the aftermath of Naga Insurgency in 1956, contributed to the spread of separateness and alienation amongst the general public. The then Chief of the Army Staff General K.S.Thimaiya is reported to have told Nehru that it required political wisdom rather that military might to solve the Naga problem[14]. The guerillas on the other hand were galvanised by idealism and romance.

The support of Pakistan and China boosted their morale and provided them a platform for anti-India propaganda.

Political initiatives in response to Naga people's conventions from 1957 to 1960 resulted in the formation of the Naga Hills Tuensang Autonomous Area in 1957 and the Nagaland State in 1963. Naga politics which had got complicated with the advent of independence, found a measure of settlement after this and particularly after the ceasefire agreement of 1964.

The belief amongst present day Nagas and amongst most Indians that there was unanimity amongst Nagas for separation from India at the time of independence and transfer of power is ill founded and mischievous. The speech by T.Aliba Imti, President of NNC at a public meeting in Kohima on 6 December 1946 where he exhorted "I have but one word to say, our country is connected with India in many ways. We should continue this connection" is revealing. This was based on the four point resolution passed by NNC on 19 June1946 and which formed part of the memorandum presented to the Cabinet Mission in June 1946.

The period from 1956 to 1963, when Nagaland became a state is marked by three conventions of All Naga Tribes people between 1957-59 bringing about a peaceful constitutional arrangement to meet the aspirations of the people and the church leaders' efforts for peaceful resolutions and ceasefire in 1964. Inspite of the break up of the peace mission and opposition of Phizo from London to the peace talks, these continued till 1967. On the breakdown of talks the period upto 1969 saw heightened insurgent activities, establishment of their links with the Chinese, intensification of SF operations and large scale captures and surrenders of Naga insurgents.

The Nagas missed a historic opportunity to find a lasting solution to the problem, when they refused Indira Gandhi's offer of a settlement not within the frame work of the Indian Constitution but within the framework of the Indian Union[15], thereby meaning that the Constitution could be amended to accommodate a settlement. Indira Gandhi was quite amendable during her talks between February 1966 and October 1967.

Indian Army's operations for the liberation of Bangladesh in 1971 dealt a strategic blow to underground Nagas, leading to the capture of key insurgents and vital documents, resulting in the banning of Federal Govt. of Nagaland (FGN) and NNO in 1972. RGN led by Scato Swu and Kughato Sukhai Sema surrendered on 16 August 1973 and Scato was nominated to the Rajya Sabha on 1 April 1974.

On imposition of President's rule in the wake of emergency in 1975, the pressure was put by the Army and peace efforts simultaneously brought about the Shillong Accord on 1 November, 1975. The newly formed NSCN dismissed the Shillong Accord on 31 January, 1980. The accord brought into focus the failure of negotiations to enter into wider negotiations before finalising the accord. Commenting in his article, "Key to peace lost in deadlock" published in the Asian Age 6 October, 1997, Sanjoy Hazarika wrote, "Shillong Accord is an issue which still divides tribes, clans and families. It raises the question of loyalty and collaboration and those who do not understand this basic truth know nothing of the Naga situation". Even today the Govt. of India is following a similar ill advised policy in negotiations with NSCN (IM).

The period of 1970s saw the centre of gravity of insurgent activities shifting to the East with China and KIA as the main source and support base. This resulted in activation of the Eastern border and areas adjoining to it in Nagaland and Manipur ushering in a new phase of insurgency which negated the Shillong accord.

Post Shillong Accord (1975–onwards)

The period since the beginning of eighties is marked with increasing overground politics getting mixed with fractious developments in the NSCN factions for furthering political power perpetuation. These go beyond the limits of human and tribal affiliations, which we have understood in the past. The game is totally political and power oriented. The nexus between the politicians, contractors, bureaucrats and the underground factions is well established, which apportions a major portion of developmental funds and people remain deprived and alienated. Forty years of confrontation in the polluted environment has resulted in the last two decades in the carrot offered to the people being eaten by the nexus and the stick falling on the people. The deals, negotiations and fights are all amongst the main players in this power game, the politicians, the bureaucrats, the contractors and the insurgent factions. The Security Forces have a situation where the main culprits are either in the Govt. or have its protection, the target is restricted to lower rank and file of insurgents. The common man (the people) is caught in this ding dong battle, with little resource to mitigation. One cannot fight insurgency only at the ground level, when its main supporters and the powerful elements behind it are left free to perpetuate it and provide it the life support. The battle is for the people and against the anti people elements. The central Govt. has been a party to the malaise by their inaction and tolerance.

The character of Naga insurgency has changed over the past decade. No Longer Guerrillas contemplate a life in the jungle hide out. The scene of action has shifted to population centres and towns. In 50s and 60s the emphasis was on mass mobilization and guerilla tactics of hit and run. Now the emphasis is on exploitation, hkjacking, kidnappings and blackmail. The community is held to ransom by fear of the militants who are running a parallel Govt. Every Govt. employee including ministers pay part of their salary to militants as taxes. So do professionals like doctors, traders, shopkeepers. For every contract commission is paid and in some cases even the award of contract is managed by insurgents and commissions directly collected from the state Treasury. The public exchequer is the main financier of insurgency.

The Naga-Kuki confrontation has further complicated the situation. This along with demands of greater Nagaland, has made the ethnic divide in Manipur more pronounced.

The year 2003 could prove to be hisvoric for the Nagas for more than one reason in spite of stray ominus clouds. The ceasefire has entered the seventh year and is holding. In January for the first time discussions were held in India in New Delhi between the NSCN (I) leadership and the Govt. of India. The Prime Minister visited Nagaland in October and acknowledged Naga sentiment and the long Naga struggle. On the question of territory he mentioned that such issues need consensus, thereby underlining the sentiments of the neigbhouring states. However, the ground swell for peace amongst the people which was surging over the last tjree years received a set back. Naga Hoho was made defunct and the Reconciliation Commision comprising of seven upright and widely respected Nagas have quit, refusing to bow to the pressure of NSCN (I) leadership and its supporters. Both had support of the Naga society and people, who have a major stake in the permanent peace. They had asked both NSCN (I) and the Govt. of India to come out openly with their position and make the process all inclusive. It should not only include all Nagas but also neighbouring communities. Ground realities dictate that no political solution contrived without genuine support of the people will succeed. It is therefore vital that Govt. does not restrict its dialogue with insurgents alone and reach out to all segments of the civil society. The parametres of peace must extend beyond political negotiations and accords with insurgent factions. The NSCN (I) leadership reported visit to India in March 2004 has been postponed due to elections. Wc hope that there is greater realisation in both the parties that the civil society needs to be heard and accommodated.

THE MEITEIS OF MANIPUR

In the last three decades, Manipur began to witness a state of social restlessness amongst its people. The growth or revival of Meitei nationality came to affect the lives of the majority Meitei community. The resurgence of Meitei nationalism has its roots in its history, culture and social structure and the movements initiated by other ethnic groups in Manipur.

Manipur, the easternmost out post of Indian civilisation presents a unique map of multi-ethnic, multilingual and multicultural social groups. Manipur, meaning the "land of the gems" is a sanskritised name given to the land when the plains people of Manipur (Meiteis) were Hinduised in the 18th Century A.D. Sanamahi Laikan, a semi historical work records the official naming of the land as Manipur during the reign of Garibnawaz (1709-1758 AD). Some of the other names recorded in the ancient texts, the Puyas, are Meitei Leipak, Poireinamthak Saron Pung, Tilli Kokton Ahanba, Mirai Pongthoklam, Hanna Semba Konna Loiba and Muwapalli. Due to its location it formed an important link between India and South-East Asia. Through it poured Mongoloid tribes, their culture and beliefs poured into Eastern India and Indian culture passed onto upper Burma and beyond. It was the melting pot on the Eastern Gateway of India, where races, languages and cultures met, influenced and ultimately intermingled.

There are twenty nine tribes belonging to the Naga or Kuki stock living in areas surrounding the valley whereas in the valley there are only six ethnic groups the Meitei, Loi/Chakpa, Yaithibi, Brahmin, Bishnupriya and Pangan Meiteis (Muslims).[16] The Meitei account for over sixty per cent of the state's population, whereas twenty nine hill tribes constitute thirty six per cent and the remaining by other groups in the valley.

There are a number of theories on the origin of the Meitei. BC. Allen opines, "From the North-West China between the upper waters of Yang-tse Kiang and Ho-ang-ho, which was the cradle of the Indo-Chinese race, successive waves of emigrants entered Assam and India. The first to arrive were the Mon-Annam who are found in Annam and Cambodia, who left a colony in Assam in the shape of Khasis. The second wave brought the Tibeto-Burmans, the ancestors of Bodo tribe, who colonized the Brahmaputra and occupied Garo, Tipperah and a portion of Naga hills. Another branch came southwards down the Chindwin, settled in chin hills and compelled by the pressure of population moved northwards into Cachar, Manipur and even the Assam Range[17]. The Tai or Siamese branch of the indo-Chinese people called Shan by the Burmese were believed to be the first to migrate from their original seat in Central Asia toward the south and settled along the rivers Mekong, Menem, Irrawadi and Brahmaputra[18]. According to Brain Houghton Hodgson, "in the Moitai of Manipur", we have the combined appellations of the Siamese Tai and the Kochin Chinese Moy.[19] P. Gogoi quoting W Shaw states that in the year 707 AD the King of Thailand defeated the King of Manipur and thereafter Manipur is said to have been ruled by the Thais for ten years[20]. This is supported by the fact that Samlung the younger brother of Sukanpha, the King of Pong stayed in Manipur for ten years at Apong Engkhol, a place east of the then Royal Palace. Since there was no independent Kingdom of Thailand in that early period, the reference is to Samlungs conquest of upper Burma and Assam including Manipur in 8th century AD. Pong appears to be the name by which upper Irawadi is still called in Manipur[21]. The various scholarly theories put forward indicate that there are two linkages between the Meiteis and the outside groups, viz, Indo-Chinese in general and the Thais in particular and the Aryan origin. The theory of Aryan origin holds no water due to lack of evidence as there is no conclusive proof that the Manipur of Mahabharata is the same as the present place by the same name. On the other hand the theory of Tai origin of Meiteis is based among others on language, movement of groups of people in the region and racial similarities. That the Meiteis are the decendents of the Thai race are also accounted for in the Burmese and Manipuri Chronicles. In the absence of historical evidence and records, the comparative ethno graphical studies suggest that Meiteis belong to the Tai race of the Indo-Chinese groups of the Mongoloids.

In the opening decades of the first century of the Christian era, the erstwhile Kingdom of Manipur was divided into seven main principalities, later amalgamated into a confederacy by Nongda Lairen Pakhangba in 33 AD. The confederacy was the union of seven Salais (clans). The first king Nongda Lairen Pakhangba (33-154 AD) of the Ningthouja Salai put his principality on firm footing and founded a long dynasty which ruled Manipur till its integration with the Indian union in 1949[22]. It existed as a fairly peaceful and independent Kingdom till about the second half of the 18th century due to distance and difficult terrain between Surma and Manipur valley. None of the great Indian Empires of Maurya, Gupta, Harshvardhan reached Manipur. Moghuls also failed to subdue Manipur. The British did not capture Manipur and it was allowed to remain a native state with a high degree of aloofness.

Manipur enjoyed a distinct political and cultural identity till the middle of 18th century AD when in 1762 Maharaja sought British help to repel the invasion from Burma. In this British saw an opportunity to establish a military outpost in this strategic area against the Burmese. The Treaty of Verelst in 1762 formalised the relationship between Manipuris and the British and was the start of the crumbling of Manipur's independence.[23] In 1824 British were again asked to repel the Burmese invasion. The Anglo-Burmese war and the resultant treaty of Yandaboo 1826 exposed to the British the weakness of Manipur, inspite of the professed friendly relations and recognition of the King as the head of the Kingdom. With the consolidation of

British power, they started regarding Manipur as a protectorate. The difference in out look resulted in the Anglo-Manipur war of 1891, when Manipur was occupied by the British. After the death of Maharaja Gambir Singh, who was installed by the British following the treaty of Yandaboo, the war of succession amongst his grandsons resulted in Kulachandra being installed and it was decided that the affairs of the state will be carried out with the advice of the Political Agent. The attempt to impose their writ led to a series of battles with Manipuris. The attempts of the British to arrest Jubraj Tikendrajit failed and British without declaring a war attacked the palacg on 24 March, 1891. After severe fighting a durbar was held to make peace; the British officers who came to attend the durbar were beheaded. The British advanced into Manipur from Kohima, Silchar and"Tamu and Manipur fell to the British on 27 April, 1891[24]. The three valiant heroes of the Anglo-Mankpur war namely Jubraj Tikendrajit Singh, Thangal General and Major Paona Brajabasi are highly revergd. While Major Paona died in the battle of Khongjom, Tikendrajit and Thangal General were tried and hanged by the British. Due to the interference of former viceroys Lord Northbrook and Lord Ripon Manipur was not formally annexed but it became a colonial dependency of the British and lost its sovergignty. The administration was conducted under British supervision, Maharaja was assisted by a Durbar and a Council, whose vice president was a British Officer. The period of British suprintency ended in 1907, when Maharaja Churachand Singh came to power but Maharaja's powers were curtailed and the vice president became its President.

After the Kuki revolt in 1917 against recruitment as labour for France, the Maharaja became responsible for the administration of the state with the counsel of the durbar but had to keep the British political officer apprised of all matters. Along with it the British Resident became responsible for administration of the hill areas on behalf of the maharaja. The bifurcation of the administration of the Imphal valley and hill areas laid the foundation of separatist tendencies and political division – the Governor of Assam was designated as the appellate authority in all matters.

Administrative changes done to suit British interest disrupted the traditional village economy and judicial system leading to unrest and protest resulting in political and social movements. The woman war (Nupi Lan) in 1933 and 1939 was a direct result of it. The main issue for the agitation was the export of rice from Manipur. This was followed by the formation of the Nikhil Hindu Manipuri Maha Sabha in 1934[25], the organisation was led by the Maharaja and H. Irabot Singh was the vice president. The aim was to promote social unity for strengthening the

Meitei nation. Later the name was changed to Nikhil Manipuri Maha Sabha in 1938 and it became a political organistaion.

Kubaw valley of Manipur was given to the Burmese in 1933 against a compensation as a gesture of goodwill by the British. Manipur had sought retrocession of Kubaw valley from Burma consistently and the efforts continued even after independence. In 1953 Pt. Nehru, during a joint visit along with U NU to Manipur, waived the claim of Manipur in favour of Burmese and Kubaw compensation paid to Manipur Durbar also ceased.

In keeping with the upsurge in the rest of India, Nikhil Manipur Mahasabha led the struggle for a democratic form of Government in 1939, demanding a legislative assembly of people's elected representatives. As a result of the agitation a Chief Court independent of the executive was established.

From the bombing of Imphal on 10 May, 1942, till 1946, Manipur remained under the spell of II World War. In 1946, Manipur State Congress was formed as a unit of the All India States Peoples Conference. With the approach of independence, the Maharaja signed the instrument of accession on 11 Aug 1947. When paramountcy lapsed, the agitation for a fully responsible Govt. intensified resulting in the Manipur State Constitution Act of 1947 and elections were held on the basis of adult franchise. The new Govt. was not responsible to the legislature, it was only 'responsive' to the legislature, a technicality devised by the Maharaja's Constitutional Pandits.

In the elections under the new Constitution Manipur Congress (earlier Manipur Mahasabha) won 24 seats out of 53 seats, the rival Krishh Sabha, Hill Areas representatives and independents won the remaining seats. A non-Congress Govt. with a left orientation came to power, which upset the Govt. of India and Maharaja was coerced into signing the instrument of merger on 21 September, 1949. The Govt. under Maharaj Kumar Priyabrata Singh as Chief Minister was dissolved and a Chief Commissioner took over the administration. In 1950 Manipur became a part 'C' state and on reorganisation of the states in 1956 it became a union territory with a territorial council which was upgraded to a territorial assembly in 1963. It was granted full statehood in 1972 after Nagaland and Meghalaya.

The period of 40s in Manipur's history was of agitation and struggle against the feudal system in which Hijam Irabot Singh's contribution towards the emancipation of the deprived is singular. His charismatic personality gave impetus to the socialist movement for which he was imprisoned in Sylhet jail. He was released in 1943 but was not permitted to enter Manipur, inspite of his assurance to raise volunteers to fight the

Japanese. He was suspected of alliance with the INA and the Japanese and warrant for his arrest was issued. He went underground and joined the Communist Party of India in Cachar. He formed Praja Sangha and Krishi Sanmeloni and advocated non-violence to put forward issues of people's suppression. He was in touch with the Communist Party of Burma. He died of typhoid in 1951. His struggle for the people of Manipur left an impact on the Manipuris mind and towards the close of 1950's the intellectuals of Manipur launched the 'Pan Mangoloid Movement' with the aim of creating a sovereign nation for the mongloid people of the North-East[26].

The Pan-Mangoloid movement acted as an incentive for the establishment of the United National Liberation Front (UNLF) in 1964 with the propagated aims of achieving self determination and a socialist society and links were established with Naga and Mizo underground. There were differences between Somarendra, who was for ideological indoctrination before launching the armed struggle, and Sudhir Kumar with more radical views, who established the Revolutionary Government of Manipur (RGM) and sought help from Pakistan. RGM raided Cachar and Tripura at the behest of Pakistan during the 1971 operation against East Pakistan. Liberation of Bangladesh resulted in detention of a large number of Meitei Extremists (ME) who were released under a general amnesty by the Govt. of Manipur. N Bisheshwar Singh, the most popular dissident leader broke away from UNLF and on return from China in 1975 formed the Peoples Liberation Army in 1978.

Due to high level of violence, Imphal valley was declared as disturbed area in September 1980 bringing the state under Armed Forces (Assam and Manipur) Special Powers Act. I took over the responsibility for Manipur and Nagaland and in relentless operations the chairman of PLA, N Bisheshwar Singh was captured. Due to continued pressure the second rung of leadership under Kunj Behari was also eliminated within a year. The situation was brought fully under control by the middle of 1982 and ME organisations maintained a low profile, while spreading its net work amongst the younger generation. In May 1990, UNLF joined NSCN (K), ULFA and KNA to form the Indo-Burma Revolutionary Front (IRBF). However each of the factions had their own agenda. The PLA took shelter in Bangladesh and formed Revolutionary Peoples Front (RPF). Its efforts to unite ME resulted in the formation of the Revolutionary Joint Committee (RJC) along with Peoples Revolutionary Party of Kanglepak (PREPAK) and Kanglepak Communist Party (KCP)

The Pangan (Manipuri Muslims) – Meitei Communal riots in May 1993 in which 97 people were killed of which 94 were Pangans, were totally out of character of the Imphal Valley's serene and communal free atmosphere. Pangans constitute seven per cent of the population, who had settled in Manipur longtime ago and had fully integrated in the life of the Imphal Valley. The propagated cause of a fracas between Pangan arms dealers and Meitei extremists could not have caused such a communal flare. It was instigated and contrived by politicians along with social and criminal elements amongst the ME and the incident of Barbri Masjid a few months earlier was used to give it a communal colour. The incident left an ugly mark on Manipur's communally free past history and gave an opportunity to fundamentalist Hindu and Muslim organisations and individuals to create religious consciousness. It also resulted in the emergence of Muslim fundamentalist organistions like the Isamic Front United Liberation Army amongst the Bangladeshi settlers in Jaribam developing links with Pakistan ISI.

A new dimension to the violence and ethnic divide was added with the eruption of clashes between Nagas and Kukis in 1992. The violence was the result of struggle between NSCN (IM) and Kuki National Army (KNA) for the control of NH 39 and the border town of Moreh. Moreh has been the nodal point for smuggling of narcotics, arms and other contraband since long. But the extension of Naga-Kuki clashes to other areas of Manipur and Nagaland was primarily due to NSCN's design to extend their areas of influence and KNA and other Kuki organisation's efforts to contest and thwart it. Both sides have support of their ethnic politicians. The Tamil-Kuki clashes in Moreh in June 1995 is a fallout of the same. Naga raid on a Kuki village set a chain reaction as Kukis suspected a Tamilian boy to be NSCN (IM) informer. Moreh has 17,000 Tamilians from Burma settled since World War II but bulk of them came across when trade was nationalised in Burma in 1960. Moreh area has majority of Kukis and Tamilians who had been paying taxes to Kukis but NSCN (IM) also started demanding taxes, thus precipitating the crisis.

Since 1995 the situation in Manipur has gradually deteriorated due to revival and escalation in the Naga – Kuki conflict, increase in ME and NSCN (IM) activities. With the cease fire in Nagaland and protracted negotiations without progress with NSCN (IM) the demand for greater Nagaland has come to the forefront. The passing of the "Greater Nagaland Demand" private members bill unanimously in Nagaland Assembly in 1994 started the old controversy. Inspite of a resolution passed in Manipur Assembly unanimously against it in 1995, the controversy goes on.

Meiteis are perturbed at the regrouping of Nagas and growing strength of Kukis. The demands for Greater Nagaland and Kukiland both go against the interest of Meiteis. Meiteis are worried and concerned ever since the Central Govt. has opened dialogue with NSCN (IM) in

1997. As a Meitei leader put it. "If the hills are cut away, the blood will flow into the valley[27]".

Politically, Manipur has been volatile since its inception as a state. It has had seven tenures of President's rule interspersed with unstable Govts. of various coalitions and configurations with none of the seven Chief Ministers completing their tenure. Congress (I) with its various splinter groups has been the dominant group in the power equations. Manipur Peoples Party (MPP), CPI, BJP and Janata Dal have splintered following. Insurgency as per state Govt's. own addmission is totally criminalised and large scale extortions continue. The present situation in Manipur is not the outcome of insurgency and terorism, it is a result of mis-governance and state abdication. The divide between the communities has deepened as a result of extension of ceasfire with the NSCN (I) to areas of Arunachal Pradesh, Assam and Manipur, and consequent mass agitation and casualties in 2001. The issue is still alive and volatile.

Historical Appraisal (Review)

Manipur located between longitudes 93.6° E and 94.48° E and latitudes 23.47° N and 25.41° N has borders with Burma in the East and South-East, Nagaland to the North and to the west lies Assam, with some common border with Mizoram in the South - West. It has two geographical regions, with Imphal valley and the surrounding hills out of a total area of 22,356 Sq. Km, the hilly areas cover 20,437 Sq. Km. and the remaining 1920 Sq.Km constitutes the valley; out of nine of its districts five are in the hills. According to 1991 census the population of Manipur was 1,8,26,714, which rose to 22,88,634 as per the 2001 census. Meiteis who inhabit the valley form over 60 per cent of the population. The hill areas are inhabited by 29 tribes of Naga and Kuki stock. To quote George Watts, "It is perhaps not far from the truth to assume that the present inhabitants of the plains and hills of Manipur have sprung from four great influences: the Kukis in South, the Nagas in the North, Shan and Burmese tribes in the East and certain hill tribes in the West related to the great Kachari family now distributed throughout the valley of Assam"[28].

Manipur, although a part of India, culturally and socially has remained aloof from the political and social trends due to its geographical location as a land locked area and has preserved its traditions and culture as none of the great Indian empires reached Manipur. The threat to Manipur came from the East in the shape of frequent wars with Burma, which resulted in its seeking help of Britishers, and thus changed its independent historical tradition. In the changing atmosphere of colonial domination national consciousness grew in the shape of political and social organisations which was further fuelled by the World War II and demand for fully responsible government grew.

When paramountcy lapsed, the maharaja acceded to the Union of India in deference to the wishes of the people. The people had got tired of the weak feudal machinery and the Colonial British administration. However, both the manner in which merger was brought about and the denial of statehood till 1972, although Nagaland was granted statehood in 1963, perhaps initiated the roots of discontent among the people of Manipur against the Central Government. The demands ranging from self determination to liberation of Manipur are based on their not accepting the instrument of Merger Act with the Indian Union in 1949. The argument is that i) The Act was not approved by the Manipur Govt. which was formed by the elected representatives of the Assembly. ii) The Maharaja was not the sole authority to govern Manipur. iii) The Maharaja signed the Agreement only in his name and that of his heirs, not in the name of Manipuris[29]. In the same context Gangumei Kabui[30] has sited three schools of thought at the time of merger of the state with India in 1949. i) The present revolutionaries under the leadership of Irabot were fighting for the establishment of a Sovereign Socialist Republic in Manipur and some parts of Burma. ii) The urban elitist congress leaders wanted integration with India as they were greatly influenced by the Indian Nationalism projected through the personalities of Mahatma Gandhi, Nehru and Subash Chandra Bose. iii) The third group—a silent majority consisting of Nationalist Meiteis who wanted to retain the independent status of Manipur with a vague idea of treaty relations with India. The revolt in the Imphal valley in 1948-51 was based on the last sentiment and influenced the Meitei extremists with socialism of Irabot providing it the ideological impetus. The rise of Meitei nationalism is thus closely linked to the Meitei insurgency in the State.

Like most tribal societies, Meiteis attach prime importance to the sanctity of community life and clans and lineages played a significant role in the Meitei society, which over the years has resulted in a cult of ancestor worship, the core of Meitei faith. The traditional religion drew its support from the institution of family of related households or village as an organisational unit. The clan (or Salai as Meiteis call) system is based on the ties of blood, marriage, adoption etc and bounded by observance of ancestral rituals. It gives them emotional security and solidarity.

Vaisnavism was declared the official religion of the Meitei during the reign of Garibnawaz and adoption of Brahmanic culture and social traditions by the Meiteis in the 18th century is a landmark in Meitei history.

Vaisnavism accommodated the tribal features to identify with the local faith and local deities. Nongpok Ningthou and Panthoibi became Siva and Durga and Pakhangba and Sanamahi were linked to Ganesh and Karttikeya, son of Siva and Parvati. The king himself found it difficult to disregard traditional deities and his attitude to traditional gods (Lai) was vacillating. Meitei had no motivation of caste and it was an egalitarian society except for the out caste Lois, who were given this status by the king for violation of certain social rules, e.g., marriage. Garibnawaz in trying to wipe out the traditional faith ordered the burning of Puyas (sacred books) concerning Meitei religion, some of which survived. The social oganisations sustained the traditional Meitei religion of ancestor cult. The ingrained age old faith which was intricately wound with social customs and traditions could not be replaced. The Meitei are probably the sole exception in the history of the world to follow two religions in the same home[31] and at the same time, the old at the cultural level and vaisnav at the religious level. Abolishment of monarchy and awareness combined with disappointment resulted in revivalism both as an escape and for consolidation of Meitei identity.

Contemporary Period

Meitei discontent, sub nationalism and secessionist feelings are the outcome of a sense of hurt due to alienation of Imphal valley land, prolonged struggle to get their culture recognized and discrimination in employment opportunities. Under the Manipur Land and Revenue Regulation, (Meiteis) are banned from acquiring land in the hills, where as hill tribals or any one else can buy land in Imphal Valley. This has not only resulted in alienation of their land but has also resulted in a demographic change, particularly in the major towns and population centres. Exclusion of Manipuri language from the eighth schedule till 1992, which has a literary history of over 2000 years is another cause for agitation. The hill people by virtue of their being categorized as scheduled tribes are entitled to reservation in jobs and education. This has resulted in tribals getting an over whelming advantage in Govt. jobs and higher education opportunities over Meiteis. The same was the case in Central Services (24 Tribals against 4 Meiteis in first 20 years), till I got the Meiteis included in the OBC list in 1994.

The above led the Meiteis to feel discriminated even when they were perceived to be part of the national mainstream. Cultural revivalism and ethnic resurgence was a natural outcome. Revival of the old Meitei (Sanamahi) culture, renouncing Hinduism and fascination for old names Kanglepak for Manipur, traditional old festivals, calendar and script and demand for evacuation of Assam Rifles from Kangla Fort in Imphal symbolises the yearning for re-establishment of the historical glory of Manipuris.

The genesis of Meitei insurgency lies in the deep hurt that Meitei psyche suffered due to the manner of merger of the state, cultural and economic deprivation and corrupt administration both political and civil coupled with mounting unemployment of the better educated Meiteis. The problem was further accentuated by issues like language, denial of Kubaw valley and monolithic society. The insurgency scenario is made worse due to drug trafficking from the Golden triangle and increasing addiction to drugs by the locals.

THE MIZOS

Physiography

Mizoram is a mountainous area with North–South parallel ranges and restricted valleys, which tapers down from the centre as they run towards North and South. Slopes are steeper in the West than in the East. The difference of elevation from the valley floors to hill tops again varies from west to east between 200m to 600m. The land form is affected by running water and resultant erosion. The ranges are believed to be the southern extension of the Cachar Hills. It has a total area of 21,087 sq km. and population of 8,91,058 (2001 census). Mizoram can be divided into three natural regions, the mountainous, ridges and high lands and low land areas. The mountainous region of North-East is above 1500 m and has low population density with marginal agricultural potential, the Central Region consists of Zopuitlang and Bualpuitlang hills and the Southern Phawngpuitlang with its highest Blue Mountain (2165 m Phawngpui) are its natural divisions. Low lands are rare and small in size, the prominent ones are in the North West near Lokichera and Bhairabi, near Demagiri, West of Tuichawng, in the East near Champai, Thenzol and North Vanlaiphai. Rain fall (June to September), soil and topography combine to give Mizoram Tropical forests in North-Western and South-Western parts which have high rainfall and subtropical mountainous forests in central and Northern Mizoram where vegetation accounts for 75% of the region. The South-Eastern parts are covered by mixed forests. Most rivers either flow north or southwards with watershed in the Central Mizoram. The main rivers Tlawng (Dhaleshwari), Tuirial (Sonai), Tuivawl provide the drainage towards the North and Tyao, Chhimtuipui and Karnfuli (Khawtlangtmpui) generally provided southward drainage.

Peripheral location, geography and climate have resulted in

isolationary trends, constraints on communication development and internal rivalries and feuds.

History

Migration of Mizo tribes from North-West Burma to South and then to West and to the Lushai Hills district was both out of motivation and insecurity. Frequent feuds with more powerful tribes forced them to move to Kabaw Valley from North West Burma in 1814[32]. Quest for safer and better lands coupled with Mautam (Famine) at regular intervals in 1882, 1911 and 1959 forced them to change their habitat. Like Nagas, early history of Mizos is largely based on legends, customs, folklore and beliefs. There is rich material available and my Mizo friends particularly LB Thanga (Ex Chief Secretary of Manipur), K.Zawla, Rev Ralte, Ex Chief Minister Lal Thanhawla, Ex Chief Minister Brig Sailo, J Lasangzuala (Ex Finance Minister) and Mizos believe that according to their ancient history they migrated from Chhingluing in Southern China. The legend has it that they came out of a cave but a more rational interpretation is that Chhingluing does not mean a cave but a prince of Chin dynasty (221-207 BC) named Chin Lung who, after an altercation with his father the king, settled in Burma[33]. Mizo's original home was in the East in Mekong Valley and they came to Chindwin Valley about 996 AD. After living there for 200 years, cruelty of the chiefs and famine drove them away but before leaving they planted a banyan tree at Khampat and took a vow to return to it. During their move they halted at Lengtlang[34]. The westward move of the Mizos from there took place between 1700 and 1730 AD. The sub-tribes were Lusei (written Lushai), Ralte, Ngente, Punte and Paite. Perpetual fear compelled them to occupy defensible higher ridges in the interior. Insecurity was the primary reason for Tibeto-Burman races along the Tibet-Chinese and Burma-Tibeto-China border to constantly move in search of secure areas. Mizos who had occupied the Kabaw valley from 8th century moved westwards due to pressure of the Shans. Even in Lushai Hills the process of readjustment between various sub groups continued till the British came in 1890s. Kukis for the same reason moved northwards due to pressure of the Lushais.

From Chhingluing to Khampat in Kabaw valley (present Shan State) and then onto Indo-Burmese frontier in Chin Hills in the 14th century, their movement was organised clanwise as were their village settlements, some of which are still in existence. The first batch crossed Tiau river and settled in present Mizoram. The name Kuki was given by the Bengalis to distinguish them from the plainsmen. These old Kukis migrated from Burma and went as far south as CHT and Tripura. The term Kuki in CHT means inhabitants of interior or inaccessible tracts. Maj Shakespear referred to them as old Kukis and Khawtlang to distinguish them from Lushais. In Cachar, Kukis means Thado or Khawtlang clan. The new and old Kuki-Chin people are the easternmost group of Indo-Mongoloid branch and linguistically similar to Burmese, Lolos and Kachins (Singphos) but culturally different and akin to Nagas and Bodos. Lushais are one of the main tribes of Kuki-Chin groups. The first batch of Mizo tribes who migrated from Chin hills into Mizoram and then to Chachar were Rangkhols, Betes or Hmars with their sub-clan. Broadly there are five major tribes Lushai, Ralte, Hmar, Pawis and Lakhers. The minor sub-tribes are known as 'Awzia'. The Lushai sub-group has ten commoners and six Chief Clans. The Chief Clans are Zadeng, Pallian, Thangluah, Rivring, Rokhum and Sailo, the commoners are Pachuau, Chhangte, Chawngte, Hauhmar, Chwnga, Chuahang, Hialise, Touchhawng, Vanchlawng and Chhakhchhuak. They established complete supremacy over North Lushai Hills in ten years from 1840 to 1850 AD.

Paites are a part of the old Kuki group and mostly in North-Eastern Mizoram between Tiau and Run rivers . Those living in Central Mizoram, have lost their distinct language and traditions but those in Churachandpur (Manipur) and North-Eastern parts of Mizoram have preserved their ancient traits. Raltes also belong to the Kuki group, they have settled in Western Lushai villages. They were subjugated by Duliens who migrated from Chin Hills but have preserved their distinct culture and traditions. Rankhol who had settled in the North near Cachar border were pushed northwards by the Thado tribe and Thado have settled in Lushai and Chin hills after pushing out Rankhol and Bete tribes. Thados in turn were pushed by Lushais into the Cachar between 1840-1850. Similarly, Thados of Chin Hills were pushed by Sokte into Manipur. Lakhers who were a part of the Shindu tribe of the Haka-Chin tribes are in South Eastern corner of Lushai Hills and South of Haka Sub Division of Chin District of Burma. They are a branch of the Lai tribe of Chin and speak a language similar to Lai.

Chakmas are in the South Western part of Mizoram and are of Indo Aryan group who belong to CHT. Their dialect Chakma is similar to South-Eastern Bengali but are distinct culturally and ethnically. They originally migrated from Arakan to CHT in the late 19th century. Among other tribes Riangs are mostly in North-West part of Mizoram bordering Tripura, while Hmars and Paites are in the North-Eastern corner of Mizoram.

Tea plantations started by the British in 1855 in Cachar were considered and resulted in perceived encroachment and threat and Mizos responded by raids and kidnappings. Since 1842, there were frequent raids by Lushais into adjoining villages in Cachar, Manipur and Sylhet. In 1844, Lulsuktala, a Chief raided a Manipuri village in Sylhet in which 20 people were killed. Punitive expeditions by Capt. Blackwood and later in 1849 by Col. Lister resulted in killing of 46 people and destruction of chief's village. In 1860, Rothangpuia raided a village in Tripura and killed 186 men. These raids and punitive expeditions continued but to no avail. This resulted in the Lushai Expedition of 1871-72, after the 1869 expeditions had failed. One column each advanced from Cachar and Chittagong. Lushais surrendered and recognized the superior power of the British. During the Burmese war 1885-86, the British took precautionary measures in Lushai hills. Killing of a British officer and two soldiers during surveillance and survey enraged the British and led to the launching of the Chin-Lushai Expedition of 1889-90 from Silchar and Chittagong. The expedition was aimed to subjugate the rebelling tribes, open up the Lushai Hills and to set up posts in the area to establish full domination of the British authority. After the successful expedition, Capt. Browne was appointed the political officer"of North Lushai Hills in April 1890 and South Lushai Hills was created as a separate district under Chittagong Division of Bengal and placed under a political officer. The officers were instructed not to interfere in internal affairs but keep an eye on happenings. After a temporary lull, the political officer at Aizawl Fort was ambushed, which led to another expedition from Silchar to recapture Aizawal and Changsil posts. The revolting chiefs were captured and deported to jails. The chiefs accepted to pay royalty and accept British domination. The two units were amalgamated and brought under jurisdiction of the Assam Govt. The Chin Hills Regulation Act of 1896 put restriction on movement of outsiders in Mizoram. This resulted in stability in the area.

Lushai Hills District was a "Scheduled District" under the Scheduled District Act of 1874, which was designated as backward area under Govt. of India Act 1919. As a result of which the popular ministry in Asssam had no jurisdiction over it and Governor of Assam was directly responsible for administration of the area. Later under Govt. of India Act of 1935, Lushai Hills District along with Naga Hills District and North Cachar Hill District were termed as "Excluded Area", while Garo and Khasi Hills and Mikir Hills as "Partially excluded" area. The administration of excluded area was carried on from 1937 to 1947 by the Governor of Assam independent of the Govt. of Assam , resulting in these hill areas being isolated and devoid of any reforms. The combination of inner line regulations and Christian missionaries taking advantage of the situation under British 'Patronage' resulted in Mizo suspicion of plains people and gave a feeling of separatism[35]. Most British Administrators showed concern for the hill people of Assam, J.P.Mills particularly was in favour of exclusion of all hill districts of Assam from reforms and favoured formation of a hill state under control of the British Govt. R.Coupland, a constitutional expert recommended a Crown Colony for hill tracts of eastern frontier region as he deemed tribals as neither Indian nor Burmese[36]. However, inspite of these opinions, security of British India was of paramount importance due to its proximity to China. The Governor of Assam Andrew Clow suggested the merger of hill areas with Assam on conditions that tribal customs and institutions be given due recognition and respect.

The Stafford Cripps Cabinet Mission in 1946, opted and suggested an advisory committee on the right of citizens, minorities and tribals of excluded areas. The Constituent Assembly set up an advisory committee on 24 January, 1947 in terms of Para 20 of the Cabinet Mission Statement of 16 May 1946. The committee appointed three subcommittees. The subcommittee for North-Eastern Frontier (Assam) Tribal Areas and Excluded areas was set up under the chairmanship of Gopi Nath Bardoloi the Chief Minister of Assam and its members were Rup Nath Brahma (Plains Tribal Leader), AV Thakkar, Rev Nickols Roy (Khasi leader) and BN Rao, the constitutional advisor to the constituent Assembly. Saprawanga and Khawtinkhuma of the Mizo Union were coopted from Mizoram. The Bardoloi sub committee visited Aizwal on 17-18 April, 1947 to record the testimony of Mizos. Phizo also visited Aizwal during the period and canvassed for the separation of Lushai Hills from India but it did not find any support from the Mizos. Mizo union submitted a memorandum to the subcommittee, the main points of which were:-

(a) Territorial unity and solidarity of the whole of Mizo population to be known as Mizo and Mizoram for Lushai Hills District.
(b) Retaining the sole proprietary rights over the land.
(c) Full autonomy within the state of Assam.
(d) All the above terms will be subject to revision according to the trends of future events even to the extent of secession after ten years[37].

A section of the Lushais under British patronage and influence were instigating separation from India and joining Chin Hills of Burma. Macdonald, the Superintendent of Lushai Hills called a conference of the leaders of commoners and the representatives of chiefs and formulated the famous Macdonald scheme to provide that[38]:

(a) There shall be a legislature which will include the representatives of the chiefs and the commoners.
(b) There shall be a judge and an auditor, a Minister and three Councilors, who will constitute the executive. The judge shall

hold office for 16 years and Minister and auditor for 4 years and other representatives for three years.

(c) There shall be a Public Service Commission for the recruitment of public personnel.

(d) The defence, external affairs and a few subjects will be transferred to Govt. of India.

(e) The territorial jurisdiction under the plan also included a part of Burma and would have access to the sea in the Bay of Bengal.

The scheme had ulterior motives of separating the Lushai Hills from India, was unworkable and was not acceptable to majority of the Mizos".

A few months later on 14 August 1947, at a meeting of 50 leading Mizos at the initiative and under the chairmanship of LL Peters the last district officer of Lushai Hills passed the following resolutions.

(a) As the Lushais have not as yet been definitely informed in detail as to what is to be proposed future constitutional form of administration of the district, the Govt. of Assam should clarify in writing what these are to be. Also if Lushais at this stage have the option of joining any other dominion, i.e., Pakistan or Burma.

(b) If they are to remain in India, their main demands are:-

  (i) The existing safeguards of their customary laws and land etc should be maintained.

  (ii) That the Chin Hills Regulation 1893 and Bengal Eastern Frontier regulation of 1893 should be retained.

  (iii) That Lushais will be allowed to opt out of the Indian Union, when they wish to, subject to a minimum period of 10 years[39]. The idea was also opposed by the Mizo Union Party.

The Bardoloi Committee had already visited Aizwal and during their meetings with a cross section of the people had collected opinion on the following points:-

(a) Whether people want to remain with Central legislature.

(b) Whether people would like representatives in the ministry to safeguard their interests.

(c) To what extent the people desire to have autonomy for the district?

The committee recommended the constitution of the Autonomous District Council democratically with powers of legislature over occupation and use of land other than reserve forest and cultivation of Jhum[40]. The district council should have powers to make laws on use of land, village forest and agriculture and entrusted with administration of justice. The committee was not in favour of Lushai Hills district to continue to be an "Excluded Area" due to advancement in the area. The committee also recommended for the provision of Regional Council to protect the interests of smaller tribes. After much debate the Constituent Assembly approved the provision of District and Regional Councils which were accommodated in the 6th schedule of the constitution. Accordingly, the Assam Govt. enacted the Assam Autonomous District (Constitution of District Council) Act in 1951. The Mizo Council for Mizos, Pawi-Lakher Regional Council for Pawi-Lakher and Chakma Tribes were set up in 1952 and 1953 respectively[41]. The fears of Mizos losing their identity were genuine. Creation of Autonomous District Council was an important step to allay these fears and to safeguard their culture and identity.

Post-independence

The Mizo Union participated in the first general elections held in 1952 and won all the three Assembly seats and majority in the Autonomous District Council. United Mizo Freedom Organisation (UMFO), under Lalnunmawia was the main opposition. The aim of UMFO initially was to bring about a unification of Lushai Hills with the Chin Hills in Burma to form a separate hill state, which received support from Eastern India Tribal Unit (EITU) a political party of Garo – Khasi and Jaintia Hills which wanted a hill state of theirs in the Indian Union. Later both merged[42]. The Mizo union also split before the next general elections in 1957, the official Mizo union retained majority in the District Council but lost two of the three assembly seats in the legislative assembly. In 1960, Mizo union participated in the formation of the All Party Hill Leaders Conference (APHLC). In 1962 general elections it won two seats and the third seat was won by EITU, a constituent of APHLC with Mizo union support. In the bye elections in 1963 due to resignation of Mizo union members on the direction of APHLC, Mizo union lost both the seats to Mizo National Front. The MNF was formed as a consequence of the Mautam Famine of 1959. Mizo National Famine Front (MNFF) was formed as a relief organisation by Laldenga, who had resigned from the District Council, to provide relief to the people. Laldenga took advantage of people's discontent due to indifference of the Assam Govt., the strained relations between the district council and Assam Govt. over the issue came in handy. In Oct 1961, MNF dropped word famine and became a political party with Laldenga as president and Lalnunmawia as vice president. The defeat of Mizo Union candidates by MNF caused a break from the APHLC and Mizo union decided to ask for a separate state in the Indian Union[43].

Laldenga and Lalnunmawia visited East Pakistan secretly to ask for Pakistan help in training MNF cadres and arms. Both were arrested on their return in 1963. On giving a written undertaking to the Chief Minister of Assam BP Chaliha, they were released in February, 1964. MNF continued with their clandestine activities to spread the seed of secession. Mizo union also launched a movement for a separate state and met Lal Bahadur Shastri, who promised that Pataskar Commission, which was examining the whole issue of autonomy for the hill areas of Assam would consider their demand. After the death of Shastri, finding the Pataskar Commission unsympathetic the Mizo union boycotted the commission when it visited Mizoram in the end of 1965. MNF submitted a memorandum demanding freedom. Soon after the visit of Pataskar Commission, MNF launched an armed uprising on 1 March 1966 and declared independence. The operation was code named 'Operation Jericho' and the lightening strike took the Govt. of India and Assam Govt. by total surprise and the total collapse of the administration in Mizoram was a major political and administrative embarrassment for them. The Army was inducted in and air strikes were carried out on rebel held areas. It took the Army one month to restore control and MNF fanned into the jungles. As a part of the Counter Insurgency operations, villages were grouped along the main Silchar-Aizwal-Lungleh road.

The insurgency continued along with the electoral process. There were no elections in 1957. In the elections to the District Council, Congress won 10 seats, MU 9 seats and Independents 3. Mizo union with the help of dissident congress members formed the Govt., (a coalition) under the banner of United Mizo Parliamentary Party. It negotiated with the Central, Govv. for its separation from Assam and Mizoram became a union territory in 1972, with an assembly of 30 elected and three nominated members and one parliamentary seat. The 1971 war dealt a severe blow to the MNF and the changed political environment resulted in surrender of hundreds of MNF cadres and Laldenga flew to West Pakistan. After a lull, the insurgency again erupted in 1974 as MNF was able to regroup in Aarakan and CHT. All the three contingents retiring from China were compromised and dispersed. But the hard core remained in tact. In the beginning of 1975 an attempt was made on the life of the Lt. Governor and the IG and some police officers were killed in the heart of Aizwal Town. Inspite of past reputation of Laldenga, peace negotiations were resumed and Peace Accord was signed on 1 July, 1976. But Laldenga failed to surrender his cadres with arms in the mutually agreed camps. The dead line for surrender was extended on Laldenga's request. The change of Govt. in Delhi in 1977, gave Laldenga another opportunity to keep the govt. guessing. The peace talks broke down finally on 20 March, 1978. MNF also showed signs of factionalism.

Brig Sailo's Peoples Conference won the May 1978 elections with an overwhelming majority. But due to his above board functioning, dissidence and antagonism of the political class, his Govt. fell. After a spell of President's rule, he again formed the Govt. in 1979, his refusal to compromise with corruption and accommodate Laldenga, polarised the Mizo polity between his supporters and that of Laldenga. Insurgency was revived and a quit order on 'vais' (outsiders) created serious law and order problems and MNF was declared illegal and Laldenga taken into custody. Indira Gandhi returned to power in 1980 and negotiations were again opened, indications were that grant of a full fledged state with Laldenga as Chief Minister will clinch the agreement. Sailo offered to step down, if it could bring peace. Victory of congress under Rajiv Gandhi gave the negotiations a fresh impetus and with the help of church leaders the memorandum of settlement was signed on 30 June 1986. The Congress Ministry headed by Lalthanhawla resigned and Laldenga headed the MNF and Congress coalition Govt. After the agreed period of six months fresh elections were held, in which MNF won 25 seats, congress 12 and PC 3. The corrupting influence of power caught up with the MNF and there were accusations of corruption and nepotism and MNF lost the next elections.

The Mizoram Accord has not only lasted but has consolidated as time has passed because by and large all segments of the society have developed a stake in peace in which the role played by the church was both persuasive and cementing. In the last one and a half decade Mizoram has made strides in economic development and displayed stability in the North East's unstable environment and can be designated as an area of hope and peace in the North-East. However it has its pockets of discord. The Hmar disgruntlement has been pacified by the agreement of 27 July 1994 and establishment of Singlung Development Council, Singlung being Hmar ancestral homeland. The Mizoram Chakma Jatiya Parishad (MCJP) demand for a union territory status and agitation continues after the ethnic flare up in 1992 when 300 Chakma houses were burnt. Along with it the anti-vais (outsider or foreigner) feelings were revived in 1993. In 1998 there was ethnic flare up against the Bru (Riang) community inhabiting west Aizwal district, resulting in hundreds of them fleeing to Tripura. Despite these hiccups, Mizoram is looking forward to progress and greater trade with Myanmar as a result of Memorandum of Understanding between India – Myanmar in 1994.

Administrative pattern of Mizoram has evolved out of its historical experience and physiography. Lushai Hills District was a backward district under the Schedule District Act of 1874. Being economically backward, centre assumed responsibility for their protection. Simon Commission in 1930, kept it out of the jurisdiction of provisional legislature and elected representatives and the area as an Excluded Area was put under the Governor as an agent.

Chakmas

Chakma inhabited areas are spread over India, Bangladesh and Burma. The root of the Chakma problem lies in the partition of India in 1947, when 90% of predominantly Chakma inhabited area of CHT was transferred to Pakistan which was a geopolitical blunder of high order. Chakma migration into India in Mizoram and Tripura to their kith and kin, resulted in their varying status as refugees, foreigners and trespassers. Culturally closer to the South-Eastern Bengalis and religiously Budhist Chakmas differ from Mizos in all respects. Their habitation in inaccessible area of the South-Western Mizoram is of great geopolitical importance. Their antagonism with Mizo is both due to ethnic, cultural and religious differences and their opposing stance during the Mizo insurgency. The continued neglect of Pawi Lakher Regional Council by various Mizoram Govts. is the main motivation for union territory demand since the 1971 negotiations. The Chakma District Council excludes 35,000 people out of 52,000 Chakmas in its jurisdiction (27,000 are only covered by the council). CDC HQ at Kamlanagar is three days march from Lunglei-Dimagiri road, is least developed, has no electricity or health centre and has just 42 primary and 2 High Schools. Education level is poor with 12 graduates, 18 PU pass and 138 matriculates out of a total population of about 60,000 compared to the high literacy amongst Mizos. Saiha, Chhimtuipui District Headquarters lies in Lakher area, with all offices located there, far off from Chakma area. Most development benefits go to Lakhers (60%), Poi (Pawi –30%), leaving little for Chakmas[44]. With the highest population amongst the three major tribes in Chhimtuipui District, Chakmas have only one seat in the legislature, while Lakhers and Pawis have two each. Chakma's desire for amalgamation of Chakma areas in Aizwal and Lunglei District under the Chakma district Council is opposed by Mizos. Mizo leaders feel that Demagiri area offers sanctuaries to immigrants from Bangladesh. It is true as Demagiri formed part of the original Chakma inhabited area of CHT, it was only transferred as part of Lushai Hills in 1893. The Chakmas feeling of neglect is genuine.

Hmars

Hmars and Thados belong to Chin-Kuki ethnic group and inhabit the Northern fringes of Mizoram and adjoining areas in Cachar (Assam and Manipur) where they were pushed by migrant Lushais and in Burma. Their total population is 1.5 lacs. They played vital role in formation of the Mizo union and Bawihhuaha and Pachhunga played a major role in Mizoram politics before independence[45]. After independence, particularly after Mizoram became a union territory and a state in 1986 when power passed into the hands of Mizos, clan based politics resulted in a challenge to Mizo unity and escalated ethnic face off. The Hmar peoples convention articulates the demand for an autonomous region comprising of Hmar areas in Mizoram, Manipur and Cachar and is training youth volunteers in arms and politics. Their leader Leichung Hmar is propagating a separate identity for Hmars. The HPC adopted an agitationist approach to further their demand for an Autonomous Hills District. The Mizoram Govt. agreed to have talks with the HPC provided its members surrendered their arms and gave up violence. After prolonged negotiations with HPC, the question of Hmar homeland was resolved by granting Singlung Hills Development Council (SDC), Singlung being Hmars ancestral home in the region. The agreement provides protection for Hmar culture, language and advisory role for SDC in formulating policy for development of Hmars. It has the support of the NSCN (I) as the area is on their transit route from Bangladesh to Cachar, Manipur and Nagaland. The dissident Hmar elements in Manipur, Cachar could foment trouble as weapons could easily be supplied by the NSCN (I).

Pois

Pois, with a total population of 30,000 inhabit the Sangan and Lawngtlai blocks in the Chhimtuipui District. They feel aggrieved against the regional policies of the Lakhers and Lushais. In 1965, Chin National Front was formed to unite the Pois in Mizoram and adjoining areas in Burma. They resent being called Mizos as is the case with Lakhers. During the insurgency MNF was not welcomed in the Pawi-Lakher area and after the accord the feeling has surfaced in the political and socio-economic field, where they resent Lushai (Mizo) dominance.

Riangs or Bru community living in West Aizawl District was the target of Mizo wrath in 1992 as a reaction to the killing of a Mizo Game Warden in Danpa Tiger Sanctuary near Tripura border resulting in retaliatory burning of 300 Riang houses by the Mizos which led to their migration to Northern Tripura. There have also been some reports of conversion of Riang Hindus to Christianity, some true and some propagated by the RSS. Riangs from adjoining areas in Manipur and

Assam have also migrated to Tripura instigated by the Bru National Liberation Front (BNLLF) in connivance with NLFT. The aim seems to be a forced concentration of Riangs in Northern Tripura. The situation has political overtones with potential for ethnic exploitation.

Anti vai (outsider or foreigner) feeling is strong in Mizoram since the 1970s, which was rejuvenated in 1993 by the issue of quit notice to all non-Mizos, although primarily it is directed against the Bengalees of Cachar Area, who represent the old Assamese dominance. Mizo youth are in the fore front in propagating it and extending it to all non-Mizos. The boundary dispute with Assam gets mixed up with the Assamese dominance. The dispute with the parent state is due to rich forest land in the foot hills.

The Mongoloid Mizos, came from South-West China during the 15th century and later occupied contiguous territories in Lushai Hills, adjoining Burma and CHT. Due to political division British called them Lushais and Mizos in India, Zomis in Burma and Kukis in CHT. The demand of Zomi National Congress (ZNC) in Churachandpur in Manipur and that of the Mizo leaders particularly T.Sailo is similar to MNF's demand. The idea of Zogam state consisting of Chin Hills of Burma, Northern CHT, Mizoram and Churachandpur is both a reflection of ethic chauvinism and a political ploy, which is often exploited.

Appraisal

Mizoram has international borders on three sides, 404 Km with Burma in the East and South and 306 Km in the west with Bangladesh. In addition it has interstate boundary of 123 Km in the North with Assam, 66 Km with Tripura in the west and 95 Km with Manipur in the East. The junction of these boundaries located in thick forests formed the core of insurgent activities and sanctuaries, which is helped by Mizoram's isolated location. Its location and borders tend to divide tribes located in Mizoram and highlights its geopolitical significance. Physiography of Mizoram encourages isolatory trends, localisation of peripheral tribes and rivalry between them and the dominant Mizos. Lakhers, Pawis and Chakmas settled in most inaccessible areas are less advanced and educated. Similarly Hmars in peripheral area feel disadvantaged. The situation is further accentuated due to cultural affinity of these tribes beyond state and international boundaries, Riangs with Tripura, Hmars and Kukis with Manipur, NC Hills and Cachar District, Chakmas with Bangladesh and Lakhers (Mars) with East Burma.

In line with its policy of keeping the hill areas of Assam isolated, Mizoram which was annexed in 1890 by the British was administered as an excluded area. The combined effect of colonial policy, spread of

Christianity and adoption of Lushai language with roman script resulted in a majority of 15 local tribes adopting a Mizo identity. As Urmila Phadnis rightly puts it, identity need not be ascriptive or given, it can also be created.[46]

The Lushai population with the dominant Sailo clan is concentrated in the middle in the Aizwal and Lunglei Districts, Lakhers (Maras) in Chhimtuipui District. The Pawi District council has its headquarters at Lawngtalai and Lakher District council at Saiha. Chakmas are mostly concentrated in the western part predominantly in Chawgate Block, Riangs are in the North-West Mizoram along Tripura border and Hmars and Paites in the North Eastern corner. The social and religious customs are common with little variation. However, chakmas maintain distinct social customs due to difference in religious practices. The egalitarian perception has made Mizo society class and casteless and agro-economic life reflects a common out look and a high sense of morality. Christianity spread education, a sense of value and coexistence. Its impact on socio-economic life imparted a sense of individualism and individualistic approach to life. The community life of Mizos is imbedded in agricultural activity which invites the whole community to share both pleasure and pain. All land in Mizoram except areas covered under the towns and protected areas belong to the community and power of allotment of land for Jhooming is vested in the village council within its jurisdiction.

Advent of Christianity, education and western orientation resulted in dilution of the traditional way of life and livelihood and gradual destabilisation and social organisations that centered around villages became victims of change. This coupled with change in power base from rural to urban resulted in old group interests giving place to elite mostly urban, which controlled large sections of the population.

Administrative pattern in Mizoram has evolved out of its historical experience and physiography. The Northern part of Lushai Hills District was Governed by Assam and the Southern by the Bengal Govt. till these were brought together under the Chief Commissioner of Assam in 1898. Lushai Hills district was a backward district under the scheduled District Act of 1874. Being economically backward, the centre assumed responsibility for its development and protection. Simon Commission in 1930, kept it out of the jurisdiction of provincial legislature and elected representatives and as an excluded area it was put directly under the Governor as an agent of the Governor General under the Govt. of India Act of 1935.

In the period prior to the transfer of Power (1946-47), the younger Mizos saw in the abolition of chieftains, participation in the legislative and democratic process by representation in the Assam legislative assembly and socio-economic advancement as their goal, which could be achieved by greater autonomy within India. While the grant of District Council under the Sixth Schedule provided internal autonomy, Assam Govt. failed to address the acute economic backwardness of hill areas. Alienation from Assam was complete due to a totally inadequate Govt. response to the famine of 1959.

Similarly, while the abolition of the traditional institution of the chiefs provided scope for people's political and economic aspirations, it also led to disgruntled elements including the chiefs to support insurgency.

The district and Regional Councils helped people to highlight the gap between policies of development and their implementation and aggravated the crisis within Mizoram.

Since the peace Accord in 1986, two major issues continue to cause friction and instability. One is the MNF demand of Greater Mizoram consisting of Mizo inhabited areas of Manipur, Tripura and South Chachar and neighbouring areas in Bangladesh and Burma which is explorted by each political party to appeal to the Mizo sentiment. The second is the issue of Chakmas, whom Mizos view as outsiders and foreigners. The basis of the problem is ethnic with social and political fall out. This feeling is also extended to other sub-tribes who seek an identity of their own beyond a Mizo identity.

TRIPURA

The state of Tripura has an area of 10,49,169 Sq.Km of which more than 60% is forest and only 28,100 Sq. Km is cultivable. The maximum length from North to South is 182 Kms and breadth East to West is 112 Km. It is almost entirely surrounded by Bangladesh, with the only opening to rest of India by land being through Assam extending to 288 Kms, its border with Bangladesh is about 839 Kms[47]. It has a population of 31,91,168 (2001 census) with a density of 304. Rajmala is the only historical record of Tripura's ancient history. The rulers of Tripura claim their descent from Chandra the moon God. Dhuhya, son of Emperor Yajali founded the State. The state is named after Tripur a descendent of Chandra, a contemporary of Yudhistra. The name Tripura is a sanskritised version of early Bodo name Tipra by which name the main tribe is known.

The kings of Tripura claimed their descent from the Lunar lines of kings. The 25th King of Lunar dynasty King Pratorddan annexed Kirat land and built his capital on the banks of Kapil or Brahmaputra and styled it as Tribeg to perpetuate the city founded by Druhyu, who had wandered south along Ganges on banishment by his father emperor

Yayati from Pratishthanpur and formed the city of Tribeg on Sagar Island in the estuary. Even a conservative estimate would assign the period of Druhya to Tripur not later than 1367 BC as Tripur was a contemporary of Yathisthria[48]. Trilochna who succeeded his father installed the images of Chaturdas Devtas and brought priests from Sagar Islands in the Sunderbans, which formed the western boundary of the kingdom. In ancient times there was a sanskrit college for pandits in Sagar Islands and their dominions spread upto Bengal, Bihar, Assam and Orrisa. According to Saktisangam Tantra, as supported by Raj Rajeshwari Tantra, the Kirat Bhumi comprised of Cachar, Sylhet, Tripura and Chittagong hill tracts.

King Dakshin moved his capital to Khalongma near the source of Barabakrah or Barak in present day Makir Hills. For nearly thirteen hundred years upto 150 BC upto the reign of Bimar they continued to rule from Khalongma. King Kumar shifted his capital to Chhambul on the banks of Manu and upto the 113th ruler Chitrasen reigned from there. Jhu-Jharu Fa moved his capital to Rangamati in 590 AD after defeating Liha Mogh and introduced the Tripura Era to commemorate his victory of Chittagong and lower Bengal. There are contrary claims as Sir Lethbridge records that it was Birraj the eighty eighth king who introduced the Tripura Era. The title of Fa was first adopted by Niladhwaja the 73rd ruler and it remained so till Manikya appellation was conferred on Ratna Fa by Tughrol Khan in 1279 AD. Muslims had already entered the scene in Bengal in 1240 AD during the reign of Kirtidhar or Singhtung Fa. Instigated by a nobleman Hirabanta Khan Nawab of Gaur attacked Tripura and King Singhtung Fa seeing the might of Nawab's Army wanted a truce but Queen of Tripura Sundari inspired the Tripura soldiers and won a glorious victory over the Pathans. The Sword used by the Queen is still worshipped[49].

The youngest son of Hariray or Dangor Fa, Ratna Fa ascended the throne in 1279 AD with the help of Mohamedan Ruler of Bengal Tughrol Khan and beheaded his brothers. He invaded the country of Jagenagar (Tipperah) and after defeating the Raja, plundered and took away a lot of wealth and one hundered elephants (Stewarts History of Bengal, p. 44). But the author of Rajmala held that Ratna Manikya got help from Sultan Samuddin who ruled from 1347 AD. Ratna Fa presented a coruscating ruby to the Sultan and got the herediatary title of "Manikya" or jewel. Hinduism spread in Tripura during his reign and he brought a large number of Bengali professionals, artisans and cultivators to improve his administration and economic activities, particularly agriculture on the line of Nawabs of Bengal. Dharma Manikya (1430-1462) was one of the greatest rulers of Tripura. He was a great patron of arts and letters and Rajmala was compiled by Baneshwar and Sukreswar during his reign. The army of Gaur was reduced by him and Sonargoan was plundered. He defeated the king of Burma and had the Arakan King reinstated on the throne. The process of greater interaction with Bengalees was given impetus during his reign and Bengalee was made the court language of Tripura. Advent of Hinduism did not result in the extinction of the tribal traditional religion.[50]. He was succeeded by his son Dhanya Manikya the greatest of the kings of Tripura, in 1463 AD and ruled till 1515 AD. His conquests included the principalities of Meher Kul, Patihara, Ganga Mandal, Bagasar, Bejura Bhanugashh, Vishhinujui and Langla. With the help of his general Rai Kachag, he subjugated Khandal (Noakhali), occupied Kuki lands in the East and extended his kingdom upto Burma. He annexed Chittagong from the Pathans. His kingdom extended from Meghna in the west to Arakan in the East and upto Cachar in the North. Dhanya Manikya was a devout Hindu and erected many temples, most famous being Tripureswari Temple of Udaipur in 1501 AD.

Vijay Manikya ruled from 1528 to 1570 AD. He defeated the Jaintia king and appointed Kalanazir as Governor of Sylhet. Sultan Sulaiman Army was defeated, his general Mamarak Khan was taken a prisoner, resulting in Sultan ceding land upto Padma in Dacca. With Moghuls coming to power in Delhi and Pathan influence decreasing in Bengal and Assam, he captured territory upto Sonargoan, Vikrampur. Ayin-I-Akbari mentions the exploits of Vijay Manikya. Tripura reached its Zenith during his rule. The next two rulers Ananta Manikya and Udai Manikya ruled for short stints upto 1576. Amar Manikya ruled from 1584 to 1601 AD, although he retrieved the lost prestige of Tripura after Vijay Manikya but he lost territory South of Udaipur to Moghuls. However Tripura was not subdued by them.

The disintegration of Kingdom commenced from the reign of Yosodhar Manikya (1613-23), who was taken as a prisoner to Jehangir's court in Delhi for failing to appease the Moghul Emperor by presenting elephants for which Tripura was famous. According to the wish of Yosodhar, Kalyan Manikya was accepted as the king in 1625 AD and ruled upto 1660 AD, he preserved Tripura's independence inspite of frequent fights. Tripura was under the Moghul rule only for two years from 1623 to 25. The subsequent history of Kingdom after Govind Manikya is a record of decline and ruin. A century of struggle resulted in Mohammeden occupation of a portion of the plains which finally came under British rule in 1765 and was held as a Zamindari by the ruler of Tripura. The rest of Tripura survived and retained a shade of its ancient prestige.

After the decline of the Mughal Empire and with the British taking over the Dewani of Bengal, Tripura lost all territories in Bengal and was reduced to its present size (Imperial Gazateer – East Bengal and Assam 1909). Tripura maintained its independent administration under the British and its kings were great patrons of music and culture. Maharaja Radha Kishore Manikya and his son Bir Bikram Kishore had association with Rabindra Nath Tagore. The state capital Agartala and Arampur were located near state's borders for easy access to rail heads in British India. During British rule tea plantations were encouraged, which attracted more Bangalees and other non-tribals. It was not only tea gardens which attracted non-tribals and Bangalees, as mentioned earlier, Tripura rulers had imported administrators, teachers and other professionals from Bengal to run the services.

Famine and economic constraints drove more Bangalee peasants to Tripura and by 1931 their number rose to 114383 (Bhattacharya SR-1989). Anti Feudal revolt of Reang tribe in 1942 known as the Ratnamani revolt was put down by the state Armed Forces. As a result of the pre-partition communal carnage at Noakhali in 1946, thousands of Hindu refugees entered Tripura (10,000 per month) and pressure on land increased. Finding in the Tribal reserves set up in 1931 and 1943 coming under pressure, the state Govt. sought denotification of the reserved tracts. These reserved areas were for settled agriculture by the five (designated) tribes, the Tripuris, Reangs, Jamatias Noatias and Halams, the initial area of 285 Sq.km was later extended to larger zone of 5050 sq. km. No land alienation was to be permitted within these reserves. However, no boundary was designated or demarcated. The zone was large, almost half of the total area of the state. Exclusion of other tribes residing in the area led to violation of the reserved areas and consequent clashes. Tripura Rajya Mukti Morcha, the Communist party's Tribal wing launched an agitation[51]. According to Sanjoy Hazarika, "the scale of migration can be assessed from the fact that in 1947, 93% of the Tripura's 6 lac population were Tribals and by 1981 they had been reduced to a minority of 28.5% of a 2.06 million population[52]." However, the official records, show Tripura's population as 173,325 in 1901, with tribals constituting 52.81 per cent of the population. The decadal increase in population of the state was 32.5 per cent (1901-11), 32.6 per cent (1911-21), 25.63 per cent (1921-31) and 34.14 per cent in 1931-41 and the tribal population was just a majority of 50.09 per cent in 1941[53]. Since then the situation worsned rapidly with a decadal increase of 78.71, in the decade 1951-61, the tribals were reduced, to 31.53 per cent of the population and by 1981 to a minority of just 28.44 per cent, which clearly cast a doubt on the authenticity of the official records. The bare fact is that figures only quantifies the problem of immigrants in Tripura but the emaciation effect on the tribals by alienation of their land is a human tragedy which is beyond words.

Tripura acceded to India on 13th August, 1947 and merged with India on 15th October, 1949. It became a part 'C' state on 26 January, 1950, a Union Territory in November 1956 and a full fledged state in 1972.

The demographic surge, economic pressure and deprivation of their lands resulted in first organised protest in the shape of formation of "Seng Krak" (clenched fist) a militant organisation of tribals, which merged into Adivasi Sansad in 1954. The CPI also organised a peasant organisation. Congress ruled till 1977 but communists were active under Nripen Chakravorty and Dasarath Deb. The defeat of Communists in 1967 came as a disappointment to educated Tribal youth and Tripura Upjati Juba Samiti (TUJS) under Sanacharan Tripura was formed with the aim of securing the creation of Autonomous Tribal District Council under the Sixth Schedule, reconstitution of tribal reserves earlier created by the maharaja and restoration of delineated tribal land to non-tribals after the TLR and LR Act of 1960 and recognition of Kok – Borok in roman script as official language. The act vests land in favour of the tiller with residuary rights over all lands not owned by individuals with the state (including rivers, forests, riverine and char land, mines and minerals). All intermediary rights were acquired on payment and some tea garden lands were declared surplus to the ceiling, section 187 of the act sought to regulate unrestricted alienation of tribals, which permitted transfer of land by non-tribals to tribals but not the reverse. The Act was amended in 1974 to legitimise all transfer of tribal land to non-tribals till upto 1 January, 1969[54]. Simultaneously, Seng Krak banned earlier was activated with the backing of MNF and 100 youth were trained for armed struggle[55].

Bejoy Harangkhwal formed Tripura Sena within TUJS. Having failed in his attempt to enter the Lok Sabha in 1978, he formed Tribal National Volunteers and by the summer of 1979, TNV started its violent activities. For some inexplicable reasons Harangkhwal dissolved the TNV only to revive it in 1982[56].

In March 1979, the state Govt. constituted an Autonomus District Council (ADC) (under the 7th schedule), which provides for constitution of district boards and other local authorities for the purpose of local self Govt. The non tribals opposed the act on the grounds that council would comprise 7131 Sq. Kms, which was ¾th of the territory of the state to serve the interests of one fourth of its population. Amar Bengali a militant organisation banned from 1973 to 75 was revived to protect the interests of the Bengalees. A stand off between Amar Bengali and TUJS led to riots in 1980 (Mandai Massacre) in which 550 were killed, 1800 were reported missing, 35,000 huts were burnt and property worth 26 crores was lost. The state Govt. never ordered any formal inquiry. The Centre set up a committee under Dinesh Singh. Harangkhwal was arrested and his trusted lieutenant Chuni Koloi disbanded TNV and formed a new organisation, called the All Tripura Peoples Liberation Organisation (ATPLO). In a rift between Chuni Koloi and Binanda Jamatia in the ATPLO, with Koloi emerging as the victor. The weakened ATPLO under Jamatia surrendered to the CPI (M) Govt. in 1983[57]. On rejuvenation of TNV in 1982, Harangkhwal demanded deportation of all Bengalees who had entered the state after October, 1947 and threatened failing which TNV will fight for full self determination[58].

The CPI (M)'s long stint in power from 1977 to 1987, saw a clean and stable Govt., with a harmonious relationship with all including the tribals. It not only recognized the tribal struggle but took concrete steps to bring TNV insurgents over ground and let TUJS as their political mouthpiece fight for them. However, dissolution of the TNV and formation of the ATPLO not only revived the insurgency but dissidence amongst tribal leaders permitted political parties to exploit the situation. While the ATPLO surrendered to CPI (M) and tribal leader Dasarath Deb's efforts to issue an amendment to TLR and LR Act were afoot for restoration of Tribal land, it met with Bengalee legal and political opposition and Bengalee militancy resulted in rejuvenation of the TNV. However, the efforts of the Govt. and particularly its leaders did not go waste and an agreement was signed on 12 August, 1988. The Mizo Accord of 1986 certainly acted as dampener for TNV. The TNV gained much more than it had hoped for by violence. The agreement provided for stopping of all further infiltration and to prevent further alienation of tribal land and TNV undertook to end all underground activities. The Tripura Tribal Areas Autonomous District Council (TTAADC) under the 6th schedule came into being by a Constitutional amendment in March, 1985. A section of the TNV cadres who were unhappy with the agreement went underground and formed the All Tripura Tribal Force (ATTF) and a section thereof took the name of All Tripura Tiger Force. Yet another section of TNV formed the National Liberation Front of Tripura (NLFT). Both militant organisations continue to indulge in acts of violence, kidnapping and killing.

Although 110,000 Bangladeshi infiltrators have been pushed back from the state since 1971 but the influx continues. The influx of Chakmas since 1980 and their continued stay has added to the problem. After the Awami League Govt. came into power in Bangladesh, an agreement was reached and deportation started but over 55,000 Chakma are still in Tripura and Arunachal Pradesh.

The period after the 1988 accord with TNV is marked with certain identifiable trends. Along with periodic surrenders militancy continues, with factional fights between ATTF and NLFT. The insurgency in Tripura since the 1990s has undergone a change and become a part of the political confrontation between CPI (M) and congress for the 20 seats reserved for the tribals in the legislative assembly. It is fuelled by resentment of the tribals against their land alienation and denial of employment. The CPI (M) won the 1998 elections but the TTAADC elections disturbed the political balance with Indigenous People's Front (IPF) winning 18 seats and CPI (M) only 8. The IPF in conjunction with one of the political parties has the potential to be a contender in power sharing. The Left Front (LF) improved its position in 2003 elections winning 40 seats and Congress (I) supported by the Indigenous Nationalist Party of Tripura (INPT) a recent incarnation of IPF won 19 seats. The LF exploited Bijoy Hrang Khawl's speech supporting the tribal insurgents in the UN working group in 2002 in Geneva. LF victory is attributed to Bengalee solidarity with the LF and its better record in implementing the Centrally Funded Development Schemes, combined with the tribal's growing fatigue with violence and fear[59]. The elections were preceded and followed by violence with each side using insurgent factions for intimidating the voters and each blaming the other for violence. The insurgency scenario has got politicised or political scenario has acquired a militant character as ATTF has links with CPI (M) and NLFT enjoys congress patronage. The level of violence in pre and post elections is high as proved by the last elections. NLFT has links with NSCN (I) and ATTF with ULFA and PLA[60], the emerging scenario is similar to the one in Nagaland and Manipur.

A closer examination of contemporary insurgency in Tripura clearly indicates that the earlier demand of TNV to secede from India was not born out of ideology but was an expression of tribal discontent. The root cause is alienation of tribal land. Militancy is not an outcome of any secessionist demand but due to deep sectarian feeling of tribal versus non tribal. It also needs to be recognized that while at the political level TUJS represents tribal opinion and sentiment, by itself it does not exercise major influence. If any thing, the party is a stumbling block to any political solution of the insurgency as a political solution will always go in favour of the ruling party and deprive TUJS of its importance (1988 Accord).

Open border with Bangladesh and limited access to the rest of the country provide militancy the conducive geographical environment to survive, which is helped by easy availability of arms to the North-East due to liberal attitude of Bangladesh. In essence insurgency in Tripura is a politico – social struggle based on tribal deprivation, which has been totally politicised in the last decade since the 1988 Accord. The structure of violence has changed in Tripura and pre- and post-election violence has become a norm. In the last decade permissiveness and corruption have made serious inroads in the Govt. functioning and the society. The only difference from rest of North-East may be that there is more equitable distribution of spoils within the party cadres, which has also led to criminalisation of militancy.

A short historical resume of immigration and its demographic fallout is attached at Appendix A as it is the core of the turmoil in Tripura.

Historical Appraisal

The turn of the 20th century historically marked the beginning of the transformation of Tripura. Colonial influence and state driven economy resulted in demographic changes, cultural submergence and changes in agrarian and social structure of the society which was primarily tribal. Sadly, most of these changes were initiated by the tribal princely order, detrimental to tribal interest but favourable for the monarchy. The first census report of India documented the effects. Tripura's transformation during the colonial period was essentially related to state power and changes were state sponsored. The tribal princely administration acted as an active agent of change.

Historically, Tripura only vaguely shared India's culture. It was sparsely populated, its tribal inhabitants practiced shifting cultivation known as Jhum. It produced paddy, cotton, oil seeds and sesamun. They paid family tax known as Ghar Chukti (calculated family tax) and export duty on cotton, which was the main source of revenue. The taxes were collected through a complex hierarchy of vasals, village headman, sardars or chiefs. The monarch was the supreme land lord and bubabgra (divine right of the king) and there was no private ownership of land. The production mode can be characterised as communal ownership of land. The adhoc technology could not meet the growing revenue demands of rulers in terms of their personal luxuries, payment to British rulers and cost of maintenance of colonial administration.

The early migrants were mostly land hungry peasants and very few Bengalee professionals and artisans. Liberal land grants and low rental policies of Tripura kings anxious to introduce settled cultivation for greater revenue attracted peasants of Bengal and Assam, which coincided with pressure of population on land and evictions in these areas. Combination of land hungry peasants of Bengal and availability of land in Tripura resulted in stagnation and lack of development in tribal rural economy. The kings were anxious to introduce settled agriculture for greater revenue. The interaction between peasant hungry land in Tripura and hungry peasants of Bengal was development of rural statification.

Although settled cultivation penetrated amongst the tribals to some extent but tribals by and large remained isolated from its benefits as better land was grabbed by the Bengalees. In 1931, 27,647 tribals out of a total population of 1,92,224 adopted this method. The tribals by and large remained isolated from the benefits of the improved system due to better land being grabbed by Bengalees. The state revenue increased steadily from 28.18 per cent in 1939 to 34.29 per cent in 1943 but the family house tax decreased from 39.3 per cent to 36.77 per cent during the same period. By the beginning of the twentieth century 30,000 hectares of land had been brought under settled cultivation.

Tripura's demographic changes resulted in a state, where immigrants became the over whelming majority and reducing the original tribal inhabitants to a small minority Demographic changes and agrarian modernisation resulted in Bengalee dominated establishment divorced from tribal interests and entirely motivated by royal (including colonial) material and economic interests. The changes sponsored by the state for its material and economic interests and administrative changes in tune with it, resulted in establishment of a bureaucratic regime attuned to princedom and colonialism. Tripura had no class division in its agrarian structure but increased settled cultivation resulted in class divisions alien to tribal agrarian structure. In 1951 in nearly half a million agrarian population 25 per cent were rent receivers, 79.5 per cent were owner cultivators and 64 per cent were agriculture labourers. There were no big landlords as in the Zamindaris of Northern India but as Nripen Chakraborti called them, there emerged a class of "Zamindari talukdars", people related to royal family or those who had its patronage who dominated the agrarian economy.

The Bengali middle class though small in numbers forms a significant part of migration to Tripura. Trade, commerce and services were mostly in their hands. Bengal renaissance of the 19th century which had an impact on Tripura's renaissance during the period of King Birendra Kishore Manikya (1909-23) was mainly brought about by the Bhadralok of Bengal, who enjoyed royal patronage. It did not involve the indigenous population as such and failed to create an agitation against the feudal monarchy as the elite and middle calss consisting of mostly Bengalees were the beneficiaries.

It was only in 1933, that the Govt. opened two free hostels for tribal students, one attached to Umakanta Academy in Agartala and the other to Khowai High School where 50 and 20 tribal students respectively were accommodated. Earlier state patronage was extended to Thakurs, who after completing their education either went to Vishva Bharti or Shanti Niketan or to Ajmer. Till 1930, only Thakur families were educated amongst the tribals. After the opening of the tribal hostels, other tribals mostly Tripuris joined the university at Calcutta and they demanded Govt. jobs, which so far only Thakurs and royal family members or Bengalees got. Educated tribals formed the Tripura State Association for Peoples' Education of which Dashrath Dev Burman was the vice president. The Maharaja's adoption of Hinduism and patronage to Bengalee art and culture resulted in cultural deprivation of their own tribal community and to the great disadvantage of their indigenous culture and language Kok Barak.

The post independence element of Bangalee immigration is the most problematic. Arriving in three surges in 1947, 67 and 71, they were the poorest and came in direct competition with the tribals for a bare subsistence and for survival. The fight for land turned into the struggle for survival leaving little space for accommodation and adjustment. It changed the agrarian structure. Settled cultivation replaced shifting cultivation, private ownership took the place of community ownership of land. While the real motive of rulers opening of Tripura was to increase land revenue but the idea was put out as a policy of development, hoping that giving large chunks of land upto 500 drones (1225 hactares) or more in a block will lead to roads and other means of development.

Modernisation of agriculture in Tripura was state sponsored and not in response to the needs of the society. Laws enacted by the state prohibited tribals from practicing Jhoom cultivation and reservation of forests where people could not practice Jhooming resulted in marginalisation of tribals. Since the beginning of the century (20th) state's forests cover of 15 sq. miles in 1908 increased to 1160.85 sq.miles in 1942 and by the end of 1943 one fourth of states area was reserve forest. This resulted in sharp fall in the area available for Jhoom and tribals had to cultivate the same land for years, resulting in decreased productivity. Tribals became dependent on money lenders and businessmen mostly Bengalees and other outsiders and alienation of land became the most potent source of ethnic conflict. State sponsored modernisation of agriculture was not out of the needs of the society but that of the royalty. The state's rolc can therefore be termed adverse.

During the rule of Maharaja, the economy was semifeudal and stagnant with self- sufficiency in food and there was no pressure on land and unemployment was not a serious challenge. Merger with India set the process of modernisation and development in motion. The tasks, apart from improving the administration and social services, were rehabilitation of millions of refugees from East Pakistan, settlement of hill tribes practicing shifting cultivation to save depleting forests. Because of communicational difficulties, diversification became difficult. 89 per cent of Tripura's population live in villages and 76 per cent of the work force was dependent on agriculture and allied services. The crisis of economy was obvious.

In the political field, the communist party of Tripura formed in 1949, through its various outlets like Janamangal Samiti, Janasiksha Samiti and Praja Mandal and finally Mukti Parishad led a wave of popular sentiment against the monarchical system. In 1952, communist party of Tripura chalked out a programme in aswer to special problems of the state. This also marked the change over from armed struggle to constitutional agitation. In the general elections of 1952, the communists were elected with thumping majority but were not only not permitted to form the Govt. as it was a part C state but were also denied the opportunity to join the council of advisors. Defeated congressmen were nominated to it. The central Govt's duplicity was exposed in 1963, when congress in the third try garnered electroal advantage in 1962 elections, the teritorial council was converted into a legislative assembly. The communist party led the people's movement on all fronts, it fought and succeeded in retention of Tripura's separate identity as against merger with Assam recommended by the States Reorganisation Commission. It got a legislative assembly in 1963 and grant of statehood in 1972. On coming to power in 1978, the communists fulfilled their commitment to democratic norms functioning and a clean and responsive administration. This ethos has undergone a change for the worse in the last two decades.

In Tripura tribal consciousness is identified with seizure and control of valuable land and its resources, local employment, preservation of their language, culture and traditional rights and territorial autonomy. This has also resulted in tribal mobilisation in the shape of indigneous organisations as a platform to articulate their economic aspirations and demand of political autonomy. The state needs to respond to these politically, socially and economically to prevent indigenous organisations within the political system being made irrelevant by tribal militant groups.

MEGHALAYA

The state of Meghalaya with an area of 22,429 sq. km. is situated between the Brahmaputra Valley in the North and Bangladesh in the South. It is bounded by the districts of Kamrup, Dhubri, Goalpara in the North, Karbi Anglong and Cachar Hills in the East and by Bangladesh in South and West. Shillong or Meghalaya plateau the abode of the clouds, has great physiographic diversity with altitude varying from 150 Meters to 1960 metres. The plateau is highly dissected and terrain is irregular in the West and North and the Southern escarpment has steep slopes. Garo

Hills covering an area of 8164 sq. Kms has an average elevation of 600 meters. It is separated from the central part of the plateau by the Maheshkhola Range. The most prominent is the Tura Range, with highest point Nokreh (1515 M), which is 13 Km. South-East of Tura town. The Khasi and Jaintia Hills form the central and eastern parts of the plateau with an area of 14758 sq. Kms. These consist of the Northern undulating hills, the central upland zone and the southern precipitous face. The highest point is the Shillong peak 1961 meters high located south of Shillong in the central uplands. The southern precipitous face of the plateau is characterised by granite topography in the Northern fringes with shallow valleys. The Myllieum Region is dominated by sand stones, with three distinct platforms the Cherrapunjee, Lyngkyrdem, and the Mawsynram.

The climate of Meghalaya plateau is influenced by elevation and relief. Alternalian pressure cells located in North West India and the depression in the Bay of Bengal and in the South have significant influence on the basis of weather conditions . There are four distinct seasons, the rainy season from May to October, cool season in October and November, the cold season from December to February and the warm in March and April. There are strong winds due to jet streams from Gangetic plains to Tibetan plateau and low pressure over the Tibetan plateau during the warm season.

The region has a variety of natural vegetation from tropical forests to pine forests. In western Meghalaya's northern and southern foot hills with warm and humid climate, there is dense tropical forest with Sal and bamboos. In the higher altitudes in the Tura Range temprate forests with pine and furs are found, whereas hard wood tropical forests are found in the northern and southern parts of the central uplands with Sal, Nahar, Champa and Gomari. Large thickets of bamboo are spread all over with wild bananas. The rolling grass lands are found between 7000 and 1350 metres with pine forests above 1350 metres mixed with willow Mangnoliaal Oak.

There are two national highways in the state, National Highway No 40, the Jorabat - Shillong – Tamabil Road, which has its complete length of 168 Kms falling within Meghalaya. The road connects Jorabat in Assam to Tamabil in Bangladesh. National Highway No. 44, Shillong - Jowai – Badarpur, Agartala Road has 174 Km within Meghalaya. In addition there are nine major state highways connecting the state headquarters with district headquarters and giving access to national highways.

The area is dominated by three principal groups: the Garos in the East and West Garo Hills, the Khasis in the central plateau (East and west Khasi Hills) and Jantia / Pnar in the Eastern section of the plateau (Jaintia Hills). They follow primarily a matrilineal system. The Khasi groups belong to the Mon – Khemar sub family of the Austeric group. The Khasis occupied the central highlands in the Khasi Hills and Pnar in the East Jaintia Hills. The people living in the Northern and Southern part of the central highland were known as "The Bhoi and War", which is akin to their classification of the hills. The further subdivision is based on location and functions performed by them. The Khasis owe their origin to the legend "U Lum Sohpet Bneng", a hill by the same name near Umiam project. It is their belief that this hill connected heaven and earth. Men lived in seven huts by the side of heaven and due to man's sins heaven was separated from the earth and man was left to himself. There are as many dialects as villages but broadly these can be divided in five groups, the Khasis of central plateau, the Pnars of Jaintia in the East, the Wars in the South, Lyngams in the West and Bhois in the North. Khasi is converted into a standard literary form based on the languages of Sohra village (Cherrapunji). The Nearest group which spoke similar language / dialects were the Mundas of the Chotanagpur plateau, the Mons of Lower Burma and the Khemars of Cambodia and Thailand. Garos are believed to belong to the Bodo group having Tibeto – Burman lineage and trace their origin to a place known as 'Tarua' in Tibet. There are two main groups hill Garos and plain Garos. Unlike Khasis, Garos are polygamous and can marry up to three wives. Major sub-groups are Marak, Sangma, Mamen and the Machong (Maharis). The major occupation is agriculture and Jhum cultivation is practiced. Main crops are rice, maize, cotton, yams, aroids, ginger, termeric, sweet potatoes and millet. The Jantias are said to have migrated to Meghalaya from South-East Asia. The Jaintia kings embraced Hinduism though their traditional belief system was akin to Khasi faith. All tribes have increasingly embraced Christianity. Like Garos and Khasis, Jaintias also do not have a recorded history and use Khasi language. The other tribal languages spoken are Bodo / Boro, Garo, Lushai, Koch, Mihir and Rabha. In addition Assamese, Bengali, Marwari, Nepali, Urdu, and Punjabi are spoken. The muslim community speaks both Bengali and Urdu.

The important immigrant communities are Bengali, the Muslims, the Nepali, the Bihari, Marwari and the Mazhabi Sikhs. They all came to the area mostly for economic reasons. Larger number of immigrant communities are in Shillong and its neighbourhood. The city was the capital of Assam and Bengal and even before the British Garo and Jaintia hills attracted non-tribals particularly Bengalis because of trade. When Assam was carved out of Bengal in 1874 on the basis of its cultural homogeneity, Shillong became its capital, which brought British officials, clergymen, Bengalis as clerks, Nepalis in Assam Rifles and Assames as bureaucrats. Khasi Hills became the nerve centre of administration and political power.

The population of the state was 23.06 lacs (2001 census), with an average density of 103 persons per sq. km, which is 0.22 per cent of the country and 5.88 per cent of the North-East region. The percentage of urban population is 8.41, rest is in the rural areas. Over 80 per cent of the population is scheduled tribes, which goes upto 97 per cent in the interior Mauzas of the Garo Hills. Non tribal population is concentrated in urban areas. The two districts of East Khasi hills and west Garo Hills constitute 47 per cent of state's area and have 64 per cent of its population. The Shillong urban agglomeration in East Khasi Hills accounts for 80 per cent of the Urban population. Percentage of literacy in 2001 was 63.31 as against 39.16 in 1991. It was highest in East Khasi Hills 48.10 per cent followed by west Garo Hills 32.07 per cent.

Level of development in the state is low, apart from Shillong and a few other centres, the area is backward and inaccessible. Development has been influenced by the twin factors of accessibility and local investible capital. Scattered and dispersed nature of exploitable resources, geographical inertia, lack of infrastructure and high cost of transportation are major factors inhibiting economic growth and development : Khasi, Jaintia and Garo Hills produce coal, Limestone, Silliminite, fire clay, white clay, Kaolm, Bolomite, Feldspar, Quartz and glass sand. Estimated coal reserves are 562 million tons, limestone 3743 million tons and fine clay 16 million tons, most of which is still untapped. Crude oil and gas resources are reported in Southern slopes of Meghalaya and ONGC has applied for prospecting licence to explore Hydro-Carbons. Most important non-agricultural produce is cement at Cheerapunjee (Chera Cement Company). There are mini cement plants at Damas in East Garo Hills and at Suluga in Jaintia Hills. Govt. is contemplating mini cement plants in the private sector. There are a number of small scale industrial units covering service sectors. The Meghalaya Electronics Development Corporation has set up the Tantalum Capacitor project at Uniam. The Meghalaya Industrial Development Corporation is in its nascent state.

In Meghalaya 83 per cent of the population depends on agriculture for their livelihood. Topography and land conditions are against extensive cultivation. Rice and maize are main crops, with a limited quantity of wheat, which has been introduced recently. Potato, Jute, Mesta, Cotton, Mustard, arecanut, ginger, turmeric, betelvine, black pepper and tezpaza are the cashcrops. Orange, pineapple, bananas, lemon, guava, litchi, jack fruit, plum, pear and peach are main horticulture crops. Recently cultivation of tea, mushroom, tomato and rubber has been undertaken.

The state has power protential of 1200 Mw. but only one sixth has been so far tapped. It is surplus in power and 36 per cent of the electricity generated is supplied to neighbouring states.

The total forest area is 8510 sq. kms with only 993 sq. kms. under state control and the rest under the district councils and private management teak, titacap, gomari, pine, bola, pine birch and makrisal are main timber trees. Forest produce includes timber, bamboo, reed, cane, ipecac, medicinal herbs and plants, cinnamon and thatch grass. Azaleas and rhododendrons grow wild in Khasi and Jantia Hills and many variety of orchids are found. Meghalaya is rich in wild life, elephants, tigers, bear, wild bore, leopards, cats of different variety and deer of different kinds are found. It has a number of lovely spots of tourist attraction.

Historical Perspective and Contemporary Manifestations

During the Ahom period, the Garo hills and the Khasi-Jaintia hills were not part of Assam. After the treaty of Yandaboo in 1826, the British annexed Garo hills first and then the Khasi and Jaintia hills. In 1874 when the province of Assam was formed under a Chief Commissioner, Shillong became its capital. This started the influx of Bengalees as part of administration, Nepalese as part of military and Marwaris as traders.

With establishment of the Welsh Presbyterian Mission in 1841 in Khasi hills and American Baptist Mission in Garo hills in 1864, Shillong gradually became a major educational centre, summer resort and a military garrison.

The Governor of Assam Shri Akbar Hydari, at the time of independence, was able to sign a standstill agreement with the Khasis on 9 August 1947 based on their broad willingness to accede to India.

By March 1948, all the Khasi Chiefs had signed the Instrument of Accession and on 26 January 1950, the united Khasi-Jaintia and Garo hills became a part of the province of Assam. Apprehensive of Assam's language policy, the tribals of Meghalaya raised the demand for a separate State under the leadership of All Party Hill Leaders Conference (APHLC). A commission on hill areas of Assam was constituted under H V Patashar in 1965. As a result of its recommendations and with some modifications to meet the demand of APHLC, Meghalaya was declared an autonomous State within Assam in 1970. Meghalaya became a full-fledged State on 21 January 1972.

As a parallel to AASU agitation in Assam, the Khasi Students Union (KSU) launched a similar stir with 1951 as the cut off year. A distinction was made between old and new settlers of Indian origin. Since 1979 there have been riots against the outsiders or 'Dkhars' as they are called.

The flashpoint has always been Shillong which has a population of 3,50,000 of which 40 per cent are non-tribals consisting of Bengalees, Assamese, Nepalese, Marwaris and others. The worst riot was in 1992.

Although land sale to non tribals is prohibited, a large number of Bangladeshi migrants are in illegal occupation of large tracts of land in Meghalaya. KSU alleges that there are 300,000 Nepalese in Meghalaya's 1.7 million population. The State Government claims to have deported 13,000 foreigners since 1989.

Rudimentary indications of militancy were detected in 1989 with the formation of Meghalaya United Movement (MUM) with the objective of all round development of Meghalaya and in due course secession. The idea was not favoured and MUM has little following and professes links with ULFA. Corruption in Garo hills and dicontentment of Garo in Kamrup and Goalpara Districts of Assam for not being recognised as scheduled tribes gave birth to Achick Liberation Matguk Army (ALMA)– a vigilant but not a secessionist movement in 1989; they also are for a separate Garo State. The movement was inspired by NSCN and also has links with ULFA. Its reported strength is about 50, has carbines, AK 47 rifles, M 20 pistols, country made revolvers and explosives. It has carried out a couple of Bank raids and its chief George Momin and an NCCN (I) accomplice were killed in an encounter. Lack of public support further demoralised ALMA in 1994 and most of its members surrendered to the State administration on terms which had been negotiated earlier.

In keeping with the tribal ethos of the North-East, in 1992 Khasis formed Hynniewtrep Voluntary Council (HVC) to eradicate evils in Khasi society particularly in the youth. At the same time Hymiewtrep Achik Liberation Council (HALC), a more militant organisation, was formed with secessionist designs as confirmed from captured pamphlets. In 1995, it voiced boycotting of Republic Day and return to traditional governance of the people. Supported by NSCN (IM), it is essentially urban based in Shillong and primarily serves the NSCN (IM) by providing guides and other help during transit from Bangladesh. Liberal terms offered by Government of Meghalaya for surrender have not evoked much response in HALC.

Meghalaya is prone to Bangladeshi infiltration both directly and through neighbouring states due to its porous borders; their number doubled during the last year to over 6000 compared to below 3000 in 1998. Similarly with the withdrawal of RAP in 1995, the influx of Nepalee nationals from Nepal has increased, which provides ISI agents another avenue for infiltration of its agents. Location of NE Militant camps in Sylhet and easy accessibility from Bangladesh has made Meghalaya a convenient transit area for them. The NE insurgents, ULFA, NSCN (I),

BLT and ME, have found Meghalaya and particularly Shillong a convenient hideout. While their presence is felt they refrain from any militant activity. It has also acted as the ideological centre of the tribal insurgent groups.

The influx of foreign nationals from Bangladesh and Nepal and outsiders has created an anti-outsider feeling particularly amongst the youth and is the main cause of anti establishment sentiment amongst them. The presence of militant organisations of the region in the state, unemployment and anti-foreigners/anti-establishment feelings have resulted in extremist organisations like HNLC, ANVC and MPLF getting active. They are provided arms, training and other help by insurgent groups like NSCN (IM), KYKL of Manipur, UNLF and BLTF of Assam. Meghalaya has an increasing problem of alcoholism, drugs, school dropouts and AIDS. Unemployment is increasing at a threatening rate.

HNLC is the only organisation which professes an anti-Indian stand but all these groups indulge in criminal activities like kidnapping, looting, extortion and murders. Extortions and kidnappings have posed a major security threat for outsiders, business community and affluent segments of the society. The Central Government is yet to ban these organisations, although the State Government has proposed the same. Meghalaya, like other states of the North-East is heading towards insurgency uless corrective measures are taken. The unstable situation in Meghalaya is further compounded by political instability marked by frequent changes in the Government. In recent years, there have been five changes in government since the 1998 elections and the state saw three Chief Ministers in the last two years. The latest change was in March 2003 when Lyngdoh lost the Chief Ministership to his own party (UDP) president Mawlong.

ARUNACHAL PRADESH

Arunachal Pradesh, situated along the North-Eastern frontier of India, is of great strategic importance. Eastern Himalayas cover the entire state which is bounded by Bhutan in the West, Tibet in the North and North-East, Myanmar in the East and South-East and Assam in the South. It lies between $26^0 28'$ N and $29^0 30'$ N latitudes and $91^0 30'$ E and $97^0 30'$ E longitudes and occupies an area of 83, 578 Sq. Km. With an altitude ranging from 150m in the foot hills to 7000m in its Northern high altitude areas. There are only two seasons, rainy reason from April to October and winter from November to March. The state is rich in minerals like dolomite, quartzite, graphite, limestone, marble, oil and natural gas. The state is rich in forest wealth like bamboo, cane and timber, forest produce is the main source of revenue. A large variety of medicinal plants grow in the area and there is a variety of wild life. Nearly 96 per cent of the total population of 10,96,702 (2001 census) is engaged in agriculture. Out of a total cultivated area of 1,33,430 hectares, a total of 56,270 hectares have been brought under Jhum cultivation and only 26 per cent is irrigated. Settled cultivation is becoming popular.

Two thirds of the population is non-tribal, the tribal population is of Tibeto-Burman stock. Sixty six communities were identified for the purpose of the People of India Project, which constitute 80 per cent of the total population, of which sixty three are scheduled tribes. Nepalese, Sonowal Kacharis, Tibetans and Chakmas are migrants. The cultural fabric of Arunachal Pradesh consists of broadly five cultural zones. From west to East these are (a) The Mon cultural zone, which covers the Tawang and Western Kameng districts and is inhabited by Monpas and Sherdukpens, the Ahas, Mijis and Khowas also belong to this zone (b) East of it lies the Nishi cultural zone encompassing the Bagnis of East Kameng district, the Nishis of upper and lower Subansiri districts and Sulungs and Apatanis. Other groups living in the zone include the Nas, Tagnis, Mikirs and Hill Miris (c) The Adi cultural zone extends from the Eastern part of upper subansiri district to the western boundary of the Dibang Valley district, covering all the Adi sub groups as well as the Khambas, Membas and Mishings/Miris. (d) The Mishmi cultural zone covering the districts of the Dibang valley and Lohit, is predominated by the three sub-groups of the Mishmi community and among them lives a small community-the Zakhring / Meyons. Other communities in the Zone are the Khamptis, Khamiyangs, Deoris, Chakmas and Tibetans who are settled in the plains bordering Assam (e) Finally the Nocte-Tangsa cultural zone is spread over the Tirap and Changlang districts. The major communities of the Zone are Noctes, Wanchos and Tangsas, with Singphos, Sonowal Kacharis, Lisus and Nepalese being the other small groups in the area[61]. Arunachal has evidence of both Hindu and Budhist influence. While the inner fringes show Hindu influence, Budhist influence is evident along the Nothern and Eastern perimeters inhabited by Monpas and Sherdukpens (Kameng), Membas (Siang) and Khamptis, Singphos and Tangsas (Lohit and Tirap). Unlike other areas of the North-East, Christian presence in Arunachal Pradesh is negligible. A large number of people follow "Donyi Polo", a form of animism which includes worship of Sun and Moon. There is no common language in Arunachal Pradesh. Nefamese (Arunachalese), a mixture of Assamese and local dialects and Hindi have become the common lingua franca with Devnagri and Roman script. English is the official language.

History[62]

The history of Arunachal Pradesh is shrouded in myths and legends. Except for a few archaeological finds there are hardly any written records. Written references to the people of Arunachal Pradesh first appeared in Ahom Buranjis (Chronicles of Ahoms) and Mughal Chronicles. The plains area was ruled by Chutiyas and the Kalitas in ancient times. The recorded history of Arunachal Pradesh starts from the 17th century. The Ahoms succeeded in gradually bringing the entire stretch from Sadiya to the Subansiri river on the North bank of Brahmaputra under their control. Ahoms contained the Hill tribals in their own area and sent punitive expeditions when there were major raids by the tribals. They followed a policy of conciliation backed by force, which was a forerunner to the British frontier policy as formulated in the following lines quoted by Machenzie (1884) "conciliate them if you can, be persistent in demanding surrender of murderers but endeaveour so to approach the tribes that a basis may be opened for friendly inter course". Ahoms had introduced a system of paying 'posa' to some tribals of Arunachal Pradesh; posa was a kind of payment made by Ahoms to the tribals in lieu of peace.

In 1826, the British replaced the Ahoms in Assam and after British annexation of the whole of Assam in 1938, they made it a Non-Regulation province of British India. In 1873, an inner line was prescribed, which passed through the Kamrup and Golpara districts towards Bhutan; the Darang District towards Bhutiyas, Akas and Daflas; the Lakhimpur District towards Daflas,"Miris, Abors, Mishmis, Khamptis, Singphos, and Nagas and Sibsagar towards Nagas. The Inner Line Regulations, stipulated that no British subjects of certain classes or foreign residents could cross it without a license and laid down rules regarding trade, possession of land and other related matters. To deal with the hill tribes of the area, the post of political officer was created in 1882, with the headquarters at Sadiya. By establishing friendly relations with the tribes, the British brought the entire area under their administrative control. To secure the frontiers of the North-East Frontier Tract with Tibet, the tripartite Simla Conference with Tibet and China in 1913, resulted in the Mc Mohan Line. In 1914, the hill areas of the northern districts of Assam were separated to form the North-East Frontier Tract and the entire area was divided into three tracts-the Balipura, Lakhimpur and Sadiya Frontier Tract units. Tirap Frontier Tract unit was created a bit later. In 1951, the plain areas all along the frontier Tracts were placed under Assam and rest was designated as North-East Frontier Agency (NEFA) and in 1954 units were reconstituted and renamed as Kameng, Subansiri, Siang, Lohit and Tirap Frontier Divisions. The Tuensang Frontier Division earlier part of NEFA was amalgamated with Nagaland in 1957. What remained became Arunachal Pradesh in 1972.

North-East Frontier Tract was directly under the Governor of Assam as "Excluded Area" who administered it under his discretion. After independence its governance was vested in the Assam Govt. and Governor was to act on the advice of the Chief Minister. However, after the commencement of the Constitution in 1950, the administration of NEFA was restored to the Governor as the agent of the centre. After independence NEFA was constitutionally a part of Assam, with governor acting as the agent of the President. The premise that NEFA would be united with Assam after it has attained a certain level of development did not materialise.

The Indian Frontier Administrative Service was created in 1956 for better administration of the border areas. In 1957, Venier Elwin enunciated this approach to the development of NEFA, in his famous book "A Philosophy for NEFA". In his words: "we cannot allow matters to drift in the tribal areas or just not take interest in them. In the world of to-day that is not possible or desirable. At the same time, we should avoid over administering these areas and in particular sending too many outsiders into tribal territory – it is between these two extreme positions that we have to function". The developmetal activities and the five year plans were guided by this philosophy.

In 1971, NEFA was detached from Assam and made a union territory under a Chief Commissioner under the North-Eastern Areas (Reorganisation) Act, and its headquarters established at Itanagar. Direct elections to the Council were introduced in 1972 but a Council of Ministers was only constituted in 1975. The Pradesh council was converted into a legislative council and Chief Commissioner was replaced by a Lieutenant Governor. The first elections were held in 1978 and it became a full fledged state in 1986.

Political and Social Structure

Almost all the communities of Arunachal Pradesh are governed by traditional forms of Govt. The heads of these governments are called by different names in different tribes. In reality these are village headmen; and each village has its own headman and the post is hereditary unless the person is found unfit. In that case village elders choose the headman. The decision of the headman or chief is final and is respected by all. The Khamptis have developed a council system presided over by a headman. They have an elaborate system of hearing and deciding cases and awarding punishment after consulting a book called "The masat". The political system of Adis is most democratic and council of elders is called

Kebang, which exercises legal and judicial powers and all social and political control. Inter-village disputes are settled by "Bango", which consists of all headmen (gams) within its jurisdiction and a few other influential villagers, who constitute the Bango council. The Govt. appointed a committee under democratic norms to be adopted in Arunachal Pradesh. The recommendations were accepted in 1969. It recommended village council with judicial and developmental functions, Anchal Samitis at block level under the SDO and a Zila Parishad under the Deputy Commissioner. The five Zila Parishads sent four members each to agency council. Though Arunachal continues to be a sixth schedule state but it adopted the Panchayati Raj system in preference to the District Council system which has strengthened the decentralisation of the democratic system. Due to vastness of the area and difficulty of the terrain, there are 12 districts today in Arunachal Pradesh to facilitate development.

Family is the smallest unit of society with father as its head. All movable and immovable property such as cultivated land, bamboo groves, palm leaves, gardens, livestock, granaries, utensils and ornaments are held commonly by the family and father as head of the family is the sole owner. After his death it is inherited by the eldest or the youngest or by all the sons equally. The societies are mostly patrilineal but polyandrous families are prevalent amongst Budhist communities like Monpas. All tribes are composed of number of clans denoted by local categories. Generally clans continue over seven generations or more till due to over population and migration they split collaterally, which gives rise to sub-clans. A lot of freedom is permitted to the young boys and girls and the dormitory provides young boys and girls opportunity for courtship and selecting their life partners. Marriages are confined to the same or a particular group of villages. Bride price is a common practice and intra-clan marriages are considered a crime and monogamy is the rule but polygamous marriages are accepted amongst the Noctes and Wanchos chiefs.

Traditional tribal religion based on beliefs in spirits is most prevalent but Budhism, Hinduism (Vashnavism) and Christianity are practiced in some communities. A section of Noctes, Tikhaks, Deoris and Nepalis living in Arunachal Pradesh are Hindus. According to 1981 census, there were 1,84,737 Hindus, 86,483 Budhists, 27,306 Christians, 5,073 Muslims, 1,231 Sikhs, 42 Jains and 3,26,000 belonged to other religions. The inner areas show Hindu influence, Budhists influence is predominent in the Northern and Eastern areas inhabited by Monpas and Sherdukpens in Kameng and Membas in Siang who follow the Mahayana School and Khamptis, Singhphos and Tangsas in Lohit and Tirap conform to

Himayana School. The influence of Donyi-polo the worship of Sun and Moon is predominent amongst the Adis, Apa, Tanis, Nishis and Tagins in Siang and Subansiri.

Contemporary Rumblings

Consequent to Dalai Lama's fleeing from Tibet in 1959, a few thousand Tibetan refugees were given shelter in Arunachal Pradesh. A few years later in the 1960's, the construction of Kaptai Dam in CHT in East Pakistan led to displacement and migration of Budhist Chakmas to Tripura and Mizoram. Due to the low density of population in Arunachal Pradesh, the central Govt. decided to relocate the Chakmas in Arunachal Pradesh. The Arunachalis thought that Chakmas were there only temporarily, a perception reinforced by the repatriation of Chakmas from Tripura in the recent past. But Bangladesh has refused to accept Chakmas, who had moved out of CHT before the emergence of Bangladesh in 1971 in terms of Indra – Mujib Agreement as Banladeshis. What has upset the tribals of Arunachal Pradesh was the insistent demands by the Chakmas for citizenship. Their number is about 60,000, which includes Hajongs. The Govt. of India had promised them Indian citizenship.

The feelings against foreigners, particularly Chakmas has been fomenting since eighties but since 1990 it has been given political overtones and student unions of Arunachal Pradesh and of the North-East have joined the agitation and quit Arunachal Pradesh notices were issued and served on the Chakmas. At the political level it has become an emotive issue that all want to exploit. Surfacing of organisations like United Liberation Army of Arunachal Pradesh and United Peoples Volunteers of Arunachal Pradesh with militant overtones is a fore-warning. The situation needs to be resolved by negotiations and political accommodation before it gets drawn into the turbulent cross currents of the North-East. Arunachal Pradesh has been experiencing the backlash of Naga insurgency for long and is affected by the activities of both the Naga insurgent groups NSCN (K) and NSCN (I) and ULFA and Bodo groups of Assam as its thick forests provide safe coridors. Changlang and Tirap districts are most effected as these provide easy access to sancturies in Northern Myanmar. The factional fights between the two Naga factions has led to extortions and intimidation of Govt. officials, which has developed political over tones. Due to ethnic loyalties Konyaks and Wanchoos are accused of siding with NSCN (K) and Noctes with NSCN (I) in retaliation. Six Ministers and Six MLA's were accused of conniving with both the insurgent groups and an inquiry was ordered by the centre, which some accuse, was motivated by centres desire to move into the local political domain[63]. This was followed by the toppling of the Congress (I) Govt. on 2 August, 2003 with just a year left for the Assembly elections. The new Govt. talked of extension of ceasfire with NSCN (I) without boundries, autonomous council for Tirap and Changlang districts and withdrawal of operations. Thus Arunachal Pradesh also fell to the power game through insurgent Nexus and political manoeuvering[64].

A part of Arunachal Pradesh has been part of the cultural system of the Brahmaputra valley. The Hindu influence penetrated along the Brahmputra upto the Dibang valley during the 11th and 13th century as is proved by the ruins of Bhishmak site in Dibang valley and of Pursuram Kund in Lohit. The Ahoms built a fort at Itanagar during the 13th and 14th century, which had ring wells and was spread over three to four kilometers. The Assamese connection is substantiated further by the presence of Deoris and other communities, who migrated through and from Assam and use Asamese language.

Since independence slavery, which was necessitated due to economic reasons (Labour) has been abolished and a new sense of self-respect is reflected by the tribes shedding the old Assamese names considered derogatory and assuming new names such as Adi for Abors (Uncontrollable) and Nishi for Daflas. Although it is small state but it is marked by linguistic heterogeneity, in all 42 languages are spoken. All of them except Assamese and Nepali which are Indo-Aryan belong to the Tibeto-Chinese family. Among the Tibeto-Chinese family Khampti-Shan belongs to the Siamese-Chinese sub family and all others to the Tibeto-Burman sub family. According to 1981 census Assamese (27,339 persons), Bengali (46,174 persons) and Hindi (32,318 persons) are the scheduled languages. There are 50,810 persons who speak Gorkhali/Nepali and 7,482 persons speak Tibetan. The tribal languages and Adi (1,22,489), Bodo/Boro (1,265), Mikir (1,255), Mishmi (23,399), Monpa (33,273), Nishi/Dafla (1,39,408), Nocte (23,668), Tangsa (10,623) and Wancho (32,419). The extra ordinary heterogeneity is the outcome of its ecological diversity which is strengthened by its tribal institutions and cultural system and tribals control over its resources. The schedule tribes are 93.94 per cent and women play a major role in economic activities but their status is low in more than 50 per cent of the communities.

The state had shown political stability since it became a union territory in 1972 and a full fledged state in 1987 till recent years, when it fell pray to the politics of expediency and insurgent pressures in August 2003. Education has made good progress and it is developing into cohesive dynamic society inspite of its heterogeneity. Depletion of forest resources is its main cause for economic worry. It is coping well with the modernisation process compared to other tribal societies of the North-East.

REFERENCES

1. Hem Barua, *The Red River and The Blue Hill*, 1956 – Lawyers Book Stall, Gawhati, pp. 12-14.
2. n1, p. 15.
3 Note of dissent by Rabi Chandra Chachari, Kameshwar Das and Sarleswar Baruah. In Govt. of Assam 1938, p. 20 as quoted in "India against itself – Sanjib Baruah.
4. *Indian Express,* 14 December 2003.
5. Dr. Ashikho, Daili Mao, *Nagas, Problems and Politics*. Ashish Publishing House, New Delhi, 1992, pp. 10-14.
6. *Ibid*, pp. 11-13.
7. VIK Sareen, *India's North East in flames*, Vikas Publishing House Pvt. Ltd., New Delhi, 1980, pp. 90-96.
8. *Ibid.*
9. *Ibid.*
10. n5, p. 31.
11. Mar Alsong Changer: *Unforgettable Memories of Nagaland*, Tribal Communication and Research, Mohok Chung, pp. 10-12.
12. n5, p. 159.
13. a) *Ibid*, p. 3 Appendix 1, p. 169.
    b) Y.D.Gundeviya, *War and Peace in Nagaland*, New Delhi, 1975, p. 57.
    c) Sanjoy Hazarika "Strangers in the Mist" Penguin Books, 1995, p. 99.
14. Nirmal Nibedon, *North East India – The Ethnic Explosion*, Lancer Publishers, 1981, p. 28.
15. B.G. Verghese, *India's North East Resurgent*, Konark Publishers Pvt. Ltd. Delhi, 1996, pp. 92-93.
16. R.K. Saha "State Formation Among the Meiteis of Manipur" in Surajit Sinha (ed), *Tribal Politics and State System in Pre-Colonial Eastern and North-Eastern India*, K.P.Bagchi and Company Ltd. Calcutta 1987, p. 213.
17. B.C. Allen, *Census of Assam*, Vol 1 (Report), Manas Publication, Delhi – 1984 (Reprint), p. 120.
18. Lt.Gen. Sir A.P.Pharye, *History of Burma*, London 1976, pp. 6-7.
19. T.C. Hodson, *The Meithens*, Low Price Publication, Delhi 1989, (Reprint), p. 10.
20. Parmeshwar Gogoi, *The Tai and Tai Kingdoms*, Dept. of Publication Guwahati University, 1968, p. 67.
21. n18, p. 12.
22. Konsam Manikchand, "The coalition of the Meitei State: A confederacy through the last two millenia" in Naoram Sanajaoba (ed) – *Manipur Past and Present* Vol.1, Mittal Publications, Delhi, 1988, p. 147.
23. R.B. Penberton, Report on the Eastern Frontier of India, Calcutta, 1835, p. 41.

24. N. Khelchandra Singh, Documents on Anglo-Manipur War 1891, Uripok Ningthoukhongjam, Leikai–Imphal, 1984.
25. Sarojini Devi, Freedom Fighters Records in the Manipur State Archives (1896-1951), Manipur State Archives, Govt. of Manipur, 1986, p. 3.
26. Phanjouban Tarapot, *Insurgency Movement in North east India*, Vikas Publishing House Pvt. Ltd., New Delhi, 1993, p. 63.
27. R. Parsana "Watching the Nagas" *The Week*, 27 July 1997.
28. Georg Watts, The Aboriginal Tribes of Manipur, Journal of the Anthropological Institute Vol 16, 1887 in the Extract – The aboriginal Tribes of Manipur, Manipur Research Society, Imphal 1991, p. 6.
29. n26, p. 63.
30. Gangumei Kabui, "Insurgency in Manipur Valley", in BL Abbi (ed) – *North east Problems and Prospects of Development*, Centre for Research in Rural and Industrial Development, Chandigarh 1984, pp. 233-34.
31. G.K.Ghosh, *Tribals and their cultures, Manipur and Nagaland* – Ashish Publishing House, New Delhi, 1992, p. 132.
32. R. Walawma, *My country and I*, Aizawl, p. 62 (In Mizo).
33. L.B.Thanga, The Mizo's 1978, Guwahati – P1 and R Pudaite, The Education of Hmar People of Manipur, 1963, pp. 21-22.
34. *Ibid*, p. 3.
35. State Reorganisation Commission Report, p. 187.
36. R. Coupland (1944), The Constitutional Problems of India Part III, p. 164.
37. n7, p. 145.
38. Proceedings of the North East Frontier (Assam) Tribal and Excluded area Sub Committee–Vol II (Evidence Part I–Constituent Assembly Debate 1949).
39. n7, p. 149.
40. Constituent Assembly Debate (CAD) Vol II, p. 112.
41. Govt. of Assam Notification No. TAD/R/10/50 dated 31 July 51 and TAD/R/15/50 dated 31 July 51.
42. n7, p. 150.
43. *Ibid*, p. 152.
44. Discussion with Chakma leaders, 1997.
45. S.K. Chaube, *Hill politics in North East India*, 1973 Calcutta, pp. 65-66.
46. Urmila Phadnis, *Ethnicity and Nation Building in South Asia*, Saje Publications, New Delhi, 1990, pp. 148-164 (Ethnic dynamics of autonomy and secession in Mizoram).
47. n7, p. 125.
48. S.B.K. Devavarman, The Tribes of Tripura, A dissertation Special series No.1, Directorate of Research, Govt. of Tripura, Agartala 2nd edition–Published in 1986, p. 3.
49. *Ibid*, p. 4.
50. n7, p. 128.
51. n15, p. 170.
52. Sanjoy Hazarika, *Strangers in the Mist*, p. 123.

53. n51 and O.S. Adhikari, *Four Immigrant Tribes of Tripura*, Directorate of Research, Tribal Welfare Department, Govt. of Tripura, 1988.
54. Law Research Institute, Guwahati, 1990.
55. n15, p. 172.
56. *Ibid*, p. 173.
57. n26, p. 93.
58. Nitin A. Gorkhale and Krishna Prasad "Big Brothers and Seven Sisters" *Outlook*, 5 March, 97.
59. *The Stateman*, 8 March 2003.
60. Tapas Roy, Conflict in Tripura, *Frontline*, 26 July 1996.
61. K. S. Singh, *People of India, Arunachal Pradesh vol. XIV*, Seagal books, Calcutta, 1995, pp. 20-21.
62. *Ibid*, pp. 10-18.
63. *The Statesman*, 12 July 2003.
64. *The Statesman*, 9 August 2003.
65. J.P. Singh, *Human Resource of North East India*, Inter India Publications, New Delhi, 1982, pp. 59-60.
66. J.B.Ganguli, The Benign Hills, Tripura Darpan Pub, Agartala, 1983, pp. 17, 37, 46.
67. B.P. Misra, *Socio-Economic Adjustment of Tribals*, Peoples Publishing House, New Delhi, 1976, p. 25 and relevant census reports.
68. n66 J.B. Ganguli, p. 47.
69. n67 B.P. Misra, p. 20.
70. n66 J.B. Ganguli, p. 14.
71. *Ibid*, p. 33.
72. *Ibid*, pp. 30-31.
73. Extracted from Tripura Durpan Tathya Panji O. Nirdeshika 1985 as cited in n53.

Appendix A

IMMIGRATION AND DEMOGRAPHIC FALLOUT

In North-East India, Tripura is the smallest administrative division, it account for 4.11 per cent of regional area and roughly 8 per cent of the population second only to Assam. During the period 1901-1971 while the per centage increase in population for India as a whole was 129.6, for the North-East, in general and Tripura in particular it was 358.4 and 797.9 respectively[65]. There can be no denying the fact that such demographic explosion is attributable to influx of immigrants than to natural increase of indigenous people. Numerically the most significant immigration into this state has been of non-tribals. How non-tribals out numbered tribals over the preceding years is illustrated by the table below[66].

	Tribal	*Non-tribal*	*Total*	*Percentage of ST Population to Total*
1901	91,544	81,781	1,73,325	52.81
1931	1,90,032	1,92,418	3,82,450	49.69
1961	3,60,070	7,81,935	11,42,005	31.53
1971	4,50,544	11,05,798	15,56,342	28.94
1981	5,83,920	14,69,138	20,53,058	28.44
1991			27,57,205	
2001			31,91,168	

Notwithstanding that these immigrants both tribal and non-tribals from other provinces and native states, the Bengalees from the adjoining districts of Sylhet, Tipperah, Noakholi, Chittagong, Chittagong Hill Tracts and Dacca constituted the bulk of immigrants settlers in Tripura. In 1901 itself, out of 43,694 immigrants, 39,807 were Bengalees hailing from these areas[67]. As many as 1,84,000 displaced persons entered Tripura in 1950-51 along with a large number of them settled here[68].

The story of non-tribal immigration to Tripura dates back to the 14th century when Raja Ratnamanikya settled 4,000 Bengalees in four places in Tripura[69]. It is however, since the end of the last quarter of the nineteenth century that immigration of Bengalees has been enormous[70]. While initially the throne was in favour of Bengalees for its own socio-political and economic interest, it is with the British intervention in the state administration, that pressure was felt by the kings to usher in administrative structure capable of implementing its modernisation plans and progress. Land settlement and agricultural activities were increased to generate additional land revenue to meet the costs of modernisation. It was with this background that large scale immigration of middle class educated professionals and agriculturists took place from Bengal. Despite all encouragement and incentives immigration on such a large scale would not have taken place except due to economic and other compulsions.

The next numerically important groups of immigrants settled in Tripura were the Manipuris. In 1931 Manipuri population was 19,200 for whom agriculture (plough cultivators) was the main occupation[71].

The total population of immigrants from provinces and states from Bengal and Assam in 1911 was 6,122, in 1921 it was 13,337; and in 1931 it was 13,175, which was insignificant. It was really the migration of Bengalees which changed the demographic composition of the state over the years.

The tribal immigrants into the state added more to its demographic varieties than to its size. Out of the nineteen enlisted tribes found in Tripura, eight namely Tripura, Reang, Noatia, Jamatia, Halam, Kuki, Chaimal and Uchai are known to have migrated in the distant historical period and are regarded as the original settlers of Tripura. The other tribes considered as immigrants are Chakmas, Mag, Garo, Khasi, Lushai, Bhutia, Lepcha, Bhil, Munda, Oraon and Santal. The Chakmas and Mags are known to have immigrated from CHT and Arakan not earlier than the 18th century, their population in 1931 were 8,730 and 5,748 respectively[72]. The princely patronage, apart from internal feuds and growing pressure on land, were responsible for their immigration as both Chakmas and Mags took to plough cultivation in the plains periphery.

Garo, Khasi and Lushai are Assam tribes who migrated to the state at different times. Immigration of Lushais from the Lushai Hills and their movement had been constant as economic pursuits particularly due to shifting cultivation. In 1931, the population of Garo and Khasi was 2,143 and 23 respectively. Khasis settled in North district and are famous for betel cultivation and because of this were in the good books of the administration, Lepchas and Bhutia's migrated from the Northern Frontier of Bhutan, Sikkim and North Bengal. In 1961, their population was 7 each, which increased to 175 and 3 respectively in 1971.

The Bhil, Mundas, Oraon and Santals migrated from Central India as labour for tea gardens in 1916 – 17. The out-immigration of Chota Nagpur tribals in 1891 was more than three lacs and increased to nine and a half lacs in 1921. 1931 census revealed that one fourth of Chota Nagpur tribals who had migrated worked in tea gardens of Assam and total number of labourers engaged in tea gardens in Tripura was 5451. The Sardar in tea gardens were engaged to bring labour from their areas.

As compared to 1971 census the population of cultivators in general and amongst tribals in particular fell in 1981 and that of agricultural labour rose. The total population of cultivators in 1971 was 2,35,292 (54.43 per cent) of which 1,07,122 (73.37 per cent) were tribals. In 1981, the total population of cultivators was 2,64,094 (43.57 per cent) of which 2,11,058 (64.03 per cent) were tribals. The comparative figures of agricultural labourers in 1971 was 86,340 (19.96 per cent) of which 28,628 (20.14 per cent) were tribals. In 1981, the total figure of labourers rose to 1,44,910 (23.91 per cent) of which tribals were 60,616 (28.72 per cent)[73].

3

Facets of Turmoil

The mosaic of the North-East represents heterogeniety at its extreme, with high level of ethnic, cultural, linguistic and religious diversity not found in any other region. Similarly, political evolution in the North-East is influenced by its divergent historical experience, social and cultural diversity and distinctiveness. Politico-administrative decisions taken by the British between 1874 and 1935 gave hill areas a distinct identity disregarding the past historic ties and socio-cultural and economic interaction. Treating hill areas successively as "Non-Regulated Areas", "Backward Tracts" and Excluded and Partially Excluded Areas" not only gave them unnatural distinctive identities but isolated them further.

By virtue of its location North-East is characterised by socio-political instability and economic backwardness. Isolation and inaccessibility continue to influence perceptions and undermine stability. Continuous inflow of immigrants, rising socio-economic aspirations, land-alienation and lack of infrastructure have all retarded the process of development and integration. The extension of administration to the peripheral areas of the North-East was viewed with suspicion and interpreted as interference in their traditional system. While out of the system the same traditional centres of power are being used to mobilise people against it. Distorted political ethos, corruption and mal-administration further compounded the situation.

The reactive nature of our policies has encouraged the belief that agitation and violence alone engage attention as our political responses generally followed agitations and insurgencies in the region. A lack of consistency and firmness in dealing with immigrants has added to insecurity amongst local communities as influx of immigrants poses economic, social and cultural threats and provides cause for conflict and violence. Ethnic mobilisation is its current facet, which automatically poses a threat to adversaries resulting in conflict.

The level of development in the hills and plains differ a lot as the level of economic activity and economics are underdeveloped but due to social structure of the societies poverty as found in many other parts of the country does not exist. Level of literacy is generally above all India standards but level of unemployment is increasing. Division of the North-East into several hill states has led to further isolation and has constrained balanced economic development. This has resulted in a conflict prone environment as conflicts in the North-East centre around human frustrations in the socio-economic fields with political articulation for registering the same.

At this stage it will be relevant to identify the major generic and historic causes of the unrest in the North-East and contemporary manifestations of the turmoil.

Isolation

The very first one is the factor of isolation. North-East has stood at the cross roads of history as much as the North-West of India, with one basic difference that the interaction of the immigrating population with the indigenous remained confined to its natural boundaries due to its geographical vastness and abundant resources. Unlike the North-West where invaders and immigrants intermixed with the local population and got assimilated. Even the great vaishnavite surge, Bhakti cult of Sankradev during the 15th and 16th century AD remained confined to the Brahmaputra valley, which later the Manipuri Kings integrated into the Imphal valley. Annexation by the British in the 19th century did not mean administering the area, it was essentially to protect their interests in the plains.

After defeating the invading Burmese and signing the Yandaboo Treaty in 1826 Assam and Manipur came under British influence and it extended its commercial interests particularly in Tea into the North-East. To protect their interests the British carried out punitive expeditions into the Naga and Lushai hills. Since it did not stop Naga and Mizo raids, the British established their presence and Administration followed by the missionaries. The combination of physical isolation, the need to protect their commercial interests in the foot hills from marauding tribesmen and their desire to leave the field clear for the missionaries resulted in deliberate measures being taken to keep the area isolated. Inner Line Regulation of 1873, Govt. of India Act, 1919 and giving the hill areas status of excluded areas under Govt. of India Act of 1935 resulted in perpetuation of physical, social, political and economic isolation. Political control of the North-East Frontier Tract under the Governor and keeping hill areas administration detached from provincial Govt. and legislation further added to isolation and separateness.

The barriers raised by the British for over 150 years as a matter of policy resulted in isolating the tribals and sowing seeds of distrust in their minds for the plainsmen. The isolation of tribals was further accentuated by the advent of western Christian missionaries in the region, who, backed and protected by the British administration, converted them to Christianity and while reclaiming them to civilisation in the process raised yet another wall, cultural and religious. This ended the constant contact that existed over the centuries between the plains people and hill tribes, whether through confrontations or through peaceful trade and interaction. However, we need to be grateful to the missionaries for bringing in a humanistic religious and modern civilisation, which imbided Christian concept of life and ethics and put an end to old custom of head hunting. It also helped the tribals to take a big leap forward from primitiveness to modernity.

The all important factor of isolation has played a pivotal role in modulating the stance of the people of the North-East. Religion and culture have greatly influenced people's mindset and perceptions. However, the North-East remained generally out of the influences of the mainland, and religion, culture and legacy of the Aryans could not penetrate the North-East except the Brahmaputra, Imphal and Barak valleys. Christianity under the British influenced the hills people and benefited them with western education, values and attitudes, thus replacing their traditional ways and values but kept them apart from the Indian mainstream. Physical land barriers and little known ways of the people of the North-East and lack of interaction with rest of India in the socio-political and economic fields perpetuated separateness and isolation. National struggle for independence only influenced Assam and Manipur leaving rest of the North-East out of it.

After independence, we perpetuated this isolation by pursuing the British policy of keeping these areas isolated. In the 1950, Constitution NEFA was restored to the Governor as an agent of the centre. "While acknowledging the need not to let matters drift in tribal areas or just not to take interest in them – we should at the same time avoid over administering these areas and in particular sending too may people in tribal areas. It is between these two positions that we have to function"[1]. We have failed to meet the middle ground while legislating measures to safeguard their tradition, culture and customs, we have failed to provide them real autonomy in their own affairs and economic independence or sustainability, without these political autonomy is meaningless.

However, it is the factor of physical isolation, which impinges on the minds of the people most as it leads to economic and social harassment. As discussed under geography of the region, partition shaped the events and left access to area confined to the narrow Siliguri corridor, our efforts to re-establish the traditional links through Bangladesh have not succeeded. The artificial division left fractured borders and disrupted relationships and created complex security problems of immigration, smuggling, infiltration and subversion. Neither have surface communications within the area and to the rest of the country improved to the desired extent. Political geography his imposed a high degree of isolation of the North-East. Similarly, the region having remained outside the central power structure and a sense of separateness has influenced their perceptions as interaction of the people of the North-East was confined to bureaucratic officers, traders, money lenders and contractors, whose corruption and high handedness could hardly bring them closer. Absence of industrialisation discouraged population movement within the North-East and between North-East and rest of India. Peace and development of Assam is vital for development and progress of the North-East. Its location, isolation and inaccessibility continue to influence the peoples' perceptions and the key to break this isolation lies in opening up the area fast and improve physical interconnectivity within the North-East.

The most stubborn of the barriers is our ignorance and lack of knowledge of the region and its people, which is largely responsible for mis-judgement and wrong decisions by the policy makers. This is largely responsible for a lack of understanding, distrust and hostility. J. H. Hutton, an authority on tribes of North-Eastern India, rightly emphasized that a just and enlightened administration of tribal affairs cannot be established and pursued without an intimate knowledge of and sympathetic interest in tribals themselves, their customs and their point of view. Only knowledge can lead to understanding and understanding generates good will and trust.

Diversity

There are over 200 ethnic groups and over 400 languages and dialects spoken in the area. In addition there is a vast cultural and religious diversity. The area is inhabited by a high per centage of scheduled tribes, 93 per cent in Mizoram, 84 per cent in Nagaland, 80 per cent in Meghalaya, 70 per cent in Arunachal Pradesh, 30 per cent in Tripura, 27 per cent in Manipur and 10 per cent in Assam. We need to appreciate that the North-East is not a homogenous region with common political, social or economic system and perspectives. Therefore search of a North-East identity will be fallacious. While searching for a solution and a holistic perspective we must be conscious of the fundamental difference at the ground level in the constituent areas of the region.

It will be pertinent to mention that one of the major in-built constraints of most of the tribal areas, particularly of the hill tribes is the close and federal nature of the society. People have been generally suspicious of any thing from outside and period of assimilation is long drawn-out, and trust and credibility have high value in their minds. The major outside constraint is ignorance, lack of detailed knowledge of each are of the North-East and its heterogeneous inhabitants, their perspectives and requirements. These not only impose constraints but are easy means of exploitation by the parochial elements.

Modernization

In the socio-political field both the good and bad effects of modernization have manifested. Unfortunately the process has not been harmonized and past values and systems are in conflict with the forces of modernization. Its two major manifestations are that the traditional rural elite has been replaced by the modern or urban elite. Similarly, the traditional self governing system has been replaced by a centralized and formal system. The tribal society is a classless society. While it is getting modernized the federal independent tribal group system still remains. There is a widespread demand for political independence/autonomy but people find it difficult to accept the emerging economic class structure. Literacy, awareness and modern political system has been accompanied by corrupt administration both civil and political and mounting economic bankruptcy and unemployment, which has proved fertile ground for exploitation both by the corrupt political set up and the insurgents. Neglect and lack of real economic development have provided incentives for exploitation, which has been accentuated by the influx of foreigners (outsiders), giving rise to ethnic parochialism. Under these conditions the question of identity has come to the forefront. The identity crisis is fomented by the fear of cultural submergence and economic and social insecurity.

Immigration

Immigration into Assam and other areas of the North-East is at the heart of the problem of the area. Historically, Muslims and Ahoms entered ancient Kamrup almost simultaneously but while Ahoms stayed on to establish their kingdom, Muslims from Bengal could not find a foothold despite various invasions. It was during the British period after treaty of Yandaboo that Assam was incorporated in the Bengal Presidency and the influx of Bangalees, Napalese, Marwaris and later on Biharis and Orissa labour for the tea estates started. The flood gates were opened by the partition of Bengal in 1905. Although the partition was undone in 1912 but large scale immigration had already taken place[2].

The observations of the then census commissioner, C. S. Mullai in the census report of 1931 are valid, "where there is waste land, thither flock Mymensinghias", a population of over half a million has transplanted itself from Bengal to Assam Valley in the previous 25 years. the role of Saadulla in his two tenures from 1937, before and during the civil disobedience movement, resulted in Muslim population of Assam quadruplicating in the 20 years from 1925. The partition of the country brought more Bengalee Hindus into Bengal, Assam and Tripura. Alongwith Hindu migrants, illegal Muslim immigration continued. The scale of migration can be seen by the fact that in Tripura tribals who were in a dominant majority have been reduced to a minority of 28.5 per cent in the span of less than a century.

The story of immigration into the North-East and Assam in particular has been covered in detail in Chapter 1, alongwith the Assam agitation and its aftermath. Unfortunately the immigration still continues. This is the single most destabilizing factor in the North-East due to change in demographic balance, which has serious economic, social and security implications. Unfortunately, neither the Central Govts. of various hues nor the State Govts. of different political parties have shown the political will to arrest the tide. They have only indulged in platitudes and exploitation of diverse groups including Muslim minorities and immigrants to serve their electoral interests. Vast machinery and physical resources employed for border guarding will serve no useful purpose in the absence of political will and administrative diligence.

Immigrants or Foreigners

The issue of foreigners evokes strong feelings amongst the people of the North-East particularly of Assam. At the same time it is highly politicised and each political party while trying to take electoral advantage has failed to face the issue squarely. Failure to implement the Assam Accord of 1985 and conflicting stand on the illegal migrants (Determination by Tribunals) Act, 1983 has further confused the situation and made the issue more volatile. This fact is borne out by the recent agitation of Assamese against Biharis during the railway recruitment for class III and IV employees in Guwahati and subsequent targeting of people of the North-East origin travelling through Bihar in November, 2003.

There is an all-round failure in India to come to grips with the problem of illegal immigrants. Unfortunately, action on this subject invariably assumes communal over tones with political parties taking position to suit the interest of their vote banks. The massive illegal immigrations pose a grave danger to our security, social harmony and economic well being. The unabated trans-border migration has altered the demographic complexion of Tripura and is threatening to change that of Assam. But, what is further alarming is that Nagaland which has no direct border with Bangladesh is also facing the brunt of illegal Bangladeshi migration. Nagaland as per 2001 census figures recorded a 64.41 per cent growth in population between 1991and 2001, much above the national average of 21.34 per cent[3], up from 56.08 per cent of the last decade, highest in the country for the last two decades. Nagaland Chief Minister S C Jamir during a meeting of the Chief Ministers of the North-East held in Shillong in January, 2000 told the Prime Minister, "Unless steps are taken to prevent the entry of people of dubious nationality into our state, Nagaland may face the same problem as that of Assam". The issue of migration and citizenship has become central in Assam and led to growth of Assamese subnationalism and to armed insurgency by the tribals of Tripura. The issue of foreigners evokes similar response in other North-Eastern states.

East Pakistan and later Bangladesh have been accused of engineering or at least supporting migration in Assam. Pakistani Premier Zulfikar Ali Bhutto in his Book, Myth of Independence, said that Pakistan was keen on including Assam in East Pakistan; he wrote: "It would be wrong to think that Kashmir is the only dispute that divides India and Pakistan, though undoubtedly it was the most significant, one at least is nearly as important as the Kashmir dispute, that of Assam and some districts adjacent to East Pakistan. To these Pakistan has good claims"[4]. But it was Sheikh Mujibur Rehman, who outlined the main cause of Bangaladeshi migration; he said "Because Eastern Pakistan must have sufficient land for its expansion and because Assam has abundant forests, mineral resources, coal, petroleum etc.. Eastern Pakistan must include Assam to be financially and economically strong"[5]. The Bangladeshi migrants have turned Assam from land of abundant tracts to land scarce areas. The conflict is over natural resources, employment and social and cultural submergence. From the security point of view the threat of demographic invasion coupled with Islamic fundamentalism can no longer be ignored.

The demographic year book published by the Registrar General recorded in its report in 1981 that as many as four million residents in India had reported their birth place as Bangladesh. The figures do not include Assam as no census was held in 1981 because of anti-foreigners agitation. Recently, dissatisfied with the functioning of the IMDT tribunals and progress on implementation of the Assam Accord, ASSU succeeded in persuading the Govt. to come up with a definition of 'indigenous people of Assam'. An agreement was reached between MHA and ASSU, 'Indigenous people', were defined as those whose names figure in 1951 National Register of Citizens (NRC) and their descendents. For seven districts where NRC is not available, the electoral rolls of 1952 were to be taken as the basic documents, thereby people who had their names in the 1952 voters lists and their descendents will be treated as indigenous Assamese. This started another controversy, United Minorities Front (UMF), All Bodo Students Union (ABSU), Autonomous State Demand Committee (ASDC) and Lok Sabha MP, S K Bwiswmuthiary representing Kokrajhar argued that the AASU is not the sole representative of people of Assam. AASU wanted 100 per cent reservation in the state legislature and states seats in Lok Sabha for the indigenous Assamese. This was based on fear of foreigners overwhelming the indigenous people and had found mention in the clause IV of the Assam Accord, which states: "Constitutional, Legislative and Administrative Safeguards, as may be appropriate, shall be provided to protect, preserve and promote the cultural, social and linguistic identity and heritage of Assamese people[6]. This is an attempt at redefinition. People opposed to it feel it will virtually push back the cut off date by 20 years from the date agreed in Assam Accord of 25 March 1971.

The minorities feel that it will be against the interest of post-partition migrants and riot affected migrants who had fled to East Pakistan but later returned. Their number is estimated to be 3,00,000 (Muslims) and they returned in different batches following the Nehru – Liyaqat Pact 1950 till about 1952, by that time the NRC 1951 and voter list 1952 had already been prepared. Similarly, Bengalee Hindu refugees from East Pakistan, whose influx began in 1950 but continued may also find their names missing in both the documents. Similar reservations were aired by Bodo and Karbi leaders U. G. Brahma and Holiram Terang[7]. The AASU and Central Govt. may find the proposal (Indigenous Assamese) handy but the legality of NRC under the Indian Evidence Act is disputed. This has further added to political turmoil in the state.

Bangladesh officially does not acknowledge the presence of any migrants from their country in the North-Eastern states but a number of their former officials and chairman of the Grameen Bank Mohammed Yunus frequently talk of a regional forum of visaless travel, borderless trade and other liberal policies which would lift restrictions on the movement of population across international borders. Similarly, since recently, Bangladeshi Track II intellectuals, who have influence and work in concert with their Govt. favour documents like work permits and propagate that migration is a natural phenomenon and cannot be stopped, the real need is to legalise and rationalise it.

Continuing trans-border migration from Bangladesh is threatening to alter the demographic profile of the North-East, particularly in Assam and Tripura. The point that Bangladesh immigrants are a source of communal and ethnic tension was well proved by the Assam agitation. There are estimated 15 to 18 million illegal Bangladeshi immigrants in India. A fair proportion of these, estimated to be 3 to 5 million, have spread to other eastern states of Bihar and West Bengal and in the North to Delhi and beyond. A bulk of them are in Assam and other North Eastern states. It has altered domestic politics and created economic crises particularly in the agricultural and labour field, the question of land alienation and unemployment is central to the crises. We need to evolve an immigration policy and establish a set up similar to the Immigration and Naturalisation Service as in the USA. In the long term a common development strategy for countries of the region and NE can only resolve the problem and prevent further conflicts.

Ethnic Dimensions and Question of Identity

Ethno-centric and religious dimensions of the conflicts are the outcome of ignoring the historic experience of the affected communities in the diverse economic, ethnic, religious, cultural and linguistic fields resulting in a sense of deprivation. It is the exploitation of the ethnic sensitivities of the communities at the time of stress that gives conflicts various shades of ethnic-activism. We have a long history of people of diverse ethnic origins coming to India throughout the ages, who were assimilated into the Indian mainsrteam by a continuous process of reconciliation. The peculiarity of this overall process of assimilation has been that immigrant groups have retained their identities. The British period is of special significance for nurturing ethnic and religious identities. To establish their authority over India, British thought it wise to encourage ethnic and religious identities, so that they could not unite against them. The idea of ethnic provinces also arose under the Council Act of 1861, 1892 and 1909. The partition of Bengal in 1905 and its reunification in 1912 let loose the forces of linguistic solidarity, resulting in the separation of Bihar and Orissa as provinces. The Indian National Congress passed a resolution in 1920 for linguistic states and reorganisation of states on linguistic basis, which after independence has heightened ethnic sensitivities. If the partition of India in 1947, had legalised the two nation theory based on religion for Pakistan, within India reorganisation of states on linguistic basis and acceding to demands of ethnic groups in the North-East to meet the ends of political expediency further sharpened ethnic feelings and parochialism. Both in itself are manageable but its exploitation has a divisive effect.

The ethnic factor is central and omnipresent in all facets of life in the North-East, particularly in hill areas inhabited by the tribals. In the very close nature of the tribal societies an outsider, even a neighbour, is a suspect. To win them, trust and credibility are essential. In the case of the plains it is a reaction to tribal ethnic assertion into their areas and threat posed by large scale immigrants. It influences politics, generates or acts as a catalyst for conflicts, is central to security, economic development and the crucial and central issues of territory and land. It is a stabilising factor at the individual, village and community level due to the social structure of the society but causes instability within the states and at the regional level. Its dynamics are based on in-built distinctions between ethnic groups since the British period, which differentiated between hills and plains and followed different approaches to politics, administration and economic development for different areas. The situation is extentuated by fractured political borders with no relationship to ethnic boundaries. In recent years political elite in conjunction with insurgent groups have exploited ethnic sensitivities in pursuance of power and for increasing areas of influence and even control of the drug trade. Ethnic politics with such dubious and distorted goals are adverse to unity and invites conflict.

A key element of the problem of growth of ethnic consciousness in the North-East is the perceived boundaries of the tribal communities. The Nagas case is a prime example. Naga tribes maintained their identities, confined themselves to their traditional areas and the present districts in Nagaland, Manipur, Assam and Tirap in Arunanchal were organised on this basis. Each tribe has its own distinct culture and tradition and institutional structure, with no common language. Nagamese commonly spoken is based on Assamese and it came up by usage primarily between Assamese of the plains and tribals in the bordering areas. Even the Naga insurgent groups drew their strength from different tribes and factional fights amongst them is aimed to dominate more tribes and areas. The slogan of Greater Nagaland does not find uniform response from Naga tribes in Nagaland and Manipur. It is really exploiting the sentiment of Naga identity by insurgents against Kukis. It has both a political and insurgent agenda of NSCN (I). The real aim is to grab territory, increase areas of influence and control drug trade. It is the main cause of Naga–Kuku conflict and Kukis arming themselves, thus adding to the ethnic conflict. The recent Meitei antagonism against extension of the cease fire is reaction to perceived Naga expansionism.

The problem of ethnicity in a developing society like ours, is essentially of deprivation and governance. Most people agree that factors of isolation, modernisation, ethno-nationalism and cultural insecurity discussed above have the cumulative and precipitating effect of deprivation. The sense of deprivation manifests in different ways.

The questions of ethnic sensitivity and identity are interlinked and not being a social scientist by training I look at their dimensions in more practical terms and to me cause and effect are more meaningful. My conclusions are based on a wide interaction with the individuals and communities of the region including radical and liberal intellectuals. I do not agree with Rangan Dutta, a former IAS officer's suggestion that a common North-East identity will help in resolving the ills of the region[8]. As a North-East identity has neither evolved nor is likely to evolve in the near future. Similarly, in this context, propagating a North-East geopolitical identity because of it being primarily Mangoloid and separated from the rest of the country by the narrow siliguri corridor is fallacious and such simplistic formulations are not accepted by the people of the North-East nor are these realistic. Intellectuals primarily administrators are the creators of this identity as a typical bureaucratic structure and over a period of time started believing in it. What started off as a regional territorial arrangement for administrative convenience in the shape of North-East Council for economic assistance and security management cannot be converted into an identity and enforced on the people with diverse historical and cultural backgrounds. This orientation has also led to failure of our developmental process in the region as both identification of people's needs and implementation were Delhi based with little participation by the people. Political expediency and clout dictated dispensation.

Both ethnicity and identity relate to people, their shared history, culture and traditions; therefore people's perceptions and feelings are important. Here my interaction with the people with North-East and outside has brought out two interesting facets of diversity and unity. Within the North-East one is a Naga, Meitei, Kuki, Assamese, Bodos, Arunachali (within Arunachal Noetes, Wanchos, Tangsas, Singhphos or Sonwal Kachari), Khasis, Garos, Reang, Jamatia or a Bangalee in Tripura and Assam. Outside of the North-East, young people of the North-East unless you ask them specifically as to which part of the North-East. On close examination one finds that in the unknown environment people from the North-East tend to stick together and help each other forgetting their differences. Their response to the outsider is both out of convenience and a feeling of uncertainty as very few outsiders know the North-East and its constituent parts. But this does not make for a common identity. In spite of this there is a regional consciousness in the making with some positive signs amongst the scholars, administrators, industrialists and economists belonging to the region. This is also evident amongst NGOs and professionals in the field of environment, bio-diversity, tourism and drug abuse. At the same time this regional consciousness is articulated in negative terms by the feeling of being left out, of being discriminated by the mainstream. Unless mindsets and politics in the states of the North-East change and a cooperative awareness comes about, whereby they work together, they will not be able to take advantage of new opportunities in the globalised liberal atmosphere. The strength of India will be tested as much by the development in the North-East as by those in Kashmir.

Within the North-East as mentioned earlier ethnic consciousness and identity crisis is fomented by fear of cultural submergence and economic and social insecurity. The main reason for this is electoral politics and the dubious role that the elite in the community have played in creating a fear psychosis to create exclusive constituencies where they can dominate land, commerce, employment and community social and economic life for their own selfish ends. Their articulation is based on hate and denial to other communities. These modern elite as well as insurgent groups have dismembered community institutions and divided homogeneous communities who have lived together for centuries sharing land and its resources for centuries (Nagas and Kukis, Meiteis's and Nagas and different communities in Meghalaya, Assam and Arunachal Pradesh). Likewise insurgent group's demands whether for extension of cease-fire or of historical claims is linked to land and territory and not to community's wellbeing. In this dirty game fear of identity and ethnic sensitivity will continue to be exploited for mobilisation for electoral politics. It is an essential fall out of modernisation and modern political system. The answer lies in incorporating traditional community institutions in the governing apparatus and bring about a concept of traditional shared home land and cooperative sharing amongst the communities. Ethnicity poses a lesser threat than communalism in the region due to our capacity to accommodate and thus blunt its divisive effect. But tension due to ethnic politics and exploitation of ethnic communities by their leaders both over and underground will continue.

State of the Economy

As argued in the earlier chapters, there can be no common identity of the North-East due to its diversity and heterogeneity. Similarly, the economies of the states of the North-East are as diverse, the level of development in the plains and hills is different, the only commonality lies in the fact that these are all underdeveloped agrarian and unbalanced economies. Much of this is due to faulty planning both at the centre and in the states, the policy has been guided by political motivations and politico-social pressures. The net result has been that economy and development has become totally dependent on central planning and financing, resulting into a bureaucratic stranglehold. In spite of vast sums being pumped into the area, there is no perceptible development and economic improvement. Political, rather than economic considerations have guided central Govt's. dispensation of finance and resources, which has resulted in patronage and not as a catalyst or promoter of economic growth and development. Declaration of the North-Eastern states as special category states has resulted in the lack of initiatives and entrepreneurship, patronage and corruption. The announcement of the last four Prime Ministers of special dispensation for the North-East over the last two decades is a testimony to it.

The North-Eastern states are deficient in food and import food items worth Rs. 2000 to Rs. 2500 crores annually[9]. The industrial sector has remained confined to tea, oil, timber and saw mills and plywood factories, which are now stagnating. The infrastructure for economic development is weak and human development inspite of high literacy is primarily service oriented. There are hardly any new industries. It is widely believed and is true that lack of transport and infrastructure has perpetuated isolation from rest of the country and within the region and contributed to agitational approach and insurgency. This coupled with the ban on acquisition of land and property and inner line restrictions in some of the hill states have resulted in denial of entrepreneurship and finance to the region. While the concept of Autonomous Hill Council under the sixth schedule to protect the tribals is good in its essence but Hill and Tribal Development Schemes have only added further fat in the shape of parochial tribal bureauracy but no real development due to lack of entrepreneurship and corruption. While protecting customary rights over land and its resources, the tribal societies have become slaves to the dogma rather than develop its natural resources to their advantage and as per their genius and requirements. The principles enunciated by Pt. Nehru for development of tribal areas in 1959 need to be reassessed for their relevance in the changing economic environment and based on past experience[10]. In spite of these drawbacks the poverty as seen in other parts of the country is non-existent due to their egalitarian social structure. One of their main constraint has been that while seeking political autonomy, tribal societies are reluctant to accept the new economic realities.

The core of most of the ills or negative manifestations in the North-East lies in the creation of the states itself as these did not have the minimum economic viability to support their administrative and non-development expenditure. Not much thought and planning had gone into developing its basic strength in the agriculture, horticulture and hydel power with the result dependence on central grants grew and any change in this was agitated against as anti-North-East. The local political leaders were the main beneficiaries and thus have a vested interest in resisting a change, a total disincentive for raising local revenue and internal resources. In addition this resulted in a narrow mindset, where interaction within the North-Eastern states and with rest of India got constrained thus stalling economic activity and development. The centre is guilty of accepting utilisation of funds allotted by it in a very routine fashion without enforcing accountability. Ever increasing non-plan revenue expenditure is a clear indication of it.

During the last decade (1990-91 to 98-99), Assam received Rs. 25000 crores from the centre, Arunachal Pradesh and Manipur received Rs. 5500 crores each, Maghalaya Rs. 5000 crores, Tripura Rs. 7200 crores, Nagaland Rs. 6600 crores and Mizoram Rs. 4800 crores, a total of Rs. 60000 crores[11]. Except in the case of Assam there is no appreciable difference between gross and net transfers from the centre. Even after deducting loans and interest payments, net devolution to the North-East is Rs. 51000 crores, whereas Orissa with the same population and economically more backward got only Rs. 25000 crores. Similarly, per capita central assistance during the 8th plan was well above national average of Rs. 1080, Rs. 36000 to Arunachal Pradesh the highest in the North-East, Rs. 32567, to Mizoram and Rs. 23177 to Nagaland. It was much more than to other special category states – Himachal Pradesh Rs. 5921, Jammu and Kashmir Rs. 9754 and Assam received on Rs. 3161. Per capita assistance to the poorest state Bihar was only Rs. 876[12]. Therefore the complaint of the North-Eastern states of neglect is totally unfounded. Moreover this does not include ten per cent earmarked by all central ministries for the North-East. In addition central Public Sector Enterprises worth Rs. 13318 crores are in the region, mostly in Assam, which is a fair 5 per cent of National Public Sector and more than 5 per cent of its employment in India.

The total debt liability of the North Eastern states was Rs. 13000 crores in 1999 with the largest share of more than 50 per cent of loans being from the centre. Assam's liability is naturally the biggest at Rs. 7000 crores. The states continue to depend on the centre to meet their non plan expenditure, rather than develop their own resources. The main sources of tax revenue are professional tax, land revenue, sales tax, taxes on property and capital transactions, taxes on vehicles and stamp and registration fees. There is very little tax on goods, passengers or entertainment. The only agricultural income in Assam is on tea. State lotteries make contribution in states like Manipur. Power and forestry contribute as does petroleum in Assam while industry contributes very little. There is no income tax for the Tribals. The Tax net work is limited and actual collections have been much less than planned and budgeted.

The ratio of tax revenue to revenue expenditure is very low from 1.4 per cent in Arunachal Pradesh to 4 to 6 per cent in Manipur, Nagaland and Tripura and in Assam and Meghalaya it is 21 and 11 per cent respectively for decade 1985-95 compared to 43 per cent of national average[13]. Prohibition policies have made a further dent into excise in Manipur and Mizoram. The potential for expanding the revenue resources lies in sales tax and exploring the possibility of taxes in the services sector. However, until administrative expenditure is cut down drastically, both capital assets and manpower from previous plan project are re-deployed and unproductive assets are diminished the situation is unlikely to improve. There is also duplication and in some instances multiplication of functions between the state and district administration and tribal institution under the sixth schedule. There is need to examine the whole administrative machinery. Gulshan Sachdeva has nicely summed up the finances of the States of the North-East. First, an overwhelming portions of receipts come from center; second, states tax revenues are low and lastly the non-plan revenue is high and unchecked.

The Potential of the North-East

In the 1980s the economic growth in the North-East except for Assam and Manipur was quite comparable to the national level. The economic reforms of 1991 slowed down the economies in the region. Agriculture, the main sphere of economic activity is seriously constrained by cultivable land, which varies from 5 per cent in Arunachal Pradesh to maximum of 50 per cent in Assam, Meghalaya and Nagaland against the national average of 64 per cent. Of this only a small portion is irrigated. However, the situation is largely made up by the high rainfall ranging from 3000 mm to 12000 mm. The other constraint is the practice of Jhum cultivation in the hilly areas. As discussed earlier except for Arunachal Pradesh all other states are food deficient in spite of the fact that more than 70 per cent of the available land is utilised for food production. Consumption of electricity and fertilisers is low. Rice is the main crop. Apart from Assam, there is Tea cultivation in Tripura and to some extent in Manipur and Mizoram. Climatic conditions are suitable for horticulture and spices, fruits, vegetables, spices and medicinal herbs are grown in most of the states. Main fruits are oranges, pineapple, coconut, jack-fruit and banana. Mizoram, Meghalaya and Arunachal produce almost half the ginger produced in the country. Some rubber plantations have come up in Tripura, Meghalaya has the potential but yet to be fully developed. The region produces two lakh tons of fish and only 20 per cent of its meat and poultry requirement. Most worrisome area for agriculture is Assam.

More than 70 per cent of the 166 large and medium industries are located in Assam and there is virtually no medium or large industry outside Assam. Industry in Assam is concentrated in Kamrup, Tinsukia and Diburgarh Districts. There are 40000 small scale units, most of them are sick as is the case with the large and medium scale. There is over-employment in industry and most of the industrial units are in food, wood and wood products, non metallic mineral products, rubber, petroleum and paper. Total manufacturing sector is 1 per cent of the national. Brahmaputra Valley with its most moderate infrastructure qualifies as the best potential area for industrial growth.

The region has 6 per cent of national roads, 13 per cent of national highways and barring Assam there is no railways worth the name. Provision of safe drinking water is a major problem. Household electrification in Manipur, Mizoram and Nagaland is better than national level (42%) while others are below it. Health infrastructure and schools in term of numbers are adequate but the quality and functioning is poor. Banking and telecom services are adequate but there are large variations from state to state.

The region has a high literacy rate, with Mizoram 88.49 per cent just behind Kerala. Except for Arunachal Pradesh (54.74%) and Meghalaya (63.31%) all other states have a higher rate of literacy than the national average (65.38%), with Assam (64.28%) as the major state just near the national average. Average female literacy rate at 62 per cent is higher than the national level at 54.16 per cent. In spite of higher literacy rates the dropout rates are high varying from 29 per cent to 65 per cent in classes I-V, 48 to 70 per cent in classes I-VIII and 67 to 81 per cent in classes I-X overall. Sixty per cent of the students leave studies before class V. The number of educational institutions in the North-East at the school, College, professional college and university level is very adequate compared to all India both in terms of area and population. All states except Mizoram have own universities and Assam has six. The number of teachers compared to all India are more than adequate but both the quality of teachers and a large number of them being of temporary status has affected the quality of education. Out of a total of 2,66,057 teachers (1998), only 45 per cent are trained compared to 87 per cent at the national level and 36 per cent of the teachers are temporary compared to less than 20 per cent at national level. Nagaland and Assam are the worst in this respect. In spite of a good student: teacher ratio and adequate infrastructure, the quality of education is poor due to low quality of teachers and this has led to higher unemployment. The educational infrastructure is an area of strength which should be encashed by improving its quality and in-service training of teachers.

CONTEMPORARY ISSUES

Deteriorating Political Ethos and Corruption

Since the early eighties there has been entirely the politics of expediency and both political parties and individual loyalties have been frequently purchased, which has led to instability and bad governance. Govt. resources have been essentially used to gain, retain and consolidate power. Insurgent factions have been used in the power game by most leaders and parties, this has provided them unlimited opportunity to gain financial and other resources at the cost of the people. This has worked to the double advantage of the insurgents. One, their resources base has widened and secondly due to denial of economic benefits of development, people feel alienated and become vulnerable to insurgent's influence and propaganda.

No discussion of the current ethos will be complete without touching on electoral politics and blatant corruption. Political will and perceptions are only confined to winning elections and perpetuating power. It has lost its sanctity and meaning as the most sacred and fundamental democratic function. In a closed society divided into small ethnic groups, particularly in smaller states, electoral politics and corruption has effected each individual and spared no one. With a limited and undeveloped economic base, political leadership, administrative officers and insurgents are digging into the common limited kitty. Financial mismanagement is of the highest order, there is no ethos of systematic utilization of funds meant for specific purposes and there is no monitoring. Denial of opportunity to entrepreneurs in the hill states has resulted in benami contractors operating on behalf of local people (mostly people in power or their relatives), who pay large sums to a local front man and insurgent nominees out of the meager development funds. In a nutshell political permissiveness and corruption are eating into the society and feeding insurgency.

Institutional Degradation

The area has highly democratic and well established traditional social and cultural institutions, which regulated all activities at the village and community level. Their authority and effectiveness has been eroded under the pretext of modernization and the modern democratic set up. We have neither absorbed them into the system nor replaced them with new ones. The motive is clear, if these are strong and effective then they will question the politicians and the administration, who want a free hand in exercising power and utilisation of meagre resources. Without rejuvenation of the institutional structure at the grass root level, neither people's genuine participation in the democratic system or development process can be ensured nor alienation of the people removed. The enactment of the 73rd and 74th amendment to the Constitution on Panchayati Raj and Municipalities is a step in the right direction but it can only succeed, if there is mandatory or direct financial devolution and there is no overlap in the functions between these institutions and the State Govt. departments; this will also prevent political interference. It will also be relevant to consider if the traditional institutions of the Village Councils and Village Developmental Boards existing in the tribal areas could be absorbed as such in place of Panchayats as they are performing the same functions.

Student Power and Student Politics

Student power and student politics always had a role in these areas. These were broad based democratic and secular. The high point of student movement was the formation of the AGP in 1985 by the student leaders of Assam Movement. Since then the student movements in Assam and other states has fragmented on ethnic and communal lines. This has happened because of the failure of the democratic parties to comprehend the dynamics of these developments. This fragmentation and its aftermath has generated its own social tensions which is being exploited by the local politicians, particularly in the smaller hill states.

Having dealt with them both in Manipur and Nagaland and having resolved a long outstanding issue of foreigners in Manipur after fourteen years of political dilly dallying, I am convinced that if the student organisations are properly oriented, then they could provide the future enlightened leadership in the North-East. Both its fragmentation on ethnic lines and its exploitation has been one of the destabilising factors at the local level. This poses a challenge for political vision of the North-East and has tremendous potential if used positively as in the case of Assam agitation, at the same time its negative impact can be tremendous if used for parochial purposes.

Nationalism and Sub-Nationalism

Nationalism and sub-nationalism in its different connotations and varieties is the most strong and exploited sentiment, particularly in the small hill states of the North-East. Real nationalism is not detrimental to local interest and identity. There are a large number of political and community leaders, particularly in the younger generation, who have faith and are convinced that their future lies with the Indian nation. But power brokers have contrived to keep them away from position of prominence and power. A review of the elections in the states of the North-East since early eighties and instability are a testimony to it. The current deteriorating situation in the area is an outcome of it and is entirely related to parochial exploitation of the sentiment.

The sentiment has been hijacked to perpetuate power. The local political leaders pose as true nationalists while dealing with Delhi and profess that national interest will suffer without them. The very same people exploit varieties of local sentiment representative of sub-nationalism to gain local support. The same is done by the insurgents. The people's interest is held as hostage to this in the power game. The motive is entirely to perpetuate power and have a free hand to resources provided by the Central Govt. In recent years different Central Govts. have shown undue tolerance to these elements for short term political gains, which has contributed to the turmoil in the area and alienated the people further.

Our federal structure of the constitution and the very federal nature of the societies in the North-East lend to accommodation and involvement but centralization and governance through a distorted polity has led to negation of both nationalism and sub-nationalism except in its exploitation, with the result that unity in diversity and democracy has become a myth due to local over-lordism. Real nationalism is not exclusive of local identity. The very ethno-centric movements if examined in depth are for local autonomy and identity and economic sustenance through indigenous self-reliance. Political autonomy also has the same connotations.

The Nature and Dimensions of Conflicts[14]

Over the last almost fifty years, the insurgencies in the North-East have remained generally under control with frequent periods of escalation and abetment except for the Mizo insurgency none of the others are any way near resolution. These have been fomenting for decades and with the passage of time developed graver dimensions and complexity. The impression that these are being permitted to linger on for parochial political, ethnic and material gains is well founded and is essentially responsible for the negative responses in the local people. The situation post-Shillong Accord has developed new complexities due to the ethnic divide and conflicts and the well entrenched politician, bureaucrat and insurgent nexus, who exploit the ballot and bullet both for perpetrating power. The instability in the region has created a conducive environment for trans-border interference and influences giving the insurgency a new dimension.

The insurgencies in the North-East are a reflection of its social, cultural, ethnic and politico-economic milieu and changes in the environment of the areas. North-East is an extremely heterogeneous region with high level of ethnic, cultural, linguistic and religious diversity.

This is reflected in the pattern of conflicts, which are varied in their nature and causes and the stance of the insurgent groups, which remain divergent and ever changing. These range from secession to autonomy, movements against foreigners and immigrants, ethnic integration and looking back to their roots as a reaction to perceived imposition of Indianness ; the common factor is resorting to violence in articulation and mobilisation for the same. Similarly, political evolution in the North-East is influenced by its divergent historical experience, social and cultural diversity and distinctiveness leading to socio-political approach to problems and violence. Of these the recent phenomenon of ethnic mobilisation automatically poses a threat to adversaries resulting in conflict. Influx of immigrants poses economic, cultural and social threats and provides a cause for conflict and violence.

The insurgency which germinated in Nagaland, spread to Mizoram, Manipur, Tripura and Assam. In addition, there are simmerings in Arunachal Pradesh and Meghalaya. Similarly, our belief that conflicts run their natural course, therefore, confront insurgencies with armed might alone, and when militancy weakens, offer negotiations and constitutional concessions that result in accords, is ill founded. These, with the exception of Mizoram, have neither put an end to insurgencies nor improved the environment, Instead insurgencies in the North-East have thrived while retaining their low key posture. A peculiarity of the North-East. Retrogression of insurgency has not resulted in its resolution and consolidation of the situation. On the contrary the insurgent groups have responded to changing situations, internally in the socio-political environment, and externally in the geostrategic field, to their advantage.

In spite of our many failures of governance and in the economic developmental field, the myth of free sovereign tribal states has been demolished due to their political and economic non-viability and the noble and great cause of independence has become defunct. It has been replaced by new slogans of greater autonomy, anti-immigrant and foreigners, Pan-Mongoloid and various manifestations of different social justice causes and the old but effective one of ethnic integration (Greater Nagaland, Greater Mizoram, Kuki Land, Bodo Land). The foreigners issue is all pervasive as it raises the issue of identity, a fear commonly shared by most people in the North-East. The level of motivation of these may not be high but these are equally lethal.

The support base of the insurgents has shifted from the rural to the urban areas as this is where the material and financial resources lie– Government money being the main source. This has necessitated that their covert presence in population centres must not only be effective but sophisticated to tap diverse sources, both private and Government; contractors and Government department payments are the major targets. Insurgents have learnt by experience that the control of population and subversion accompanied by planned acts of violence and terrorism are rewarding, at minimum cost. The emphasis is on exploiting ethnic bonds to influence events in all fields–political, economic, social and cultural– in the area. Insurgent links and influence with the politicians, bureaucrats and elite in all fields are motivated by the same. Insurgency in the North-East will continue to thrive while retaining a low key posture, with limited periods of high intensity violence and remaining under control for prolonged periods. Increasing acts of terrorism and subversion and a greater degree of collusion amongst the insurgent groups will be the hallmark of insurgency in the North-East.

The core of insurgents will remain separatist and anti-establishment, and ethnic for support amongst the people. The politician-bureaucrat-elite-insurgent nexus in the North-East particularly in the Hill states, unless checked, will continue to provide support to insurgency to achieve their diverse aims and further intensify deprivation and alienation of the people.

Because of the presence of large immigrant Bangladeshi population over the entire North-East, a fertile ground for ISI's anti Indian designs with full connivance of Bangladesh DGFI exists. The ISI has established outposts in the border areas of Bangladesh and is spreading its tentacles in Assam and bordering areas of Manipur, Nagaland and Meghalaya. Mizoram, though relatively peaceful, has the Hmar and the Bru ethnic dissidence. Similarly, Tripura too has tribal insurgency. Both these states, due to their location and open borders with Myanmar and Bangladesh, are highly vulnerable to trans-border influences. The threat has acquired regional dimensions, which needs to be countered both at the strategic and tactical levels.

Extortion and misuse and diversion of resources meant for development are the two ugly fall outs of the Central Govt's policy of pumping more money when under pressure and to meet the requirements of political expediency. Political leaders and bureaucrats have used their offices to siphon off developmental funds at the cost of real development. Since 1981, more than Rs. 30,000 crores have been pumped into Nagaland, with nothing to show in terms of development for the people in agriculture, health, education and civic services. Modern buildings, some finished and others unfinished both Govt. and private (of the elite) are the sole testimony as this is where the contracts and opportunities for sponging are found.

In an all pervading atmosphere of corruption, money power and violence governed by narrow ethnic loyalties, most of the politicians and insurgents are found to be motivated and propelled by narrow parochial gains. Insurgency in the North-East has become an industry in which main motive is profit for the people in power both through the ballot and bullet. In this struggle the common people remain poor and the Security Forces are the "Fall Guys" for all the three—politicians, the insurgents and the people. In spite of all the noises against the Security Forces, all of them want the Security Forces to be present in order to survive against each other.

Most of the accords in the North-East except Mizoram Accord of 1986 have become milestones of discord as these were the outcome of political expediencies and not really intended for implementation. They all lacked credibility, sincerity and political will and machinery for implementation. Such political arrangements create disillusionment and provide issues for mobilization of ethnic groups by local politicians and insurgents.

Government's approach to conflicts has been primarily at the tactical level dealing with its law and order dimensions. Strategic issues of political-responses and conflict resolution measures in the social and economic fields are given a go by. This has resulted in conflicts re-escalating after periods of regression and not being resolved. It is equally true of ethno-centric conflicts, where communities are passing through a period of transition, which is painful and conflict prone. The conflicts are not just in terms of its visible violent manifestations, the more painful and deep are the inner turmoils. Violence is only an outcome of the internal conflicts and contradictions. Law and order is a problem but not the whole problem, there are social, economic and political issues which affect peoples lives and contribute to their feeling of deprivation. Attending to these can only resolve the problem in the long run. Low key insurgencies in the North-East are like slow poison on our sores which require prolonged treatment in holistic manner.

Conclusion

The major area of concern by and large for the entire North-East is the increasing alienation of the people of the region from the national mainstream. Primarily, it is due to our failure to recognize the peculiar historical, social and cultural factors of each area of the North-East with the common effect of isolation. The various facets of this isolation vary from area to area. Of this the factor of physical isolation impinges on the minds of the people the most. The road communication and railway network is totally inadequate. Movement into and within the region is restricted and puts people to economic and social harassment by the neighbouring states. The problem is further compounded by the flooding of Brahmaputra River as Assam is the heart of the North-East.

Alienation of land is one of the major causes of ferment in the North-East. Studies have revealed that in the plain area of the North-East particularly in Assam, alienation of land is primarily due to perpetuation of land based development process and unchecked immigration, particularly from Bangladesh, erstwhile East Pakistan. In the hills and the tribal areas (including plains), it is as a result of the perversion of the traditional jurisdiction of the community on land and land based resources due to greed and manipulation of the local political elite and political economy of the neighbouring countries. In this immigration of Bangladeshis has played a major role, particularly in Assam and Tripura.

REFERENCES

1. Elwin V., "A Philosophy of NEFA", 1959.
2. B.B. Kumar, *Tension and Conflict in North East India*, Cosmo Publications, 1995, New Delhi, p. 7.
3. *Times of India*, 15 August, 2001.
4. Report on Illegal Migration into Assam to the President of India by Lt. Gen. (Retd.) S. K. Sinha, Governor of Assam, 1998, p. 6.
5. Sheikh Mujibur Rehman, Eastern Pakistan: Its Population and Economics– Report on illegal migration into Assam as sited in Sanjib Baruah, *India Against itself, Assam and Politics of Nationality*, Oxford University Press, New Delhi, 1999, p. 44.
6. Assam Accord 1985.
7. UMF leader Hafiz Rashidh Choudhry in *North East Daily*, 17 April 2000.
8. *The Statesman*, 11 October 2003, North East Page.
9. Report of the committee for educated unemployed in the NE Region 1997, p. 11.
10. Foreword to second edition, *A Philosophy for NEFA*, by Elwin V, 1959.
11. Gulshan Sachdeva, *Economy of the North East*, Konark Publications Pvt. Ltd., New Delhi, 2000, pp. 69-78.
12. *Ibid*.
13. *Ibid*, p. 84-90.
14. These observations and conclusions are based on author's recent study of Low Intensity Conflicts and extracted from his book, "Low Intensity Conflicts in India", published by the United Services Institution of India, New Delhi, 2000.

4

The Way Forward

A trilogy of obstacles has sealed off the North-East from rest of the country. The most formidable of these has been our ignorance and lack of knowledge. The ignorance has led to distrust, ill will and hostility. We need to break this with knowledge, which will lead to understanding, good will and trust. Ignorance has been responsible for mis-judgement and wrong decisions on the part of Delhi and its executors on the ground. The handling of the extension of cease-fire with NSCN (I) to areas of Manipur, Arunachal Pradesh and Assam which led to bloodshed in Manipur and resentment in other states is the most recent example of our ignorance of the ground realities and sensitivities of the people. The other barrier is of isolation, which extends beyond physical to the cultural, social and economic field, the dimensions of this isolation vary from area to area. Lastly, the physical barriers due to inaccessible terrain and lack of communications cannot be wished away, its physical, economic, social and psychological effect on the minds of the people is to be experienced to be believed. The cumulative effect of these over the last fifty years has resulted in a deeply negative mindset amongst the people of the North-East, which is the main cause of alienation.

The negative mindset has its foundations in the contemporary experience of the people of the North-East and extends in all fields of life. It extends from the treatment meted out to Chief Ministers of the North Eastern States by the central ministers to lowly bureaucrats in various ministries. The Chief Ministers seldom get an appointment to meet the Prime Minister, the planning commission dismisses them in a few minutes during plan discussions by telling them what will be their allocation, they are hardly asked about their requirements and problems, neither they are taken to task for mismanagement, both administrative and financial. Both corruption and political manipulation are arts which the North-Eastern politicians learnt from their elders at the centre and now they are blamed for being better in these fields. This has had an adverse effect on the minds of the people and they have developed a feeling of hopelessness so that nothing can be done to improve things. It was the single most formidable obstacle I met in Manipur, when I went back after ten years in 1993. My response was, not to talk but do things and with their participation. It generated responses beyond expectations. The narration of this negative mindset will be incomplete without mentioning the impact it has had on the younger generation. Students from the North-East are looked upon as foreigners in their own country and they tend to stick together. Most Indians need to realise that apart from Aryans and Dravidians the Mongoloid races inhabiting most of our North-East are as much Indian and unless this realisation spreads, do not blame the North-East for calling you outsiders in their area. The mainstream (reluctantly for want of a better word) India is to be blamed for it. Also to be blamed is the leadership in the North-East, which has a stake in perpetuating this negative feeling to pass on the blame to Delhi for all their failures and inaction. The key to breaking this negative mindset is trust and participation. Centre should stop dictating to the North-Eastern states what is good for them; instead, should help and participate to identify it. Alongwith it should go the accountability and the capacity to tell them it is your problem you resolve it. Make the North-East self sustaining and not dependent. The essence is very aptly put in the Shukla Committee report of 1997; it observed that there was a "two way deficit of understanding with the rest of the country" and that "the development of tranquility is also a national security interest and can offer regional solutions to national problems". It then recommended that "the country must assist the North-East to realise its full potential and avail of opportunities within and around it". The commission felt that "the people of the North-East cannot remain cocooned and wish to take their place as full and equal partners, contributing to the great enterprise that is Project India. It is right not to want to be swamped by Indians from outside the region, even less by an influx of foreigners. But the region does not need to fear 'outsiders' and lapse into 'localism'. Violence, insurgency and easy money are no solution to the problem, real or imagined. These eruptions and bands, extortion, kidnappings, leakage, and the sulking and cynical indifference they have engendered in section of the populace, can only delay and could even deny peace, progress and prosperity that every one seeks". Keep electoral politics like the recent ones in Arunachal Pradesh and Nagaland out, if you want the North-East to respond positively. With such a mindset and orientation we should address the problems facing the North-East; we should learn from history and not repeat it.

The most damaging of the contemporary manifestation of the turmoil has been the ethnic and religious divide in the North-East particularly in Assam. It has led to a deepening sense of alienation and deprivation amongst the communities of the North-East. The Assam agitation and prolonged struggle by the Assamese against their neglect and demographic invasion in the early eighties and non-implementation of the Assam Acord 1985 have left the communities divided and society fragmented Foreigners, bulk of whom were Muslims from Bangladesh, initially got identified with Bengalis, within these two major ethnic groups religion further narrowed their political and social stances. In the aftermath of this turmoil, tribals both in upper and lower Assam were compelled to seek their own identities with greater vigour as historically and culturally they are different and any alignment with Assamese or with Bengali would submerge them. The language is another issue which crops up when tensions are high, in spite of the fact that a large number of migrants have opted for Assamese to shed the stigma of foreigners. Caste and religious agitations in the shape of Mandal/anti-mandal and Ram Janam Bhumi and Barbri Masjid confrontations have also left some impact. Similarly, fragmentation of student organisations along ethnic and communal lines has not only resulted in giving impetus to ethnic and religious divide but added to social tensions amongst the younger generation. This social alienation and tension in the North-East needs attention.

The abundant land in Assam attracted the immigrants, who have now made inroads in the hill states of Nagaland and Meghalaya as cheap labour. They have now even spread to metropolitan cities in the North, particularly Delhi. Alongwith them came the politics of religion, which in the absence of a realistic policy and action has resulted in socio-political tensions. The demand of Muslim leaders in Assam to shift their stance of identification of foreigners based on 1991 census from 1971 census and reaction of the ASSU and other ethnic organisations including the tribals against it will add to the tensions; and the issue of protection of indigenous communities has gained strength and legitimacy. The issue needs to be resolved as suggested in the portion dealing with immigrants.

The role of religion has become more pronounced in the North-East in the last two decades, with pronounced ethnic and political overtones. The Christian church played an important role in the social and educational fields in the hill states of Nagaland, Mizoram and Meghalaya played a vital role in bringing about negotiations between insurgents and the Government. But a section of it has also been have been found abetting insurgency and providing it support. Its role in the last decades has also come to light in the politico-ethnic resurgence in Tripura,

Manipur and Meghalaya; of these the Naga–Kuki clashes and support to the tribal insurgencies is of significance. The North-East and particularly Assam was free of Hindu-Muslim religious tensions except immediately after partition and language was the main contentious issue. Muslim migrants accepted Assamese as their language thus allaying Assamese fear. But the anti-foreigners agitation provided opportunity to the few Hindu fundamentalists to harp on the Muslim immigrants theme, amongst the Assamese and Bengali Hindus and the fact that no Hindu was considered a foreigner inspite of the fact that a large number of illegal immigrants from East Pakistan and Bangladesh are Hindus and their continued trickle added to the communal sensitiveness. In spite of vast majority being secular had resisted such efforts, there were clashes at Nelle, Chamaria and Gohpur in 1983. This coupled with changing stance of Muslim leaders in Assam on the issue of migrants, in the aftermath of the demolution of Barbri Masjid resulted in tensions and greater sensitivity of the Muslims in Assam and in the North-East. Use of religion to build political bases and to mobilise people on emotive religious plank is a recent phenomenon in Assam and the North-East. The indulgence shown to Hinduvta by some political parties and religious discrimination against Christianity and Islam have eroded secular ethos and values.

Most of the social and ethnic tensions in the North-East are generated by the clash of interest of the new elites that are emerging in the middle classes of the communities. Earlier it was confined to the clash of interest between the middle classes of Assamese and Bengalis to gain political power, for economic gains and employment and language was the most potent weapon. But with the emergence of new generation of educated from tribal, backward societies and from the immigrants, the tussle for power, jobs and economic opportunities increased. Due to lack of a large and growing economic base, the entire struggle got oriented to state sector, hence demands for reservation in education and employment. With the passage of time economic demands became political and the new elite started to exploit ethnic and religions identities for mobilising communities. This also resulted in the elite of the societies becoming corrupt and siphoning of resources from public funds for their own self-interest in power perpetuation. Land alienation and disruption of its relationship with the community are two of the major causes of alienation of the North-East. The discovery of tea changed every thing and it was the beginning of the end. All good high lands were acquired and given to the planters. Grant of huge tracts of land for refugee and immigrant resettlement would not have been possible if the traditional community custodial right over land had been preserved. Most of the current demand for autonomy are related to control over the land and its resources.

Dilution of traditional custodial rights has also resulted in exploitation of forests by the politician, bureaucrat and contractor nexus. It would have also prevented tribal areas being submerged by immigrants. Conflicting with it is the requirement of land for development purposes but if the authority is with the community then it will be possible to maintain a balance. We need to revise our laws in keeping with these divergent requirements.

The North-East is infested with wide-spread insurgencies and ethnic conflicts. The socio-political, economic and ethnic dimensions leading to these conflicts have been discussed in the earlier chapter. But understanding the dynamics of conflict is essential as conflicts are part of the North-East environment. While writing on "Low Intensity Conflicts", I had good opportunity to interact with social and behavioural scientists, intellectuals, state officials and the people affected by the conflicts in the North-East. They all agreed that agitations and conflicts are essentially due to a deep sense of perceived denial of what is their just due. This sense of denial generates insecurity and has the effect of deprivation. The various dimensions of it are reflected in the shape and nature of insurgencies and ethnic conflicts. These vary from political in the shape of independence and autonomy, to land alienation and lack of development in the economic field, lack of employment and land alienation due to migration and influx of outsiders which leads to both economic and social insecurity and ethnic integration which poses a threat to other communities. Land appears to be central to all these insecurities and sense of deprivation. Similarly, differential treatment in the shape of reservations and scheduling tends to sharpen ethnic sensitivities due to a sense of comparative deprivation and add to inter community hostilities and conflicts.

Conflicts and the perceived sense of denial or deprivation have a mutually sustaining relationship as conflicts add to deprivation, which in turn fuels conflict. Effect of both constrains economic development and wellbeing of the people and becomes a permanent sources of alienation and deprivation of the common man. This is exploited both by the insurgents and the politicians and they develop a stake in conflicts. The real aim of resolving conflicts is to remove the deprivation of the people. Conflicts deny access to each other's markets and resources and breaks inter-dependability. It diverts resources to unproductive interest groups, which is abundantly visible in the North-East. Conflicts also give undue prominence to security and raises the bogey of security and diverts attention from the main aim of addressing deprivation. In a conflict environment civil society, which should be part of the democratic and development process and its main beneficiary, gets side-lined. In the developmental field, conflicts distort both requirements and priorities and lead to corruption, thus adding to the sense of deprivation. The key to resolving conflicts is to mitigate the sense of deprivation of the people, and since it relates to people therefore it should be our focus in finding a solution.

The first step in this direction has to be in trying to understand the North-East. Luckily there is greater awareness but this awareness is essentially based on the perspectives developed by main stream academicians, policy makers and economists. The first issue which needs to be dispelled is the issue of a North-East identity or of a North-East personality. North-East is a melting pot of two great civilisations and cultures, while the Indo-Gangetic civilisation was introduced through the river valleys, the South-East Asian culture entered through the Hills. Inspite of intermingling, these two broad parts are distinct and different, with large variations in each part of the region. The only commonality of approach lies into the security field due to the large 2500 km. international border and economic planning for infrastructure for the entire geographical region but micro level planning has to be related to each constituent unit.

Dealing with Migration

We need to recognize the geographical configuration and historical links within South Asia. India having common land and maritime borders with the neighbouring countries encourages migration into India from all directions. The partition of India in 1947, resulted in shifting of an estimated 14 million people. Over 10 million people fled to India during the military crackdown in East Pakistan in 1971, most of whom were repatriated back on the birth of Bangladesh in December, 1971. Such forced migration has occurred the world over due to national crisis in the post-cold-war era. Other major migrations include 10,00,000 Burmese Indians during the period 1948-65, 10,00,000 Srilankan Indians and Tamils since 1954, flight of 10,000 Chakmas in 1981, approximately 1,00,000 Tibetans to India from 1958 to 1963 and continuous flow from and to between India and Nepal. Over-riding all this is 1,50,00,000 Bangladeshis to India. To complete the picture of South Asia migration, it will be worth while to record that there are 3,00,000 stranded Pakistanis (of Bihari origin) in Bangladesh; 2,00,000 Burmese Muslims flew to Bangladesh in 1978, nearly 30,00,000 fled from Afghanistan to Pakistan during 1978-93 of whom approximately 20,00,000 have returned and nearly 60,000 Bhutanese of Nepali origin to Nepal during 1990-91. There are different reasons for these migrations within South Asia, varying from state failure (Afghanistan), internal conflicts due to ethnic, communal and sectarian violence (Sri Lanka), and coercive state authority (Bhutan's Nepalese population) but underlying all these is the crisis in nation building and governance, which include economic deprivation and compulsions[1]. The above underlines the fact that migrations are a fact of life irrespective of its reasons and rhetoric's and political mudslinging cannot resolve the issue, if any it can make situations worse. The problem needs a rational approach to control and manage it.

Confining to the North-East, the history and dimensions of migration has been broadly discussed in chapters 1 and 3 but it will be relevant to restate both the nature and dimensions of migration in the region. The report of group of ministers on National Security notes : "Today, we have about 15 million Bangladeshis, 2.2 million Nepalese, 70,000 Sri Lankan Tamils and about one lakh Tibetan migrants living in India". Demographic changes have been brought about in the border belts. As per the latest Intelligence Bureau (IB) reports, of the 15 million Bangladesh immigrants in India 80 lakhs (8 million) are in West Bengal, 50 lakhs (5 million) in Assam, 3.75 lakhs in Tripura, 4 lakhs in Delhi and 4.75 in Bihar[2].

There are all the indications that in the coming decades, Bangladesh will face a serious crisis of lebensraum and a natural overflow of population pressure is very much on the cards and will not be restrainable by physical means of barbed wire fence and border patrols. The natural trend of population overflow from Bangladesh is towards the sparsely populated lands in South East in the Arakans and to the North-East India. Such a demographic pressure will not be sustainable within Bangladesh. This combined with the poor or at best the indifferent state of its economy, Bangladeshis will continue the process of migration to neighbouring areas particularly to the North-East due to its ethnic and traditional affinity. The intellectual elite, economists, former diplomats and leading think tanks have been advocating free movement of people as their interest is better served by border-less competitive trade of labour and they argue as to why regional cooperations cannot be worked out to plan and execute population movements and settlements. The idea of sub-regional cooperation between Eastern India, Bangladesh, Bhutan and Nepal under the SAARC but distinct from it is strongly articulated. These include Farook Sobhan, former Foreign Secretary and High Commissioner to India, Chairman of the Grameen Bank, Mohammed Yunus and S A Malik, Political Advisor to former Bangladesh Prime Minister Sheikh Hasina[3]. The above is complimented by the Indian Chamber of Commerce initiative of sub-regional cooperation called the Greater Ganga–Brahmaputra–Meghna Initiative (GGBMI) for Eastern South Asian Sub Regional Economic Cooperation, with the help of leaders in Industry, foreign policy, and bankers of East India, Bangladesh, Nepal and Bhutan. It has the support of the Manila based Asian Development Bank (ADB). The GGBMI meeting in New Delhi in 2000 to give shape to the project are convinced that it will improve access to resources, improve linkeages, reduce non tariff barriers and bigger markets and scale of economies will benefit all. With the likelihood of SAFTA coming into place soon, its chances are bright. Bangladesh as per the statement of its commerce Minister Amir Khasru Mahmud Chowdhry in December 2001 was keen to open a corridor between Bangladesh and India for trade, thus enabling Indian manufacturers to sell their products in East India using Bangladesh territory as it will also help to introduce its products to Eastern India.

The feeling that South Asia has to come together was amply highlighted by the erstwhile Prime Minister Atal Bihari Vajpayee during his address to the Hindustan Times Leadership Initiative Peace Dividend on December 12, 2003. The theme of his speech was "Enlightened self-interest demands an integrated South Asia". The main thrust was economic benefits of such a move— he outlined seven key factors of rich and varied human resources, comparatively younger population, technological advances which have put us in the vanguard of today's knowledge, economy, the size of South Asia's combined purchasing power which will create economies of scales for cost effective production, efficient exploitation of our energies can enhance intra-regional trade, region's massive untapped hydro power and untapped hydrocarbons, the rich diversity of our bio-resources and finally the combined political weight and economic strength gives us considerable lever to pursue the objective of a cooperative multipolar world order. He emphasised that in today's context, collective regional interest is an expression of enlightened self-interest[4]. The above is a clear indication of the Indian ruling establishment's desire to resolve issues with the neighbours and Prime Minister's initiative and response to it by Pakistan and the thaw with Indo-Pak stand off on Kashmir are its manifestations. The issue of illegal migrants requires a similar approach.

From the above it should be amply clear that with globalisation and liberalisation of trade, commerce and economy, open borders with minimum impediments is the thing of the future. This will entail movement of labour and goods as such fences will be redundant and migration cannot be stopped by it. We need to think of more rational and effective means to control and manage migration across the borders.

We can resolve, control and manage the illegal Bangladeshi migrants provided we can enunciate a clear cut policy beyond political mud slinging and rhetoric's as these only raise passions and political pressures influence decisions. First of all there has to be a consensus of all the political parties and the North Eastern states on the issue of cut off date. This rationally speaking has to be 25 March 1971 as agreed in the Assam Accord of 1985, going back to 1951 as agreed between AASU and the MHA during the discussion on indigenous people of Assam in 2000 will only invite a political upheaval and denegrade the sanctity of Govt. of India's agreement. There is also a need in this regard to incorporate the closest date after 25 March, 1971 based on the NRC closest to it in the definition of indigenous people if such a definition is the common demand of all the North-Eastern states but I am not in favour of it as it will raise similar demands in other states. Recent resentment against Biharis during railway recruitment in Maharashtra is a case in issue. This all will ultimately make the recruitment and managing of central services and enterprises more difficult. This also raises the issue of updating and publication of NRC by the Registrar General of Census at regular frequencies.

The IMDT Act of 1983 has proved totally ineffective and should be scrapped and Foreigners Act of 1952 should be made applicable to Assam as well. Connected with it also a period of cooling off before a declared legal migrant has the opportunity to become a citizen of India, a fact which we must recognize in keeping with international norms. In this regard Articles 5, 6 and 7 of the Constitution and section 3, 4, 5 and 6 of the Citizenship Act need to be enforced.

Having recognized the fact that trade related issues and labour movement in the region will continue to be requirement in the liberalized economic environment, there is greater need to put in place a system of work permits. However, this can only work if a properly thought out Immigration and Naturalization Regime similar to the one in USA is put into place and such work permits are in accordance with it. The work permit system can only be made to function effectively if our own citizens have identity cards. I am fully in agreement with Sanjoy Hazarika who has done very detailed work on Bangladeshi immigrants on both sides of the border and holds that work permits and job cards are necessary to manage the problem[5]. This should preferably be done by groups and by authorities at the place of work or employment. The current system of issue of certificates by states other than the state of residence and employment has to be discontinued.

During the above discussion, there are clear indications that economic interdependence, free flow of trade and commerce and work force will be the hallmark of future regional cooperative ventures and there is no getting away from it. Therefore, growth and well being of Bangladesh along with the North-East is vital for stability of the region and thus strengthening of SAARC is vital, if problem of mutual concern has to be tackled, immigration is one such issue.

The discussion on the illegal immigrants from Bangladesh will be incomplete without an examination of its security dimensions. The North-Eastern states of Assam (262 km), Tripura (856 km), Meghalaya (443 km) and Mizoram (318 km) share a 1879 km long border with Bangladesh, which is fractured and riverine with habitations in close proximity and conducive to infiltration. The influx has led to disruption of internal polities, smuggling and other illegal activities and porous borders have resulted in insurgents seeking shelter in Bangladesh and populations migrating when their security is threatened. All these combined have posed threat to social, ethnic and religious harmony in the region. The security dimensions go beyond the normal trans-border movement and sanctuaries provided to the Indian insurgents, due to Pak intelligence agency ISI presence and connivance of Bangladesh. Field Intelligence and right wing Jammat and mushrooming of mosques and Madarsas along Indo-Bangladesh and Indo-Nepal borders. According to the latest IB reports Assam itself has 2002 madarsas. Misuse of madarsas by nationals of Pakistan, Bangladesh and Saudi Arabia[6] has come to notice.

The mushrooming of Muslim extremist organisations in Assam has already been discussed earlier in Chapter 1. These have serious internal security dimensions and the vast immigrant Bangladeshi population present in the region can be exploited for anti-India activities. Therefore, a tight border regime functioning under a unified system is essential. This will require proper managing of the border by the BSF, a well placed immigration regime and effective local administration, for in the ultimate analyses it is only the administration at the ground level which can determine who is an outsider. Fencing is only a physical barrier which can be easily overcome by determined people. It cannot be cost effective unless manned and patrolled effectively, is extremely high on maintenance and manpower with our vast borders in difficult terrain. We need to seriously reconsider our policy of fencing the border along its entire length.

You cannot deal with the complex problem of immigration in the North-East, without a policy framework. Some of the issues requiring immediate attention in this context are: the identity cards be made mandatory for all Indian residents in the North-East and national citizenship law be reviewed to plug loopholes, which enables illegal settlers to become virtual citizens in a short time using touts, politicians and petty officials. Local administration and communities be involved in the monitoring of our borders along with the local police and Border Security Force. Entry of names of citizens into electoral rolls should be made only after verification by local authorities and based on identity cards. A national commission be set up by law to examine the issues of work permits for migrants, Identity Cards for Indian Citizens, a National Migration Law, Citizenship Act, Illegal Migrations Determination Act and Foreigners Act. Finally, setting up of a proper Immigration and Naturalisation Regime as a permanent department should be considered.

Economic Revival

The root causes of the problem in the North-East are deprivation, ethnic nationalism and cultural insecurity. Both are being fed by people's sense of alienation and deprivation. Unless we attack these unrest will continue. The focus has to be on deprivation of the people, and way to tackle it lies in the economic development and security field. In my opinion the debate between security and development is pointless as both are complimentary and have to be tackled simultaneously. Also most informed opinions agree that improvement in the economy of the North-East will help in removing alienation and peoples' sense of deprivation. The second aspect is that so far policy pronouncements and initiatives in the political and economic realm negate each other and thereby the impact of these measures. The announcements by the last four Prime Ministers indicate the continuation of the old policy of pumping in money without accountability and perpetuation of subsidies without measures to phase these out in a given time frame. The other issue is whether the local leadership has the capacity to respond to the demand of the liberalised market economy policies adopted by the centre. The solution probably lies in a shift towards Ideal Politik and economic common sense oriented to peoples' requirements.

Two major considerations for economic planning should be geographical isolation and constraint of hill area economics and thereby emphasis on infrastructure and deprivation; both also condition perceptions therefore should be priority. Our approach to economic development should be on two plains. At macro level on development of core sectors of infrastructure, power, communications and human resource development, particularly education. These should be decided in consultation with the states but implemented/executed by central agencies with NEC playing the role of the central watch dog. The cost of infrastructure may be high and will have to be primarily in the private sector, which will only come forward if encouraged in a conducive environment for investment. The subsidies and incentives announced under the New Industrial Policy 1997 and by the state Governments should act as an incentive. An active North-East Development Finance Corporation can play a vital role by creating a data base, commissioning feasibility studies and identifying entrepreneurs for ancillary projects and services. The recent initiatives by the Confederation of Indian Industry and Federation of Indian Chambers and Commerce and Industry (FICCI) are in the right direction. Reliance Industries has committed to major projects of Rs. 4,000 crores Tenga Khat Gas Cracker Plant and Telecommunications. The gas cracker plant construction is delayed due to shifting of its site and issues of quantum and price of feed stock, which are still to be resolved. To give encouragement to Industry, changes in land policy, labour laws and infrastructure management are required. Surprisingly, power which in the region has a great potential is not a priority in any of the states. Similarly, privatisation of state owned industries is a prime requirement . At micro level emphasis should be on processing industries in agro and horticulture sectors and fisheries etc. and improvement of civic facilities like water, electricity, sanitation, community development and health. Weaving and other cottage industries should be included. These should be state particular, planned and executed by the state. Public Distribution System (PDS) is a vital factor due to physical features of the area.

For any infrastructure expansion and industrialisation in the North-East Assam is the key. Apart from the highest population, its location and common borders with all the other states, access to rest of the country and being the commercial hub of the region is key to the economic development of the region. Infrastructure expansion, industrialisation and trade and commence can only expand outwards from Assam to other areas of the region, it cannot be otherwise. For development of Assam and communications to the region, control of floods in Brahmaputra River in vulnerable areas and its development as a major water way for transportation of goods and passengers is vital. This should be kept in mind while planning and formulating hydel power projects in the adjoining areas.

The transfer and devolution of resources from the centre, through statutory grants and based on finance commission recommendations, planning commission, discretionary grants through ministries have reached their optimum. With the liberation of economic policy initiated by the centre, centre will find it difficult even to sustain these levels and the question of any increases is out of question. The recommendations of the Shukla Committee to bridge the gaps in infrastructure and basic minimum services Rs. 93,618 thousand crores, report of the committee on unemployed youth, North-East sub-plan in each ministry (10 per cent of its allocation) and promise of full funding of all ongoing projects will add to a staggering amount. It is doubtful if Centre on its own is capable of meeting the infrastructure requirements, the answer lies in private investment and inviting foreign capital. Some of initiatives and responses in this regard have been mentioned above, this will have to be a major area of concern and effort. This will require first of all certain policy changes in land tenure system in the North-Eastern states. Unless land is made available to investor both for industry and agro related activities, no private investor is likely to come in, land could be on lease for long periods or on ownership basis. This will also help in modernisation and commercialisation of agriculture. All cash crops which are possible in the North-East e.g., tea, rubber, horticulture and floriculture require higher level of technologies, skilled labour and organised marketing. There are a number of reports by eminent persons on the issue. Economists are unanimous in the opinion that North-East is deficient in both skilled and unskilled labour. This is well brought out by the preponderance of Bangladesh immigrants both in agriculture, fishery, animal husbandry and in construction business. If industry and modern agriculture has to be attracted then both land and labour will be required. This should not be mixed with the issue of immigrants and the leadership of the North-Eastern states need to take a view on it. Control measures will be necessary; it is better to regulate it than to allow an uncontrolled influx of wrong people. While an overall improvement in the infrastructure is necessary but for economic development and particularly when you want to invite industry and modernise agriculture with major help coming in from the Private Sector, power becomes a prime requirement and should be a priority area for all states. Against an estimated potential of 30,000 to 40,000 MW, only a fraction is developed. The power projects under execution (fifteen) should be completed. Since this area has major portion of infrastructure outlay (Rs. 60,000 crores), this area should be a major area of attention of the Centre and States; Potential of clean industries based on power is high. While local technologies may be primitive but manpower is literate and proficient. Therefore, upgradation of technological base will not only be easy and cost effective but also productive. This will require reorientation of education with emphasis on science and technology and improvement in vocational training facilities, with a network of IAT's based on local requirements.

Trading is an important part of the economic activity in the North-East, which is mainly in the hands of the Marwaris, banias and other outsiders, who operate in collusion with corrupt politicians and bureaucrats. Border trade with Myanmar was opened in 1995, with Moreh and Champai in India and Tamu and Hri in Myanmar, other border trading areas may be opened by mutual agreement. One gate is for movement of goods under the EXIM policy, which includes rice, pulses, groundnut, vegetables and fruits, betelnuts, turmeric, ginger, coriander, chillies, poppy seeds and wood of specific thickness. The second gate (Transit point) is for head loads exchange of local inhabitants living within 20 km. on either side of border. This includes twenty locally produced items. The total value of trade is estimated to be Rs. 2000 crores annually at Moreh alone.

Trade with Myanmar is marred by high cost of transportation, interruption and payment to insurgents. Estimates go upto Rs. 50,000 from Dimapur to Moreh and Rs. 35,000 from Imphal to Guwahati. Trade with Myanmar has great potential both economically and for employment but it will become another area of resentment unless value addition comes to locals, so far bulk of it is in the hands of outsiders. The local youth need to be trained in trading (including foreign), secretarial services, hospitality services, communications and IT. A beginning was made by me in Manipur in 1994 after the agreement with Myanmar was signed but there are too many vested interests. Border trade agreement with Bangladesh was signed in 1972, to regulate trade between people living within 16 Kms of border but the agreement was not implemented and all trade is informal. Value of official trade between Tripura and Bangladesh was only Rs. 18.7 crores of which Rs. 12 crores were imports. However, the illegal trade is estimated to be between Rs. 500 to 1000 crores.

There is vast potential of trade for mutual benefit of the states of the North-East, its neighbours and the South-East Asia. However, this can only be possible once North-East is able to meet the demands of economic liberalisation and dynamics of market economy. Essential part of this will be improvement of infrastructure and flow of investments which depends on stability and level and quality of administration. Most North-East watchers agree and have propagated the need for linking the North-East with Dynamic South-East Asia. However, as Sanjib Baruah has clearly brought out that without using the North-East as a conduit, India's wooing of South-East Asia will fail[7]. He has strongly recommended that we adopt the Chinese model of making Yunan as the hub of its regional economic activity. When China invited experts and business people from the region (own Chinese, Myanmar, Bangladesh and India) to its capital Kumming, the venue underscored the geographical locational advantage of Yunan and its cultural ties and affinities with its neighbours and to restore Yunan's historical role as a bridge to South Asia and South-East Asia. Whereas India in return hosted the Forum of Regional Economic Cooperation created by the Kumming initiative in New Delhi by-passing the North-East. While Yunan Provincial Govt. and its institutions play a direct role in the greater Meakong sub region, our North-Eastern states have no role in BIMSTEC (Bangladesh, India, Myanmar, Sri Lanka, Thailand Economic Cooperation). Whereas our North-East has even stronger cultural and ethnic ties with South-East Asia, Thai-Ahoms, Khasis, Balanese Hindus etc. Both Thai Ahoms and Khasis have a Yunan connection. It is an irony that China, a communist country, has understood the demand of globalisation of economy, whereas India as a democracy has failed to meet the challenge.

No discussion on the economy and development of the North-East can be complete without mentioning the role of the North-Eastern Council established in 1972 under the NEC Act of 1971. Its role has undergone changes from an advisory body to that of a mini planning commission. Most states have lost confidence and respect for it as they feel dispensation and financing of projects is based on political clout and equations. Recent cosmetic changes in its constitution are not dictated by requirement. In the changed economic environment, it should expand its role to that of a corporation with financial, technological and providing capability. It should identify projects, seek investments, identify agencies for implementation and act as a watchdog. To be able to perform these functions it should be freed of political and bureaucratic hold. While it cannot entirely shed political control but it must enjoy autonomy of functioning. This can only happen if it is managed by professionals, technocrats and corporate managers.

If economic development in the North-East has to take off, first of all it will require a change in the mindset of the leadership and people of the North-East. A stage has come when they cannot continue blaming Centre or rest of the country for their ills. They have to do their bit and accept responsibility. If you want peace and prosperity you have to work for it, it cannot be doled out. A change in attitudes is a primary requirement, then only will North-East become investor friendly and attract investment and entrepreneurs. Private investment, industrialisation and modernisation of agriculture are key to rejuvenation of the North-East. This is possible only with new policy initiatives and an outward looking mindset.

Parameters for Resolution of Conflicts

The North-East is an interesting study in negotiations for political solution of conflicts ending in various failed and defunct accords. It is so because of our failure to understand the core of these conflicts and its internal and external dynamics. Some of the salient dimensions and nature of the conflicts have been discussed in the previous chapter. Here I will primarily concentrate on possible approach to conflict resolution. Conflict resolution and efficient conflict management require a holistic approach incorporating political, socio-economic and law and order aspects. The overall policy framework for conflict resolution provides the long term strategic orientation and within these parameters conflict management deals with the tactical aspects in all spheres at the ground level. Such a policy framework helps in creating synergy between the various organs of the state. Conflict is a dynamic process and all factors which contribute, effect and interact with it are relevant to the conflict environment. Being a dynamic process, it comprises phases of initiation, escalation, controlled maintenance, abetment and termination or resolution. When parties to a conflict employ competitive means of dealing with the situation, whereby they pursue their perception of mutually incompatible goals of physically damaging each other or eliminating each other physically and psychologically. Our approach to conflicts in the North-East has been primarily competitive and therefore essentially confined to the law and order field.

It is argued that aggression is the main outcome of frustration. In the case of a system of individuals, it may take the form of crime; in a system of groups, the form of revolution and in a system of nations, the form of wars/ conflicts. One of the major reasons for proliferation of conflicts is that it allows less developed communities, groups and nations to compensate partially in a military sense for the disparity it suffers in its relationship with more developed societies and nations. Poverty, disparity actual or perceived and environmental decline leading to economic stagnation breeds frustration, resentment, political turmoil and violence. Similarly, threat and violation of basic needs for security, identity and life increase the probability of violent responses to the perceived source. The frustration of needs / aggression nexus is both stimulated by and in turn stimulates ethnic centrism and real politik. The reasons for initiation of violent conflicts and their escalation have implications for conflict resolution as this is the basis on which foundation of conflict resolution should be laid.

The basic paradigms relevant to conflict resolution and management are Real Politik and Ideal Politik, these are poles apart, the basic difference is one of nature and nurture. While one makes the best of a negative situation, the other emphasises the changeability of the situation. These also are the foundations of the two approaches to conflict, competitive and cooperative. Conflict as a process should be handled so that real politik driven competitiveness can be replaced by an ideal politik based process of conflict resolution.

It has been the experience of those who have handled conflict situations involving terrorism, insurgency or proxy war in Kashmir and in the North-East that once the situation has been brought under control and the retrogression phase sets in, efforts to consolidate gains and bring in normalcy have not fructified. This is primarily due to lack of understanding of the Low-Intensity Conflict (LIC) phenomenon in general and the way to handle its retrogression phase, in particular.

Counter Insurgency (CI) includes various measures to frustrate insurgency with minimum overt action. The principles are equally applicable to subversion, terrorism and proxy war, with variations in emphasis and modifications related to each situation. The aim is to nullify the elements on which insurgency thrives. Counter Insurgency starts with a political structure, a responsible civil administration and a cohesive security apparatus including the paramilitary, police, intelligence, armed forces, and a judicial system geared to meet the requirements. This must be supported by an economic infrastructure (material resources, finance, transport, communications, a public distribution system and civic services), information and propaganda set-ups, and diplomatic effort to gain recognition and support for such efforts. Counter Insurgency also includes population and resources control, civic action, psychological operations, political and administrative measures and larger socio-economic reforms. It thus includes both preventive and remedial measures to control, contain and defeat insurgency.

It is not possible to demarcate various phases and stages of insurgency, but retrogression of insurgency starts when insurgent leaders are eliminated or won over and replacements are difficult, there are positive gains in favour of the majority or the populace, people feel secure, voluntary support and cooperation starts coming, and socio-economic and rehabilitation measures show progress to satisfy the needs of the people. In real terms, it means a backward movement of insurgency and a forward movement towards normalisation. The slide back is a frequent contemporary experience of all those who have handled the situations. The reason for this is a failure to sustain the application of CI measures with understanding, imagination, unflinching will and determination. The battle is for the hearts and minds of the people, therefore only genuine socio-economic changes in the living conditions of the people will retrogress insurgency. Measures based on tokenism, superficial socio-economic changes brought about by charity, or on a paternalistic approach of the elite which helps only a few individuals are bound to fail. One has seen such efforts failing and adding to the frustration of the people.

Retrogression

Like insurgency, retrogression of insurgency has overlapping psychological, political, military and mobilisational phases. It may be more prudent to call them 'facets of retrogression of insurgency' and deal with them as such. The process of retrogression of insurgency can be hastened by observing some simple yet important guidelines derived from experience.

Political

Political will and determined commitment of the government to execute CI measures is essential to defeat insurgency, as in its absence there cannot either be a cohesive policy or rational and effective execution. This also helps in conservation of resources and sharpens the capability of the government's instruments. It establishes the government's credibility and legitimacy.

Command Structure

Unified command at all levels is essential to coordinate political, economic, social and military actions. The activities in each field are complementary and supportive; disjointed efforts in any field impose constraints or nullify action in other fields. This can only be achieved by a unified command structure. Proper tasking and goals have to be laid as progress is made and their achievement monitored. There are no short cuts in counter-insurgency, and actions once started in any field must be taken to their logical fulfilment.

Responsive Administration

The battle for the hearts and minds of the people is won by socio-economic, administrative and psychological measures (food, clothing, shelter, health care and civic services which affect all human beings). Insurgency thrives on deprivation. Only an administration which can fulfill these and provide security can be called responsive. It is our failure in this field that insurgency on the decline gets new life and the process of retrogression is arrested. We have failed to consolidate on our SF achievements much too often, and the bureaucracy gets away with it. This is what governance in a CI environment is all about.

Security Forces

Security forces (including the intelligence agencies) must function in a coordinated fashion. This can only be achieved by proper orientation, a common perception of the problem based on an overall national perspective, and tasking derived from these. If this is done, then human values automatically get built into their ethos and there is a minimum of aberrations. It will provide the ideological orientation, moral parameters and physical preparation for CI tasks. All must act within the framework of the law and of human values, including the counter-insurgents.

Permanent retrogression of insurgency is a long-drawn-out process, which can only be achieved by stabilisation of recovery in each field and territorial area, followed by consolidation in the political and socio-economic fields. The indicators that insurgency is on the wane and nearing its end are; when people start participating in large numbers in political activities and economic development, are vocal against insurgency, and feel due to improved standards of living that they have a stake in maintaining peace, and for social and cultural affairs. The perspective should be to involve people in resolving their own problems; the state should be perceived to be a provider and helper.

Political Management of Conflicts

The discussion on conflict resolution and conflict management and the retrogression phase of counter-insurgency has clearly demarcated the pivotal role of political will and political management. Most advanced nations have developed effective systems of management of their external and internal security problems, and political management is part and parcel of their security systems. Unfortunately, this is lacking in most developing countries, essentially due to the lack of a strategic culture, and India is no exception. India now has a National Security Council which is charged with deliberating on security and foreign affairs. In spite of the fact that most of the key cabinet ministers (e.g., the prime minister, the home, defence, external affairs and finance ministers) are part of this committee, the political management of our security problems is inadequate.

Handling these problems while in the army and later in Manipur and Nagaland, I found that political management of security problems was only confined to short-term reactions to immediate events. This is particularly true of our internal conflict situations, political management of external conflicts and the external components of internal conflicts is better. Political management of conflicts in the North-East, Punjab and more recently in J&K is a testimony to the failures of all accords, with the lone exception of the Mizoram accord of 1986. The primary reason is that while all aspects of the problems get monitored to some degree, this is done in isolation. The political management is left essentially to the political party in power in the state and at the Centre, whose perceptions are coloured by the compulsions of retaining power. National interest is the ultimate casualty. The local political elite has understood the requirement well and have exploited it for staying in power.

The issue of political management of conflicts is vital to provide consistency and political guidelines for conflict management, in the absence of which the law-and-order dimensions of conflicts are tackled in isolation, and there is no coordination between the efforts of the SF to improve the law-and-order situation and other measures in the economic, social, cultural, ethnic and religious fields. Most of all, a lack of sound political management leads to political expediency and distortion or even conflict between the political establishments and other agencies, particularly the SF.

The above analysis clearly underlines the fact that there cannot be a purely military solution to the problem of insurgencies in the North-East as else where. Academicians, intellectuals, politicians, bureaucrats and most of all Army endorse this view. Our experience also shows that negotiations with the exception of Mizoram have failed to find a lasting solution. In the case of Mizoram, the entire community backed by the church wanted peace and no politician or insurgent could afford to go against it. The role of the civil society was substantial and a determining factor . Moreover, political space provided by Lalthanawala for the MNF to join the main stream clinched the issue; it was a shift from real politik to ideal politik. The MNF are once again in power in Mizoram with people's mandate. The destroyers have become the builders of Mizoram. The situation in Nagaland, Assam, Tripura and Manipur is different. However, this does not mitigate against a solution or that it lies beyond the politician's domain. It only clarifies that political initiatives still remain in strategic arena. The solution cannot be found by negotiating with the insurgents and the very political parties who are responsible for the mess. The civil society which is the main victim of conflict is a party to it. The very fact that the civil society's efforts for reconciliation and peace have been sidelined by the NSCN (I) in Nagaland and it has established a proxy presence in the state by helping politicians sympathetic to it is an indication of their desire for power through coercive means, does not bid for peace. Moreover, there are a large number of insurgent factions in Nagaland and Manipur with conflicting interests. In such a situation civil society is central to resolution and should be our focus. The case of Tripura is different, where IPF can bring together both NLFT and ATTF, act in the larger interest of the tribal society for a solution, and help in removal of alienation and deprivation of the tribals. In the case of ULFA in Assam, both their relevance and status in Assamese perception are questionable. So it can only be a case of surrender and rehabilitation of its cadres.

The ongoing conflicts in the North-East are armed insurgencies in which peoples' support is derived through ethnic links, which is supplemented by the sense of deprivation amongst people, wherein they see insurgent groups representing their frustration. There is an element of external support in the shape of sanctuaries and material and moral support. Further, the North-East, due to its location, is characterised by socio-political instability, isolation and inaccessibility, which continue to influence perceptions. Lack of infrastructure, land alienation and continuing inflow of migrants have retarded the process of development and integration. Political integration without economic and social interaction remains weak. Distorted political ethos, corruption and maladministration has further aggravated the situation and created a conflict prone environment.

With the above back ground and considering the nature of the conflicts, the paradigms of conflict resolution and management relevant to the situation in the North-East are Ideal Politik and cooperative approach. The present environment in the country is that of Real Politik and a competitive one, if any a bit worse in the North-East. One hears people often mentioning that real world of politics cannot be changed. Therefore, let us look elsewhere for solution. I am afraid such perceptions are dangerous and can only lead to disaster as it encourages a confrontational course, which is adversal and power oriented and presents a win or lose approach to conflict resolution. You cannot talk of peace and a political solution while still persisting with policies of Real Politik. These are contradictory. We have to have a change in the mindset and start veering towards Ideal Politik to change the environment for the better. The start of Ideal Politik is in the minds of the policy makers by understanding the causes of people's frustrations and willingness to work towards removing these. However, this does not mean that response to violence does not have to be effective. In reality it means that violence has to be dealt with effectively and simultaneously we should bring about a change for the better in the political, social, economic and other systems to eliminate causes and conditions responsible for the conflict.

The other issue is orientation or focus of our policy of Ideal Politik and cooperative response. The core issue is of frustration, deprivation and denial and it essentially relates to the people, the common man. My experience in the North-East and particularly in Manipur has proved beyond doubt that Ideal Politik focussed on peoples deprivation can only resolve the problem and is the real political solution. So far our focus has been on politics and thereby on politicians and insurgent groups. Its implementation requires good governance more than the political accords. The foundations of the shift to Ideal Politiks is laid on a declared policy, transparency, people's participation, then only legitimacy and credibility of the Govt. can be established.

While talking of peace and resolution of conflicts, one cannot ignore the methodology. Here again the Govt's. approach is faulty. They having essentially fallen back on their intelligence personnel and the bureaucracy as negotiators. Both are seen as an extension of the establishment and as such are suspect in the eyes of the opposite party and the civil society.

The very basis of conflict resolution are laid on trust and such a mutual trust can only be established by genuine peace mediators, who are respected and have the confidence of both sides due to their independence, sincerity, tact, modesty and knowledgeable understanding of the situation. Their stature and mindset helps to reduce confrontations between opposing parties and keep the peace process going. Their knowledge and understanding helps to keep history away from the negotiations as history normally is a detriment to peace. Good and genuine peace negotiators also keep the civil society and its feelings in mind while guiding the negotiations as they understand the binding influence of society on peace.

Governance

Fifty six years of democratic governance has resulted only in expansion of Govt. and less of governance. While this is true of the entire country but in the disturbed environment of the North-East (equally true of J & K) it has added to the problems beseiging the area. The failure of the state to deliver has led to alienation and negative responses of the people and created hurdles for integration. The instruments of governance and constitutional provisions made in the early days after independence have only created multiplicity without real empowerment resulting in their dissociation with the development process even in areas of their immediate concern. The institutional structure has become unwieldy, self-consuming, ineffective and competitive within itself for power. The constitutional framework implied that sovereignty rests with the people and their elected representatives govern on their behalf for their betterment. Instead they have assumed powers as colonial rulers and treated the citizens as subjects to be dispensed with as state feels with total disregard of fundamental rights and directive principles of state policy. While the constitution is democratic but Indian polity in its practice has become power oriented, feudal in attitude and self-serving. Federalism has been dispensed with and power centralised. The biggest sufferer is the common man and civil society is sidelined.

In the context of the North-East specifically, we need to examine the constitutional frame work, state structure and the short falls in the area of governance. The basic structure of the constitution is people oriented, provides "justice, social, economic and political; liberty of thought, expression, belief, faith and worship; equality of status and opportunity and to promote amongst them (the citizens) fraternity assuring dignity of the individual and unity and integrity of the nation". It is flexible to respond to the aspirations of the communities that constitute the citizens of India. In the case of the North-East, the 13th

amendment (1962) created the state of Nagaland and Article 371 (A) provided safeguards for their traditions, culture, customs and protection of their jurisdiction over land and its resources, the 27th amendment (1971) resulted in the creation of the union territory of Mizoram, and statehood was conferred on Mizoram under the 53rd amendment (1986) and Article 371 (G) provided safeguard for Mizo identity similar to those given to Nagas earlier. The 72nd amendment (1992) provided tribals in Tripura greater share in governance. The fact that the constitution is accommodating was further borne out by the fact that as early as 1967 when Indira Gandhi offered a settlement to the Nagas "not within the framework of Indian Constitution but within the framework of the Indian Union", thereby meaning that the constitution could be amended to accommodate a settlement. The extension of the 6th Schedule to the hill areas of tribals and 5th Schedule to the plains tribals has not resulted in either meeting the aspirations of the local people or their participation in the developmental and democratic process, if any people's alienation has increased. It has divided people on narrow ethnic lines and clamour by small ethnic groups to obtain a similar and separate status has increased. This has also provided opportunity to the parochial community elite to exploit the ethnic sentiment for furthering their interests, the same is true of the insurgents. The people have been left high and dry with no voice in their future and resulted in furthering their disillusionment and greater deprivation. Governance has failed to benefit them and people have lost faith in its instruments. The above underscores the point that over fifty years of the practice of democracy and political accords has left people dissatisfied and deprived resulting in their alienation both from the political structure and institutions of governance.

There is a perceptible change in the functioning of the North-Eastern states and their administration since the 1970. The emphasis has shifted from administration with involvement by the old Indian Frontier Administrative Service (IFAS) cadre to that of a bureaucratic white collar administration by the IAS cadre. Neither people's requirements are identified nor are these implemented with people's participation. Cadres are overscribed by local officers who are inducted and empanelled based on ethnic and parochial considerations. Such a situation is convenient for the local politicians, who treat the administration as an extension of their personal, political and ethnic designs. Upright and professional officers are sidelined or eliminated. Administration in the smaller hill districts is virtually non-functional due to structural defects, wrong manning and influence of local politicians, ethnic elite and insurgents. This requires reorganisation, evolution and revamping. At the district level there is multiplicity of functioning between Panchayats,

Autonomous District Councils, Local MLAs (who are also being allotted funds like the MPs), District Administration and state departments, all want control over financial allocations. There is no financial allocation based on priortised requirements and needs and the state finance commissions are non-functional. Therefore, there is an urgent need to look at the political and state structure based on our experience, particularly in the hilly states and areas.

As discussed in the earlier chapter, the area has very democratic and well established institutions at the grass roots level, these have been ignored due to the very process of modernisation and the new institutions have not taken roots. In this state of flux the political elite and bureaucracy have a free hand in mis-management and corruption, which is the main cause of deprivation and alienation. To ensure good governance, accountability and participation of the people through the traditional institution of Angs, Gaon Buras, Village Councils in the hill areas and Panchayats in the plains should be incorporated in the system and made effective. Similarly, in the districts, the District Councils and development organisations of BDO and DDOs are running parallel fiefdoms with little achievements. They have become self-consuming entities with meagre output. We need to take a hard look at the totality of institutions particularly in the hill areas. In the hill areas the institutional structure should be derived from the traditional tribal structure at the village and tribe level and elected representatives at the district and state level. These should be elected on tribe basis at the district and a combination of tribes within the state and in districts which have more than one tribe. The aim should be to give representation to all tribes at all levels of the state.

The case of Assam is different as it was always a part of the political system during the British period and continued to be part of it even after independence. The present smaller hill states except for Tripura and Manipur, which were princely states were districts of Assam and administered as such. We are well aware of the developments leading to their statehood. Since becoming states there has been a general deterioration in their functioning and their present state is marked by a high state of permissiveness in state functioning, corruption, ethnic parochialism, retarded economic growth and disenchanted people. Economically people have been denied the benefits of resources poured in and denial of private capital and entrepreneurship. The present system has failed and is a hostage to the designs of powerful elite, insurgents and the contractors. The local political leadership lacks vision and will to deal with the situation. The need is for a requirement based structure to meet the challenge. Such a structure should be based on past practices and experience and a well informed approach, with people's participation and aspirations as our guide. It was the experience of the British and our own after independence that tribals trusted and responded warmly to a well informed person, whether he was a superintendent, a commissioner, a governor or an army officer. Tribals like straight dealings and find interacting with individual whom they can trust, and to know where they stand and respond to and go by the credibility of such individuals. Till today they recognize and respond to the individual institutions of the Governor, General Officer Commanding or a Commissioner and respect these. Chief Minister and Ministers are part of them, who have failed to carve a place for the institutions they represent and for themselves due to their corrupt and self-serving practices, which is so alien to tribal ethos and traditions, where community comes first. Tribals are most democratic in their own functioning and follow a rigid system of values but while dealing with the authority or Govt. they are individual and personality oriented. Both the process of modernisation and democratic growth as seen by them in the contemporary period has been a sad experience for them and their general feeling is that it is unlikely to improve or change for the better. This feeling is also the reason for their looking back to their roots/past and demand for autonomy in their affairs. There is an urgent need to have an interim arrangement till we build up their trust and they feel part of the country and its system. They must willingly, consciously and effectively participate in the democratic system. Perpetration of the present system will only lead to further disenchantment and distancing from the nation and its people. I have discussed the interim arrangement with tribal leaders and some well informed intellectuals and practiced it in Manipur with success. This is an interim measure to break the present impasse of corruption and non-progressive set up and ethos. Continuation of present system will lead to further failures. I am not against true democracy but certainly against the sham being practiced in the name of democracy.

The interim arrangement has to be a mix of individual institutions and democratically elected true representatives of the people. The general consensus of the tribal people is that individual institutions should be minimum and manned by well informed, experienced, dedicated and upright people. The head of the interim set up should be a Governor with full executive powers, to be exercised through administrative channels directly with secretaries of departments. There should be an elected State Advisory Council with a representative of each district, in addition there should be a provision to nominate one or two members to provide representation to smaller tribes and any other un-represented people. At the grass roots level the present structure of village councils and panchayats should be left untouched and elections to these bodies should be as per their traditional system. The election to the District Council should be on tribe and its area basis, based on population but on non-political basis, i.e., no political parties. The election to the state Advisory Council should be by the representatives of District Council, so that they feel their district is best represented. For states, representation at the national level, Members of Parliament should continue to be elected as at present. The Governor should function as Governor in Council, with Advisory Council members coopted as required. In the case of financial planning and development, education and revenue matters all members of the advisory council shall attend as also in the case of any other policy formulation.

The above will ensure people's participation at the village, district, state and national level. The advisors to the Governor as appointed during President Rule are not required and are redundant and will only be a bureaucratic hindrance without accountability. To meet the security requirements, the senior army officer and the DGP at the state, and at the district level their representatives should be coopted to the Advisory Council and the District Council respectively. The election to District Councils and State Advisory Council should be held every three years, which could be staggered to alternate years to provide continuity.

The political parties in the interim arrangement have no place but as individuals they are part of the process. Depending on the growth of institutions, the political structure should develop, so that states are administered politically through elected representatives representing political parties. The above will ensure that democratic political ethos grows as per people's genius and political parties and arrangements that come up are people oriented and accountable to people. Such a state apparatus will be inspired, responsive, cohesive and accountable. In the development field it will result in correct identification and prioritisation, ensure implementation and increased accountability. The district plans should be formulated and executed by the District Councils, with technical assistance where required from the state departments. The district administration and development apparatus should function in conjunction with the District Council and departments at the district level and should be accountable to the district council. The Village Development Board (VDB) as constituted and organised in Nagaland were a great success and need to be revived and adopted by the other hill states.

Democracy is about representation, participation and empowerment. We have failed in the latter two aspects and it is a cause for worry. The Indian ethos essentially has been of democracy at the grass roots level and a magnanimous ruler or king on top. In keeping with it, the almighty Ram had to bow to the wishes of the people and banish Sita. However, in practice of democracy our elected representatives have failed to emulate the magnanimous ruler, who functioned as per the wishes of the people. Instead they have debarred the masses both from the democratic and development process and empowered themselves to the exclusiveness of the masses. The British followed a policy of divide and rule, partial empowerment and exclusion of certain segments of the society in the peripheral areas. By and large, we have followed similar policies. The basic issue is of empowerment and participation in areas of their concern. Since both democracy and empowerment has to start at the grass root level, therefore, it will be valid in this context to examine the provisions of the 6th Schedule and the 73rd and 74th Amendments on the Panchayati Raj and the Nagarpalikas. The matter has become the focus at the national and state level and amongst the people.

The Sixth Schedule operates in parts of Assam, Mizoram and Tripura and throughout the state of Meghalaya. Assam barring two districts covered by the Sixth Schedule, Arunachal Pradesh and Manipur have passed legislation bringing local bodies under the 73rd and 74th Constitution Amendments. The tribals of other regions in India are covered under the 5th Schedule. Nagaland is a case apart due to Article 371A of the Constitution. In addition there is the Nagaland Tribe, Area, Range and Village Council Act of 1966, which provides, a Tribal Council for each tribe, an Area Council for Kohima and Dimapur, a Range Council in the recognized ranges in Mokokchung and Kohima Districts and village councils for one or two villages in Kohima and Mokokchung as deemed necessary by the Deputy Commissioner. A few of these have been set up since the Act became effective. The village council act is highly centralised and gives no effective role to local bodies, the only exception is the VDBs and the setting up of a regional council for Tuensang under sub clause (d) of clause 1 of Article 371A. In addition the Governor enjoys special powers to act with regard to internal disturbances and administration of Tuensang.

The provisions of the 6th Schedule as enacted and practiced by the states have great variance and need to be examined in each case. In the case of Autonomous District Councils (ADC) in Assam, the right to vote is decided by access to traditional land and length of stay. The ADC has legislative, judicial, executive and financial powers. The legislative powers related to 30 allocated subjects which requires Governor's assent. While the Karbi Anglong and North Cachar Hills ADCs have strengthened their position in relation to the state Govt. but their record of internal democracy, transparency and representation from the grassroots level is not good. The centralisation of power in the hands of executive committee and centralised planning and implementation of development are the main lacunae. The situation is made worse by politicisation of these councils and financial mismanagement as a necessary corollary. The elections should be based on adult franchise and creation of village councils including a degree of representations to traditional institutions of chiefs and Gaon Buras should be introduced and elected every four years. Without it there can be no grassroot level democracy or empowerment. In the case of Bodoland Autonomous Council (BAC) which has been functioning under its own laws as a consequence of 1993 Agreement. Bodos want to pursue the same, whereas the Assam Govt. feels it could be under the 73rd Amendment. In the absence of its notification as a scheduled area and considering the demographic profile and presence of other tribals, it will probably require a different package altogether.

In Meghalaya, the ADC, the traditional ruling system and the state are in a perpetual conflict for influence at the grass roots level. The Syiems (rajas) of Khasi Hills, Dolois of the Jaintia Hills and Nokmas of the Garo Hills represent the traditional system. While sysiems are well organised but the Dolois of Jaintia Hills and Nokmas, the traditional headmen are not influential and have been marginalised by the political process. Non-tribals are not barred but are not welcome to participate in District Council elections, there has been few exceptions in the Garo Hills. Similarly, there is no role for women. The main problem is the multiplicity of role of the State, ADC and traditional institutions in a highly politicised unstable environment. The process does not cater for democratisation and gender justice like elsewhere and there is no representation from the grassroot level. The matrilineal system of inheritance has made representation of women a sensitive political and social issue.

The TTADC, set up in 1985 in Tripura in real terms represents the aspirations of the tribals to control tribal rights and their control over natural wealth, particularly after Indigenous Peoples Front of Tripura (IPFT) came to power in the last elections in 2000. The main problem in the functioning of the TTADC has been devolution of power and functions of which funding has been a most contentious issue. This flows from years of alienation. Tribals consider TTADC head quarters at Khumulang as their capital and chief executive as their Chief Minister. This can only be overcome by equitable sharing of power and resources for development of their area which is 2/3 of the state's area.

The three ADCs in Mizoram are in the minority areas of Lai, Mara and Chakmas and known by the same name, with the largest Lai of 40,000 population. These are less developed with Chakmas area being the least developed. The state Govt. has a dispute with Article 275, which they feel is faulty in relation to the current environment in the state, which is different after statehood. There is a natural antagonism to minorities in the state. In the absence of state finance commission, the devolution of resources to the ADC is inadequate. Keeping in mind the simmerings in the Hmar and Bru areas the need for devolution of power on equitable basis is a prime requirement. This certainly cannot be met by state Govts. proposal to form district development boards under the local MLA's in these areas.

The tribal villages in the Hill areas of Manipur were traditionally administered by village councils consisting of Khunbu, Luplaka and other village elders headed by Khullakpa the village headman. The council settled all disputes of civil, criminal, religious and social nature. They derived their judicial and civil powers under the Manipur State Courts Act of 1947. Chiefs are ex-officio Chairmen of village authority system and elected members of the village authority are included in Block Development Committees. Manipur has six ADC's constituted under the Manipur (Hill Area) District Council Act of 1971, of which Senapati District has two ADCs and other four districts of Tamenglong, Chura Chandpur, Chandel and Ukhrul has one each. The elections to the ADCs have not been held for one reason or the other. The ADCs have limited powers and what they have are subject to state control, the Hill Area Committee of the Legislative Assembly has further eroded their authority. The idea of extension of the Sixth Schedule to the hill area evokes response in the hills essentially instigated by NSCN (IN) through Naga organisations and violent opposition in the Valley as they perceive it is linked to the issue of greater Nagaland. Naga / Kuki Cashes in 1990's and extension of cease fire beyond Nagaland territory added fuel to fire resulting in violent agitation. Subsequent efforts of the state to pass legislation to grant District Council status to Hill areas is lost in the maze of Nagas demand of Sixth Schedule, threat of greater Nagaland and fear of Meiteis and Kukis.

Apart from the infirmities of the Sixth Schedule discussed above, it does not provide adequate framework for democratic management of towns and cities. The town committees under various acts of the states cannot meet the challenges posed by rapid urbanisation in the hilly Sixth Schedule States. The amendments to ADC or adoption and modification to current acts and legislations will not meet the requirements of a well managed city/town with the desired civic amenities. Town committees established in Nagaland, under the Jaintia Hills Autonomous District, Village and Town Administration Act of 1974 compared to the Municipalities in Meghalaya and the state of towns and cities in Mizoram are a clear testimony that local tribal ethos and claim of local politicians being able to run the city administration without elected bodies with proper town management procedures and rules is fore-warning of the catastrophe of denial of civic facilities[8] to there urban people. I have personal experience of it in Nagaland and Manipur. Most states and general opinion in the North-East favour adoption of the 74th amendment for management of towns and cities by a network of Nagarpalikas, the names are of little consequence.

The 73rd and 74th Amendment have been enacted in the non Sixth Schedule states and areas in the North-East in Assam, Manipur, Tripura and Arunachal Pradesh. Assam passed the Assam Panchayat Act in 1994 and in spite of various hiccups and opposition in BAC area the elections were held. The three tier structure consists of Gaon Panchayats, Aanchalik Panchayats and Zila Parishads. The incorporation of Mels (an assembly of village elders) as a social institution, Mohkuma (sub divisional level) could be considered based on area, population and accessibility. Assam has had sufficient experience since the first Panchayati Bill in 1948, Acts of 1959, 1964, 1972 and 1986. On the issue of empowerment, except for Kerala and Madhya Pradesh other states limit the powers of Gram Panchayats drastically. Similarly, all states with the exception of Bihar have accepted the recommendations of the state finance commissions partially or fully on financial devolution. It varies from 25 per cent surcharge on stamp duty, MV tax and court fees to panchayats in Kerala. West Bengal recommended 16 per cent of all state taxes, Karnataka 36 per cent of non-loan gross revenue receipts, Madhaya Pradesh had recommended 3.24 per cent of the net revenue of the preceding year and 40 per cent of plan funds. Punjab State Finance Commission recommended 20 per cent of Stamp Duty, Entertainment Tax, MV Tax and Electricity Duty. Tamilnadu State Finance Commission recommended 15 per cent of the Tax revenue. In the North-East, Tripura State Finance Commission recommended 20 per cent of states share of central taxes, 50 per cent of revenue from sales tax, purchase and luxury tax, 35 per cent of agricultural income tax and land revenue and 15 per cent of forest revenue. In the case of Assam, the State Finance Commission recommended only 2 per cent of state taxes and ten per cent of MV Tax[9].

Panchayat System existed in valley in Manipur since long and was introduced in 1960 formally in these areas. Although elections have been held but the system has failed to function due to politicisation of the system and lack of devolution of powers. Manipur adopted the Panchayat Act in 1994 and the latest elections were held in 2001 but the state Govt. has failed to devolve a number of subjects to the Panchayats and there has been agitation and strike by the elected members.

Arunachal Pradesh was the first hill state in the North-East to introduce Panchayati Raj System even before becoming a state. The NEFA Panchayati Raj Regulation was promulgated in 1967 on recommendations of the Dying Ering Committee. With Gram Panchayat at the village level, Anchal Samiti at the block level and Zila Parishad at the district level and an apex body called the Agency Council. According to Panchayati Raj Regulation 1967, there was a Gram Panchayat member for every hundred persons and Gram Panchayat must have a minimum of three hundred electors. Village level Govt. functionaries were ex-officio members with no voting rights. Every Gram Panchayat elected one member for the Anchal Samiti, which could have a maximum of 25 members, with five nominated members of tribes not represented. The President and Executive Officer were appointed by the DC, heads of all Govt. departments were associated with the Samiti for the preparation of development schemes. It coordinated activities of Gram Panchayat. It could create assets from aid from Govt. and could earn revenue from earmarked areas of forests from its produce. Zila Parishad comprised of one elected member from each Samiti and their vice presidents. The deputy commissioner was the head and departmental heads were coopted. It was an advisory body with no executive power. The act of 1967 which made it effective, deviated from Dying Ering recommendation, although Gram Sabhas were made elective bodies but it was not given any specific function except electing the Anchal Samiti members, it also did not have a president or vice president. While Panchayati Raj Institution have brought about uniformity in village level institutions of the state and created greater awareness of modern political system but it has failed to act as an agent of development at the grass root level. The Arunachal Pradesh Panchayati Raj Bill of 1994 did not meet the requirements of 73rd amendment and was not given Presidential assent. The Arunachal Pradesh Panchayati Raj Act was passed in 1994 but elections could not be held due to dispute over a central bill delineating the schedule castes of the state and making provisions for them for reservation. The state Govt's. contention is that there are no scheduled castes in the state. The Govt. of Arunachal Pradesh sent a bill to that effect for the President's assent. Once that is done the Panchayat Act will come into effect. The main issues for consideration are the role of the traditional institutions, their integration with Panchayati Raj Institutions or as parallel social bodies, the empowerment of women by reservation of 33-1/3 per cent. These institutions have limited capability of raising funds in a tax free state and will depend on Govt. funding. Financial devolution, or direct funding and empowerment to decide and execute local projects is the demand of these institutions.

Tripura adopted the UP Panchayati Raj Act of 1947 with a few modifications. Under its rules of 1961, a single tier of Gaon Sabhas and Nyaya Panchayats were established. The Nyaya Panchayats were abolished in 1983 and Gaon Sabhas were replaced by Gaon Panchayats. The Gaon Panchayat's strength varied from 7 to 15 and its members were elected through secret ballot, the tenure was 5 years. The Act of 1983, provided a wide range of functions to Gaon Panchayats and they were entrusted with Govt. programmes and schemes and empowered them to look after all spheres of community activities, such as agriculture, education, industry, commerce and public utilities. They could undertake profitable business, impose taxes, could appoint, punish and dismiss staff. The Govt. used it as a means to reach people and implement its schemes of rural development and employment generation. After 73rd Amendment, the Tripura Panchayat Act of 1993, provides for a three tier Panchayati Raj structure at the village, block and district level. (The Tripura Panchayats Act was passed in 2001).

Having broadly discussed the constitutional provisions and the functioning of the grass root level institutions under the Sixth Schedule and PRI under the 73rd Amendment, it is but natural to compare the relative merits of the systems as the aim is to have democracy and development with participation at the lowest level in the best possible manner. The new Panchayati Raj system has better institutional structure for self governance due to its clearly demarcated operational areas, adequate power and authority commensurate with its responsibilities, the right human and financial resources to manage their affairs, if the state finance commissions function properly and diligently and have functional autonomy. The developmental functions have been incorporated in Article 234 G and the 73rd Amendment Act of 1992. The ADCs by and large differ structurally and operationally and have greater dependence on the states. Para 12 A of the Sixth Schedule gives overriding powers to the state legislatures and autonomy of the ADCs depends on their political relationship with state leaders and in the absence of a finance commission they are on the mercy of the state departments. The PRIs are mandated to be elective at all levels, which is not the case entirely with the ADCs and village councils. Reservation of one third seats and chairpersons is provided for women, SCs / STs and OBCs, in the PRIs whereas under the 6th Schedule women are relegated, with decision making power and responsibility for male tribesmen in the Hill areas. The ADCs have no development and welfare functions and are dependent on assignment of these by the state. The PRIs are going to be vested with a lot of power and money in the coming years. The allotment of Rs. 30,000 crores in the 8th plan for rural development and suggested allocation of 36 per cent of total outlay for sub-state level planning bodies, with 30 per cent as lumpsum grant for expenditure on rural water supply, roads, electricity, education and other schemes, 5% for district and village bodies at their discretion, the remaining 1% for poverty alleviation and employment generation. This comparative study is not complete or comprehensive but is fully supported by informed opinion in the North-East. Decentralisation of power under the provisions of the 73rd amendment act received a favourable response from people of Mizoram and the State Govt. constituted the states administrative reforms commission to study the implications of the 73rd and 74th amendment acts and explore possibilities of its implementation in 1995. All political parties and village council activists agreed to its applicability. The draft bill was sent to the select committee of the State Assembly. The only dissent was by Mizo Students Union. Due to the expiry of the life of the state legislature the bill is pending but if any demand for its implementation is rising. I would strongly recommend that the civil society in the Sixth Schedule states and areas study the 73rd Amendment Act of 1993 and debate its merit vis-à-vis the Sixth Schedule. While saying so, I also feel that the traditional tribal Institutions at the grassroot level which have been guiding and providing self-rule at the village level should be incorporated in the PRI structure as these will provide legitimacy to the PRI without disturbing its basic structure. Names are important but not more than the ethos of PRI and its implementation.

To strengthen the Panchayati Raj Institution and fulfil its aim, there is need to strengthen it in some respects. It should be made obligatory for the states to devolve the subjects under the Eleventh Schedule by law and devolution of the 36 per cent of plan funds to panchayats, failure to do so would deny them allocations or alternately fund should be allotted to Panchayats directly. The state finance commissions also be set up in Sixth Schedule states and allocation by them as per centre's directions be overseen by the CAG. With the PRI, the Govt. role in DRDA should be removed and chairman of Zila Parishad should be chairman of DRDA. The power to dissolve lower level panchayats should rest with the Zila Parishad and not with the state, to establish peer group accountability. Panchayats can develop units of self governance only if bureaucratic and Govt. control is reduced. This will only be possible if relevant structures of power and administrative level are cut down in tune with the Eleventh Schedule. The district plans must evolve from below through PRI structure and this with other sectoral outlays should constitute district plan budget to be reflected in state budget. Panchayats should be given policing and judicial powers to maintain law and order in their areas. There should be transparency and all PRI account displayed publicly and audited. Finally, alongwith other devolutions, the system will only function if political interference is reduced. This can be done if elections to PRIs up to Zila Parishad level are held on non-party basis and MLAs and MPs as mandated currently should be excluded from their functioning. Constitution and legislation are as good as these are implemented. This requires political will cutting across party lines to achieve the mandate.

Conclusion

The problems of the North-East are no different from the problems in rest of the country and for that matter else where in the developing world. These appear to be complex because of lack of understanding and vision and ground realities. There is a wide gap in the perceptions of the decision makers and the people of the North-East, which need to be bridged in looking for solutions. The pace of modernisation has left communities groping for solution to emerging problems in the political, socio-economic and cultural fields. Failure to provide the requisite space and openings to meet the new challenges has resulted in conflict situations. The violent manifestations of their conflicts has engaged all the attention and action of the authorities. The inner conflicts which the communities in transition are experiencing are the real conflicts. Our main concern should be to help the ethnic communities resolve these inner contradictions by the process of reconciliation, accommodation and understanding. The main challenges are in the social and economic fields and not in the political or law and order domain.

REFERENCES

1. S. D. Muni and Lok Raj Baral, Refugees and Regional Security in South Asia, Konark Publishers Pvt. Ltd., Delhi, 1996, pp. 7-24.
2. *Hindustan Times*, 7 November, 2003.
3. *North East Daily*, 16 June 2000.
4. *Hindustan Times*, 15 December 2003.
5. Sanjoy Hazarika, "Rites of Passage", Penguin Books, New Delhi, 2000, pp. 261-262.
6. *Hindustan Times*, 6 June 2002 and 7 July 2002.
7. *Indian Express*, 12 December 2003.
8. Meghalaya Cabinet Minister in a workshop in New Delhi in 2000 – as quoted in 'A Consultation Paper on-Empowering and Strengthening of Panchayati Raj Institutions/Autonomous District Councils/Traditional Governing Institutions in North-East India; by the National Commission to Review the Working of the Constitution, p. 27.
9. *Ibid*, p. 78.

Part II

Jammu and Kashmir

Roots of Discord

5

Historical Perspective and Geopolitical Dynamics

Like elsewhere history and geography have influenced the lives, attitudes and perspectives of the people of Jammu and Kashmir. Kashmiri historical experience has varied from independence, isolation and solidarity to subjugation and repression by one or the other outsider. The second quarter of the current century ushered in a period of reassertion marked by rejuvenation of its secular and composite identity and democratic and economic revival. This coincided with the struggle for independence in India and Jammu and Kashmir was greatly influenced by events and happenings during the period. The contemporary period since independence particularly after Sheikh Mohammad Abdulla's dismissal in 1953 is a period of readjustments, reassessments and turmoils culminating into the decade of violence and bloodshed since 1989. It is therefore relevant to examine the historical perspective of the Kashmiri experience and contemporary trends in Jammu and Kashmir, which have conditioned the perspective of the Kashmiris in particular and those of the people in Jammu and Kashmir is general.

HISTORICAL PERSPECTIVE

Ancient Period

Shaivism was founded by Vasugupta in late 8th century AD and for 600 years up to the 14th century it guided the personal and community life of the Kashimiris. With the advent of Buddhism in 3rd century BC, fusion of best of both the religions resulted in Shaivite philosophy, and reactionary Brahamanism with its caste consciousness was eliminated from ancient Kashmir of the period. This blending of the Vedic and Budhistic culture is in keeping with all the traditional Indian philosophies[1]. Islam came through gradual conversions in the wake of foreign adventures from the South and Central Asia. Individual conversions had been going on for some time, particularly after the local Buddhist ruler Rinchen embraced Islam in 1320 under the influence of Faqir Bulbul Shah. Shah Mir who ruled after Rinchen Shah for a short period (3 years) was just, human and generous like Rinchen. He was considered the saviour of his people for healing the wounds of two centuries of anarchy and misrule.

Qutub-u-Din's regime from 1374 to 89, saw the arrival of Sayyids from Iran, most notable of them being Hazrat Amir-I-Kabir Sayyid Ali Hamadani popularly known as Shah-I-Hamadan, a revered and remarkable personality of the 14th century muslim world. He is regarded as the real founder of Islam in Kashmir [2]. This was the period of large scale conversions to Islam through persuasions and preachings. A contemporary of Sayyid Ali, hermitess Lalladed (born 1335) having assimilated the basic teachings of both Shiavism and Islam became the harbinger of resurgence movement laying the foundation of composite culture of Kashmir devoid of differences of caste, creed, birth and position. She was a true apostle of religious humanism in Kashmir. Lalla was the spiritual progenitor of Nandrishi (Sheikh Noor Din) and their relationship has a special spiritual and symbolic significance. It is said that while he refused to take milk of his own mother, he drank from the breast of Lalleswari. He grew up in her spiritual patronage and acknowledged her preeminence as a spiritual heritage of Kashmir and undertook to carry it forward. In this sense, Muslim Rishis of Kashmir represent continuity of this tradition. They introduced Islam not as a revolt or as a destroyer of tradition as is the case in many parts of India but as a preserver, consolidator and perpetrator of tradition[3]. Opposed by Brahmanism, appreciated by Shaiva philosophy, the new philosophy culminated in the composite culture of humanism expounded by Lalladed and her disciple Sheikh Noor Din (Nand Rishi).

Sikander ascended the throne in 1389 after his father's death and enforced Muslim law with great strictness. He was an able ruler and great builder (Jama Masjid and Khankah-I-Mualla). After Ali Shah, Sikander's elder son (1413-1420), his younger son Zain-ul-Aabidin ruled for 50 years. Popularly known as Badshah or great king, he was one of the most remarkable rulers of Kashmir. He revoked all discriminatory laws against Hindus, recalled Brahmins who had fled during his father's regime. He recovered Ladakh and Baltistan and extended his kingdom from Peshawar to Sarhind. He was a great builder and founded many towns, constructed the Mar canal and the first wooden bridge over Jhelum. A patron of learning, arts and craft, Rajtarangni and Mahabharata were translated into Persian by Mulla Ahmad, Kashmiri poet laureate during his reign. It was a period of tolerance and progress.

Dissensions amongst the successors of Zain-ul-Aabidin resulted in the downfall of the great Shahmir dynasty. The kingdoms of Ladakh, Baltistan, Jammu and Rajouri declared independence. Mughals intervened on the invitation of the nobles and Kashmir was divided amongst them. In 1531, Mughals again invaded Kashmir but had to withdraw against stiff resistance of the Kashmir forces under Kaji Chak. Kashmir was placed under the cruel rule of Mirza Haider, a Mongol, by Humayun. He followed a policy of persecution of Chaks who were mostly Shias and executed Daniyal, the son of Mir Shams-ud-Din, principal Shia missionary, in 1558. Mirza Haider was killed by Kashmiris in 1561 and Chaks under Ghazi Chak seized the throne of Kashmir.

The Chaks had migrated from Dardistan and settled in Trehgam and Kupwara and the two factions who had split before settlement in Kashmir are known as Trehgami and Kupwari Chaks. Ghazi Chak was an efficient and able administrator, practiced religious tolerance and abolished forced labour. His brother Hussain Chak succeeded him in 1563 and his reign of 7 years was a period of tolerance, sympathy towards his subjects and a period of learning. Ali Chak replaced him in 1570, maintained a liberal outlook, and encouraged literature, arts and craft. After Ali Chak's death a war of succession took place and Yusuf Chak after taking shelter with the Moghuls during the rebellion regained his throne. He ruled for a short period and encouraged music, poetry and literature. He is regarded as one of the most cultured rulers of Kashmir.

Moghuls invaded Kashmir in 1585; Yusuf Chak agreed to pay homage to the Imperial Court but never returned. Moghuls withdrew after establishing their sovereignty over saffron cultivation and shawl manufacturing. Yakub Chak resisted the Moghuls but he offended Sunni nobles by his intolerance and inefficiency. On the invitation of Sunni nobles and scholars Moghul forces entered Kashmir in 1586 and Akbar was proclaimed the sovereign of Kashmir and the Kingdom thereafter ceased to be independent.

An appraisal of the ancient history of Kashmir up to the Sultanate period at this stage will be relevant as this period marks the first watershed in their long history of independence, isolation and solidarity in which people of Kashmir developed a distinct culture and identity. A remarkable fusion of composite cultures promoted further by tolerant kings like Zain-ul-Aabidin and teachings of Lalladed and Nand Rishi resulted in the average Kashmiri Muslim's orientation to Sufism. Apart from achievements in all fields Sultanate period was marked with emergence of regional personality consciousness. The two great Kashmiris of the period Lalladed, a Hindu yogini and Sheikh Noorud-Din Wali a muslim saint may be described as the fountain head of the ideology of Kashmiriyat[4].

Kashmiri culture developed through the silent process of history rather than by imposition. It is free of dogmas and its literature reflects the traditions of the Indian sub-continent[5]. The development of a rich language as an admixture of Sanskrit and Persian highlights the historical connection of the Hindu and later Muslim periods. The Koshur – as the language is called by the Kashmiris has 600 years of recorded literary heritage. The original Dardic language has supplied the skeleton, Sanskrit has given it flesh and Islam has given it life[6]. Kashmir language is polyglot in character. Out of every 100 words, 25 are Sanskrit, 40 Persian, 15 Hindustani and 10 Arabic. The remaining 10 may be Tibetan, Turkish, Dogri and Punjabi. In modern times there has been a sprinkling of English words also.

Islam in Kashmir was not imposed but accepted by choice, neither was it a revolt to destroy old culture, religion or traditions. As a matter of fact in spite of conversion to Islam, Kashmir never forgot its old culture and traditions, on the contrary it preserved, consolidated and perpetuated the traditions. Kashmiri Muslims after conversion did not abandon the way of life and mental outlook of their forefathers, cultivated through thousands of years of history. A Kashmiri Muslim shares in common with his Hindu compatriots many inhibitions, superstitions, adulations, practices as well as social liberties and intellectual freedom, which are unknown to Islam. Lawrence says, "I attribute much of the delightful tolerance which exists between followers of the two religions to the fact that the Kashmiri muslim never really gave up their old religion of the country. Similarly, Islam influenced the attitude and perceptions of the Kshmiri Hindus[7]. The Kashmiri Brahmans were different from the orthodox Hindus, they had no reservations in sharing water and food with their Muslim brethren.

CENTURIES OF SUBJUGATION AND REPRESSION

Mughal Period

Annexation of Kashmir by Akbar to a large extent resolved the crisis in Islam due to Shia-Sunni discord as he treated Shias, Sunnis and Hindus on equal footing. He brought peace and order to the land as Jazia was abolished and Hindus were appointed to position of prominence. However, it ended Kashmir's independence and commenced the impoverishment of its cultural heritage. Art and culture sought patronage of the Mughal courts and to be a Kashmiri became a disqualification[8]. Vilification of Kashmiri's started with the forcing of men to wear Phiran, a woolen overdress, denying recruitment in Army and forbidding carriage of arms by them. Srinagar was turned into a cantonment and Hari Parbat fort was constructed. Moghul soldiers suppressed and tortured the population destroying their martial spirits. Emperor was declared owner of all cultivable land, thus denying the Kahmiris ownership of their own land. The great Moghul road across Pir Panjal was made with forced labour and a famine during his regime resulted in large scale starvation deaths. This worked on the psyche of the Kashmiris and apart from a feeling of subjugation and repression, it dealt a damaging blow to their self-respect. Kashmir was ruled through six Governors during Akbar's regime.

Jehangir succeeded Akbar and ruled through seven Governors and some of them were repressive. The first Governor Kubleh Khan had to be dismissed on complaints from the Kashmiri Pandits for his excessive oppression. Beautiful gardens were laid at Verinag, Achabal and Nishat Garden. Forced labour and harsh taxes added to the misery of the people. During Shah Jehan's regime the beautiful Chashma Shahi garden was laid. After Shah Jehan, Aurangzab ruled through twelve Governors (1658-1707). He followed a discriminatory policy against the Hindus and taxed them heavily. He encouraged sectarian clashes to keep the place socially and culturally fragmented. The biggest Shia-Sunni clash in Kashmir history took place in 1685, resulting in mass scale loss of life and property. During the period natural calamities of flood and earthquake added to people's misery. After Aurangzeb's death, 57 Governors ruled Kashmir with little control by Delhi, resulting in sectarian conflicts, starvation and poverty and a lot of people left for safer areas. On the invitation of some nobles of Kashmir, the Afghans annexed Kashmir in 1753. Yusuf Shah Chak has been acclaimed a national hero who fought Moghuls to save the honour, integrity and independence of Kashmir[9]. Moghul imperialism period of 166 years was by and large a period of internal feuds, misery and impoverishment.

Afghan Period

On the invitation of Kashmiri nobles Ahmad Shah Abdali invaded Kashmir and absorbed it into the Afghan Kingdom and Kabul replaced Delhi as the central authority for Kashmir. In all 28 Afghan Governors ruled over Kashmir, most of them indulged in robbing Kashmir of its wealth, torture and killings due to their uncertain future. It was a period of tyranny and worst cruelty in Kashmir's history[10]. Jazia, a poll tax on Hindus, was imposed and many either fled or converted to Islam. The last of the martial tradition of Kashmiris ebbed and they became timid.

At the same time more Kashmiri Pandits were elevated to the highest posts and most businesses and occupations were held by them.

The extent of looting can be imagined from the fact that the first Afghan Governor Abdulla Khan carried a wealth of over one crore in just six months of his rule. He was replaced by Raja Sukh Jewan an Afghan Hindu, who declared independence from Kabul, when he could not meet the exorbitant demands of additional revenue. He was defeated, captured and killed. Hindus had some respite during his period. According to Lawrence, Amir Khan Jawan Shir is the only Governor who is remembered as a great builder and admired as a Governor. He proclaimed Kashmir's independence after Abdali's death for a short period. Azad Khan was the most repressive and brutal of all the Governors, his name meant instant horror for the Kashmiris. The people were most dispirited, humiliated and broken.

Ironically, it was Birbal Dhar, a powerful Hindu revenue official who, after mass scale embezzlement, flew to Ranjit Singh's Durbar and persuaded him to invade Kashmir. In 1819, Misri Dewan Chand accompanied by Raja Gulab Singh invaded Kashmir and 500 years of Muslim rule ended.

Sikh Rule

The Sikh rule lasted for 27 years from 1819 to 1848 during which period eleven governors ruled the state. The Sikhs were no less cruel, intolerant and rapacious than the Afghans. The first Governor Misiri Chand lasted six months, he was recalled when lawlessness created by the Sikh soldiers got totally out of hand. Property was looted, men killed and women folk molested. His successor Moti Ram made cow slaughter punishable by death and whole families were burnt alive on suspicion of killing a cow. Muslims were deprived of their land, which was distributed to non-Muslims. Mosques were closed and Pather Masjid was converted into a grain store. Kan-Kahi Maulla was spared due to strong public resentment. Moti Ram was replaced by Hari Singh Nalwa, who was removed by Ranjit Singh due to his misdeeds and amassing wealth. Moti Ram returned and the reign of terror, poverty and starvation continued, which has been recorded by Moore Craft, an English Veterinary surgeon.[11] . It was during this period that Birbar Dhar who had monopolised the revenue administration committed large scale embezzlements, was jailed and died. The distress, misery and agony of the people continued ruler after ruler. Severe famine during Ranjit Singh's son Sher Singh's Governorship took a huge toll of life due to mismanagement by Jamadar Khushal Singh. The only redeeming period is of Colonel Mian Singh (1834-41), who imported grain to feed the starving population, remitted taxes on marriages and improved the administration. Unfortunately he was put to death by his own mutinous soldiers.

Gulab Singh of Jammu after restoring order withdrew and a period of relative peace under Sheikh Mohi-ud-Din, a Punjabi musalman (1841-46) followed and Jama Masjid was opened for prayers in deference to popular sentiment. He had to face onslaught from Bombas of lower Jhelum. He was succeeded by his son Imam-ud-Din. The crown in Lahore was with Dalip Singh, who was only six year old. The Britishers defeated Sikhs at Sabroan in 1846 and Kashmir passed on to them as war indemnity. The English passed on Kashmir and the whole tract situated east of Indus and westwards of Ravi to Maharaja Gulab Singh for a sum of seventy five lakh rupees under the Treaty of Amritsar, in March 1846, However, Imam-ud-Din did not surrender and with help of valiant Bombas defeated the Dogra forces and killed its commander Dewan Lakhpat Rai. The English forces moved in and Imam-ud-Din surrendered. Gulab Singh entered Srinagar as its new ruler on 9 November, 1846.

In 1835, three European visitors, Hugal, Vigie and Henderson vividly recorded the divide between the affluent aristocracy living in palatial palaces and the abject poverty of the common man[12]. Sikh rule was a continuation of the degeneration, poverty and deprivation of the people of Kashmir, worse than the Afghans.

Dogra Rule

Dogra rule under Gulab Singh for ten years was a sad story of greed, repression and exploitation by a totally feudalistic regime. People were deprived of their hereditary rights of ownership and occupancy over the land and King became the owner of all lands, forests and even mountains. People became tenants and paid revenue to king. People's resentment was ruthlessly suppressed. Maharaja's greed, corrupt officials and rule of money lenders squeezed the population. The system of Begar (forced labour without payment) not only hurt the pride of Kashmiris, it took human toll while carrying loads to the frontier in inclement weather and due to inhuman treatment. Heavy taxation on agriculture (1/3 of crop) and on shawl weavers finished agriculture and industry and people fled Kashmir. He taxed every vocation. This invited British intervention and Henry Lawrence, the Agent of Governor General at Lahore had to warn the Maharaja that British Govt. will not tolerate such tyranny and may adopt measures for protection of the hill people. The British interference in the state increased due to complaints by the people, although for a time they were misled by Maharaja's henchmen[13].

Ranbir Singh succeeded Gulab Singh in 1856. He continued the same way as Gulab Singh. He kept the Britishers pleased with cash and kind to crush the 1857 uprising and was honoured with the title of 'Star of India'[14]. He captured Gilgit in 1860 and was suspected by the British of forging close contacts with the Russians. A British agent was posted in Kashmir. He distributed and managed cultivation of estates through tenants by establishing a new type of Zamindari under the Kardars. The practice of Begars continued and got worse with people being sent to far off Gilgit. Over taxation, poverty, disease and grief gave birth to social evils like prostitution and sale of girls. The rule symbolised misery, starvation and death for subjects and privileges and profits for rulers and the administration mostly Rajputs, Pandits and other Hindus. Anger born out of misery drove the shawl weavers to march in protest to Governor's residence, the marchers were fired upon and 20 died in the stampede. Discriminatory policy against Muslims, left vast majority of them illiterate. In spite of the appointment of an advisory council in1882. Under British pressure, matters did not improve as people manning the administration had a vested interest. Robort Thorpe in his book 'Kashmir Misgovernment' blamed the Britishers entirely for imposing such a repressive rule against all tenets of modern civilisation.

On the death of Ranbir Singh in 1885, his son Pratap Singh took over the reigns. He was distrusted by the Britishers and under the garb of administrative reforms they appointed a powerful resident in the state and Maharaja's authority was gradually eroded. During his 40 years of rule he enacted the land settlement rules, the distinguishing features of which included occupancy rights of land, reforms in the system of revenue collection and abolition of forced labour. This resulted in agriculturists settling down on their land, easy payment of revenue thus saving in soldiers and officials for the same. This helped in the improvement in the agricultural economy[15]. But shawl industry remained in the dark[16]. In the education field some progress was made by establishment of Missionary and Islamic schools. Epidemics, floods and famines took toll of life due to inadequacy of health, sanitation and medical facilities. British set up a four member council to tighten their grip over the administration due to continued distrust of Pratap Singh. Later, the Council was disbanded and Pratap Singh's powers were restored. Pratap Singh took measures to improve social and economic state of his people. Education was his chief priority and aid was given to Islamic schools and other Islamic institutions, scholarships were given to Muslim students and Muslim representation in the administration started growing. His regime was a vast improvement over the earlier Dogra Kings. Road from Baramula to Kohala (Jhelum Valley Road) was opened for car traffic thus improving trade and communications. Development in Czarist Russia and World War I made British further suspect of Pratap Singh and a new state council was instituted in 1922, with Hari Singh as its senior member. A year later under pressure he renounced his position as president of council in favour of Hari Singh. Pratap Singh died in dismay in 1925.

The last ruler Hari Singh ruled for 23 years, he lived in his own world of comforts and luxury quite oblivious to the conditions of abject poverty of his subjects. According to Sir Albian Banereiji[17] his own political and foreign minister, "the people were like dumb cattle" who had no say in the administration. He charged the rulers of pursuing a discriminatory policy towards the population, keeping them deliberately illiterate and inflicting utmost poverty on them[18]. He resigned in disgust in 1929. Hari Singh treated the state as his personal preserve and squandered his wealth in pleasure, with little regard for his people. Peasants mostly Muslims were subjected to violence for collection of taxes and were forced to migrate to Punjab as labourers during winter. There was forced labour (Begar) in military service under extreme climatic and terrain conditions in Gilgit.

All in all this prolonged period left bitter memories for the Kashmiris and it is only the resilience of its basic cultural strength that motivated revival of Kashmiriyat and traditional composite culture of the Kashmiris.

Kashmiri Reassertion

Period from 1930 onwards is of special significance to understand the contemporary situation as it was the start of the agitation by Kashmiri Muslims, being the oppressed lot. The events of June and July 1931, in which a non-Kashmiri Abdul Qadeer from North West Frontier was tried for treason for his vehement appeal against Maharaja's rule, are of significance. Firing on agitated public outside Srinagar Jail where trial was being held on 13 July 1931, in which 22 demonstrators were killed can be termed as the start of the end of the Maharaja's regime. The day is observed as the 'Martyrs Day'. Under pressure Maharaja released all political prisoners including Sheikh Mohd Abdullah. Eleven Muslim leaders presented a memorandum of demands to the Maharaja. As a result of which Glancy commission to look into the grievances was set up. Based on the recommendation of the Glancy commission, land rights to occupancy tenants were granted, improvement in educational facilities to Muslims and more jobs in education department, adequate share to all communities in Government departments, abolition of several taxes, freedom of Press, restoration of religious places to Muslims and abolition of the practice of Begar were implemented. A legislative assembly was also set up. It paved the way for formation of Muslim Conference, which took up the mantle of guiding the upsurge for their rights. This brought reaction from Kashmiri Pandits in the shape of Roti Agitation demanding job security.

Hindu reaction and factionalism within the Muslim conference between Mirwaiz Mohd Yusuf Shah and Sheikh Mohd Abdullah during the period 1932 to 1938 brought out very clearly to the Muslim leadership that a politico-social reforms programme would require a larger mass base consisting of all segments of the state's communities to further the political struggle. As a consequence of this Muslim Conference was renamed as All Jammu and Kashmir National Conference in 1938. In this Sheikh was greatly influenced by the leadership of Gandhi, Nehru and Frontier Gandhi – Khan, Abdul Gaffar Khan. In keeping with the wishes of the delegates in its first session at Anantnag in October 1939, it decided to keep itself away from both the Indian National Congress and Muslim League ideologies. It also adopted its separate flag.

Naya (New) Kashmir

Forties was the period of conflicting ideas and ideologies in Jammu and Kashmir like rest of India. Both Muslim League and Congress were busy extending their influence in the state, visits by Jinnah and Nehru had their influence. Simultaneously, the radical and the so called progressive elements, which came under the spell of Marxism influenced the members of the National Conference and by 1942, CPI was able to open a study circle in Srinagar, of which Miss Mahmooda, GM Sadiq and Bakshi Gulam Muhamad were members, it influenced the struggle decisively. Secularisation of National Conference created strong links between it and the Congress Party and people from all walks of life threw their weight in support of National Conference's demand for a responsible govt. During his visit to Kashmir Nehru openly asked for all communities to strengthen Sheikh Abdulla's hands against communal and conservative forces[19]. In 1944, Jinnah was invited both by the National Conference and Muslim Conference, he played the Muslim Card, and this was not acceptable to Sheikh Abdulla. He asked Jinnah to leave the state and the people of the state to their fate. The divide was complete. Nehru along with Badshah Khan arrived at the same time and they were accorded a royal welcome. Badshah Khan called Sheikh the gift of God and asked people to follow him[20].

The CPI progressives in the National Conference influenced its strategy and provided the authorship of the Naya Kashmir Manifesto of the National Conference in 1944. It covered both the constitutional and the economic structure. This provided a radical change to the approach of the National Conference resulting in the launching of the Quit Kashmir Movement in 1946. In a memorandum submitted to the Cabinet Mission to India in 1946, it demanded an absolute right to freedom and an end to the autocratic rule of the Maharaja. Explaining the demand on the eve of his arrest in a Public meeting, Sheikh Abdullah emphasized that the princely order should quit as a logical extension of the policy of "Quit India". It received the support of the All India State Peoples Conference under Nehru. In spite of Pandit Nehru's effort to provide defence for Sheikh Mohd Abdullah he was tried for treason. He emphasized that time has come to tear the Treaty of Amritsar and Quit Kashmir is not a question of revolt. It is a matter of right[21].

As independence approached, the Prime Minster of Jammu and Kashmir sent telegrams to both Indian and Pakistani governments, suggesting a stand still agreement. According to it, 'the existing arrangements should continue pending settlement of details. 'The government of Pakistan agreed to the stand still agreement, whereas the government of India asked for a meeting with the Prime Minister or any other Minister of Jammu and Kashmir for negotiating such an agreement.[22] With the passage of the Indian Independence Act by the British Parliament the paramountcy lapsed. The Maharaja delayed the decision and toyed with the idea of independence, till the rebellion in Poonch and invasion of the Kashmir Valley compelled him to accede to India on the suggestion of Lord Mountbettan, the Viceroy. The accession was made subject to a plebiscite to determine the peoples' desire after raiders were evicted and complete Jammu and Kashmir was liberated. This was accepted by Pandit Nehru. Kashmir was granted a special status in the Union of India under Article 370 of the Constitution.

The Partition

The period after the partition is most relevant for understanding the overall contemporary situation and needs detailed analysis to get a clear perspective. It is a historical fact that the tired Indian political leadership, who had fought the long campaign for freedom, reluctantly accepted the partition of the country to gain independence. While throughout its struggle for freedom the Nation stood together but for the final act they succumbed to British manipulations and Muslim League's pressure for partition, which were not fully representative for the vast Muslim majority in the subcontinent. In the 1937 elections Muslim League won only 22 per cent of Muslim seats (109 out of 491). The idea of Pakistan took roots only in ten odd years between 1937 and 1946 and the slogan of Pakistan was adopted only in March 1940 at Muslim League's meeting at Lahore. During the forties, most of the Congress leaders were in Jail, which left the field open for the Muslim League and it won 429 seats out of 491 in the 1946 elections. The Sixth Schedule of the Government of

India Act 1935, prescribed different qualifications in different provinces for the right to vote. These included ownership of land or a building, paying house tax or even cantonment fee to be able to vote. Consequently only thirteen per cent of the Indian population exercised their franchise. Out of 79 million Muslims (as per census of 1941), only 6 million Muslims voted, of which 4.5 million voted for Pakistan implying that a mere 16 per cent of adult Muslims in India participated. The Muslim vote was garnered by the Muslim league in areas where Muslims were in minority and nationalists in the Muslim majority areas could not vote. The point is that it was not representative both in desire of the people or in principle, therefore, it was bound to evoke different perceptions and emotions in different people in its aftermath. [23]

Similarly, the hurried implementation of the partition plan, without due preparation and agreement on the basic issues of the boundary between the two new nations, division of assets, rationalisation of sharing of river waters and other interdependent infrastructure left each side with a series of woes and suspicions.

The British recommended that the princely states (some odd 560) should accede either to India or Pakistan based on two criteria given below:-

(a) The rulers of Muslim majority states should accede to Pakistan and those with Hindu majority populations to India.

(b) Accession to Pakistan by rulers of Muslim majority states should occur only if their states were geographically contiguous to either East or West Pakistan[24].

This, coupled with the desire of some of the ruling princes, both Hindu and Muslim (in Hyderabad, Travarncore and Jodhpur) to carve out independent states for themselves, created further complications. The realisation dawned on India only when Sardar Patel took over the Ministry of States. The case of Junagarh set the tone for confrontation, when it being a Hindu majority state acceded to Pakistan. It had to be 'disciplined' before it merged with India. It's Dewan Shah Nawaz Bhutto, father of Zulfikar Ali, flew to his native place in Sindh. This has contributed to a large extent to the anti-India attitude of the Bhutto family. Therefore the principles of partition as laid down were neither sound nor observed. In the case of Kashmir Pakistan's initiative to grab it with force initially through raiders, due to the Maharaja's vacillation, added to the problem. Kashmiri leadership, which was already struggling against the Maharaja with the help of the Indian nationalist leadership, forced the Maharaja to decide for India. This was also because of the failure of Muslim League to convince the Muslim majority leadership of Kashmir to opt for Pakistan.

Kashmir's accession if on one hand was considered essential for India's secular image on the other hand it being a Muslim majority state opting for India, went against the very foundation of the two nation theory on which Pakistan's national identity was to be carved. This set the stage for Indo-Pak confrontation with Kashmir as the centre-piece. To make the situation worse, India accepted Mountbatten's suggestion to make accession subject to the determination of the will of the people of the state, once hostilities were over and forces were withdrawn unlike any other state. Here again sentiment prevailed and Nehru accepted the suggestion, it was a clear case of lack of political, geo-strategic and even legal wisdom. Taking the case to the UN Security Council further compounded the problem. The advancement of the date of partition from 1 July, 1948 to 15 August, 1947 added fuel to fire because of inadequate preparation in respect of transfer of population and assets and the absence of a boundary till after the partition. [25]

Besides Pakistan's emotional attachment to Kashmir, its importance lies in the fact that it provides strategic depth to Pakistan, its rivers are its source of energy and irrigation system and most of all, the dispute over Kashmir represents the extension of the two-nation theory. This is in spite of the fact that while the partition of India was accepted the two-nation theory is flawed as events within Pakistan and the birth of Bangladesh proved.

The setting up of the emergency Administration under Abdullah was followed by installation of a popular Govt. under him on 17 March 1949. India taking the Kashmir dispute to the UN on 1 January, 1949 and UN resolution on Kashmir, elections to the state Constituent Assembly, Delhi Agreement of 1952 and abolition of hereditary monarchy in 1952, are events of great significance. These brought out on one hand the need for a democratic and secular set up within the overall umbrella of the Indian Constitution and secondly, the need for autonomy, which was viewed differently within Kashmir and outside. The problem also developed from the very beginning security overtones both for India and Pakistan. Predominantly Hindu reaction in Jammu to the Kashmiri rule in the shape of Praja Parished Agitation in 1952 (one constitution, one flag, one president for Kashmir and India) and support extended to it, possibly led to ambivalence in Abdullah's position about accession. According to S.Gopal, Nehru failed to isolate the communal nucleus of the agitation by supporting and establishing that the Sheikh Abdullah's Administration was secular broad minded and national.[26] Sheikh Abdullah's speech on Martyr's Day 13 July, 1953 in the presence of officials of US Embassy led to a cabinet upheaval and Sheikh's dismissal and arrest. During this short period the state achieved political goals of self-rule and elimination of monarchy, in the economic field agrarian reforms to restore land to the tillers after confiscation of Jagir without compensation, reforms in the field of education and establishment of the first university, greater share in administration by the Kashmiri Muslims and establishment of the Jammu & Kashmir Militia, with opportunity to Kashmiris for military training.

Sheikh Abdullah's urge to promote drastic political and economic reforms with little regard to its consequences or for the circumstances had its fallout. Sheikh Mohd Abdullah's controversial and dictatorial style of functioning was manifested in another field of democratic functioning, the electoral field. While the 1934 elections were a sequel to the movement in early thirties, articulating the demand for representative institutions. However, during the first elections to the state Constituent Assembly in 1951, the National Conference won a landslide victory, it won all the 75 Assembly seats with 73 of its members returning unopposed. The nomination of the Praja Parishad candidates was rejected. There is no doubt that in a fair election Praja Parishad would have won few sets and it would have made no difference to the fortunes of National Conference.[27] It would have strengthened the people's belief in the process. This was to set a trend in the manipulation of democratic process with adverse effect in later years.

Both the partition of India on independence and the events related to the accession of Jammu and Kashmir state have left a legacy of conflict of which Kashmir has become the centrepiece.

Integration and Estrangement

Bakshi Gulam Mohd, while maintaining a stance of autonomy but legally consolidated its ties with rest of the country. State Assembly ratified the state's accession to India on 6 February, 1954 and states new position was endorsed by the presidential order in May, 1954 observing the legalities of the Article 370. State constitution was adopted in November, 1956 and measures adopted to further strengthen state's ties with rest of the country, notably adoption of fundamental rights, extension of functions of supreme court, transfer of services to the union list, extension of authority of Auditor General, approval of state development programmes by the Planning Commission and financial allocation from the center and abolition of Customs barriers. In Jan. 1960 by a presidential order, jurisdiction of the supreme court and election commission were extended to J & K. A few days before Bakshi Gulam Mohd relinquished office in a memorandum sent to the Sadar-e-Riyasat, in October 1963, he asked for the designation of Sadar-e-Riyasat and the Prime Minister of the state be changed to that of Governor and Chief Minister.

Bakshi during his regime abolished Mujhawaza, compulsory procurement of food grain, introduced ration subsidy of up to 75%, removed monopoly of cooperatives which had became a symbol of tyranny and education was made free at all levels. He established Medical and Engineering Colleges at Srinagar, Agricultural Research Institute at Pampore and several other institutions. Employments in Industries went up and progress was recorded in the field of agriculture, horticulture and development of power. However, simultaneously, a regime of repression against opponents and corruption came into being. Due to excesses mainly but possibly also due to his championship of autonomy as some people suspect he was made to resign in 1963.

Birth of Plebiscite Front

Immediately after the arrest of Sheikh Abdullah a war council was formed to muster support for his cause, which was converted into Plebiscite Front, whose politics centered around opposition to the so called imposed system and main plank remained accession and self determination. The activities of the Plebiscite Front increased after the withdrawal of conspiracy case and the demands of self determination were voiced in foreign countries and in foreign media and resulted in detention of Sheikh Mohd Abdullah and Mirza Afzal Beg on return from Haj in May 1965. Kashmiri youth organized under banner of Al.Fatah and later JKLF also adopted the main stance of self-determination. This also brought together Sheikh and Awami Majlis Amal (Awami Action Committee) of late Mirwaiz Farookh on the common platform of self-determination in 1964 and their actions were in concert with each other till 1974. The period from the dismissal of Sheikh Abdullah till before the signing of the Indira–Sheikh Accord in 1975 also gave Pakistan the opportunity to ferment the anti-Indian feeling and meddle in Kashmir affairs. Provision of Rs.7.5 crores during this period to these elements is only a symbol of it.[28]

The holy relic agitation and its aftermath resulted in fresh initiatives on Kashmir, release of Sheikh Abdullah followed by his visit to Pakistan, resulted in all-round failure, when Sheikh's idea of confederation was rejected by Pakistan.[29] With Nehru's death, stance of subsequent Govt. hardened and rapport between Kashmiri leaders and national leaders broke down. Vide presidential order, articles 356 and 357 were made applicable to Kashmir. Along with constitutional integration, political integration of NC with the Congress took place in January, 1965. This was followed by adoption of the 6th Amendment Bill adopted by the state legislature in April, 1965 changing the nomenclature of Sadar-I-Riyasat and PM to Governor and Chief Minister, resulted in greater opposition to the Indian state and reinforcement of the sentiment of separation. This also possibly provided impetus to infiltration by Pak resulting in the 1965 conflict. With the death of Sadiq, Mr. Qasim, though his rival continued, with the same policies. His biggest challenge was to keep balance between the Congress and Sheikh's followers. He was keen to retrieve the situation and this helped in the second Kashmir Accord.

After the 1965 war parleys between the Centre and State Government continued resulting in peoples' convention in 1968. Sheikh while addressing the convention adopted a conciliatory tone and Shri Jaya Prakash who inaugurated the convention, stressed the need for stabilizing the accession of Kashmir and setting the problem within the constitutional framework of India. It is after the Indian victory over Pakistan in 1971 and signing of the Shimla agreement that Sheikh Abdullah again adopted a moderate tone saying: "our quarrel with Government of India is not about accession but about the quantum of autonomy".[30]

In the parliamentary elections in 1972, Plebiscite Front was banned and entry of its leaders in J & K was banned. After protracted talks over three years the six point Accord was signed in November 1974, making article 370 a permanent feature for the Constitution of India.

Unhealthy Electoral Experience

It was also during this period that the pattern set by Sheikh Abdulla in 1951 in the elections to the constitutional Assembly was repeated by his dissident successors in the legislative elections in 1957 (55% of votes polled) under the new constitution adopted in 1956. Party captured 68 seats of 75, with 41 unopposed including 5 from Jammu. Similar trends continued in the 1962, and 1967 elections under the Elections Commission of India. National Conference captured 70 of the 75 seats, 32 unopposed (63% of the votes polled). This was a systematic effort to eliminate political opposition and was adversely commented upon across the nation. In 1967 unopposed returns dropped from 32 to 22. Plebiscite Front gave a boycott call for the 1968 by-election. In Safakadal and Budgaon, 98% of voters abstained. The situation improved in 1972 elections, where Plebiscite front and Jamait-I-Islami put up candidates and later won 6 seats and uncontested returns dropped to 5.

The General Elections of 1977 were possibly the fairest, freely contested, with Janata Dal, formerly of the Plebiscite Front, and Congress in a fierce contest with NC. There were no unopposed returns, NC won 39 of the 42 seats in Kashmir Valley, 7 out of 32 in Jammu and both the seats in Ladakh. The election in 1983 were also sufficiently fair, in spite of the instigation to the contrary by the Congress and its central leadership. However, electoral process went into the lowest ebb in 1987. In some constituencies the margin of votes declared invalid was larger than the margin of winning by the National Conference candidates. This is acceptably regarded as the breaking point and resulted in boycott of Lok Sabha Election in 1989.

Balraj Puri, writing in the Economic and Political Weekly about the alliance observed that "The best way of making the border people disloyal to their country is to require them to prove their loyalty by the additional test of demonstrating their loyalty to the party at the centre[31] .The question that comes up is that are we following the British legacy of divide and rule.

The coming together of the Muslim United Front (MUF), a conglomeration of the opposition parties in Kashmir was a retort to the National Conference and Congress alliance to what was perceived to be primarily Kashmiri Muslim interest. But the rigging of elections denied them the legitimate constitutional outlet, led to violence and finally militancy, ground work for which had already been provided through the Jamait-i-Islami madarsa system. This also resulted in the youth turning away from the established leadership. This was a big price to pay for 10 to 15 seats that MUF would have won. This was followed by the boycott of 1989 Lok Sabha Elections by the militant elements and its resultant fallout turned it into a farce and further eroded the faith of the people in the legitimacy of the system, aggravated the feeling of alienation of the people and provided an impetus to militancy.

At this stage it will be pertinent to examine the effect of Farooq Abdullah's dismissal without giving him an opportunity to prove his majority was similar to Sheikh's in 1953 in as much as that a popular Kashmiri leader was removed in a partisan fashion. His return similarly on conditions of power sharing with the Congress again conveyed that the state's leadership will be dictated by the Centre, thereby eroding the hold of established leadership on the masses. This largely resulted in the intellectuals and youth gravitating towards MUF, impetus to which was provided by the communal riots of March, 1986, followed by persecution of the local youth by the state police, imposition of Governor's rule and return of Farooq Abdullah on Centre's terms imposed on the already disturbed and agitated Kashmiri mind. The situation was rife for Pakistani interference and to put her subversive design into play.

Geopolitical Dynamics

The state of Jammu and Kashmir (J & K) is a conglomeration of several diverse geopolitical entities carved out in the 19th Century. The origin goes back to 1820, when Maharaja Ranjit Singh made Gulab Singh, a Dogra Chieftain, Raja of Jammu and his brother Dyan Singh was granted the Jagir of Poonch. Gulab Singh extended his empire to Ladakh in 1830 and to Baltistan in 1840. The valley of Kashmir became a part of the state, when it was sold to the maharaja in 1846 for rupees seventy five lakhs by the British to recover the cost of the First Sikh war and a reward for Maharaja remaining neutral in the Anglo-Sikh wars, or as Lionel Trotter says in plainer English, as a reward for his secret desertion of a failing cause[32]. Poonch, though always a part of Jammu, became integral to it formally in 1936. The Gilgit agency, which was never firmly under its control was leased out to the British for 60 years in 1935. Chitral once under the suzerainty of J & K was made a separate state by the British in 1936.

The state of J & K is bounded by Sinkiang and Tibet in the North and East, by Afghanistan in the North-West and West, Pakistan in the West And South-West and states of Himachal Pradesh and Punjab in he south east and south. The central Asian Republics are its close neighbours. The total area of the state is 222, 236.2 Sq.km, of which 78,114 sq.kms is under illegal occupation of Pakistan and 5,180 Sq.Km in Shaksgam Valley was illegally ceded by Pakistan to China in 1963.The northern frontiers of the undivided state ran along the high Karakoram and associated ranges, which form the watershed between the Tarim basin (in Sinkiang) and Indus river in Jammu and Kashmir. Two major passes provide the main routes of ingress into the sub continent over the Karakoram range, in the east Karakoram and Haji Langar from Khotam and Kashgar (Kasha) on to Leh and then Srinagar. East of Karakoram pass the boundary is disputed and area is under Chinese Occupation. The Aksai Chin road built by the Chinese enters this area from Tibet and traverses Soda plains and Haji Langar before entering Xing jiang.

The western route or the Gilgit route is under Pakistan. From Kashghar (Kasha) it passes through Mintika – Khunjerab and Shinshal passes to Hunza – Gilgit and Rawal-pindi. The Karakoram highway follows this route. The northern territories of Gilgit and Hunza are directly administered by Pakistan and are not under Pakistan occupied Kashmir (P O K) administration.

Both the Eastern and Western routes provide major avenues of ingress to the Chinese. We have a tenuous hold in the Shyok and Nubra Valleys in Turtok, Siachen and in the area of Karakoram pass. The alignment of the line of control itself is disputed between India and Pakistan in the Siachen area.

For centuries, the Chinese, the Moghuls, the Afghans, British and Russians have displayed interest in the area and maneuvered for position of advantage in the area. Chinese interest in the northern area is direct, therefore indirectly in J and K. Pakistan considers southern areas in POK vital as these provide it much wanted strategic depth. Her interest in Kashmir geo-politically is an extension of the same.

Topography[33]

The main Himalayan range running in a north westerly direction forms the watershed between the catchment areas of Chenab and Jhelum on one side and the Indus on the other. In the east it separates Lahul in Himachal Pradesh (HP) from Rupshu in South-East Ladakh and in the west it separates Kishtwar and Kashmir Valley from Ladakh and Baltistan. The main passes East to West are Baralacha pass (4890 meters) on Leh-Manali route, Umasi La 5294 meters) from Kishtwar to Zaskar valley Chillung (4401 meters) which leads to the desolate watershed between the head waters of Zashar and Suru rivers in Ladakh, the Zojila (3529 meters) on the great caravan route and present national highway between Srinagar and Leh and the Kamri and Burzil passes (4198 meters) are on the route from Srinagar to Gilgit. The mighty range ends on the massive massif of Nanga Parbat (8126 meters) but a spur continues South-west till it reaches the South bank of Jhelum river near Muzaffarbad, where it faces the Pir Panjal range across the Jhelum gorge.

The great Himalayan range near the western border of spiti throws South – the Pir Panjal range, which runs parallel to and west of the parent Himalayan range for 480 kms up to Baramula and Uri and the Jhelum Gorge only Chenab river cuts through it near Kishtwar. The eastern half of the Pir Panjal divides the drainage of Chenab from those of Beas and Ravi rivers. It separates Lahul from Kulu in the East and Kishtwar and Paden from Chamba in the West. It forms the southern wall of the Kashmir valley, separating it from Jammu and other outer hills of Akhnur, Kolti, Mirpur, Bhimber, Naushara, Rajauri and Poonch. The average height of the range is 4572 meters and the main passes are Rohtang pass (3978 meters) joining Kulu to Lahul, Banihal (2743) carrying main NH from Jammu to Srinagar, the Pir Panjal Pass (3494 meters) from Rajouri to the valley, Nilkanta Pass (3636 meters) from Poonch to Gulmarg and a number of minor passes suitable for foot and animal traffic.

Near Zojila, from the main Himalayan range, two sub ranges branch off, one running south separating the Chenab drainage from Jhelum forming the eastern wall of the Kashmir Valley. On nearing Chenab near Kishtwar, this turns to the west and joins up the Pir Panjal range near Banihal. Its higher heights are 4572 meters with few difficult passes (over 3333 meters) providing precarious access from the valley to Kishtwar. The prominent heights of Kolahoi (5425 meters) and Mahadeo (3966 meters) located on a prominent major Southern spur near Amarnath Cave are visible from the Valley. This spur formed the Southern wall of the Sind Valley.

The second major spur from Zojila runs west, separating the main valley of the main Kishen Ganga river from the Kashmir Valley. The range is crossed over Rajdiangan Pass (3638 meters) on the Srinagar – Gilgit route and it continues along the left bank of Kishanganga river and then turning south reaching Jhelum river near Uri. The southern extension is also known as the Kazinag mountains, home of rare Markhor goats. This range forms the western wall of the Kashmir valley. Beyond the great Himalayan range lie Ladakh and Baltistan.

In the North and Parallel to the Himalayan range is the Zaskar range, with an average height over 6000 meters. The area between Zaskar and the Himalayan ranges is desolate and drained by snow fed streams, which form the Zaskar river, which joins Indus river just west of Leh. There are grazing routes across Zaskar range joining Leh with Kulu and Shimla. Indus runs parallel to Zaskar ranges and Leh, Kargil and Skardu are located in the valleys of its tributaries. Leh had been the focal point of caravan routes to Yarkand, Lhasa, Srinagar, Gilgit and Shimla. To the North of the Indus Valley runs the Ladakh range, separating it from the Shyok Valley. Shyok river falls into Indus north of Skardu in the gap between the Ladakh and Haramosh range of Karakoram range. North of Shyok is the Karakoram range, culminating into the mighty glaciers of Baltoro and Siachen, with peaks above 7620 meters including the second highest peak K2 (8610 meters). Either side of these glaciers run the caravan routes from Leh to Yarkand over Karakoram pass 5575 meters and Gilgit to Kashgar via Mintaka pass (4709 meters).

These mountain ranges divide the state into clear geographical regions of Jammu and the outer hills, the Kashmir Valley and the high mountain regions of the North. Jammu province lies between Punjab border and the Pir Panjal range, which consists of the plains area and the outer hills. The plains average height is 366 meters and outer hills rise from 610 to 1220 meters in ridge lines parallel to Pir Panjal range, sloping up from South to North.

The valley of Kashmir to 135 Kms. in length and 30 to 40 Kms. in width, with Jhelum river running in a South-Westerly direction through Wullar Lake, towards Baramula, Uri, Muzaffrabad and then into West Punjab (Pakistan). The Northern region is separated from the Kashmir Valley by the great Himalayan range. The western region constitutes the Gilgit agency.

Communications

Prior to 1947, the state of Jammu and Kashmir was mainly dependent on West Punjab (now in Pakistan) for its economic needs and was linked with it by fairly developed roads . Srinagar was connected by an all weather road which ran along the Southern bank of Jhelum up to Domel then along the Eastern Bank up to Kohala Bridge, where it entered the state of J & K, then onto Rawalpindi. The road from Wah through Abottabad also converged at Domel, this was a better and preferred road as the hill section of the Rawalpindi road on either side of Murree had a number of hair pin bends was prone to landslides. In the South Jammu was connected by the major road from Wazirabad on GT road through Suchetgarh, Rambirsingpura to Jammu and then to Srinagar. Jammu-Srinagar portion remained closed during winters due to heavy snow on Banihal Pass, In 1955, it was made on all weather roads by boring the Banihal tunnel. The only link from India was 112 km long fair weather road from Pathankot in Gurdaspur Distt, which had been given to India in the Radcliffe award, through Kathua, Samba and then to Jammu. There was no bridge over Ravi river and over many of its streams and tributaries which had to be crossed on a ferry. Inspite of communal disturbances due to the partition and Pakistani interference this road was improved and Ravi river and the many streams were bridged by the summer of 1948 and it became the vital life line for J and K not only for induction and maintenance of troops but to support J and K logistically.

From Srinagar three motorable roads in good condition connected the holiday resorts of Gulmarg, Bandipur on Wular Lake and Pahalgam in the Lidder Valley. Jammu was connected to Poonch by a fair weather road via Aknoor on the bank of Chenab River, Naushera, Jhangar and Kolli, at places the road was only jeepable. A fair weather lateral road connected Poonch with Uri through the Hajipir pass (2638 meters). Srinagar was also connected to Leh and Gilgit by tracks which were not motorable but strategically very important. The route from Srinagar entered the valley of Sind River, climbed to 3528 meters crossed the great Himalayan Range at Zojila, then descending to Kargil through Dras and beyond Kargil crossed over at Fotu La at 4094 meters travelled along the Indus River to Leh, a total distance of 389 Km. From Leh one route continued North through Shyok Valley, crossed Karakoram Pass at 5575 meters and then along Yarkand stream up to Yarkand town, a distance of 771 km. Another route went to east along Indus River to Gartok and Lhasa in Tibet. These were the routes used by central Asian Caravans for trade with China and Tibet. The route from Srinagar to Gilgit was a level and motorable stretch up to Bandipur, then it climbs up to Rajdiangar (Rajdhani) pass 3638 meters on the water shed between Jhelum and Kishanganga, with a superb view of Nanga Parbart. The track descends into the valley of Kishanganga, past the meadows of Gurais and crossing over to the right bank climbs the steep slopes of the main Himalayan range, it bifurcates, one going across the range Kamri Pass (4075 meters) and the other across Burzil Pass (4198 meters) . Both the routes join up on the far side descending into the Astor River gorge, cross the stream at Ranghat, (only 1158 meters above sea level) pass through Bunji, cross Indus River over a frail bridge, up to Gilgit River till reaching Gilgit. The total distance is 365 Kms and was vital to move troops and supplies for the garrisons in the Gilgit area. Gilgit was not only the District Headquarter of a turbulent area, it was also connected to Kashghar in Sinkiang (Xinjiang) by the Caravan route, which went up the gorge of Hunza River and crossed the Karakoram at the Mintaka pass 4709 meters. Gilgit was connected by a motorable road to Abbotabad in Pakistan via Chilas. Gilgit was also connected to Ladakh by a track along the Indus River up to Skardu, where it split into two, The northern track joined the Leh-Yarkand route beyond the Shyok Valley and the Southern track joined the Srinagar – Leh route at Kargil.

Ladakh was also connected to India by a very difficult and long route, south of Leh till it entered the Lahul and Spiti Valley; after crossing Bara Lacha LA 6094 meters and Manali Pass 3826 metres, it joined the Pathankot-Manali Road in Kangra District of Himachal Pradesh. India later constructed a motorable road along the same alignment, it remains snow bound during winters.

In 1947, the only rail link available was from Sialkot (in Pakistan) to Jammu. Since then rail links from Pathankot to Jammu have been extended and planned to extend to the Kashmir Valley via Udhampur. The air strips at Srinagar and Jammu were undeveloped and only used by the Maharaja. Inspite of primitive facilities air strip at Srinagar was used for induction of troops in October, 1947. These have been developed into all weather commercial airfields. In addition an operational airfield has been constructed at Awantipur near Srinagar. The airstrip at Leh has been developed to take on most commercial aircrafts. These have provided a tremendous boost to tourist and domestic air traffic. In addition air strips at Poonch and Kargil are being developed for emergency use.

The lack of communications between India and J and K and its total dependence on West Punjab were fully exploited by Pakistan to pressure Maharaja to accede to Pakistan but events of October, 1947 exposed Pakistan's design resulting in J and K acceding to India.

Geo-political Realities After Independence

The British foreign policy aimed at securing India's territorial integrity by ensuring that the potential enemies were kept away from the border. In the West it was to ensure that Russia did not come any where near the borders. For this purpose they ensured a neutral Afghanistan as a buffer between India and Russia. The success of the policy can be gauged by the fact that in the Anglo-Russian convention of 1907, Russia recognized that Afghanistan was not within the sphere of Russian influence. Russia also agreed to conduct its relations with Afghanistan through the Govt. of India. Similarly, in the North the British Govt. ensured that no foreign influence operated in Tibet. The weakness of the Imperial Chinese Govt. also resulted in the Tibetan Govt. to pursue an independent policy. To counter the Russian influence in Tibet and to ensure that Tibet did not follow too independent a policy, military mission was sent to Tibet under colonel Sir Francis Younghusband under Lord Gurzon's orders resulting in the Treaty of Lhasa in 1904. Great Britain was given complete control of the foreign policy of Tibet. No part of the Territory was to be given to any other country and no concessions were to be given to any other foreign power in the form of roads, railways and telegraph.

Kashmir occupied a central place in British strategic policy right up to the transfer of power, so much so that it prompted one historian to say that everything that happened in the state of Jammu and Kashmir between 1846 and 1947 was in some way a product of this strategic policy"[34]. This perception was adopted both by India and Pakistan the successor states as is evident by the fact that Pandit Nehru in his cable to the British Prime Minister Clement Attlee on 25th October, 1947 explaining the rendering of military assistance to J and K stressed the fact that "Kashmir's Northern frontiers run in common with those of Afghanistan, USSR and China. "Security of Kashmir is vital for security of India"[35]. Similarly, Liaquat Ali Khan, the Pakistani Prime Minister, in his radio broadcast termed the accession of the state of Jammu and Kashmir to India a "threat to the security of Pakistan". With the Partition of the country J and K itself became of greater strategic value. Kashmir is essential for defence of Ladakh and Northern borders against China.

The cold war between USA and USSR impinged on Indo-Pak confrontation over Jammu and Kashmir, resulting in Pakistan joining west sponsored alliances of the 1950 and USA tilt towards it as the barrier against Soviet expansion in the region. India while remaining formally non-aligned, established strategic & economic relationship with USSR. Both shared disputed borders with China and thus had common strategic interests. These resulted in Pakistan acquiring large quantities of western arms and diplomatic support in UN and India countering it with USSR support and arms purchases from her.

The Chinese take over of Tibet in 1950 deprived India of the traditional and vital buffer in the North and added to the strategic pressure on Kashmir. The invasion used routes from Xinjiang through Aksai Chin to Tibet. Chinese interest in Jammu and Kashmir emerged fully after the Tibetan rebellion of 1959 and in the border war of 1962, it annexed

Aksai Chin. China signed Sino-Pak Border Agreement in 1963, which signaled acceptance of Pakistan position that Jammu and Kashmir is a disputed territory. Under the agreement Pakistan relinquished claim over 1500 sq. miles of its territory (not under its actual control) and Chinese ceded to Pakistan 750 Sq. miles including access to K2 actually administered by China[36]. The growing nexus resulted in the building of the strategic Karakoram Highway. During the cold war China, also saw this relationship useful to counter USSR influence and helped in Afghan resistance in Afghanistan. China recognized India's independent foreign policy post-1971 and the 1980's saw improvement of relations and Chinese terming the Jammu and Kashmir dispute a bilateral one. However in the post-cold war period Pakistan is likely to continue as an ally of China as is proved by her assistance in the nuclear and missile fields to counter perceived Indian designs in South Asia.

Independence was followed by major changes in independent India's boundaries. In the West, the Radcliffe boundary award resulted in division of Punjab, the boundary ran through the desert of Rajasthan and resulted in the division of the Rann of Kutch. The natural barrier of mountains disappeared, instead it passed through the densely populated areas in Punjab, desert and saline swarms of Kutch.. In the East, we got three international borders, one between West Bengal and East Pakistan (now Bangladesh) running through densely populated areas, second between Meghalaya, Assam and Tripura and East Pakistan (now Bangladesh) and the third a hilly jungle border with Burma. The new borders had no natural geographical barriers and involved defence or guarding rigorously of thousands of miles of border territory. Worst of all, it broke centuries of relationship amongst people, who were socially, culturally and economically one. The net result was complex security problems due to immigrations triggered by communal and ethnic tensions and economic pressure. The new artificial division has been most prone to smuggling, infiltration and subversion. The total length of the boundary of approximately 15,000 Kms. (9,315 miles) is live with some or the other type of tension and violence.

The Northern borders with China, inspite of improvement in relations in the last two decades continues to be a potential source of tension due to their claim of 32,300 Sq miles in Arunachal Pradesh and 12,000 Sq. miles in Ladakh and few disputed points in the central sector. The borders with Pakistan have been a source of tension and physical belligerence of Pakistan in Punjab and now Kashmir has held Indo Pak relations in all fields hostage to it.

Major Inferences

Geographically, the mountains compartmentalize Jammu and Kashmir into distinct regions with separate identities. The plains sector of Jammu in the south is a maze of rolling plains with swift following rivers with its outer hills. In the North these hills rise to meet the Pir Panjal range, which separates Jammu from the Valley of Kashmir, is rugged and remains snow bound for half the year. The Kashmir Valley is surrounded by high mountains of the great Himalayan range in the North and Pir Panjal range from the South and West, which have kept it isolated from out side influences. Ladakh is separated in small compartments by high ranges. The Ladakh range forms the water shed between Indus and Shyok Valleys and several ranges in the North divide Ladakh into small in accessible pockets.

Jammu is a Hindu majority area with some pockets of mixed population and pockets of Muslim majority areas in the Western and North-Eastern parts. The valley of Kashmir is a 90 per cent Muslim majority area, with a distinct Kashmiri dominated identity and culturally different from other areas of Jammu and Kashmir. The population of Ladakh is Buddhist and Shia Muslims are ethnically closer to Tibet. Kargil and Suru valley have a Shia majority and the Buddhist majority is generally confined to upper Indus Valley. The people of Hunza and Gilgit area overwhelmingly Shia Muslims belonging to the twelve Shia seat.

Several natural barriers in Jammu and Kashmir containing different ethnic and religious groups inhabit integration. The state is an assorted assembly of diverse regions with inherent tendency of falling apart. The terrain and geography of Jammu and Kashmir militates against a united independent state due to diverse cultural, ethnic and socio-political milieu of various regions accentuated by virtual partition of the state in 1949. Lord Bird Wood in his book, "Two Nations and Kashmir", aptly notes, the delimitation of a line on a map of Central Asia, which on political considerations enclosed a completely artificial area, a geographical monstrosity, which then assumed the name of the land of Jhelum Valley "Kashmir". The Kashmir Valley cannot geographically sustain itself without surface routes from India or Pakistan. But the bigger threat to Kashmiris will always be from the West due to social and cultural submergence as has been historically proved.

The cease fire line (CFL) and later Line of Control (LoC) created through arrangements with Pakistan does not follow well defined geographical features and its vagueness in certain sensitive areas (Siachin) leads to varied interpretations and is a source of continuous tension, which heightens with each India and Pakistan-confrontation. Similarly,

Line of Actual Control (LAC) in Aksai chin area is the second front against China in Jammu and Kashmir.

The creation of POK Shrank the Western borders of J and K and provided Pakistan the much needed strategic depth to its heartland. The artificial frontier of the LC created by the Karachi Agreement of 1949 has created a strategic threat in perpetuity by a hostile Pakistan in collusion with a belligerent China in J and K to the disadvantage of India.

The geo-strategic importance of the state of Jammu and Kashmir and its three sub-regions in the subcontinent is obvious as besides Pakistan, China has major strategic interests, particularly in Ladakh and Northern areas. The Siachen problem needs to be viewed in this overall context. Ladakh's logistical nightmare dictates that the Aksai chin problem be resolved with China on priority.

REFERENCES

1. Gul Mohd Wani and Nasir A Naqash, *Reflections on Kashmir Politics*, Ashish Publishing House, New Delhi, 1993, p. 10-11.
2. Naser A Naqash and GM Shah, *Kashmir crisis to crisis*, APH publishing corporation, New Delhi, 1997, p. 20.
3. *Ibid*, p. 22.
4. n1, p. 14.
5. *Ibid*, p. 10
6. *Ibid*, p. 15
7. Walter Lawrence, Valley of Kashmir, p. 189 *Encyclopaedia Britannica*, Vol. XIII (1974), p. 290.
8. M Ishaq Khan, *Perspectives on Kashmir*, 1983, Srinagar Gulshan Pub, 1983, p. 47.
9. n1, p. 17.
10. n7, p. 197.
11. n2, p. 34.
12. *Ibid*, p. 35.
13. T Biscoe, *Kashmir Under Shade and Light*, London, 1922, p. 108
14. M.S.Pampori, *Kashmir in Chains*. Srinagar Pampori Publications, 1992, p. 37.
15. *Ibid*, p. 58.
16. Lawrence, *The Valley of Kashmir*, London OUP, 1985, p. 396.
17. P.N.Bazaz, *A History of Struggle of Freedom in Kashmir*, p. 140.
18. Interview with Associated Press – 15 March, 1929. As quoted on, p. 49, n2.
19. n7, p. 180.
20. M.J. Akbar, *Kashmir- Behind the Vale*, p. 87.
21. M.J. Akbar, *India-The Siege Within*, Penguin, 1985, pp. 227-228.
22. *The Story of Kashmir, Yesterday and Today*, Vol. III, Deep and Deep Publications, New Delhi, 1995, p. 106.

23. Mani Shankar Aiyar, *Pakistan Papers* (New Delhi: UPSPD, 1994, pp. 94-98.
24. Raju GC Thomas, *Perspectives on Kashmir*, p. 19.
25. Article on Mountbatten, *The Times of India*, 26 June 1994.
26. S.Gopal, *Jawahar Lal Nehru – A Biography*, p. 123 Delhi Oxford University Press, 1979 Vol–2.
27. Z.M. Quraishi, *Elections and State Politics in India: A Case Study of Kashmir*, p. 48.
28. IE Report 26 June 1976.
29. Mohd Ayub Khan, *Friends Not Masters*, London OUP, 1967.
30. *London Times*, 10 March 1972. As quoted in Gul Mohd Wani, *Kashmir Politics – Problems and Prospects,* Ashish Publishing House, New Delhi, 1993, p. 76.
31. Quoted by Iqbal Masood in *Indian Express* Magazine, 17 September 1989.
32. Trotter, British Empire, p. 72 as quoted in Schofield, Victoria, *Kashmir in Cross Fire*, Viva Books, 1997.
33. Extracted from the official history of 1947-48 war with Pakistan.
34. Lamb, *Kashmir: A Disputed Legacy* – 1946-1990, p. 17.
35. White Paper on Jammu and Kashmir, pp. 45–46.
36. Robert Warsing, *Pakistan Security under Zia*, 1977-1988, p. 147.

6

Multiplex Dimensions of Turmoil

Geography like history has played an important role in preserving the Kashmiri identity. Unless compelled by force of circumstances, a Kashmiri is reluctant to move out of the valley even today as in the past. While this has helped the Kashmiris in preserving their culture and identity, at the same time it has perpetuated a sense of isolation, which has been exploited by the local elite and has remained a barrier in coping with ever expanding outside influences. The mountain ranges as we have examined earlier, divide the state into distinct geographical regions of Jammu, the Kashmir Valley and high mountain regions of the North and North-East (Ladakh including Kargil is part of this region), which socially, culturally, ethnically and religion-wise are divergent and mitigate against inter-action.

Discussion of the historic perspective and events of the contemporary period has brought into sharp focus the major factors of political ineptness and changes in the geo-strategic environment after partition and its impact on Indo-Pak relations with Kashmir as the centre point. Islamic resurgence in Afghanistan and Islamisation of Pakistan has resulted in emergence of Muslim fundamentalism, which has had its fallout in Jammu and Kashmir. Islamisation of Pakistan under Zia-ul-haq provided both the opportunity and resources to Pakistan to further their subversive designs in Kashmir.

Political ineptness in dealing with Jammu and Kashmir has resulted in Kashmiris feeling isolated from the national mainstream and within the state itself. Central Govt's confrontationist and overbearing stance towards National Conference resulted in Sheikh Abdulla and later Farooq Abdulla adopting a protectionist policy towards their main constituency in the Kashmir Valley, which further accentuated the Kashmiri isolation.

This isolation over a prolonged period turned into alienation and provided fertile ground for Muslim fundamentalism to take roots and grow. Central Govt.'s tolerance and connivance with corruption for short term political gains resulted in denial of fruits of economic development to the people, made them wary of their own leaders and suspicious of Indian States concern for the them added to the people's sense of alienation.

It will therefore be valid to say that the genesis of the turmoil and current insurgency is founded on the historic and contemporary experience of the people of Kashmir and their interaction or lack of it with people of other regions of the state and with outside the state which had had a fall out in the political, socio-economic and religious fields, with internal and external dimensions. The external dimensions extend beyond Indo-Pak bilateralism and are the result of the geo-political dynamics of the region interacting with the emerging geo-strategic realities. Of these, Islamisation of the region with its militant posture represents its major and all prevailing dimension.

Islamic Resurgence and Fundamentalism

Islamic fundamentalism is a world wide phenomenon and the Western Christian World's views are influenced by its historic perspective of the 17th and 18th century, when the encounter was between the Europeans and the Muslims (the Ottoman Empire). Europe was quite satisfied when the struggle developed into an intra-Islamic fight between the Wahabi Arabs and the Ottoman Turks during the end of 18th and beginning of 19th century. The Western powers have dealt with Islamic regimes guided by the twin factors of convergent strategic interests and the division between the fundamentalist and the moderate Islamists. Lawrence of Arabia mobilised the Arabs to defeat the Ottoman Turks. During the cold war, USA and the West developed alliances with Muslim countries to contain USSR, which was not confined to moderate Islamic countries alone as in the case of alliance with Saudi Arabia (Fountainhead of Wahhabism) and enemy of Shiaite Iran. Nearer at home USA supported and promoted Afghan militancy to oppose Soviet expansion into Afghanistan and to secure western economic and military interests in the Gulf region. The west wants allies in the Muslim world to further its strategic interests and Muslim countries want arms or money or both. The danger of Muslim fundamentalism is warded off and diverted from the west by alliances or by maintaining intra-Islamic fault lines and divisions. However it has spread into Central, South and South-Eastern and Eastern Asia and poses a threat to the states in the region and is of concern to them.

Historically and geographically Afghanistan has been the gateway for spread of Islam in the South Asia subcontinent. Arab armies conquered Sind as far back as 712 but it was only in the 10th century when Islam had been established in Afghanistan that the Muslim invasions of Jammu

& Kashmir and India began.[1] The Afghans fought and defeated the British in wars, which in their perception had both a national and religious character. Similarly, the Russian expansion in Central Asia was viewed as the work of Kafirs (Infidels).[2] Islamic volatility, which existed in the Middle East has manifested in Iran, Afghanistan and in the Indian subcontinent in the recent past. It has also spread into Xinjiang in China and in Indonesia, Malaysia and Philippines in South-East Asia.

Wahhabism has its roots in the Arab movement and was inspired by the achievements of Mohammad. In 1806, Wahabi forces led by Mohammad-al-Saud occupied Mecca and ordered that public prayers be read in his name instead of that of the Ootaman Sultan. Its present day appeal is for Islamic solidarity rather than Arab solidarity[3]. It is because of this orientation that it opposes Communism, Zionism, Socialism (Egypt) and Sufism (J & K)[4]. Wahhabism is the manifestation of militant Islam; it has developed strong roots in Pakistan and was the driving force of the Afghan Talibans. Pakistan in conjunction with Saudi Arabia since 1980 has emerged as the main propagator of militant Islam into the region, in Afghanistan, Jammu & Kashmir, Xinjiang and Central and South East-Asia. It has influence from Chechniya to as far as Philippines[5]. It is in contention with Shiaite orthodoxy in Iran and has its fall out in the internal politics of Pakistan and other South-Asian countries.

Till 1970, Afghanistan appeared to Pakistan as a political irritant and a resentful neighbour due to the Pusthun movement. To the Afghan, tribal and ethnic loyalties mattered more than the common religious bonds. In 1974, Gulbuddin Hekmatyar and other leaders of Afghanistan took shelter in Pakistan to escape persecution at the hands of the leftist regime. Pakistan helped them to raise an army of young dissident Pusthuns for covert operations against the communist regime in Afghanistan. These leaders grew to be fire-brand fundamentalists after adopting the Pan-Islamic policy propagated by Pakistan. This relationship between Pakistan and Afghan Mujahideen was further cemented by the Russian intervention in Afghanistan. Eventually, Pakistan successfully transformed the Afghan nationalistic movement against communism into a Jehad against the Godless Communists. This also provided Pakistan the opportunity to acquire the status of a frontline Islamic state, interfere in internal affairs of Afghanistan with apparent legitimacy and carve out an area of influence to compensate for the loss of East Pakistan in 1971. Pakistan exploited radicalisation of Afghan politics to siphon off large quantity of arms and money for its design in Jammu & Kashmir and to covertly train Afghan and Kashmir terrorist groups.[6] The American and Pakistani strategic interests coincided at this point of time and Pakistan became the main conduit for supply of arms for Afghan resistance. Saudi

Arabia used this opportunity to promote Wahabism and a rigid Sunni-Wahabi code was being propagated with official patronage much to the dismay of Shias of Afghanistan, Pakistan and their Iranian supporters.

Radical Islamic groups in Pakistan and Afghanistan are obsessed by the belief that Islamic tenets as interpreted by them must prevail. They justify the use of force against Muslim states which do not follow their interpretation of Shariah and the Quran. Their aim is to impose rigid Wahabi traditions in Muslims of South and Central Asian region. To them western, secular and democratic norms are an enigma and they have generated ethnic and sectarian violence to impose their will. Pakistan since its inception has been the supporter of Pan Islamic movement. The rationale of the Pakistani State is an Islamic consensus that is expected to transcend geographical and ethnic divisions. The Islamic dimension in Pakistan has been all prevailing in the context of Indo-Pakistan situation by equating India-Pakistan to Hindu-Muslim in all its political, cultural, diplomatic and military encounters with India. Strategic considerations and religions' affinities has enabled Pakistan political and military class to exploit internal conflicts within India to maintain its own domestic cohesion. Pakistan has always visualised religion as a means to enlarge its strategic arena to Central Asia, Afghanistan and Iran, Feroze Khan Noon, spoke of such a confederation as far back as 1958.

Islamisation of West Asian variety came to Pakistan during Bhutto's tenure even before the Iranian revolution and the visit of Gaddafi followed by organization of Islamic conference during which Bhutto asked King Faisal to lead the prayers at the Badshahi Masjid were its pre-runner. This gave opportunity to large numbers of Pakistanis to find jobs in oil kingdoms. Along with prosperity it brought Islam through the petro-dollars. This was followed by Ikhwan-ul-Muslmeen (Muslim Brotherhood) youth squads on fraternal visits to conventions organised by youth wing of Jamaat-i-Islami. Then came Afghanistan when Bhutto offered protection to Islamic parties after Daoud's Coup of 1973, well before the 1978 revolution. The role played by Gulbuddin Hekmatyar in the Islamic insurgency is substantial. Bhutto also saw in it great opportunity to shift its historic orientation to West Asia from South Asia, with the twin aims of a place in the Islamic world and to foster its nuclear ambitions (Islamic Bomb) against India. Bhutto's view was that he was sent to the gallows for having defied US imperialism and Israeli Zionism on the nuclear issue. Zia's Islamic orientation was out of conviction based on conservative Islam that he had always practiced. Zia saw the Afghan struggle as an opportunity to take over the Islamic struggle but to do so Islamisation of Pakistan was essential. In this he found willing partners in the Islamic parties and young Pakistanis organised by them into youth squads and Islamic indoctrination of the Pakistani Army. A defeated Pakistani Army felt rejuvinated by the success it brought about in Afghanistan and looked toward Kashmir and other areas in the neighbourhood supported and goaded by the Islamist Parties as it furthered their aims of Islamisation and fundamentalism. Ironically, it was the defeat by India in 1971 that made Pakistan to look beyond its boundaries and find its Islamic moorings in West Asia. This also influenced the strategic thinking of Pakistan as Islamisation provided it greater territorial depth and geopolitical opportunities. Bhutto and Zia viewed Pakistan's nuclear programme in this context as well in the Indian context.

Islamisation of Pakistan was part of Pakistan Muslim League's (PML) election agenda. After the nuclear tests the Islamisation of Pakistan was announced by Nawaz Sharif in August 1998 due to pressure of Islamist parties after the USA missile attack on South Sudan and Afghanistan.[7]

The1979 Islamic revolution in Iran and later Jehad in Afghanistan against the Soviet occupation (1979-89) opened the flood gates of money and arms for Pakistan from the USA and Saudi Arabia due to fear of Soviet expansion and Iranian type of anti-monarchy and anti-West radical Islam. It led to greater radical Islamisation as Pakistan became the launch pad of various militant Islamic groups fighting in Afghanistan. Activists came in not only from Afghanistan, but also from the Arab world as far as Egypt, Sudan and Algeria and Muslims settled in the west. Some of the activists were already fighting their own Govts whom they saw as stooges of the West. Islamic parties in Pakistan—Jamaat-l-Islamic, Jamat-i-ulama-i-Islam and Jamaat-i-ulama-Pakistan—joined the Jehad and established their own Madarssas and militant groups but some of these were based on sectarian affiliation. Inflow of arms combined with sectarian militancy resulted in internal conflicts between Shias and Sunnis and amongst Sunnis between Deobandis and Barelvis. Islam also became a ploy to support the military regime, whose legitimacy was being challenged. Linked to the Islamisation project was Kashmir and a free democratic Kashmir did not fit into the scheme of things. This resulted in marginalization of nationalists (JKLF) and cultivation of radical JEI and HM. After the Mujahideen's victory in Afghanistan, Pakistan turned full attention to Kashmir and Pakistani Jehadis started playing a key role in Kashmir. However, with increasing criticism by the West of Pakistani establishment's role in sponsoring terrorism an increasing privitisation of Jehad took place. That the Pakistani Jehadis were playing a key role in Kashmir is well brought out by the fact that in the year 2000 it was estimated that there were 2750 pro-Pakistan Islamist militants in Kashmir, the nationalists mainly represented by JKLF had only 60. While Pakistan based Jehadi organizations claim to be independent of the Pakistani state but in fact they are totally dependent on it for survival and patronage. Most of the groups have very small Kashmiri component and virtually none at the leadership level. One of the main reasons for marginalization of Kashmiris is due to their reluctance to carry out large scale killing of Hindus to reduce their population and create a communal divide. Whereas Pakistani Islamic groups have no such compulsion and it is a part of their agenda. The part played by the Jehadi organizations in Pakistan is of vital concern to us and needs examination.

The most prominent of the Pakistani Islamic group operating in Pakistan are Harkut-ul-Ansar also known as Harkut-ul-Jehad-i-Islami, Jaish-e-Mohammed, Al Jehad, Al Badr, Jammait-ul-Mujahideen and the most prominent and important of all Lashkar-e-Toiba (LET). LET is closely linked with the Pakistani establishment and JEI of Pakistan. LET is the military wing of Markaz Da'awat-ul-Irshad set up in 1986 by professors Hafiz Muhammad Sayeed and Zafar Iqbal. Its headquarters is located at Muridke 30 km from Lahore. It is affiliated to Salafi or Ahl-i-Hidith school and apposed to Sufism. It is closely linked to Pakistani establishment, particularly ISI, originally designed to serve the Afghan Jehad. It established its training centres at Jaji in Patkia and in Kurnar province. As Markaz's activities grew it divided into two sections of Islamic education and Jehadic. The Jehadic and militant wing was named as LET, which established centres in Pakistan and Afghanistan. Militants trained by LET played a key role in Afghanistan. It first entered Kashmir in 1990 and its presence has enlarged since 1995. LET has aimed to dominate the border districts of Rajourie, Poonch and Doda. It has indulged in mass killings of Hindus in isolated villages to cause their exodus and thus create Muslim majority areas, which they feel Kashmiri militants are incapable of. Islamic groups Harkut-ul-Mujahideen, Tehrik-i-Jehad, Al Badr along with LET were part of the kargil intrusions. When forced to withdraw they spread into the entire state of Jammu and Kashmir. Its cadre specializes in Fidai (suicide) missions, the attack on Badamibagh cantonment in Srinagar was by them. Jehad launched by LET is not confined to Jammu and Kashmir but is spreading to the rest of India.

The theme of armed Jehad is central to Markaz's ideological framework. Like other Islamist groups Markaz sees Islam as a perfect all embracing system and way of life and social and personal life is to be governed by the Shariat laws. For establishment of an Islamic system an Islamic state is essential. It implies that the present division of Muslims into various states should be done away with. For Islamic call to reach all people an Islamic state must carry it to new lands. It will lead to conflict with other states and ideologies, which must be resolved diplomatically but if it fails then through an armed Jehad. Global Jehad vision of Markaz is presented as liberalization of suffering Muslims including from their own Western oriented elite. The biggest problem of Muslims according to Markaz is subjugation to the West, thus Jehad against the West and particularly the USA is justified. The eight specific objectives laid for the Jehad are:

(a) to end persecution and turmoil,
(b) to enforce the Islamic world order,
(c) to force the disbelievers to pay Jazia,
(d) to protect and shield the weak and the oppressed from oppression,
(e) to avenge the millions of Muslims who were and are being mercilessly slaughtered in various parts of the world,
(f) to punish those who have broken covenants made with the Muslims,
(g) to restore Muslim possession of the territories now occupied by non-believers, e.g., Spain, India, Jerusalem, Turkistan (within Xinjiang),
(h) to protect the Muslims continuously facing offensive from disbelievers[8].

Jehad is seen as the secret of Muslim power in the past when much of the known world was under Muslim rule. Markaz argues that when Muslims abandoned Jehad they began to degenerate. They argue that the present world situation warrants that all Muslims must be involved in Jehad one way or the other. The struggle in Kashmir is viewed as a war between two opposing ideologies of Islam and Kufr and not a territorial dispute or a clash of cultures. The roots of Kashmir problems are seen as the replacement of its Muslim rulers by the Sikhs and later by the Hindu Dogra ruler through British assistance. Since 1947 a reign of terror is seen to have been unleashed on Kashmiri Muslims. Hence the moral duty of all Muslims to wage Jehad against Hindu India. This represents radicalization of Kashmiri Jehad; such anti-Hindu or India rhetoric was not even a part of Gilani's discourse as we shall see later. According to Hafiz Mohammed Sayeed, Amir of Markaz, Jehad is not only about Kashmir it encompasses the whole of India. The disintegration of India followed by its take over by Pakistan and establishment of an Islamic state is justified by elaborate arguments that use the rhetoric of liberation[9].

The Islamic parties in Pakistan due to their limited electoral appeal are trying to increase their political base by lobbying for Islamic

Constitution and Shariah laws by fuelling Sunni-Shia social and political violence and recruitment of Islamic oriented youth into the Army and the Govt machinery. The Islamic parties winning 67 seats under the banner of Muthida Majlis-E-Amal (MMA) and a clear majority in the frontier provinces of Baluchistan and NWFP during the 2002 Oct. elections are a clear indication of their increasing influence. Religion in Pakistan has grown from a cultural plain to a political option with institutional and constitutional arrangements and a principle of diplomatic strategy in international relations. Militant Islam apart from its internal dimensions wants to exploit external frontiers in its neighborhood in the shape of revolutionary violence. With its orientation of ideological and religious fanaticism, it has transformed the internal institutions of the Govt. and military in Pakistan and externally it aims at an Islamic society in its neighborhood, which is evident by the association of Pakistan Military and intelligence agencies with Taliban in Afghanistan and various militant organisations in Jammu & Kashmir, Punjab and Islamic forces in central Asia. Islamic militancy is a political and military strategy which seeks to islamise domestic, political arrangements as well as external strategic relationships. The changes are revolutionary and pose a challenge to the institution of the state, to the principle of the rule of law and to the democratic process.

To understand the motivation of Islamic militant groups a brief on the Jamaat-i-Islami in South Asia and Ikhwan-ul-Muslmeen (Muslim Brotherhood) of Egypt is attached as annexure.

Pakistan has used religion based parties to raise militant groups, which were organised for terrorist and guerilla warfare in Bosnia, Jammu & Kashmir, Central Asia and Xinjiang. The support of religious war in Afghanistan and subversion and terrorism in Jammu & Kashmir became the two main ingredients of Pakistan Pan-Islamic foreign policy. Amongst the various militant groups inducted in Jammu & Kashmir Hizb-ul-Mujahideen (HM), Harkat-ul-Ansar (HUA) and Laskhar-e-Taiba (LET) are the most motivated and draw their cadres from Afghan veterans; these were more trusted than JKLF standing for Azadi as they were considered soft to deal with the enemy of God and infidels[10].

Most segments of Muslims in Central Asia and Jammu & Kashmir were not willing to accept rigid Wahabi codes and therefore a violent programme of coercion, intimidation and terror was launched in these areas. The resentment against it generated sectarian, ethnic and cultural violence and sowed the seeds of internal conflicts and political upheavals in the region. The ISI further stoked the fire by diverting sophisticated arms in large quantities to terrorist groups from Afghan resistance. The efforts to radicalise moderate Muslim population of India, Bangladesh and Central Asian Republics will continue. Terror is being used to further Wahabi dictates and promote Pak-Saudi Arab interests.

Religious upsurge in Kashmir

The Kashmiri independence movement has its roots in the popular uprising against the Dogra regime in the 1930's for a proper representation for Kashmiri Muslims. It succeeded primarily due to Sheikh Mohd Abdullah's charismatic leadership and Muslim Conference changing into All Jammu and Kashmir National Conference which widened its mass base so essential for a politico – social struggle. After 1947 due to a decline in Sheikh Abdullah's charisma, failure of the National Conference to meet people's aspirations and to safe guard the autonomy of the state, the Kashmiri struggle assumed the form of a liberation movement within. Disillusionment by Sheikh and other Kashmiri leaders' complicity with the Indian state, modern educated young Kashmiris voiced their anger in the shape of self-determination/plebiscite. They advocated an independent, secular and democratic state of Jammu and Kashmir based on the ideology of Kashmiriat. JKLF was in the forefront of this movement.

However, parallel to this nationalistic main stream, beginning in 1930's also saw the emergence of an Islamist movement, roots of which can be traced to the Ahl-i-Hadith reformist movement established in 1925. They see themselves as the inheritors of the legacy of prophet Mohammed but due to deep rooted Sufi traditions amongst the Kashmiri Muslims they failed to develop much of a following. It was only in 1941 when Sayed Abu Ala Maudoodi formed the JEI that seed for Islamisation were sowed[11]. The JEI constitution although based on Shariat but propagated democratic means of peaceful persuasion to achieve its goal. It confined its activities to influencing people through Islamic literature, publications, establishing libraries, organizing discussions and a network of Madarssas. It entered the political and electoral arena during the 1969 Panchayat elections, which were held on non-party basis as it felt remaining outside the electoral politics it will be rendered ineffective. JEI participated in successive state elections but failed to win an impressive number of seats both due to lack of enthusiasm for its agenda and large scale rigging by the government of the day. It participated in the 1987 elections as a part of the eleven party alliance of MUF, however due to mass scale rigging MUF won only 4 seats. Although it had remained a marginal force till 1980 but with the launching of the armed struggle in 1989, its role became central in Kashmiri politics. MUf initially hesitated in joining the armed struggle and JEI's chief ideologue Sayed Ali Shah Gilani retained his seat in the assembly along with other MUF MLAs. However, the rising tide of JKLF armed struggle proved too overpowering for the JEI to ignore and its members resigned in 1989. JEI decided to join the militants and in 1990 set up its militant wing Hizb-ul-Mujahideen (HM), the holy warriors.

JEI sees the struggle as a war between Muslims and others and does not accept the notion of a separate Kashmiri national identity and propagates that Kashmiri Muslims are a part of the worldwide Ummah. JEI efforts were given an impetus by the growing intervention of Islamist groups based in Pakistan. It seeks to displace the Kashmiri struggle for a free Kashmir in favour of an Islamist agenda incorporating Kashmir into Islamic Pakistan as a part of the broader Islamic project.

Islamic agenda of the JEI is well illustrated in Sayed Ali Shah Gilani's writings since 1990, where his focus is mainly on Kashmir's freedom from Indian control, the struggle is Jehad, the goal of which is merger of Kashmir with Pakistan and establishment of an Islamic state. According to him the armed struggle is not a war of liberation but a Jehad between Islam and forces of disbelief (Kufr), he justifies it on India's denial of the right of self-determination to Kashmiris, its brutal suppression and rapid rise of Hindu chauvinism against Muslims. Jehad is directed against the Indian state, not Hindus or Indians, it has the limited goal of freeing Kashmir from Indian control. To prove he is not anti-Hindu, he asserts that migration of Kashmiri Pandits (KP) was instigated by Indian authorities to project Kashmiri struggle as an Islamic terrorist movement to discredit it. Gilani sees Islam and nationalism in complete contradiction of each other, which is also his justification for denial of a Kashmiri identity. He considers Hindus and Muslims as two nations though living in the same territory. He fears that Muslims in a Hindu majority area will get absorbed due to Hinduism's great capacity to absorb. Hence for Islam to be preserved and promoted, it is necessary for Kashmir to be separated from India and be with Pakistan. This is the initial step towards eventual unity of all Muslims. He categorized nationalist groups like JKLF as un-Islamic. In a pamphlet titled, *Masla ka Hal* (Solution of the problem) he emphasised that to advocate that one Muslim group (qaum) to be kept apart from the rest would be against the very definition of Millat. While seeking help from Pakistan, he bitterly criticized Pakistan for their alleged policy of "taking everyone together" initially and supporting nationalist groups like JKLF in addition to the Islamist. This was also motivated by a feeling of frustration, as one of the major hurdles faced by JEI in pursuance of its agenda was the popularity of JKLF amongst Kashmiri Muslims. The other hurdle for the JEI was the popular Sufi Islamic tradition, which is the dominant part of Islamic expression in Kashmir. JEI propagated that the solution to their problems lay in what they projected. This countered both Indian occupation and demand for independence- a shift in strategy for liberation struggle. Islam and not Kashmiriat and accession to Pakistan were presented as a solution. Rise of Hindu radical groups in India and destruction of the Barbari Masjid in 1992 and its aftermath helped JEI to justify their Islamic agenda.

One cannot deny the fact that since 1990, there has been a marked shift in the orientation of the armed militancy in Kashmir; the nationalists have been sidelined by the Islamists under the control of the radical groups in Pakistan supported by the JEI. The success of the JEI is due to their successfully cultivating the middle class (student, traders and Govt employees) who were disillusioned by the politics of the secular parties the National Conference and Congress. The failure of National Conference both under Sheikh Abdulla and Farook to articulate and respond to Kashmiri aspirations, corruption and collusion with the ruling party at the centre to subvert autonomy and democracy in the state resulted in increasing unemployment and economic deprivation. The resultant, anger and disillusionment of the youth pushed them towards the Islamists. To encash on the developing situation, the JEI established Madarssas system came in handy, where village level baitulmals for collection and distribution of Zakat funds, education and social programme and distribution of Islamic material helped in widening its mass base. The issue of plebiscite and self-determination came in handy. The anti-Muslim stance of radical Hindus and violence against Muslims in India was fully exploited by JEI and Pakistani Jehadi groups, with greater assertion of Kashmir's Islamic identity.

While the Islamists may be having an upper hand in the militancy field and Pakistani factor is predominant due to the support of Pakistan based Islamist groups and it establishment but their relevance to the Kashmiri struggle has decreased and they are primarily following Pakistani strategic interest. The marginalization of JKLF due to targeting by the security forces and the Islamists and denial of support by Pakistan can only be viewed in the military sense but the nationalists still represent the aspirations of the majority of Kashmiris as Islamists like the LET have a very marginal Kashmiri component. The vast majority of Kashmiri Muslims are war weary and do not show much enthusiasm for the Jehadi rhetoric. The Afghan experience and their own past experience, the turmoil within Pakistan has convinced Kashmiris that there future does not lie there. Similarly, in spite of all its claim JEI has failed to turn the majority of Kashmiri Muslims away from their Sufi Islam and radical Wahabism has few takers amongst the Kashmiri Muslims.

Most Kashmiri intellectuals acknowledge that Islamic resurgence is essentially a reaction to corrupt and inefficient regimes and failures in the practice of democracy to meet the aspirations of the common man and to alleviate their grievances, with Islam acting as an alternative source for inspiration and motivation. Impetus to it was provided by Islamic revolutions in Iran, consolidation of Zia's regime with overt and covert means to subvert Kashmiri mind and emergence of Islamic militant groups in Afghanistan providing the teeth to it and Jamaat-i-Islami of Kashmir providing the vehicle for its propagation. Collapse of USSR, provided the natural vacuum for Islam to fill it[12].

The Jamaat-i-Islami of Kashmir is closely linked with Jamaat-i-Islami in Pakistan and is totally independent of its counterpart in India. It is because of this orientation that it sees itself as a part of the wider Islamic movement and is totally influenced by Pakistan in its anti-India and anti-secular image. The aims and objectives of Jamaat-i-Islami are clearly outlined in Sayed Ali Shah Gilani's book "Ye Bhee Tha Ek Rukh Tasveer-e-Kashmir Ka" (This was also a side of a picture of Kashmir) and Mukadma-Illhaq (Trial of Accession). Finding the older generation of Muslim indifferent to it, Jamaat-i-Islami, set up over 125 Madarasas in the valley initially to indoctrinate the youth and spread its influence to colleges and university campuses by articulating student's demands and initiating debates and seminars on religio-political themes. Jamaait intensified its activities after Sheikh's death, it changed the stance and extended its base more in the political fields than ideology to exploit the feeling of alienation and isolation which were not finding an outlet.

The impact of Jamaait on Kashmiris was felt both in the social and educational field. Socially, it openly came out against family planning schemes of Govt. of India by terming these as Govt. designs to reduce Muslim population. In the educational field it established Madarssas (Islamic Schools) which indulged in fundamentalist parochialism. Impetus to it was provided by the Middle-Eastern countries particularly Saudi Arabia by pumping large resources. A Madina University delegation in 1980 openly emphasised the need for preparing for an Islamic revolution. The fundamentalist ideologies of Ahl-e-Hadis were preached while most of the Kashmiris are Ahl-e-Itikadh (Kashmiris recognise the role of saints in Islamic life and are believers in Sufism).

The sense of alienation of the Kashmiris and Kashmiri psyche of a sense of discrimination and aversion to corruption was given a religious outlet. Disenchanted by their own lot they fell prey to the call of establishment of an order (Nizam-e-Mustafa) where corruption and negative aspects of western culture would be punished. With the death of Sheikh Abdulla, the Islamists intensified their struggle and widened their base.

Growth of Muslim fundamentalism in Kashmir has unfortunately been more by default and to meet the ends of political expediency by political leaders of the state, with either inaction or connivance of central political leaders. This came about with full knowledge of Farook Abdulla and his National Conference and Congress (I) coalition Govt. A situation which perfectly suited Zia's strategy of fomenting trouble in India and denting its secular ethos. In this regard rise of Jamaat-i-Islami and Madarasas education is of special relevance.

To judge the success or failure of Muslim fundamentalism and allied terrorism propagated by Pakistan in Jammu & Kashmir, we need to take the following into account. The movement launched by JKLF for demanding Azadi was hijacked by the ISI of Pakistan and transformed into a campaign of terror. The movement was taken over by radical Islamist groups, with terrorism, insurgency and ethnic cleansing as its main weapons. Pakistan propaganda presented it as part of indigenous Muslim uprising against Hindu India. The ploy failed due to lack of genuine indigenous elements and their disenchantment with Pakistan. Similarly, imposition of rigid Wahabi code of conduct like closing of cinema halls, liquor shops, attack on Christian Schools, Hijab (Veil) and rigid dress code enforced by force failed in the long run as it could never be rationalised in Kashmiri Muslim mind.

The supporters of terrorism in the initial phases, the local press, religious leaders, lawyers and doctors, who make public opinion, started evading the dictates of the militants. The Wahabi campaign against Sufism became extremely unpopular as terrorists destroyed Sufi Shrines dear to the people, which represented centuries of their religion and culture of Kashmiriyat.

While insurgency in Kashmir has been controlled and yet not eliminated, on balance it can be said that Wahabi fundamentalist terrorist movement sponsored by Pakistan has failed due to excesses committed by them in the name of religion. The failure is manifested in their failure to wrest any area by armed action (Kargil) or political alternative and to transform the moderate Sufi culture of Kashmir into fundamentalist one.

A recent 5 years study on fundamentalism by a US foundation led by Prof Appleby, who was its main coordinator, has come to the following main conclusions.[13]

(a) The fundamentalist groups are often at odds with each other but they are unified in their pursuit of political power. Usually they are peaceful but occasionally their fight back philosophy leads to riots, terrorism and death.

(b) Every thing in fundamentalist world is we versus them, God versus Satan, Black versus White– to be persecuted or spoken against is sin, and they alone have the truth.

(c) All such movements – despite their internal differences, "want to change the society and they believe that they and they alone have the answer"

(d) While these zealots "emphasize non-violence, they can find an escape hatch", a statement in a holy book, a teaching of Guru (that may say) that the faith itself is under moral attack. This makes head lines and encourages irrationality.

(e) They are shrewd observes and initiators of secular politics – even when their messages are obscurantist and out dated, "they think modern communications and technology are perfectly fine to be manipulated for the glory of (their) God".

(f) Fundamentalist may not share a religions doctrine but they all are anti-feminist, anti-pluralist and anti-liberal.

(g) They don't believe in compromises and so there are no negotiations.

(h) They believe that the notion that majority should rule and notion of political parties are all western notions".

The above not only fit into what the Islamic fundamentalism have been propagating but their zeal, enthusiasm and resorting to violence and terrorist acts prove that they feel that the only right course is theirs and terrorism to achieve their political goals is not only justified but their sacred duty for the Jehad.

THE PAKISTAN FACTOR

History of Belligerence

In 1947, in spite of the fact that the Maharaja of Jammu and Kashmir had signed a standstill agreement with Pakistan; it followed an intimidating and coercive policy. All major routes and road communications to J and K ran through Pakistan. Pakistan imposed a ban on movement of all essential commodities, interrupted its telegraphic communication and used threat and allurement. Maj. Shah, Mr.Jinnah's Military Secretary, threatened the Prime Minister of Jammu & Kashmir Mr. MC Mahajan with sword in one hand and the instrument of accession in the other. When threat did not work, he conveyed Mr.Jinnah's personal assurance to the Maharaja that his privileges, status and position will be protected and there was no need for the Maharaja to worry about Sheikh Abdulla and the National Conference. Perhaps Maharaja wanted to maintain an independent status as such, their tactics did not work.

The blockade of Jammu and Kashmir by Pakistan, which was causing a number of problems to the state and hardship to its people was followed by border raids, which unnerved the Maharaja and his appeals to the British Prime Minister followed by appeals to Jinnah failed to get any response. Instead, thousands of tribal people led by Pakistan Army regulars were unleashed under its well planned operation 'Gulmarg' in October 1947. Raiders had initial success at Muzaffarabad and Uri and reached Baramula, when Maharaja acceded to India resulting in the induction of Indian troops and the Indo-Pak war of 1947-49. People of J and K rallied under Sheikh Abdulla and the cry was – "Hamla awar Khabardar, ham Kashmiri Hain Taiyar" (Invaders beware; we Kashmiris are ready to repulse you) "Sher-i-Kashmir Ka Kya irshad? Hindu, Muslim-Sikh Itihaad" (What does lion of Kashmir (Sheikh Abdullah) desires – Hindu-Muslim – Sikh Unity.

In the later phases of Operation "Gulmarg" Pakistani and Indian Army were locked in war ending in the ceasefire on 1 January 1949. The ceasefire line (CFL) created an artificial and unnatural division. In spite of Pakistan's failure to grab Jammu and Kashmir, it resulted in major strategic gains for it. Areas from Hajipir Bulge to Kotli and Mirpur in the South provided depth to Rawalpindi, Islamabad, Jhelum and Mangla Dam. Occupation of Muzaffarabad-Bugina-Neelam Valley areas gives depth to areas extending from Abbotabad to Peshawar. Occupation of Gilgit, Shardu areas with Kamri and Buzil passes provide depth to strategic links with the Chinese in the Korakoram Range and resulted in the construction of Korakoram Highway. The captured areas in POK and Northern areas not only gave Pakistan a foothold in J and K but provided it windows of mischief for the future into our front yard in Jammu and Kashmir.

While it is doubtful if Pakistan foresaw these advantages when it embarked on its venture in 1947, but one thing is certain that Pakistan's desire for seeking accession of Jammu and Kashmir went beyond emotional attachment merely because it was a Muslim majority area. Pakistan definitely had strategic and political designs probably contrived by British. With British Generals in Command both in India and Pakistan and all available indications that Earl Mountbatten was keen for Jammu and Kashmir to accede to Pakistan, the motives of the western world to preseek its strategic and political advantages cannot be disregarded. The subsequent conniving of Mountbatten for taking the dispute to UNO, ceasefire and introduction of a referendum to determine peoples' will as a condition to Maharaja's accession are all indicative of it. The scheme misfired to some extent due to Jinnah's impatience and Pakistan Army's limited capability. Because of repeated failures to grab Jammu and Kashmir, frustration has been converted into a politico-emotional issue by the ruling elite and the army in Pakistan to gain support within the country. West has looked at Jammu and Kashmir from their own strategic perception, which guided the massive military aid to Pakistan from USA in the fifties and sixties.

Indian military debacle in 1962 against the Chinese gave Pakistan renewed hopes on Kashmir, resulting in infiltration in August, 1965 under Operation "Gibraltor" followed by the Indo-Pak war of 1965. Failure resulted in both Ayub Khan and Bhutto quitting. Tashkent Agreement resulted in restoration of status quo ante in J and K, particularly in the Hajipur bulge and areas in Kargil being returned to Pakistan.

In 1971, Pakistan's humiliating defeat and emergence of Bangladesh, resulted in Shimla agreement which was departure from the past. The agreement, besides other issues, stipulated:-

(a) Differences were to be resolved by peaceful means through bilateral negotiations.
(b) The existing Cease Fire Line (CFL) was to be determined and delineated by the field commanders of the two armies and would be called "Line of Control (LoC). It was pledged that both sides would respect LoC without prejudice to the recognised position of the other.
(c) UNO was not to be involved in dispute and violation of the LoC; these matters were to be settled by bilateral negotiations at appropriate levels.

The UNCIP resolutions of 1948-49 were abandoned by both sides in 1965, therefore after Shimla Agreement there was no question of self-determination. The emphasis was for durable peace and a final settlement of J and K.

Post 1971

Period post-Shimla agreement is of special relevance for the contemporary situation. The Indian victory in the war of liberation of Bangladesh in 1971 not only resulted in the severing of the Eastern Pakistan and birth of a new nation but also in the capture of 94,000 POWs. Pakistan was a shattered nation physically, emotionally and ideologically. It was under these circumstances that Zulfikar Ali Bhutto, the biggest India baiter, arrived at Shimla to seek peace. Armed Forces of India had given her a great advantage but the Indian Political leadership let the only opportunity to impose a settlement over Kashmir escape. The Indian team was outmaneuvered; neither did they settle the Kashmir problem on the basis of the existing cease fire line (1949) nor ending the UN role. All that was achieved was that the cease fire line was converted into a Line of Control (a defacto Indo-Pak boundary in Kashmir) and the Kashmir issue became an Indo-Pak affair. But Bhutto never had bilateralism in mind as is borne out by clause 1 (I) and 6 of the agreement. Which states; clause 1 (I), that the principle and purposes of the charter of United Nations shall govern the relations between the two countries; clause 6, Both Govts agree that their heads will meet again at a mutually convenient time in the future. In the meanwhile, the representatives of two sides will meet to discuss further the modalities and arrangements for establishment of a durable peace and normalization of relations including the question of repatriation of POW and civilian internees, a final settlement of Jammu and Kashmir and resumption of diplomatic relations.

The Shimla Agreement left the Kashmir problem where it was and let Pakistan receive formal recognition of its position on Kashmir. This is also the basis of Pakistan's continued referring to Kashmir problem as the major irritant. In his first broadcast to the nation, Bhutto asserted his country's determination to take revenge and also referred to Indo-Pak confrontation as a confrontation of thousand years. He also referred to emergence of Bangladesh as an outcome of India's hegemonistic designs. Bhutto reiterated that he signed the agreement to guard Pakistan's immediate national interests and never for a moment did he resile from the position that the final solution of Indo - Pak problem lay in acceptance of the United Nations resolutions on Kashmir.[14] While consumed by its desire to take revenge Pakistan is conscious of its military limitations vis-a-vis India.

However, it was late Gen. Zia-ul-Haq who took the stance in categorical terms that Kashmir is the centre piece of Pakistan's policy and the issue can only be resolved based on UN resolutions of August 19, 1948 and January 1949. Under his leadership Pakistan never missed an opportunity to raise the Kashmir issue in international forums. Consequent to the hanging of Bhutto, Zia went ahead with the islamisation of Pakistan. With the Soviet invasion of Afghanistan, from his image as a tyrant in the Western eyes, Zia became bulwark of the free world against Soviet Communism.[15] In keeping with his concept of Pan-Islamism he improved his relations with Saudi Arabia, Jordon, Indonesia and Iran and extended full support to the Afghanistan Mujahideen. His foreign policy had three basic elements:

(a) Convergence of geo-strategic interests of Washington and Islamabad in the region.
(b) Annexation of Jammu and Kashmir and Afghanistan.
(c) Revival of concept of Pan-Islamism with Pakistan spearheading the movement.[16]

To complete the unfinished business of partition, separation of Kashmir from the Indian Union was key to it. Based on past experience the key to Kashmir in Zia's view lay in the fact that an open conflict in unlikely to succeed and would compromise Pakistan's position in the eyes of the world. Liberation of Kashmir should be contrived from within, with military option only as a "Coup de grace" when situation is ripe.

In his assessment the Kashmiris did not have the potential to achieve it on their own. He however felt that they had a few qualities which could be exploited. These were Kashmiri's qualities of shrewdness and intelligence, perseverance and that he is the master of political intrigue. The answer lay in providing him the means through which he can utilise these qualities[17]. The Pak strategy on Kashmir centered on two propagated views: one, in Pakistani perception the Kashmiri Muslim is shrewd, persevering in adversity and is a master of political intrigue. Secondly, the freedom struggle in the valley is indigenous and aimed at their right of self-determination. With this basis they will continue to renew the demand for plebiscite and self-determination, without showing undue concern for assimilation with Pakistan initially. [18]

The USA strategy on Afghanistan initiated and implemented by CIA, involved large quantities of arms and ammunition being pumped in the area for Afghan Mujahideen leaders through Pakistan's ISI. This massive induction of arms provided Zia the wherewithal for his designs to destabilize India. At least 400,000 Kalashnikov assault rifles were supplied to the ISI by USA and there were other suppliers too. The CIA reportedly purchased 60,000 rifles, 8,000 light machine guns and over a 100 million rounds of ammunition from Turkey alone. It also acquired stinger missiles and launchers, Chinese type-56 rifles (AK 47 produced under license), a variety of land mines and Oerlikon anti-aircraft guns. In 1983 over 10,000 tons of weaponry was sent through the pipeline and the figure rose to 65,000 tons in 1987, just before the Kashmir insurgency[19]. The pipeline continuously leaked or was made to leak due to the lack of accountability of the intelligence agencies of USA and Pakistan, CIA and ISI. It is generally believed that Mujahdeen's may have received as little as 40% of the arms supplied to ISI. A former head of ISI has been quoted as saying that ISI has still access to 3 million packed and greased Kalashnikov assault rifles. [20]

Pakistan's support to secessionists and militancy in Punjab and her exploitation of the situation in the aftermath of Operation "Blue Star" is another story but relevant to the Kashmir situation in as much as it was a forerunner to the proxy war in Kashmir and a part of overall design of Zia to destabilize India. Simultaneously, Pakistan had been sponsoring foreign expeditions from their side into the Siachin Glacier region to denounce the permanent boundary in Jammu & Kashmir along the LoC beyond NJ 9842. To thwart Pakistani designs India took the initiative and occupied the dominating Saltaro Ridge in the area in 1984. Pakistani efforts to throw India out of the Siachen Area failed. The Indian Army's aim was to keep it confined to the limits of a local incident and diffuse the situation during military sectoral level meetings. Pakistan who had suffered heavy casualties was quite amendable to the suggestion. We would have withdrawn after establishing the line of control beyond NJ 9842 and leaving surveillance and protective elements in key areas. Unfortunately due to military and political leadership's ineptness, it got sucked into the Indo-Pak confrontation and became yet another area of confrontation. This is contrary to what some of the Indian and foreign historians have led the public to believe[21].

A systematic proxy war was launched in August 1988, just prior to Zia's death and subsequent Pakistan Governments have followed the same strategy. The proxy war as it progressed broadly followed the pattern as outlined by a group of Indian Army retired officers on the likely developments in Jammu and Kashmir under the title "OP Topac – The Kashmir Imbroglio" in the Defence Review of July 1989. This caused some discomfort in the higher echelons of the Army and possibly the Government, who felt comfortable with the situation being handled by the state government and the journal was banned for some time. However, 'OP Topac' was often referred to and related to the ongoing proxy war and developments in Jammu and Kashmir by the intelligence agencies and in the deliberations of the Joint Intelligence Committee and later even in the National Security Council Secretariate with regards to the Kargil intrusions in 1999. I carried out a comparative analysis of O P Topac and "Operation Gibraltar" of 1965 in my book "Threat From Within"[22].

The strategy of subverting Kashmir and arming and training of disgruntled Kashmiri youth by exploiting the Islamic sentiment to fight an internal war became central to Pak strategy. Benazir Bhutto in spite of her propagation of democracy pursued the same line and went to the extent of reiterating the slogan of a thousand year war with India and could not deviate from the established line of Zia due to domestic political compulsions.

INTERNAL DIMENSIONS

Subjugation and Repression to Democracy and its Failure

The early sixteen centuries history of Kashmir up to Sultanate period before the Moghuls is marked by independence, splendid isolation and solidarity based on tolerance and secular spirit of Sufism, a result of fusion of old Hindu and Buddhist religions with moderate Sufi Islam and an identity based on the ideology of Kashmiriat. The period of three and a half centuries of Kashmiri history from the Moghul period up to 1930 was a total contrast to its earlier history. It was the period of subjugation and repression and a blow to their self-respect by one or the other invader. The composite culture and identity came under stress and the worst of it was during Aurangzeb's period due to his discriminatory and partisan attitude towards Hindus, which fragmented the Kashmiri society socially and culturally. Afghan, Sikh and Dogra periods are equally marked by tyranny, plunder and repression. In spite of these, Kashmiris survived due to their basic social and cultural strength and it also motivated the revival of its urge for reassertion.

The period post-1930 till Sheikh Abdulla's dismissal and arrest in 1953, a period of 23 years is marked by Kashmiri reassertion of its composite and secular identity underlined by the sentiment of Kashmiriat, democratic and economic revival after shedding feudal anarchical rule. It reestablished Kashmiri ownership of its own land, self-esteem and confidence and achievement of the political goal of self-rule. The process of democratization and constitutional reforms also raised the issue of autonomy or independence based on past experience and fears. Suspicion and distrust were to haunt the future relationship of Kashmiris with the Indian State due to failure of Indian leadership to consolidate the secular and nationalistic base of Kashmir politics under Sheikh Abdulla on one hand and Sheikh's autocratic ways of functioning on the other hand. While the constitutional and political integration of Kashmir became the main thrust, instead of economic, social and cultural accommodation based on mutual trust and partnership. These trends were to have far reaching impact on Kashmiri mind particularly of its leadership and encourage Pakistan to play its destabilizing role. National conference and Sheikh's desire to play an all dominating role in Jammu and Kashmir political future resulted in distortion of the democratic system and set trends for future regional imbalances within the state.

Events post-Indra-Sheikh accord 1975 and up to 1989, need to be examined both in the political spectrum of national and state politics as these had become entangled prior to the accord. While Sheikh Abdulla propagated the accord as a reestablishment of trust[23], Indira Gandhi treated the accord to bring Sheikh back into power, while talking of the essence of the accord in the parliament. She acknowledged Sheikh's past role and treated the intervening period as period of disagreement and estrangement, "since he is willing to work for unity and secularism, he is welcome" [24].

However, trust was besieged by differing perceptions of the intervening period, which became the main source of irritation. Sheikh did not reconcile to be a Chief Minister in the new environment and demanded a pre-1953 position. Mrs. Gandhi on return to power in 1980 attacked Sheikh Abdulla and Jammu and Kashmir Govt.'s Grant of Permit for Resettlement Act of 1982 provided another cause of Centre-State political rift. There were differences in perceptions on economic development and the issue of revision of some of the unimportant central laws and constitutional provisions applied to Jammu and Kashmir. Sheikh felt that in this regard the commitment was not honoured. The differences came out in the open, when he refused to dissolve the National Conference and instead demanded the dissolution of the State Congress Party. During Sheikh's period democracy was revived in a legitimate manner and improvement was noticed in the employment, education tourism and banking sectors. But his promise of clean administration remained unfulfilled; on the contrary it received a boost. Similarly, Governor's ordinance for provision of land to outsiders for industry did not go well with Kashmiris.

After Sheikh's death, Farooq Abdulla was installed as the Chief Minister with centre's backing. The assembly was dissolved paving the way for 1983 elections. In spite of Farooq Abdulla consistently upholding of accession to India, elections brought out bitter rivalry between the National Conference and Congress. He termed the elections as a plebiscite between National Conference and Congress and demanded the restoration of the pre-1953 autonomy. He forged an alliance with the Awami Action Committee of Mir Waiz Maulvi Mohd Farooq. During the election Congress Hinduised the party and connived with RSS and Hindu Parishad in Jammu. National Conference won the elections and congress bagged 23 of the 32 seats in Jammu. Congress did not accept the verdict and dismissed Farooq Abdulla in July 1984, after engineering defections and installed GM Shah with its support. During GM Shah's regime, the worst ever communal disturbances took place and both the National Conference and Congress were equally responsible for it. In March, 1986, Shah's ministry was dismissed on the same grounds as Farooq's.

During the Governor's rule, politicians mounted pressure for getting back to power, resulting in the expediency of Rajiv – Farooq accord and Farooq Abdulla returned to power in November 1986 and elections were called in March 1987. Rajiv – Farooq accord was essentially an understanding of power sharing, which resulted in further estrangement of the people and formation of the Muslim United Front (MUF). The National Conference and Congress alliance won with National Conference wining 38 seats, Congress 28, MUF 4, BJP 2 and 4 seats were won by independents. The seats won by the opposition were not proportionate to the percentage of votes polled. This was the turning point and accusation of rigged poles plunged the reputation of Farooq Abdulla and the Congress and made deep impact on the psyche of the Kashmiris.

Most observers feel that 1987 elections was the turning point in Jammu and Kashmir recent history, which turned the simmering discontent into insurgency. The period was also the high point of corruption, nepotism and inefficiency, already deep rooted in state's political and administrative culture, which further alienated the people. A local observer very aptly summed up the situation: the state was divided between two secular and nationalist parties, those dissatisfied with the local Govt. voted for the congress and those with the Central Govt. for National Conference. There was no room for a third force. It also provided two channels for integration both based on dissatisfaction. Congress encouragement to Jamaait and MUF was to break the monolith character of the National Conference in the Valley and cut Farooq to size, thereby make him dependent on the Congress. Congress blunder was to reach for power without developing a political base. In some ways, having Farooq in opposition is better as he, like his father, would inevitably be anti-centre rather than anti-national.

The period since 1953 from Sheikh's first dismissal till 1989 can be rightly termed as a period of inner turmoil and convulsions marked by Indian leadership's apathy combined with political expediency overriding all other considerations politically, the dominant theme was division of the state between two secular and nationalistic forces (National Conference and Congress) each aligning with communal forces to outdo the other thus encouraging anti Indian sentiment. They could not do without each other but could not live together for the greater good of the Kashmiri and Indian cause. In this competitive game rigged elections, political expediency to wield power subverted democracy. In spite of economic progress and well being, the above stance led to dynastic consolidation of power, corruption, dissatisfaction and finally alienation of the people.

The political environment was further vitiated by communalisation of politics, a fertile ground for insurgency and Pakistani interference. Insurgency is fallout of prolonged bad politics and exploitation of the historic sentiment of subjugation and isolation, where every act of the establishment is seen as suppression.

Corruption and Alienation

Corruption has its roots in the disruption of the political process consequent of Sheikh's dismissal in 1953 and the perceived threat from the newly formed Plebiscite Front; wherein corruption as model to bring about integration was applied to Jammu and Kashmir.[25]. The approach was distribution of spoils and patronage to appease people and particularly the elite in the shape of liberal Central Govt. aid, building up of a subsidised economy, discretionary sanction of permits, contracts, licenses and permits for quotas. Per capita, grant in aid to Kashmir was almost seven times of that of the average of other states of the country[26]. Corruption in all walks of life became the order of the day, and politicians, bureaucrats and businessmen nexus to perpetuate it became well established. The situation resulted in the ordering of one man enquiry commission against Bakshi Ghulam Mohammed in 1965. On becoming chief minister of Jammu and Kashmir in 1975, Sheikh Mohammed Abdulla proclaimed that he will give the highest priority to eradication of corruption but the reality is that it only increased. Sheikh and his family assets were valued over rupees twenty crores.[27] This apart, Sheikh Mohammed Abdulla became a protector of dishonest and corrupt people, income tax raids against corrupt businessmen were thwarted and Income Tax Officers were physically attacked and prevented from unearthing ill gotten wealth of such people. The jurisdiction of the Central Vigilance Commission was not extended to Jammu and Kashmir, similarly, the presidential order of 1954, which brought all matters in the union list under purview of the Parliament, excluded the power of CBI to investigate corruption in Jammu and Kashmir[28]. The cumulative effect of all pervading corruption was the emergence of a neo rich urban elite consisting of politicians, bureaucrats and businessmen, lack of development and unemployment resulting in social tensions, disillusionment and finally alienation.

Both the propagated anti-Indian sentiment and alienation of Kashmiri masses are cumulative facets of the Kashmiri contemporary experience, which provided the ground work for Pakistan's subversive designs resulting in revolt and insurgency. It has its roots in the politics of expediency played both by the Kashmiri leaders and central leaders. The Indian leaders dealt with J and K through Kashmiri leaders, some of them were not genuine or sincere to J and K and the Indian nation. Loyalties were modulated to requirements of political leaders in power both at the centre and in J and K. To maintain their political base intact Sheikh and other Kashmiri leaders kept Kashmir isolated from the national mainstream and from other regions within the state, their political stance varying between the desires for independence and coming to terms with the ruling party at the Centre to regain power. The Kashmiri masses in this inept political power game became pawns and remained isolated and deprived, resulting in a sense of alienation. Sentiment of autonomy and independence is hostage to this power game.

The other facet of alienation is corruption as a result of which resources meant for development were cornered by the neo rich elite and the common man remained deprived and did not participate both in the democratic and development process. While J and K may have shown improvement in economic terms and compares very favourably in allocation of central funds, the common man remained deprived of minimum requirements and no employment avenues were created for the younger generation.

Political ineptness, corruption and failure of democratic institutions to meet people's genuine aspiration resulted in frustration. At the political level this frustration was mixed with protectionism, which apart from isolation distorted their identity into a religion dominant one, which fell pray to fundamentalism.

Autonomy

The question of autonomy is as much a sentimental issue as a political one, both at the national level as well as within Jammu and Kashmir. The perceptions on autonomy within Jammu and Kashmir vary from region to region and it has been an exploitative and dismal experience for the people of Jammu and Ladakh. It may be prudent to first discuss the shape and content of regional autonomy within the state, for what you cannot give and share with your constituents, asking it for the state may repeat the past experience. It would therefore be only correct to get to the core of the regional imbalance and formulate the parameters of the regional autonomy.

The fate of the two Autonomy Committees, one under Dr.Karan Singh to determine state's autonomy and the Regional Autonomy Committee under Sh. Balraj Puri are forerunners of the failures on both fronts. Dr. Karan Singh resigned within a couple of months and Dr.Balraj Puri a few months later— the reasons were simple. The National Conference and the Kashmiri leadership at large had an agenda of their own and wanted to write the script accordingly. While division of Jammu into Hindu and Muslim majority areas and of Ladakh into Muslim majority region of Kargil and the Buddhist majority region of Leh may be politically convenient for the Kashmiris but the trap is that it is in consonance with the current Islamic orientation of militancy and is no different from the recommendations of the US based Kashmir Study Group, with sympathetic response from Pakistan. The issue is discussed in detail later. Such a distortion of both the autonomy packets will be disastrous both for India and Jammu and Kashmir.

The State Autonomy Committee report was tabled in the State Legislative Assembly on14th April '99 and was distributed to legislators and the media. The report seeks that the state be restored all subjects except, defense, foreign affairs and communications. It envisaged that all modifications made in the Article 246 in its application to the state subsequent to the 1950 order should be rescinded. The 184 page report prepared by the nine member panel of the ruling National Conference has recommended that the word temporary in regard to Article 370 be deleted and replaced by word 'special', thereby this article giving special status to the state be made permanent. The report also recommends that the Articles 248, 249 and 251, whether applied in original or modified or substituted be omitted from their application to the state. It aims at reverting to the 1952 status when state under the Delhi Agreement had full sovereignty, its own flag and Constitution.

But it is the recommendation of the Regional Autonomy Committee (RAC) which is of greater significance and should have rung alarm bells, which unfortunately has gone unnoticed. The report recommends the creation of eight new provinces, each with an elected provincial council. In the Kashmir valley the RAC recommended the creation of three provinces, Kamraz province made of the districts of Baramulla and Kupwara, Nundabad consisting of Budgam and Srinagar districts and Maraz from Anantnag and Pulwama districts. Ladakh was to be broken into two districts, predominantly Buddhist Leh and Muslim Kargil. Acute divide already visible by the exclusion of the Kargil from the Ladakh Autonomous Council will be further sharpened by the ethnic and communal divide. The most dramatic impact of RAC recommendation if accepted will be on Jammu. The Muslim dominated District of Doda and Mahore teshil from the Udhampur district have been grouped into the new Chenab Valley Province. Jammu will only retain the Hindu dominant districts of Jammu, Udhampur minus some areas and Kathua districts. The Poonch and Rajouri Districts will form the third province of Pir Panjal. The communal divide would be complete. The stated rationale for the above reorganisation was that the "prevailing classification of provinces/divisions are hampering social and human" development. The above recommendations present a mosaic of exclusive ethno-religious divide, which the communalists in the National Conference and the Hindu Chauvinists have devised to further their political agenda. Insurgency was the outcome of prolonged Kashmir alienation and fundamentalism was the fallout of alienation and corruption with resultant deprivation. The regional committee's recommendations if accepted will only stabilise the communal boundaries that the Islamists have aimed for. Farooq Abdulla and the BJP's local and National leadership who seem to give it tacit support will only be encouraging communal and fundamentalist elements. You cannot even remotely be seen to be accepting such a communal agenda and still be fighting the Islamic Jehad in Jammu and Kashmir. This is purely playing politics of religion and ethnic divide and is the high point of inept political games which the Kashmiri leadership and our central leadership has been playing and is the core of the problem in Jammu and Kashmir.

The regional rivalries and imbalances have long since been evident in view of divergent historical, social and cultural background. The Glancy Commission of 1931, Gajendragadkar Commission in 1976 and the Sikri Commission of 1978 are a testimony to the failure of the state to resolve these imbalances, and with the passage of time it has accentuated regional tensions. The provinces of Jammu and Kashmir should have proportionate representation in the State Cabinet and Deputy Chief Minister should be from Jammu region. Ethnic, linguistic and religious minorities must have seats reserved for them in the legislation. The Ladakh Autonomous Hill Development Council should be strengthened and given police powers and the District Authorities made accountable to them.

As regards the autonomy to the state, its discussion in the historical perspective alone may also not be totally relevant. We must realise that the ground situation has radically changed and the fact of Pakistan's continued involvement with Kashmir militancy and the threat that it poses to the state and integrity of the nation after the Kargil episode cannot be disregarded. Moreover we cannot ignore the fact that previous state governments including those of National Conference are equally guilty by accepting the erosion of state autonomy and using it as a vehicle of political expediency to perpetuate power in connivance with the Govts. in power at the Centre and is the main cause of inter regional friction and distrust. We cannot afford to repeat failures of the past and neither can we wish away the events of the past two decades. The six point Indira-Sheikh pact of 1975 (signed in 1974) is close to the realities of the current situation. It maintains the sanctity of Article 370 and state's interests, without compromising the sovereignty and territorial integrity of the country. It is also in keeping with the federal structure as provided in the constitution and recommended by the Sarkaria Commission. It gives the state Govt. the latitude to do away with some of the laws imposed on it. Moreover, the validity of the above agreement was endorsed by the 1977 elections, which have been acknowledged by all as the most free and fair elections. It should therefore act as a credible start point.

Keeping in view the recent cases of corruption at the national level, the deteriorating political ethos and state's past history, it will be in its interest not to interfere with the jurisdiction of the Supreme Court and the established judicial system, the Controller and Auditor General of

India and the Election Commission's jurisdiction. In the economic field the state apart from having to catch up with the last 14 years void in development field, it has to go in for massive reconstruction and rejuvenation of its economy for which vast resources would be required. It cannot entirely depend on the centre for it; it will require private capital and participation at a large scale. This is only possible if outside entrepreneurs both Indian and Foreign feel secure and state is part of the emerging liberalised economic structure of the country. In the financial and developmental fields greater autonomy to all states as outlined in the Sarkaria Commission should be granted. However, a word of caution is due about the proper utilisation of resources. Utilisation of resources and assistance unless made more transparent and monitored by a central independent agency, will perpetuate corruption and will continue to be a means of political manipulations as in the past. However, having said this, there is a definite case for restoration of residuary powers of the state and changes brought under article 248 in 1985 should be restored to status quo as per President's Constitutional Order of 1954 (applicable to Jammu and Kashmir).

Both the reports of the State Autonomy Committee and the RAC smack of unrealistic and motivated political agenda of the National Conference Kashmiri leadership to perpetuate its political hold over the state. The agenda has a communal, anti-people and anti-India stance. It needs to be reviewed by a committee of all political parties representing all communities.

THE OTHER SIDE OF THE HILL

Pakistan Occupied Kashmir[29]

Any talk of autonomy brings into natural focus the Pakistan Occupied Kashmir (POK) and Northern areas directly being controlled by Pakistan. Self-determination in Pakistan does not mean Azadi but accession to Pakistan. Not trusting POK to handle the strategically important Northern Areas (Gilgit, Baltistan and Hunza) these have been incorporated in Pakistan. The Karachi Agreement signed on 24 April 1949 by Nawaz Mustaq Gurmani on behalf of Pakistan; Sardar Mohd Ibrahim on behalf of POK and Political leader Ghulam Abbas on behalf of Muslim Conference institutionalised Kashmiri subservience to Pakistan. POK Govt. was left only with overseeing policy with regard to administration, general supervision of administration and publicity with regard to its own activities. Political charter of Muslim Conference was restricted to publicity on plebiscite and general guidance of POK Govt. A joint secretary in the Pakistan Govt. appointed by Ministry of Kashmir Affairs was the de-facto ruler of POK.

Under Gen Ayub Khan, all political activities in POK were banned. Under the Azad Jammu and Kashmir Basic Democracies Act of 1960, like in the rest of Pakistan, the POK President and council was to be elected from 1200 indirectly elected basic democrats of POK and 1200 representing Kashmiri refugees. K. H. Khurshid, the first President was sacked in 1964, when he started asserting himself; he wanted POK to be a party to the Indus Water Treaty. Commenting on his dismissal 'OutLook' of Karachi on 14 August 1964 said: "The uncomfortable truth is that the Ministry of Kashmir Affairs has acquired a vested interest of its own. It treats 'Azad Kashmir' territory and Gilgit and Baltistan as its own domain". The ministry likes to deal with puppets and not with Presidents who take their position literally. In 1968 some cosmetic changes were made, abolishing the practice of selection of Azad Kashmir President by Ministry for Kashmir Affairs, instead he was to be chosen by the state council of twelve members, eight elected through basic democracies and four nominated by the President of Pakistan.

After the Shimla Agreement in 1972, realising the implications of renunciation of UN role and conversion of ceasefire line (CFL) into line of control (LOC), Bhutto started greater assimilation of POK into Pakistan. An interim constitution of POK was promulgated in November 1975, which made the Prime Minister of Pakistan the Chief Executive of POK instead of its President. The new Azad Jammu and Kashmir council had thirteen members of which six members were to be nominated by Govt. of Pakistan. Chairmanship with six federal nominees gave Pakistan the majority. Zia-ul-Haq on assuming power dissolved the POK assembly and appointed Maj. Gen. (Retd.) Abdul Rehman as Chief Executive and Sardar Ibrahim continued as nominal President. After a year Gen. Abdul Rehman was replaced by Brig (Retd.) Mohd Hayat Khan, who took over as President and Chief Executive on declaration of Martial Law in July, 1979, all political activities were suspended till 1985. Abdul Qayyum Khan took over as president after elections, restricted to registered parties thus keeping PPP out. Qayyum Khan followed Zia's radical agenda, introduced 'Zakat' and 'Ushr' as taxes in POK.

Constitution and all laws framed for POK singularly aim at ultimate accession to Pakistan. Some examples are:-

(a) Part 2 of section 7 of POK Constitution States: No person or political party in Azad Jammu and Kashmir shall be permitted to propagate against or take part in activities prejudicial or detrimental to the ideology of state's accession to Pakistan.

(b) Section 5(2) (VII) of Azad Jammu and Kashmir Legislative Assembly Election ordinance of 1970: a person would be disqualified for propagating any opinion or action in any manner prejudicial to the ideology of Pakistan, the ideology of states accession to Pakistan or the sovereignty and integrity of Pakistan. The same caveat applies to any one who defames or brings into ridicule the judiciary of Azad Jammu and Kashmir or Pakistan or Armed Forces of Pakistan.

(c) Section 9 of the POK constitution while granting freedom of speech imposes reasonable restriction (in their view) in the interest of the security of Azad Jammu and Kashmir and friendly relations with Pakistan. The oath of any office in POK right from the President downwards includes "I will remain loyal to the country and cause of accession of the state of J and K to Pakistan".

(d) Section 56 of the POK constitution gives Pakistan Govt. all the rights including the right to dismiss POK Govt.

POK was devoid of franchise till 1960 as no elections were held and election from 1960 to 1975 were indirect. Pakistan arrested the Prime Minister of POK, rigged the state elections in 1991 resulting in alienation of the people and their demand for independence[30]. Same was the fate of Sikander Hayat Khan, who was elected president in June 1996 election and was removed through a voice vote in the assembly.

The relationship between Pakistan and POK has been one way traffic. People ousted as a result of Mangla Dam went away to UK and other places in the west. There are 3, 00,000 Mirpuris in UK itself. Their remittances are a major source of foreign earnings. Mangla Dam supplies electricity to vast areas but POK gets no royalties. Before the 1996 elections Abdul Qayyum Khan demanded Rs.50, 000 crores as royalty from the federal Govt.

Northern Areas

Northern Areas form a wedge between Afghanistan and Sinkiang and strategically it outflanks both Kabul and Srinagar. Britishers considered Gilgit as one of the Northern gateways to India. That is why Pakistan wants to keep it under its direct control. An area of 2700 Sq. miles in Hunza was ceded to China in 1963 and the Karakoram Highway built through Northern Areas (old silk route) gives Pakistan direct access to China for clandestine transfer of nuclear and missile components and material.

The status of Northern Areas is anomalous and it has been purposely contrived by Pakistan as such. None of the Constitutions of Pakistan—

1956, 1962, 1972 and 1973—recognize Northern Areas as Pakistan territories and neither does the 1974 Interim Constitution of POK includes Gilgit and Baltistan. This resulted in passing of "Legal Framework Order" which placed Northern Areas under control of the Ministry of Kashmir but Pakistan persists that it is not part of POK. In 1990, two representatives of the Northern Area Council Malik Mohammed Miskeen and Haji Amir Jan along with an advocate of Muzzaffarabad Sheikh Abdul Aziz filed a writ petition under Section 44 of the Interim Constitution as bonafide citizens of Jammu and Kashmir and challenged the Pakistan Govt. statement that Northern Areas were not part of Kashmir but part of Pakistan. They also concluded that although Gilgit was leased to the British Govt. in 1935 but restored to the State Govt. on 1 August 1947. Even under the Dogra rule Gilgit and Baltistan were represented in the State Assembly and in 1941 Mr.Jagmot Dodal, Raja of Leh (Buddhist), represented the Ladakh Wazarat, Chewing Rinchen represented Leh town, Fateh Ali Khan, Skardu Teshil, Ahmad Ali Khan Kargil, and Raja Ghulam Raza Khan represented the Gilgit Teshil (Civil List 1941). During the July 1947 elections held to the Kashmir state Assembly, Raja Jagmot Dodal, Chewing Rinchen, Raja Fateh Ali, Ahmad Ali Khan, Raja Ghulam Khan and Muhammad Javed Ansari were elected. Pakistan Govt. pleaded that Govt. of Pakistan was not functioning or operating in the territory of Azad Jammu and Kashmir and as such it was not subject to the jurisdiction of the POK High Court and also denied the well known Karachi Agreement of 1949. The High Court decided that the so called Northern Areas were part of POK and after arguing the case, court came to the conclusion that "we, therefore hold that no legitimate cause has been shown by respondents No. 1 and 2 to keep the Northern Areas and their residents (state subjects) detached from Azad Jammu and Kashmir under separate and arbitrary administrative system and deprive them of fundamental rights" (POK High Court Judgment writ petition No. 61 of 1990, decided on 8.3.93).

The 1.5 million population has never voted because it had no legislature to vote for after 1947. They have the distinction of not being represented any where, neither at the national level nor locally[31]. What is worse is that Gilgit over the last five decades is continued to be ruled by Frontier Crime Regulation of the British meant for marauding Pathan tribesmen of those days; every resident has to report to a police station once a month. The Northern Area Council is headed by the Minister of Ministry of Kashmir and Northern Area (KANA) and meets only when minister desires. The council has no Legislative and administrative powers, it can only suggest developmental issues. It is ceremonial only meant to receive Pakistani dignitaries. The rights of the people of the

Northern areas were usurped under the agreement reached by POK leaders and Pakistan under the Karachi Agreement of 1949.

To add to the problems of Northern areas sectarian violence between Shias and Sunnis is rampant since Zia-ul-Haq's time when JEI was given money and weapons to counter the influence of the youth wing of PPP. There has been continuous unrest in Northern areas and Gilgit and in June 1996, there were clashes between students and the police resulting in several casualties. The procession was held under the aegis of Gilgit-Baltistan United Action Forum for self-rule. There have been systematic efforts to reduce the local population of Gilgit and Baltistan to a minority by settling more and more Pathans in the area.

Both the main stream political parties (Muslim League) and PPP in Pakistan have been eyeing POK. Elections have been reduced to a farce and the musical chairs game between Sardar Ibrahim and Abdul Qayyum has got exposed. Qayyum has warned Pakistan to stay away from POK politics. He reinforced three negations on 14 May 1996: "No dissolution, no resignation and no dictation". In run up to the elections 34 candidates refused to sign the declaration calling POK accession to Pakistan an article of faith, they also refused to sign "allegiance to the sovereignty and integrity of Pakistan. There was large scale rigging and results shocked Muslim Conference: PPP 31, Muslim Conference 9, PML (Junejo) 3, JEJ 1 and JK PP (Ibrahim) 1 and Independents 3. The elections reflect a changing relationship between Pakistan and POK. Pakistan's game of berating the elections in Jammu and Kashmir is exposed by the mess in its backyard.

POK is an area which is neither a country nor a province but an occupied territory in real sense, deprived of political rights, practice and exposed to economic and social depredation of the highest order. It is important for our Kashmir brethren to understand the actual situation, vis-à-vis the freedom and democracy prevailing in J and K, irrespective of its constraints and bad performance in their eyes. The other side of the hill is downwards in all respects.

Ethnicity, Identity and Emerging Politics of Religion and Ethnicity

Ethnic resurgence is a worldwide phenomenon and ethno-nationalism could be of two varieties. First, the process is closely linked with politicisation of ethnic, religious and cultural identities due to process of modernisation and development. This conflict has been pronounced in states with heterogeneous population. Secondly, the national self-awareness of ethnic groups concentrated in compact geographical areas, which have retained or have developed or are in the process of developing self-awareness. Kashmir constitutes the second variety of ethnic identity formation.[32] At this stage it will also be pertinent to understand the meaning of ethnicity. An ethnic group can be defined as historically formed aggregate of people having a real or imaginary association with a special territory, a shared cluster of beliefs and values connoting its distinctiveness in relation to similar groups and recognition by others of its group differentiation[33].

Ethnicity, however is a flexible concept, a stress in changed circumstances for example on religion instead of language will transform an ethno-linguistic community into a communal one. Ethnic group identities are also affected by external factors such as migration, redefinition of territorial boundaries, economic advances and changing political system will result in ethnic groups dividing, amalgamating, disappearing or reappearing in completely different forms. One fundamental attribute characterising Kashmiri behaviour is its ethno centrism. Ethnicity permeates beyond the horizon of Kashmiri personality to that of Kashmiri identity. The identity not only possesses objective marks of identification but is subjectively conscious of its evolution. While scanning the pages of Kashmiri history, the inevitably multifaceted dimensions of its composite culture emerge and influence the course of its history. The composite cultural mainstream can be broken into two variables that interact with each other and avoid falling into extremes of either regional chauvinism or religious intolerance. The divisions are: one, the regional, linguistic and cultural and secondly, religious urges cum Pan-Islamic tendencies [34]

A larger section of the Kashmiri society (including JKLF) stresses a supra-religious 'Kashmiriyat" as the basis of Kashmir's identity in an ideological and strategic sense, so as not to alienate Buddhists in Ladakh and Hindus of Jammu from the predominantly Muslim population of Kashmir. The other section, on the contrary, led by Jamaat-i-Islami, while banking on territorial sub-nationalism stresses the religious component of Kashmir's identity, which contrives them to join Pakistan in true tradition of the Millat. Those favouring independence or a fully autonomous profile of the state draw support from regional and extra regional quarters. While the Islamic fundamentalists draw their support from the Islamic world primarily modulated by Pakistan in keeping with her self-assumed role as the spearhead of Islam in the region. Both are motivated and not fully supported by the Kashmiris. It is really exploitation of their sentiment on both accounts due to alienation. India's stand that Jammu and Kashmir is its integral part[35] and Pakistan's persistent interest in Kashmir add an international dimension making it a geo-political issue.

It is their land, geography and history which shapes their ethnic profile, and a common language bound them as a cultural grouping. The sum total being Kashmiriat, which is secular in essence and tolerant on the religious plane, within which both the Kashmiri Muslims and Pandits devised their indigenous religious philosophies, traditions and practices. What has gone wrong is the distortion of these due to external factors both from within India and from outside. From within India it is a reaction to state sponsored Pan-Indians and the emerging Hindu nationalism. It is also influenced by the fact that Kashmiri Pandits who laid the foundation of Kashmiri identity distanced themselves from it for political and economic reasons and their exodus further sharpened the divide. Externally, Pakistan's part in fomenting Islamisation of their identity in conjunction with Jamaat-i-Islami has been discussed and needs no further elaboration. The Kashmiris are caught amongst these two pulls and it will be prudent for the Indian state to provide the requisite space to the Kashmiri identity and encourage it to prevent ethno-nationalism or sub nationalism changing into a communal identity.

The response of the authorities and the intellectual community has been entirely conditioned by the political and divergent perceived international opinions, particularly in its Indo-Pak context. The ground reality is that Kashmiri Muslim population does not represent the entire state of Jammu and Kashmir. Even in the valley itself there are ethnic and religious differences. In the overall context the state of Jammu and Kashmir has a number of ethnic and religious groups and their political and socio-economic perceptions are diverse and in some cases conflicting. J & K is a multi-lingual, multi-ethnic and multi-religious state.

The largest region of the state is Ladakh with an area of 96,701 square kilometers and is predominantly (52%) Buddhist. Jammu region is next in size with an area of 26,293 square kilometers and is predominantly Hindu (66.3%) with 29.7 per cent Muslims and 3.58 per cent Sikhs. Kashmir province is the smallest in land area of 15.853 square kilometers, is predominantly Muslim 94.85% with 3.89% Hindu and 1.04% Sikh. The overall position of the religious groups as per 1981 census is 38, 31,292 Muslims (64.3%), 19, 08,288 Hindus (32.1%), 1, 29,393 Sikh (2.17%), 69,796 Buddhist (1.17% and 6,916 Christians (0.12%). These religious groups are further divided into a number of social and ethnic groups, some of the major ones are Kashmiris, Dogras, Gujjars and Bakerwals, Dards, Baltis, Gaddis, Ladakhis and Pothwari speaking Muslims and non-Muslims. Kashmiris are mainly concentrated in Kashmir Valley, Dogras are spread over the Jammu region, Gujjars and Bakerwals inhabit the Mountainous and Kandi areas, the Dard and Baltis Muslims are in Gurej, Tilel and Dras, Gaddis are found in the

South Eastern part of the middle mountain ranges of Jammu, Pothwari speaking Muslims and non-Muslims live between Chenab and Jhelum and Ladakhis in Ladakh. The principal languages spoken are Kashmiri, Dogri, Pothwari, Balti, Ladakhi, Gojri, Dardi, Punjabi and Urdu.

During discussions with the leaders of various ethnic and religious groups, it came out clearly that the core of militancy is confined to the Kashmiri sympathisers of Jamaat-i-Islami amongst the Sunnis in the Jhelum Valley, who have a pro-Pakistan element amongst them. The majority of Kashmiris - Shias, Gujjars, Bakerwals and other ethnic groups consider themselves victims of both the militants and security forces with a deep sense of neglect and resentment and feel alienated from the Indian state. This sense of grievance and victimization responds favourably to the cry of independence and autonomy as a way out of their misery both from Pakistani inflicted militancy and neglect from the Indian State. The sentiment or cry for merger with Pakistan is confined to JEI hard core and ISI controlled HM under Salahudin in POK and does not find favour with bulk of Kashmiri's. This was amply proved by the MODI's sample survey in the valley in 2002 and by subsequent elections in October in Jammu and Kashmir. They feel that their fate will be no better than that of Ahmedias and Mohajirs in Pakistan. It is unfortunate that the Indian state has failed to respond to these feelings. One million Shias in Jammu and Kashmir have been discriminated against by Pakistan supported militants of Hizb-ul-Mujahideen and their coreligionists the Kashmiri Sunnis. The Muslim population of Kashmir can be divided into Kashmiri Muslims, Gujjar and Bakarwals, Dard and Baltis, nearly eight lakh Kashmiris are Shias and remainder Sunnis (almost half). One lakh Shias live in Kargil district of Ladakh and one lakh in different parts of Jammu region. The distribution of Gujjars and Bakarwals of over 12 lakh population is, in Poonch one and half lakh, Rajouri two lakh , Udhampur one lakh, Jammu eighty thousand, Kathua fifteen thousand, Baramula one and half lakh, Pulwama one lakh, Kupwara one and a half lakh, Srinagar fifty thousand and Badgam thirty thousand. The population of Puthwari speaking Muslims and non-Muslims is four lakh— one lakh in Poonch, eighty thousand in Kupwara, fifty thousand in Baramula, thirty thousand in Srinagar and one lakh in Rajouri.

The resentment against the state's politico-bureaucratic elite which is predominantly Kashmiri Sunni amongst the other ethnic groups is high. Gujjars, Bakarwals, Shias, Dards, Baltis, Kashmiri Pandits and Sikhs constitute 55 per cent of the Kashmiri population and dominate 16 of the assembly constituencies but have never been allotted more than 10 per cent of the seats (4 out of 42) in the Kashmir region. On the contrary,

Valley Sunnis who form 45 per cent of Kashmiris and 22 per cent of the states population have all along retained no less than 38 legislators in the 76 member assembly as they control all the political parties, National Conference, Congress, Janata Dal, CPI, CPI (M), the Peoples Conference and Jamaat-i-Islami. Even Kashmiri Sunnis are divided over the issue of merger with Pakistan, Pre-1953 status, independence and full integration. In finding a solution we cannot ignore the interests of diverse ethnic and religious groups.

Clash of Identities

The composite Kashmiri culture and identity forged by the fusion of Hindu Shaivism and Buddhism and reinforced by religious humanism of Islam based on the ideology of "Kashmiriat" has stood the onslaught of the Moghuls, Afghans, Sikhs and the Dogras to reassert itself as a secular and composite identity at the time of independence. The sentiment of Kashmiriat was underlined by economic and democratic revival and raised the issues of autonomy and independence.

Kashmiri identity enjoyed a special status within the Indian state due to Jammu and Kashmir's accession as distinct from merger of other princely states in the Indian Union. It was the fall out of Pakistani invasion of Jammu and Kashmir in 1947 and India's stand to hold a plebiscite to determine the will of the people. Due to changed situation and Pakistan's failure to vacate areas occupied by it, the plebiscite offer no longer remains valid. However, developments within Jammu and Kashmir and rest of India need to be examined as these have had an influence in conditioning the minds of the people of Jammu and Kashmir.

Developments consequent to the removal of Sheikh Abdulla set in motion the process of integration of Jammu and Kashmir into the Indian Union, albeit Kashmiri identity a sub-national identity was subordinated to the national identity in the perception of Kashmiris. Sheikh's efforts to create an independent state in Jammu and Kashmir were countered by withering down of state's autonomy as a corollary to integration.

At the all India level Congress having a majority at the Centre, felt threatened by political mobilisation essentially along sub-national identities into electoral majority at the state and regional levels. The Congress response under Mrs. Gandhi was dictated by her parochial stance of identifying Congress with the Indian nation and state. Her response to Jammu and Kashmir was also totally in keeping with this stance as applied to other states. As in other states it not only denied legitimacy to the sub-national identity of Kashmiris but went a step further to impose her and Congress party's political choice on Jammu and Kashmir. It resulted in her effort to replace National Conference with

Congress, debarring Plebiscite Front from state elections and thereby the democratic process. Her refusal to roll back the erosion of Jammu and Kashmir's autonomy in the 1975 accord, turning down Sheikh Abdulla's pleas for fresh elections and withdrawal of support in 1977 after Congress's defeat in general elections were part of the same design.

In 1980's Mrs. Gandhi's efforts to woo Hindus had its adverse fallout on minorities. In Jammu and Kashmir it made Kashmiri Muslims suspicions, and provided encouragement to Ladakhis and Jammu Hindus to adopt a belligerent attitude towards Kashmiris, who were already antagonised due to dominant Kashmiri role in the state. She promoted Jamaat-i-Islami to undercut the National Conference and its secular ethos, thereby the secular foundation of Kashmiri identity. It started the process of communalisation of Kashmiri politics and Kashmiri identity. This was backed by strong arm tactics and abuse of Central Authority in dismissing Farooq Abdulla Govt. Later, Rajiv Gandhi coercing the National Conference into an electoral alliance with the Congress and rigging of 1987 elections was the last straw. Kashmiris were convinced that they would remain disenfranchised under the prevalent political set up and revolted. Denial of a conducive environment for the growth of Kashmiri identity, combined with political ineptness pushed the Kashmiris into a path of confrontation and secession.

In retrospect, it needs to be understood that the success of the political movement in Kashmir against the powerful Dogra Maharaja's rule was due to its ability to expand its narrow ethno-religious stance of Muslim Conference to all powerful National Conference, embracing all state subjects, in the words of Sheikh Abdulla "nor the Muslims, nor the Hindus and Sikhs alone, nor the untouchables alone and Buddhists alone but all those live in the state". It was the composite identity which won mass support, as "Naya Kashmir" had created stakes for everyone in the new political dispensation. However, once Sheikh Abdulla acquired power, his efforts to unify people of Jammu and Ladakh under Kashmiri domination in the constitutional, political and economic fields, alienated and marginalised the non-Kashmiri population including the Gujjars and Shia Muslims. It not only fermented consciousness amongst the Ladakhis, Buddhists and Jammu Hindu majority but politicised their identities demanding Jammu and Kashmir state's closer integration with the Indian state and a separate union territory in Ladakh.

Jammu and Kashmir state's Unitary Constitution, under representation of Jammu in the legislative and state services, neglect and discrimination in socio-economic development of these regions created imbalance and pitted these regions against the Kashmir Valley. Kashmiris' popular slogan of the right of self determination has no appeal in Jammu and Ladakh as independence will put them at the mercy of dominant Kashmiris. Their stance on the issue of restoration of Jammu and Kashmir's autonomy is also guided by similar considerations.

Islamisation of Kashmiri identity in 1990 and Kashmiri Pundits' exodus from the Valley politicised and separated them from the Kashmiri identity demanding a separate home land in the Valley. It also made them voice their opposition to J & K's special status. The question of independence and autonomy is a hostage to these emerging narrow political identities within the state and self defeating to Kashmiri demand of independence or greater autonomy. Kashmiri leadership's insistence that its special status can only be a source of greater unity and closer association with the Indian State is only valid if it accepts that as the dominant majority they need to pay heed to Jammu and Ladakh's argument that greater autonomy within the region will act as a unifying force for people of all the regions. The internal contradictions remain unchanged.

The Kashmiri identity from the "Naya Kashmir" period has undergone a change from Kashmiri people of the Valley in 1950 to Kashmiri Muslims in 1989 and to further division within Kashmiri Muslims on the political goal of independence or greater autonomy to joining Pakistan.

National Conference winning the Assembly Elections in 1996 by two third majority was an indication that unlike the past when it drew its mandate from the Valley but ruled all the state, its victory was more representative. It also depicts a change in the political configuration at the national and state level with the regional and sub-regional forces playing the part. However, we should not forget that due to militancy a large section of the youth and antagonised population did not vote. Kashmiri violent secessionist movement may be on the decline but gun dominated the political process and yet rejection of gun culture was the single most important verdict.

While these trends exist both at the political and grass root level, at the same time there are undercurrents of communalisation and disintegration of the overall Kashmiri identity and its composite nature with adverse political and socio-economic fallout. There is demographic spread of Muslims from the Valley astride the national highway 1A into Doda and Udhampur districts and of Pahari Muslims from Poonch and Rajouri into Jammu region. The demand of Paharis to be recognised as a separate ethnic identity bulk of whom are Muslims akin to the people of POK in Muzaffrabad and Mirpur is motivated and instigated to perpetuate Muslim domination with pro-Pakistan leaning. In the overall context the demographic spread coupled with such demands will give

Jammu & Kashmir greater Muslim domination in State politics and continued Kashmir Muslim dominance within this Muslim identity. Within this overall dominant Muslim identity, separate ethnic groups will try and project separate identities as Gujjars, Bakarwals Shia Muslim, Paharis, Dardi and Baltis. Recognition of Paharis as a separate backward ethnic group (which they are not) will result in Gujjars who are in majority in border and Pir Panjal areas becoming a minority, once the logical step of delimitation of constituencies takes place.

Demographic invasion by Muslims from the Valley and Poonch and Rajouri areas had the tacit support of the NC state Govt. and is part of a design. It is resulting in Jammu town being surrounded by various Muslim ethnic groups. There are also under-currents of proposals as part of the same design to divide and delimit Jammu Division into Doda, Jammu and Rajouri and Poonch, which will make all areas of present Jammu division into Muslim dominant areas.

The worst fears in this regard are confirmed by the release of the Regional Autonomy Committee Report on 13 April 1999. The reforms will further widen the communal divide rather than bring communities together. Its original chairman Balraj Puri resigned in protest against the communal approach of the Committee. The report is reported to be masterminded by Finance Minister Mohammad Shafi Uri and Surankot MLA Mustaq Ahmed Bukhari and was supported by the BJP MP Chaman Lal Gupta and his brother Ramesh Gupta. It seems to have support of Farooq Abdulla and some leaders of the Congress Party. The plan is remarkably similar to the proposal by Owen Dixon, the United Nations Mediator in Kashmir in 1950, which called for international border to run broadly North of Chenab River, thus cutting predominantly Muslim Doda, Rajouri and Poonch from Jammu and joining it with Kashmir with Hindu dominated Jammu and Kathua staying with India. The plan was revived and propagated by the influential United States Think Tank "Kashmir Study Group" in recent years amongst the elite groups in India.

It is a sad commentary on the so called nationalistic leadership of Jammu and Kashmir and India that what Pakistan desired after partition but could not achieve after three wars and over a decade of Insurgency, the political leadership of India and Jammu and Kashmir is offering on a platter for small political gains. Even if the plan is not executed the psychological sellout is total. Why blame Pakistan Foreign Minister Sartaj Azis in asking for a district wise plebiscite if our own people are preparing the agenda for Pakistan designs. The sinister design of our politicians is apparent by the manner in which the media blacked out views of Balraj Puri and others opposed to this and did not publicise the earlier version of the RAC report under him, which had evolved a consensus for reconciling the interests and aspirations of all diversities in the multi-ethnic state of Jammu & Kashmir. In the absence of a strong and committed secular formation in Kashmir, the pro-Pakistan elements led by All Party Hurriyat Conference and JEI will find the resistance in Jammu and Kashmir crumbling and Kashmir will again be victim of cultural, social and religious invasion from the North-West.

REFERENCES

1. Peter Mansfield, *The Arabs*, New York, 1981, as quoted by Ashok Kapur in Militant Islam and Internal Conflict in South Asia and Beyond, 1999, p. 21.
2. G.H.Jansen, *Militant Islam*, Pan Books London, 1979, p. 99.
3. Mansfield n1, pp. 123, 156, 167, 219, 240 and 400 on role of Wahhabism.
4. Ibid, 402, and Jansen n 2, p. 42
5. The Chechen Knot "Directorate of Strategic Analysis, Department of National Defense, Canada, Research Paper No.98/01, February 1998.
6. Behera, Ajay Darshan, in *Strategic Analysis*, p. 1375 Jan.–Feb, 1997, IDSA.
7. Indian Express, 29 August 1998.
8. Dr. Yoginder Sikand, *Economic and Political Weekly* (Reproduced under the title "Changing Course of the Kashmiri Struggle, from National Liberation to Islamist Jehad?") in Peace Initiatives, vol. VI, nos. IV-VI, Jul-Dec 2000.
9. n 8
10. Sreedhar, Nitesh and Nilesh Baghat, *Pakistan A Withering State*, Wordsmiths, Delhi, 1999, p. 94.
11. Ashik Kashmiri, Tarikh-I-Tahrik-I-Islam, Jammu aur Kashmir Aghaz-I-Islam se 1947 Tak and Tarikh-I-Tahrik-I-Islam Jammu aur Kashmir 1947 se 1970 Tak, Department of Publications and Publicity, Jamaait-I-Islami Jammu and Kashmir,1984.
12. Gul Mohammad Wani, *Kashmiri Politics – Problems and Prospects*, pp. 111-114.
13. Extracted from "Foot Prints of Fundamentalism by I.K. Gurjal, *Outlook*, September 21, 1998.
14. Gul Mohammad Wani, *Kashmir Politics and Problems*, p. 116.
15. Maroof Raza, *War and No Peace over Kashmir*, 1996, p.61.
16. V.D.Chopra, *Genesis of Indo-Pak conflict, Kashmir Patriot*, 1990, pp. 116-117.
17. *Ibid*, pp. 14-116.
18. V.K.Nayar, *Threat from Within*, 79.
19. Chris Smith, Light weapons and ethnic conflict in South Asia, p. 64 and IDSA paper on Light Weapons and International Security, 1995
20. *India To-day*, 15 May 1994.
21. Robert Wiring *Pakistan Security under Zia, 1977-88*, Mac Millian London, 1991, pp. 170 and 172 to 175
22. n18, pp. 80-83.

23. Sheikh's speech in the Legislative Assembly, 1975.
24. Indira Gandhi's speech in the Lok Sabha, 24 February 1975.
25. Rijaz Punjabi, Corruption A Factor in Kashmiri Alienation, *Mainstream*, March 16, 1991.
26. Rijaz Punjabi's Paper in a *Seminar* "Kashmir, Economy, Society and Polity" at Srinagar, 31 October 1989.
27. Abid Hussain, *Life of Sheikh Mohammad Abdulla – An Open Book.*
28. M.C. Jain, *The Constitution of India*, 1995.
29. Most of the information is derived from a very comprehensive and detailed paper titled 'Pakistan Occupied Kashmir' (A history of Deprivation) by K.N. Daruwalla, Published by South Asian Centre for Strategic Studies, New Delhi.
30. Benazir Bhutto's statement to *India Today* as quoted in R Kadian, The Kashmir Tangle, West View Press, 1993, p. 140.
31. Editorial in *The Nation*, 27 April 1994.
32. Nasir A Naqash and G.M. Shah, *Kashmir Crisis to Crisis* p. 2.
33. Urmila Phadnis- '*Ethnicity and Nation Building in South Asia*, Sage Publications, Delhi, 1989, p. 14.
34. G.M. Wani and N.A. Naqash, *Reflections on Kashmir Politics*, Ashish Publishing House, New Delhi, 1993, p. 9.
35. M.S. Pampori, *Kashmir in Chains*, p. 1.

Annexure

BREIF NOTE ON JAMAAT-I-ISLAMI AND IKHWAN-UL-MUSLMEEN (MUSLIM BROTHERHOOD OF EGYPT)

The Jamaat-i-Islami (JI) along with its affiliated wings of Pakistan and Tablighi-Jamaat (TJ) are the two most organized Islamic Movements of South Asia. JI aims at establishing an Islamic State in Pakistan with Quran and Sunna (the way of prophet) as its constitution and Sharia as its basic law. Tablighi movement on the other hand wants to inculcate Islamic values in individual Muslims. Both are basically fundamentalists.[1]

The influence and organisation of JI and TJ extend to most Muslim countries of the world. The apolitical stance of the TJ makes it more acceptable to both Muslim and non-Muslim societies. JI faces restriction and opposition due to its religio-political agenda. Both have appeal and ability to mobilise Muslims in the sub-continent, which has implications for politics of the countries of the sub-continent. JI was founded in 1941 in undivided India. In 1947, with the partition, JI split, Maududi, its founder, moved to Lahore and founded JI Pakistan. Maulana Lais Islahi a close associate of Maududi stayed back and reorganised the JI in India, which purely concentrates on religious issues like Muslim Personal law and is apolitical. JI Pakistan drifted from the parent JI and there is only little formal contact left. JI (Pak) became an aggressive propagant of establishing an Islamic state in Pakistan. It has large cadres, who advocate fundamentalism and it has along with the Muslim brotherhood of Egypt served as the model for Muslim revivalism and has links with Dar-ul-Islam of Indonesia, The Islamic National Front of Sudan, the Islam Tendency Society in Tunis, the Party Islam Se-Malaysia and Rafah Party of Turkey—all fundamental organisations aiming to establish idealised Islamic systems.[2] JI justifies political activities and believes Islam being a complete system and all aspects of Muslims life, political, social, cultural and economic cannot be separated from religion. Its vision is Pan-Islamic and recognizes the importance of gaining political power.

The leaders of the Muslim Brotherhood of Egypt, founded in 1928, Abul Ala Mahadudi and Hassan-Al-Barna have similar rigid stance against non-Islamic societies, which laid the foundation of the militant Islam in Egypt. Sayyid Qutb, a prominent leader of Muslim Brotherhood, advocated a bloody revolution against the assertive secularism of Nasser in Egypt. He justified terrorism, subversion and armed Jehad against infidels. According to this concept religiously motivated violence was justified against Muslims who strayed from the straight path and those who refused to join Jehad. It also divided the world into an abode of peace (Dar-ul-Islam) and an abode of war (Dar-ul-Harb); non-Islam world was abode of war, therefore violence against it was justified. Mosques and Madarsas have become the focal point for spreading the word of radical Islam and training of terrorist and subversive groups assumed an organised form to perpetuate violence in the aid of religious fundamentalism. About 8,000 Sunni Madarsas came into being during Zia-ul-Haq regime. These were funded by Saudi Arabia, Iraq and CIA. The latter wanted to use motivated students to fight and bleed Soviet forces in Afghanistan. This led to anti-Shia violence in Pakistan, Punjab, NWFP, Gilgit and Baltistan. Iraq responded by helping Shia organisations to fight Sunni attacks. The coalition of Pak army's ISI, Taliban (Sunnis) and Madarsas, which emerged in 1980s is still effective in Afghan and Pak politics. The growth of Shia-Sunni violence is a sign that Pakistan itself is an ideological and military battle field and militant Islam is not only involved in conflicts in Jammu and Kashmir, Punjab and Afghanistan but also internally within Pakistan.

REFERENCES

1. Ahmed, Mumtaz, 1994, "Islamic Fundamentalism in South Asia in Martin E Harty and R Scott Applely (ed)- fundamentalism observed, Chicago. The University of Chicago Press, p. 458.
2. *Ibid*, p. 459.

7

Movement for Azadi, Militancy, Proxy War and its Islamic Agenda and War on Global Terrorism

The events of the past fourteen years have centered around the proxy war and it has had a fall out on the internal and external dynamics of the situation in Jammu and Kashmir. The configuration of the Low Intensity Conflict or proxy war itself has undergone changes in its military and politico-social content. The indigenous content in both the fields has reduced due to our success in the military and political field. The foreign and Pakistani content with Pan Islamic orientation has become predominant, giving primacy to her Politico-strategic goals. A brief examination of the proxy war since 1989 will therefore be relevant in this context.

Gestation Period

It will be prudent to accept that this phase commenced after the rigged elections of 1987, when a large number of Kashmiri youth crossed over the Line of Control (LoC) for training in Pakistan and induction of arms and ammunition in the Valley started. Various estimates put the figures between 15,000 and 20,000 during 1988 and 1989. This has to be viewed in the backdrop of events in Afghanistan and the ISI's reported diversion of almost 60 per cent of the arms and ammunition delivered by the West for Afghanistan, and Pakistan's experience in Punjab. This was aided and abetted by Jamaait-i-Islami cadres by injecting fundamentalism in the body politic and society.

The period was marked by mass agitations, demonstrations, bomb blasts and selected targeting of Kashmiri Pandits to give it communal overtones. This was followed by the terrorising of the general public through arson, destruction of government property like schools, bridges, administrative buildings and intimidating government functionaries to undermine Government authority and establish the writ of the militants. This phase was marked by three events which encouraged and gave credence to militancy. One was the kidnapping of Rubiyya Sayeed, the then Home Minister's daughter (March 1990). The second was the killing of Mirwaiz Maulana Mohammed Farooq, Chairman of Awami Action Committee (24 March, 1990), by the terrorists and firing on his funeral procession by panicky CRPF personnel in which 57 civilians were killed. Third, the high point of political ineptness, when Farooq Abdulla was provoked to resign on the appointment of Jag Mohan as Governor. This was also marked with mass Kashmiri Pandit migration to outside the Valley thus bringing the Central Government in direct confrontation with the situation. All these events put together can be termed as political and strategic failures of the highest order.

Till March, 1990, the Army was manning the Line of Control (LoC), as hitherto, against armed military intrusions and overt Pakistani action. It did not interfere with civilian movement. In the period before March 1990 major infiltration and exfiltration had taken place to and from Kashmir. This was both a political and military failure of high magnitude. In particular terms it was the failure of all the intelligence agencies, central, local and military. This put us to a disadvantage and was the beginning of a reactive syndrome and gave Pakistan the initiative.

Insurgency to Proxy War

The process of ethnic cleansing, arson, destruction of property and process of undermining the Government's authority continued during the summer of 1990. The period was marked by escalation in militant strikes against selected targets, militant operations enlarged to cover dispersed areas of the Valley and operational aspects of military gained ascendancy.

Insurgency had started in the summer of 1990.Realisation on the Government dawned and military responses to deal with the situation were set in motion. Valley and the 20 Km belt of Rajouri and Poonch areas were declared disturbed on 5 July 1990. and process of undermining the Government's authority continued during the summer of 1990.

The years 1991-92 saw escalation in militant activities and intensification of counter-insurgency operations by the security forces. Army tightened the anti-infiltration and exfiltration measures along the LoC and areas immediately in depth. These efforts met with notable success in Kupwara and Uri sectors, which drew violent responses from Pakistan in the shape of limited attacks on some army posts, artillery duels and heightened activities along LoC in Kashmir, Poonch and Rajouri. The Indian response was professional, controlled and aggressive resulting in heavy casualties to Pakistan and few casualties on our side as well. This changed the configuration of the LoC and more troops were inducted and CI operations were intensified, resulting in the killing of militants in increasing numbers and capture of a large quantity of arms and militants. Interrogation of captured militants and events along the LoC gradually revealed the design of proxy war by the end of 1992.

During this period while military responses to meet the situation were built up, the civil administration took further beating due to the strike by Government employees. The Government's functioning was disrupted and public distribution system and civic services and Government infrastructure broke down, resulting in greater hardship to the people and further alienation.

Allegations of mass rape at Kunan, Poshpora in Kupwara in February 1991 and other incidents were exploited by militants to put pressure on the Government. Murli Manohar Joshi's Ekta Yatra and Amanullah Khan's efforts to organise a people's march, which was prevented by the Pakistan Government, were other events of significance.

The situation turned around during the summer of 1993. The anti-militancy drive centred around the formulation of a unified concept at the state and field levels to plan, co-ordinate and execute CI operations, establishment of a CI Grid, better management of LoC, improvement of intelligence and rebuilding the police force.

The year 1993 and the beginning of 1994 saw huge losses to the militants, increase in criminal activities and people gradually turning away from the militants. The period also marked a high rate of drop outs of Kashmiri militants both due to heavy casualties and maltreatment by Pakistan authorities. Decline in the effectiveness of Kashmiri militants forced ISI to induct greater numbers of mercenaries resulting in greater disillusionment of the Kashmiris. 1995 and the period after this is marked by a pronounced change in the configuration and orientation of insurgency. From a combination of Pro-Azadi and Pro-Pakistan militancy, it is mainly thriving as a Pro-Pak proxy war.

The militancy picture is not complete without taking into account the events of Hazratbal in October 1993 and the Charar-e-Sharif incident of March 1995. While the first was a success, the second can be termed as a failure. It was followed by the kidnapping of the six western hostages by Al Faran.

The years 1996 and 1997 were marked by pro-active initiatives in the political field by holding elections to the Jammu and Kashmir Assembly and installation of an elected Government in November 1996. This was followed by elections to the Lok Sabha in February/March 1998 which completed the political process.

Along with the above political process, the situation was marked by two major trends. One, that the proxy war had passed into the hands of the foreign mercenaries operating under the direct control of ISI. Secondly, that it has spread and taken root in areas of Poonch, Rajouri and Pir Panjal Range. Attacks on isolated Hindu villages in the upper reaches of the Pir Panjal in Udhampur district and adjoining areas were a part of ISI design to perpetuate ethnic cleansing in dispersed areas to give it a further communal colour and create Muslim dominant areas in conjunction with local fundamentalist forces.

With the installation of a popular government there was the expected dilution of CI strategy formulated earlier, whereas the need was to reinforce it in view of the emerging proxy war threat. Nuclear explosions both by India and Pakistan in May 1998 and weaponisation of this capability by both will take time to stabilise and did not make any changes to Pakistani designs of proxy war. If any, there was escalation of it both in its dimensions and intensity.

Till end March 1999, the army had killed 7,994 militants and 24,251 had been apprehended including 900 foreign mercenaries killed and 150 apprehended. 1,858 militants had surrendered to the Army. The figures do not include results achieved by the PMF and Jammu and Kashmir Police. Army casualties included 1,005 killed and 3,017 wounded and 23,817 weapons of various sorts were recovered. Militancy has claimed the lives of over 29,000 innocent civilians and about 2, 80,000 persons have been rendered homeless. The loss to public and private property is estimated to be Rs.2, 000 crores[1].

Finding their design floundering, Pakistan raised the ante by massive intrusion in the Dras and Kargil sector in May, 1999; this was totally against the hopes generated by the Lahore declaration of February, 1999.

The intrusions in Kargil should primarily be viewed as an extension of the proxy war to boost the flagging insurgency and raise the stakes in Jammu and Kashmir and internationally. With insurgency having been brought under control and normally making strides in Jammu and Kashmir, Pakistan had to rejuvenate the proxy war. In keeping with her design of Islamisation of the proxy war, its expansion into Doda, Jammu, Udhampur and Poonch and Rajouri areas to create and enlarge Muslim dominated areas. She achieved success but it did not disturb the overall situation as after initial successes her efforts in this regard were contained. Moreover, terrorist strikes against innocent civilians beyond a point were proving counter productive as world conscience against sponsorship of terrorism had been sufficiently stirred. The next obvious areas were on the LoC and Kargil that fulfilled the requirements of a Muslim dominated and a vulnerable area, which had been softened by artillery shelling since

1997. In Pakistan perception the recently acquired nuclear parity against India minimized the chances of a conventional war or a major conventional response in another area. Therefore Pakistan could indulge in a sizeable conventional intrusion across LOC to draw international attention, for insurgency does not convey the same as heightened military activity in the disputed territory (Pakistan perception) across the LOC like Kargil and Siachen do. Militarily, a large scale intrusion apart from drawing international attention will extend the Indian Army, create fresh avenues of infiltration, threaten the vital lines of communication to Ladakh and do a Siachen to India. After the 1971 defeat, Siachen rankles in the Pakistani, particularly its military, mind the most.

The Indian Army's response to Kargil intrusions after the initial shock was most professional and in tune with the prevailing geo-strategic situation. India's decision not to cross the LoC, in spite of the constraints that it imposed militarily, was politically and diplomatically wise and the country reaped rich dividends internationally. The junior leadership from battalion commander and below has done us proud and their valour and dedication remains unsurpassed. Much against professional estimates they threw out the intruders by 10th July '99, whereas most estimates had considered success before onset of winter as an excellent going. However, a heavy cost in terms of human lives with 400 killed about 900 wounded and in material sources and finances had to be paid. It has also imposed long term costs in material and human resources due to imperative higher level of deployments in the area. The episode has left a lot of grey areas.

Without being privy to the information or intelligence available to the Army, the intelligence agencies and to the Government, to a professional mind there should be no doubt that there was failure at the operational level, in the intelligence field and above all there was serious failure in perception to appreciate the growing dimensions of the ongoing proxy war.

In a assessment given out during a lecture on the proxy war in July 1998 at the United Services Institution[2] author had pointed out that the proxy war has been totally Islamised and passed into the hands of the Pakistan Army and ISI, with execution mainly through foreign Mujahideens. It had also become imperative for Pakistan to create Muslim dominated areas and extend the proxy war to these areas and to ferment a communal divide. Terrain wise, for this design to succeed the outer core of the LoC and the Pir Panjal spine had become vital to enlarge the scope of the proxy war. LoC was of particular importance as discussed above. The increased activity in Kargil was a part of the design but we failed to read it inspite of intelligence indicators. May be euphoria of Lahore bus ride clouded even the professional minds.

Having suffered a major military defeat in Kargil, Pakistan agreed to withdraw across the LoC under world pressure. Nawaz Sharief lost politically and diplomatically, repercussions of which are manifesting against Pakistan Govt., both internally and abroad, of which economic crisis will be a major challenge. But the managers of the proxy war are beyond any accountability. In August, militants attacked a BSF Camp, the Rashtriya Rifles (RR) camp, at Kupwara on 6th August and next day killed the commanding officer of the RR and then attacked the brigade headquarters. In all there were 18 attacks on Security Forces resulting in 48 deaths.[3] This was followed by disrupting the election process by killing candidates and intimidating the voters. The militants belonged to Harkat-ul-Ansar (An Afghan and Pakistani Tanzeem), Al Badr Mujahideen (owe allegiance to Osama Bin Laden) and Lashkar-e-Toeiba (Lahore based), all Pakistani and foreign mercenaries. There was a large haul of RDX (Over 100 Kg) from places as apart as Delhi, Haryana, Punjab, Bengal and Assam. Cells of Lashkar-e-Toeiba have been located in Punjab, Haryana, Andhra Pradesh and Mumbai.

Having failed in Kargil, escalation of the situation was to be expected. The strikes are entirely by the well trained, seasoned and motivated Mujahideen of the Taliban variety and the complexion of militancy is entirely Islamic and Jehadi with little indigenous participation.

It is estimated that over 2000-3000 Jehadis were infiltrated during the summer of 1999 itself, they were equipped with more sophisticated weapons like RPG's, SAM's, mines and explosives. However Jehadis suffered heavy casualties, 1278 were killed in 1999 compared to 1111 in 1998, and our casualties were also higher 278 in 1999 compared to 230 in 1998.

The years 2000 and 2001 continued to witness higher levels of militant activities and there was a spurt in IED and bomb blasts and attacks on SF. For the first time Sikhs were targeted by the Jehadi militants, when 36 Sikhs were killed in Chatti Singhpura on 20 March 2000 in pursuance of their policy of ethnic cleansing in the valley and to create communal divide.

In the political field, the APHC leaders were released in April 2000 but efforts to talk to them since have not met with any success; neither have the cease fire of July 2000 by Abdul Majid Dar, Dy Supreme Commander of HM and a later one by the Central Government in November 2000 fructified. Farooq Abdullah floated the autonomy balloon by passing the autonomy resolution in the State assembly in July 2000, which was promptly rejected by the Central Government. The failure of Agra Summit in July 2001 added on to the confrontation. Jehadi militants have also been able to target Amarnath Yatris both in 2001 and 2002.

The terrorist attacks on the Jammu and Kashmir Assembly in Srinagar on 2 October 2001 and on the Indian Parliament on 13 December 2001 put further pressure on the Government. The response was prompt and government ordered full scale mobilisation of the armed forces and moved them to their battle locations, where they continued for over a year. Such a prolonged deployment was bound to have an adverse effect on the armed forces and the Government motives were questioned: were these political? With American troops present in Pakistan and war against terrorism going on in Afghanistan, the chances of our having gone to war with Pakistan were remote. The cost of such a prolonged deployment is bound to effect the economy, essentially it will retard the armed forces modernisation. The argument that the cost for Pakistan is higher is disputed as Pakistan knows that war is unlikely due to American presence. America cannot let down Pakistan for its own reasons. The happenings in Gujrat further eroded our credibility internationally and pressure on the Government domestically added to its problems.

A Fair and a Faulted Election

Two elections held back to back, one in J & K and the other in Pakistan have two entirely different stories to tell; the only commonality was a fractured political verdict. The one in Pakistan in spite Musharraf's pre-election rigging and manipulation and the one in J & K due to its fairness and in spite of Pakistan backed militants perpetrating large scale violence.

The four phased elections in Jammu and Kashmir during September and October 2002 can be rightly termed as the fairest but the bloodiest elections in the state. During the 45 days of campaigning 46 political activists mostly of the ruling National Conference including a minister were killed compared to 13 in 1996. The credit must essentially go to the people of Jammu and Kashmir for their resolve for peaceful solution through constitutional means. The voter turnout varied from 47.25 per cent in the first round to the highest of 52 per cent in the final round, the lowest being 40.60% in the second phase. The ruling National Conference (NC) paid the price for misgovernance during six years of its tenure. The final tally was NC-29, Congress-30, Peoples Democratic Party (PDP)-16 and others including independents-22. The results are a reflection of people seeking a change both in governance and solution through a different dispensation.

The elections have established the credibility and legitimacy of Indian intentions to seek a solution in the world and to large extent internally amongst the people of Jammu and Kashmir. The rejection of the idea of trifurcation of the state by the people of Jammu and Kashmir is also a triumph for the secular and democratic elements in the state.

Ultimately India and the people of Jammu and Kashmir are the real winners. The Chief Elections Commissioner and his dedicated teams deserve all the credit for making it possible.

The mandate clearly indicates that the problem can only be resolved by a political consensus, as the new Government has a strong regional component and natural balance in dealing with the problem. Political rhetorics during the elections should be forgotten and substantial issues and governance should be the focus. This will require statesmanship and accommodation by the Central leaders and understanding by the new Government in Jammu and Kashmir. In the security field issues bothering the minds of the people should be addressed, without diluting our security posture or maligning the SF. The threat of Proxy war in years to come is likely to escalate due to pressure of hardliners on Musharraf, who will be a part of the government in Pakistan.

Compared to the elections in Jammu and Kashmir, elections in Pakistan on 10 October 2002 to the National Assembly were termed by most neutral observers as pre-rigged. EU considered them as flawed and the Commonwealth Observer Group alleged misuse of government machinery in favour of a certain political party PML (QA). In spite of reducing the voting age to 18 years, the turn out was low. Bush administration was forced to muffle its disappointment as too hard a push for democracy could produce a worse alternative. However, USA Today had protested on 10 October that Musharraf's political abuses deserve loud condemnation. The British press led by the *Guardian* and *Financial Times* were more forthright in their condemnation. While the former went on to say that if Bush's war on terrorism was remotely rational or even roughly reasoned their next target might be Pakistan and not Iraq. *The Financial Times* said that the USA must be warned that these highly restricted elections will not produce a stable ally. *The Time* had predicted that the likely beneficiary of general elections will be the religious right and he had given them freer reign in the campaign than the two main political parties, which were his main rivals.

In spite of Musharraf's best efforts to get his Kings Party PML (QA), it could win only 77 seats, PPP got 62 and the Alliance of six hard-line religious parties Muthahida Majlis E-Amal (MMA) walked away with 67 seats. What is more worrisome is that it gained clear majority in the frontier provinces of Baluchistan and NWFP and formed their government in these provinces. It also made serious in-roads into MQM's preserve in Karachi. This is the first time that religious parties will have such a formidable presence in the National Assembly and control borders with Afghanistan. MMA has started putting pressure on Musharraf by announcing that they will take oath under the 1973 constitution and not as amended my Musharraf. They also want American air-base at Jacobabad to be vacated and US troops to leave and impose the Islamic Shariat law. Its general secretary Maulana Fazlur Rehman Khalili was the leader of the banned Harkat-ul-Mujahideen and one of the signatories to Osama bin Laden's 1998 Fatwa calling for an attack on US interests. It has already shown its clout by releasing pro-Taliban prisoners from the central jail in Quetta by declaring them as white.

While the future dispensation in Pakistan may give greater leverage to Musharraf to extract concession from USA, the war against terrorism will be seriously hampered by the MMA in control of the border with Afghanistan and with a substantial presence in the National Assembly. With MMA's Pan Islamic orientation and known support of elements within it to Osama bin Laden and Taliban, stability in Afghanistan is seriously threatened and militancy in Jammu and Kashmir is already showing an upward trend. The war against terrorism is heading for a stone wall.

Kashmir 2003

On 22 March 2003, Abdul Majeed Dar was gunned down in Sopore by suspected HM factions loyal to Salahudin. The rift between Majeed Dar and Salahudin had widened when Majeed Dar declared ceasefire in 2000 and opted to stay away with some top commanders in the valley to re-group his cadres. He was expelled in 2002 by Salahudin under instructions of the ISI to marginalise the pro-peace lobby. There had been clashes between the Dar's cadres and Salahudin loyalist in POK and Dar was making preparations to go to POK to take control of his cadres. This was followed by the massacre on the 24 of March 52 Kashmiri Pandits in Nandimarg in Pulwama district on the 23 March 2003 by suspected militants of LET dressed in army uniforms. The police post established to provide protection to Kashmiri Pandits surrendered meekly without firing a shot. Two days later militants chopped off the noses of 6 Muslims in Panihad village in Poonch suspecting them of helping the security forces but it passed off unnoticed. Can security forces and the state afford to ignore people who help in eliminating Pakistani Jehadis? We must realise that these are all modulations of Pakistan Proxy War to eliminate all opposition to Jehadis and perpetrate a communal divide. Mufti's softness is not to blame as during the National Conference regime now termed hard on the Jehadis, there were greater killings during a similar period. Despite what critics may say Mufti's "healing touch policy" has started bearing results. The people of Jammu and Ladakh have appropriate representation in the government, he got Farooq Abdulla elected to the Rajya Sabha with PDP support and his insistence with the Centre to start a dialogue with all sections of Kashmiris has been taken in hand by the centre by appointing N.N. Vohra as the chief negotiator.

Prime Minister Atal Bihari Vajpayee during his historic visit to Srinagar on 18-19 April 2003 laid the foundation of what could possibly be a breakthrough in the stalemated situation. He mentioned peace with Pakistan, asserted that gun was no solution, negotiations were; and that the government was fully behind Jammu and Kashmir Chief Minister Mufti Mohammed Sayeed[4]. At the Kashmir University convocation he spoke of Hindu-Muslim unity, Sufi philosophy and valley's composite culture[5]. He also referred to the happenings in Iraq as a warning and need for India and Pakistan to sit down and sort out their problems, inviting a third party will only expand the problem. Later addressing the parliament, he informed that he has assured the people of Jammu and Kashmir "we wish to resolve all issues both domestic and external through talks." He stressed that gun can solve no problem, brotherhood can. Issues can be resolved by the principles of *Insaniyat* (humanism), *Jamhooriat* (democracy) and *Kashmiriyat* (Kashmir's composite culture).[6] Immediately following his visit there were fidaeen attacks at Bandipore, Radio Kashmir in Srinagar, Tral (Pulwama) and Drugmullah in Kupwara. There has been no let up in militant activities and there are reports of a large number waiting to infiltrate.

The Prime Minister's peace offer drew immediate response from Pakistan and Mir Zafarullah Khan Jamali the Prime Minister of Pakistan spoke to him on the 28 April, welcoming his peace initiatives, saying that Pakistan was willing to talk to India at any level and hoping that these will cover all issues including Kashmir. He offered to send the High Commissioner, giving landing rights to Indian aircrafts and releasing fisherman, some Sikhs and crew members of a cargo ship in Pakistan jails but kept silent on the issue of cross-border terrorism[7]. India responded by appointing a High Commissioner to Pakistan, restoring civil aviation links on a reciprocal basis and restoring relations to the level prior to the terrorist attacks on the parliament in December 2001. With the thaw in the Indo-Pak relations, India's stance from "we won't talk unless you end cross-border terrorism" to a less absolutist position of "we will talk, but you must end cross-border terrorism"[8]. While realising the need to act on India's offer, it is important for Pakistan to assure the fundamentalist groups that it has not compromised. Foreign Minister Kasuri's offer to do something to lower the temperature but India must reciprocate by non-initiation of operations as in the past[9].

Further impetus to the peace process was provided by Pakistan responding favourably to Prime Minister Vajpayee's twelve point peace proposals for confidence building, while some were accepted immediately, the response to other was open and these were to be part of the dialogue process. If the Srinagar initiative broke the ice and saw return of High Commissioners; resumption of train and air services and discussion on new routes to connect the two countries including Srinagar-Muzaffarabad added to the thaw in the Indo-Pak relations. Pakistan's offer of cease-fire along the LoC and extending it to the entire border and Siachen provided indications of change in the proxy war environment. Infiltration had come down, people along the LoC heaved a sigh of relief and divided families exchanged news and views. It rekindled hope for the future and peace looked a possibility. As dates of the 12th SAARC summit were announced momentum for peace built up and there were all the indications that President Musharraf did not wish to lose the opportunity. His declaration of putting the UN Resolution and the failed Agra summit behind were healthy indicators. The statesman in Vajpayee responded by announcing his participation in the summit in January 2004.

2004–Change of Winds

Deeply conscious of what he had said repeatedly, that this was his third and last chance for peace, Prime Minister Vajpayee sent his Principal Secretary and National Security Advisor Brijesh Mishra to Islamabad for behind door negotiations with Musharraf's key advisors. This was part of the scheme to take the peace process forward, after weeks of deliberate thought and interaction with his key advisors. The inaugural session of the SAARC summit set the tone, when Pakistan Prime Minister Mir Zafarullah Khan Jamali omitted any reference to Kashmir or UN resolutions. Prime Minister's response was equally positive, when he told the heads of the states assembled at the summit, "History can remind us, guide us, teach us or warn us. It should not shackle us"[10]. The handshake between the two prime ministers after inaugural session followed by a courtesy call on the Pakistan Prime Minister convinced Prime Minister Vajpayee that time was ripe to change the dynamics of interaction between the two countries and the movement was in the right direction. It set the stage for the meeting between President Musharraf and Prime Minister Vajpayee next day. Greeting Prime Minister Vajpayee warmly, President Musharraf complimented him on his vision. Prime Minister Vajpayee responded by saying that we should consolidate what has been achieved by innumerable Confidence Building Measures over the past few months. President Musharraf seized the opportunity to address India's Prime concern of cross border terrorism. He said, "we have taken steps against terrorism and now it has become our common enemy", citing the recent attempts on his life (December 2003)[11]. The joint press statement issued on 5 January 2004 reflects the same sprit.

President Musharraf during his press conference the next day emphasized on simultaneity, insisting there could be no movement on one issue without movement on all other issues. Demining of border and other de-escalation measures followed the agreement. The world community has welcomed the thaw and start of negotiations on different issues in February 2004. Pressure by USA on India and to a greater degree on Pakistan is generally sited as the catalyst for the peace process. Irrespective of reasons, progress both in Indo-Pak relations and the agreements during the 12th summit of SAARC bid well for South Asia.

Simultaneously, a breakthrough was made on the domestic front by nomination of the Dy. Prime Minister LK Advani as the centre's interculator and the first meeting with the Hurriyat leaders was held on 22 January 2004. The situation in the valley, in spite of Security Forces successes in killing of top HM Commander Ghulam Rasool a. k. a. Ghazi Naseerudin on 16 January and Abdul Majid Wani, outfit's Anantnag District Chief, had a set back when seven civilians were killed in separate incidents. This brought both the Mufti Govt's policy of healing touch and Hurriyat under pressure before the next round talks in March 2004.

The Centre reacted promptly and both the Dy. Prime Minister and the Defence Minister took the Security Forces to task and asked them to reinforce human rights norms and avoid collateral civilian casualties during anti-militant operations. Use of porters during operations and detention of suspects in Army camps was forbidden. As the prime mover of dialogue with separatists and his healing touch policy, Mufti Mohammad Sayeed and his PDP cadres have become prime targets of the militants; Mufti himself escaped an attempt on him on 27 February at a rally near Badgam. With JKLF, Jamaat-e-Islami and Peoples League boycotting the talks and Fazal Haq Quereshi leaving after the first round, the pressure on Hurriyat is mounting. This could be the dark cloud over the peace process.

The second round of talks between the Hurriyat and the Dy. Prime Minister L. K. Advani took place on 27 March as scheduled. The meeting ended on a positive note both for the Govt. and the Hurriyat. While Hurriyat gave their consent for not boycotting the Lok Sabha Elections due next month and Govt. agreeing to release more separatist leaders from detention provided there are no criminal cases against them. But what is of added significance is that Maulvi Abbas Ansari made it clear that talks with Dy. Prime Minister L. K. Advani would continue despite reservations in certain quarters. Hurriyat leaders also made it clear to the visiting PPP leaders from Pakistan. "the time to play Kashmir politics was over and Pakistan would do well to put behind the decades old hatred and join the process to usher in peace in the region". They also said peace and not Kashmir should be the central issue[12]. The next round is scheduled in June 2004 after the elections, it is hoped that substantial issues will be discussed.

Efforts of the militants to disrupt the peace process by targeting PDP leaders continue, they targeted Mehbooba Mufti convoy while going for an election meeting on 27 March 2004 and the PDP's rally at Uri on 9 April demanding the opening of the Srinagar-Muzafarabad Road killing 9 persons and wounding 60 including two PDP ministers Muzaffar Husain Beigh and Ghulam Hassan Mir. The terrorist attacks are against the peace process and its supporters. Mehbooba Mufti, PDP president who was also present blamed the attack on political rivalry.

Hurriyat while condemning the attack backtracked from their earlier stand and voiced opposition to the Lok Sabha elections in April/May 2004, clearly indicating pressure of extremists and anti-dialogue lobby. They even asked for a cease-fire in the valley. A call for cease-fire against Pakistani Islamic militants and their changed stance defy logic. It also raises the issue, whether Hurriyat has the mass backing to negotiate a solution. The militants also started targeting Congress rallies in April. During National Conference election rallies Omar Abdulla asked for initiation of talks with Ali Shah Gillani, Yasin Malik and Shabir Shah and not just Hurriyat led by Maulvi Abbas Ansari. He also accused the Chief Minister Mufti Mohammad Sayeed of being an agent of the Centre. Such rehetorics may be good for elections but can hardly add to peace and local security. Simultaneously, during Friday congregation on 16 April Mirwaiz Umar Farrook asked the political parties PDP and National Conference to join their Kashmir movement as they speak in the same language. Shabir Shah had said the same a day earlier. He said elections and dialogue are two separate issues[13]. The heat and dust kicked up during elections may leave some sand to be removed before serious dialogue and real issues can be addressed.

However, Musharraf once again queered the pitch during his speech in the *India To-day* conclave in March by saying that, "Kashmir issue lies at the heart of India – Pakistan confrontation and is a source of disunity in South Asia. If there is no movement towards a solution on Kashmir[14], I am afraid everything will slide back to square one". Colin Powel during his visit during the same period while visiting India and Pakistan declared the USA was raising Pakistan's status to that of a Major Non-NATO ally (MNNA), no mention of it was made to the Indian leaders in New Delhi earlier. This quickly followed the lifting of the sanctions imposed on Pakistan following General Musharraf Coup. The moot question is, where does it leave US-India strategic partnership?

Global War against Terrorism

Terrorist attacks on the World Trade Centre twin towers and the Pentagon in the USA on 11 September 2001 changed the dynamics of terrorism globally both in its dimensions and reach. It is the biggest challenge that the USA, the only superpower, has faced after the cold war. The war launched by the USA and its allies against terrorism generally drew positive response world over. While most nations showed willingness to participate in the war against terrorism even amongst NATO allies and other European countries only the U.K., Canada, Norway, Denmark and Germany opted for direct involvement. Russia offered cooperation in the intelligence field and agreed to the use of its air space but refused joint operations. In return it wanted US cooperation in Chechanya. It is fair to assume that provision of bases and facilities in the central Asian states of Turkmenistan, Tajikistan (air-bases), Kyrgyzstan, Uzbekistan (main air base) and Kazakhstan (air bases) had tacit Russian approval as their utility would be limited without Russian air space and intelligence. Iran which has provided shelter to Afghan refugees and Pastun warlord Hekmatyar, while not responding, maintained a neutral stance. China offered cooperation against terrorism under the UN Security Council Resolution 1373 of 28 September 2001 and in return asked for USA and the west's understanding about separatist movements in Taiwan, Tibet and the Xinjiang area. French deployed part of its Navy to support US operations, Japan undertook refueling of coalition ship in the Indian Ocean, Turkey extended refueling facilities to the US air force and Spain and South Korea extended logistical support. Each nation was guided by its own interests and strategic imperatives.

US led war against terrorism in Afghanistan has had partial success so far. It has succeeded in its political objectives of replacing the radical Taliban by a more broad based regime under Karzai. However the military objectives of killing or capturing Osama bin Laden, the Al Queda and the Taliban leadership could not be achieved and most of them managed to escape and are still at large in the border districts of NWFP and Baluchistan in Pakistan, which is only possible with Pakistan's connivance. Although Pakistan appears to have permitted US intelligence and covert operations by its Special Forces, but these are unlikely to succeed without the full cooperation of Pakistan. While the war against Osama bin Laden, Al Queda and Taliban is still on, US launched its second phase of its war against terrorism on the 11 March by providing contingents to train local forces in the Philippines, Georgia, and Yemen. The aim is essentially political to demonstrate momentum of the war against terrorism, deploy training assistance teams in friendly countries, show flag and hope for some success. The US is unlikely to commit its manpower in these areas to fight terrorism.

The nature of the US military action so far clearly indicated US dilemma to act but still caters for anti-US sentiment in the Islamic world. From a crusade, it has changed to a war against terrorism, with clear enunciation of it not being anti-Islamic. "Operation Infinite Justice" was changed to "Operation Enduring Freedom". The US realises that its prime targets Osama and his Al Queda group have a wide network which draws its strength from the strong anti-US sentiment in the Islamic world. It is very strong in the Middle East, in South Asia, in Afghanistan and Pakistan, South-East Asia and Islamic countries in Africa. The core of the sentiment lies in Palestine/Israeli conflict, in US support to Israel, aggression against Iraq and Iran, the control of the Persian Gulf and US support to monarchies and dictatorial regimes in the Islamic countries. To succeed US military actions have to be wide spread but such a strategy is constrained by fear of civilian casualties, which are bound to intensify anti-US feelings and weaken the coalition against terrorism. In the Islamic countries Saudi Arabia, Egypt and Jordan that support the USA, it will strengthen domestic opposition and terrorist groups.

Given the devastating effect of the 9/11 attacks on the USA and the outcry against it world over the Jehadis are likely to reorient their strategy, for such attacks in the future may prove to be counterproductive as it will consolidate opposition to it and cement the alliance against terrorism further. A greater sophistication by selective use of chemical and biological agents against widely distributed targets would equally incapacitate nations and government and keep the US and the alliance partners under pressure. This was well proved by very limited use of Anthrax in the USA and Australia and the fear it generated worldwide.

To Musharraf in Pakistan it was a God-sent opportunity and he made the best use of it. Under pressure due to dire economic state (35 billion US dollars loan outstanding) and the Jehadi group and their symphathisers he joined the war against terrorism. To safeguard what he called Pakistan National Interests, security (against external threat, read India), revive the economy, protect strategic missile and nuclear capability (which the American's had threatened to take out) and the cause in Kashmir. He has gained both domestically and internationally. For his own survival he has removed pro-Taliban and hard line elements in the army and in return has resurrected economic and arms aid. From almost a terrorist state, Pakistan has emerged as a frontline state, an ally that the USA cannot do without due to its geo-strategic location and deep involvement in Afghanistan. Cross border terrorism sponsored against India is secondary as has been proved by the US responses on the issue so far.

The situation within Pakistan is however showing signs of destabilisation and Musharraf seems to be running out of options. While the Supreme Court of Pakistan has decreed the referendum on the 30 April 2002 won by Musharraf, unlike the earlier occasions, in public perceptions its credibility is doubtful. Jehadis' in connivance with fundamentalist organisations and the polity are likely to exploit Musharraf's anti-Jehad policy and the anti-US sentiments.

More than two years after the start of war against terrorism, USA is still submerged in the quagmire of Afghanistan and is far from achieving fully its military and political aims. Osama-bin-Laden, his Al Queda group and Taliban have escaped to tribal areas bordering Afghanistan in Pakistan and some have gone to sanctuaries all over the world. Except for the capture of Abu Zubaidah a senior Al Queda leader near Jalalabad there is nothing to show except for the unconfirmed claims of 3000-4000 having been killed in "OP Anaconda" in Tora Bora Caves Complex. It is now confirmed that only 200-300 Al Queda fighters hid in Tora Bora Caves to misdirect US Special Forces, while rest escaped to Pakistan. It is also widely believed that during the battle of Kunduz, before its fall in November 2001, 3000 Al-Queda fighters were surreptitiously evacuated to Persian Gulf and Africa along with Pakistanis. Evacuation of Pakistanis was part of the silent agreement with US[15].

The law and order situation in Afghanistan has remained disturbed in the last two years and Interim Government under Karzai has not been able to mitigate peoples' hardships. Its writ runs only in Kabul and the Internal Security Assistance Force (5000) finds it difficult to control Kabul itself. The elections to the constitutional Loya Jirga in December 2003 were marred by vote buying, death threats and intimidation and warlords or their proxies were mostly elected. Even the regional elections in Kabul under the very nose of Interim Govt., UN officials and hundreds of journalists resulted in the election of the feared Mujahideen leader Abdul Rabb-al-Rasul Sayyaf. President Kaizai's efforts with the warlords to get a constitution with a strong President may succeed but a strong presidency on paper only is unlikely to resolve Afghanistan's problems as warlords and roving bands of gunmen are the problem itself[16]. The presidential and parliamentary elections slated for June 2004 have been postponed to September 2004.

Pakistan has extended full support to the FBI to control terrorism, which has established Transaction Tracking Servers (TTS) at the Karachi and Lahore Airports, which is connected to the FBI databanks for surveillance of Pakistani citizens. FBI has been given access to Pakistan's communication network and it has set up 28 field stations[17]. Pakistani troops in conjunction with USA Special Forces launched operations in tribal belt bordering Afghanistan in March 2004, the operation was called off after Pakistani Security Forces suffered casualties and 14 Pakistani officials were captured[18].

Al Queda has been able to launch seven more major attacks internationally after 9/11 resulting in over six hundred deaths, the latest being on 11 March 2004 in Madrid in Spain in which at least 198 people were killed[19]. While Al Queda may be a bit down but Jehadi terrorism inspired by it far from being under control. Jehadis attacked President Musharraf twice during December 2003 unsuccessfully. The Jehadi capability to target American surrogates, allies and western interests is wide-spread. These attacks are not being directed by Al Qaeda but inspired by it. This is the new face of terrorism where scores of local groups world wide are connected and inspired by a common ideology across states with societies as their support base.

War in Iraq

The United States war on Iraq ended as expected leaving behind a comparatively higher degree of destruction than human casualties all around, the unresolved myth of Weapons of Mass Destruction and lurking danger to the Iraqi nation after the so called freedom. Glen Ranwala and Raymond Whitaker listed 20 falsehoods which President Bush and Prime Minister Blair projected to justify war against Iraq. These included: Iraq was responsible for September 11 attacks, Iraq's link with Al Queda, and uranium from Niger for nuclear weapons programme, import of aluminum tubes, WMD, chemical and biological weapons, Iraq could deploy its WMD in 45 minutes, previous inspections have failed and the USA and British claims were supported by weapon inspectors amongst others[20]. The death of Dr. David Kelley British defense scientist and weapons advisor on the 18 July 2003 cast further shadow on the British Prime Minister Tony Blair's credibility on the issue of WMD's in Iraq. Dr. David e-mailed a reporter before he went missing describing "many dark actors playing games"[21]. Uday and Qusay sons of Saddam Hussein along with one bodyguard and Qusay's teenage son were killed in Mosul on the 22 July 2003, when a loyalist who had given them shelter informed Americans for the prize money. Death of Saddam's sons bought no respite in the guerilla campaign against the Americans. The delay in showing the bodies after treating them brought further anger amongst the Iraqis and their casualties increased. The war laid bare the uni-polar trends in international relations, raised the issue of the UN role and effectiveness in future conflicts and left Europe and NATO divided. It has generated strong Muslim sentiment and posed a challenge to Arab nationalism and solidarity. The internal dynamics of Iraqi society with the Kurdish desire of a free state in the North and Shia-Suni stand off may draw its neighbours into the conflict. If the USA pursues its policy to dismantle the axis of evil further than greater turmoil and destabilisation in the Middle East can be expected. Similarly, democracy cannot be implanted, it has to grow indigenously with genuine support from outside.

While the USA declared that the war against Iraq had been won on 1 May 2003 but resentment against the USA and its allies has been growing. This is primarily due to failure of the allies to provide effective civil administration and civic services. Lack of water, electricity, health care and above all non-involvement of the Iraqis in reconstruction and rehabilitation has resulted in anger turning into resentment and finally violent agitation. The USA has suffered up to September 2003 over 140 casualties due to sabotage and terrorist acts. It may be the beginning of the Low Intensity War against allies. This was confirmed by the new central command chief Gen. John Abizaid who took over from Gen. Tommy Frank in July 2003. Attacks included one surface to air missile attack on a US transport plane C130, the second attack since the fall of Iraq on 9 April. Gen. Abizaid predicted a long deployment of a year. He estimated that remnants of the Special Republican Guard and Iraqi intelligence and security agencies have organised at the regional level in a cellular structure, helped by terrorist groups like Ansar al-Islam and perhaps Al Queda[22]. The sham act of constructing an Iraqi advisory council of lackeys of USA would hardly convince the Iraqis of the sincerity of the USA and allies. While future unfolds itself in the Middle East it is bound to have its effect in South Asia and on our security.

The capture of Saddam Hussain on 13 December 2003 brought no relief and attacks on the Americans grew more focused and deadly. A year ago pulling down of Saddam Hussain's statue on 9 April 2003 signalled the American triamph in war against Saddam, his WMD and eliminating the possibility of Al Queda's strategic link with the dictator. The truth is no weapons of mass destruction have been found and except for a solitary base of Ansar-ul-Islam in Kurdish North, nothing was discovered. America has failed to realise that dislike of Saddam would not automatically translate into a liking for the invader and that Iraqi national pride was hurt. The American and allies casualties are mounting and kidnapping and hostage taking are frequent. While on one hand they are battling the Sunnis in the North and negotiating for a cease fire in Fallujah the epicentre of resistance in the Sunni triangle. In the South the Mahadi Army of Shia Cleric Muqtada al Sadr in the South in Kufa, Najaf and Karbala the two Shiaite holy cities have been declared the red lines, which Americans should not cross in their confrontation with Muqtada al Sadr. The four top Shiaite clerics including Ali-al-Sistani have been able to maintain their sanctity. Under stress, US is hoping for UN envoy's plan for a caretaker Govt. to replace the US Administration in Iraq[23] to succeed. The recent discovery of maltreatment of Iraqi prisoners by the American and British troops and its wide publicity in the western media has added further to the problems of the Americans and its allies. This is also bound to create further resentment in the Muslim world and fuel terrorist attacks against America and the west.

While condemning the Nandmarg massacre on 24 March 2003 both thee USA and the UK called for a dialogue with Pakistan. This drew some thoughtless reaction from India with Foreign Minister Yashwant Sinha equating Iraq and Pakistan and describing Pakistan as a fit case for preemptive strikes, which drew instant retribution from the USA. This totally disturbed the middle path adopted by India on Iraq and by implication justifying US action in Iraq. The parliamentary resolution on Iraq on the 9 April 2003 further compounded the situation, coming at a time when the war had almost been won by the US and its allies. Even the strongest critics of the USA, France Russia China and Germany had not gone to the same extent. We need to learn that domestic sentiment need not always be converted into diplomatic responses. In this regard India's refusal to send troops to Iraq to join USA and its allies in peace keeping has been a very legitimate and valid response keeping in view India's long term interests in the Middle East. We certainly don't want to be seen acting at the behest of and in accordance with the USA requirements in total regard of the strong Iraqi sentiment and thereby loosing our historic long friendship within the Muslim and Arab world.

Comparatively, Pakistan continued to follow quietly the parallel twin strategy of helping the USA in capturing and elimination of Al Queda terrorists and simultaneously releasing local Jehadi leaders like Hafiz Sayeed and helping local terrorist groups to re-group and prepare for strikes in Kashmir. So far Musharraf has succeed in his aims as is evident from the $1.5 billion new grants, over $5 billion in loans, waving off a $1 billion loan and rescheduling of $2.3 billion over the next 38 years[24]. From above it is clear that the USA has bypassed the Symington amendment in spite of North Korea and Pakistan's WMD and nuclear links discovered last year.

India need to take a lesson from the above that while we continue to be part of the global war against terrorism but its limits are defined by the USA and countering cross border terrorism does not figure in it, neither punishing Pakistan with preemptive strikes which upsets the equilibrium established by it in South Asia. Our diplomatic and military responses have to face this reality, dragging Indo-Pak standoff into the international arena would be counter-productive. Similarly, military responses have to centre around better intelligence, harder strikes against militants and resolving internal dissidence by dialogue.

Conclusions

While Pakistan continues to propagate internationally that Kashmir is a disputed territory and the struggle is motivated by their desire for self determination, its implementation is based on exploitation of Kashmiri sense of alienation with increasing fundamentalist stance – suppression of Muslims and giving it a communal colour. A covert plan to introduce Muslim fundamentalism through the madarsa system with the connivance of the Jamaait-I-Islami had been undertaken since the beginning of eighties. Legitimacy to it was provided by us by dismissal of Farooq Abdulla Govt. in 1984 and denial of participation in the constitutional process to the MUF in 1987 elections. This was followed by mass demonstrations and hartals in population centres to exploit peoples' alienation and anger, and Kashmiri Pandits and selected Muslims were targeted to ferment communal divide. They propagated Jehad and in keeping with its ethos targeted liberal values of Kashmiriat and its democratic and secular culture. The situation was compounded by the inability of the Government to ensure Kashmiri Pandits' presence in the valley, which was a major political and strategic lapse in countering Pakistani designs. The ISI and pro-Pakistani agents infiltrated into vitals of the Govt. and paralysed the Govt. and the administration causing hardships to the people. Dissatisfaction, alienation and indiscreet handling of the public protests using strong arm tactics of the police resulted in repression. People revolted against it providing fertile ground for Pakistani sponsored violence.

Initially Pakistan exploited the sentiment of Azadi and JKLF's commitment to perpetuate violence and garner indigenous support. This resulted in JKLF's drawing main attention of the security forces and in its diminution. During this initial phase time was utilised by Pakistan to establish and sponsor pro-Pakistani Tanzeens and the stage was set for the movement passing into the hands of pro-Pakistani militants and control by ISI of Pakistan. Simultaneously Pakistan stopped arms and material support to JKLF. Pro-Azadi militants represented by JKLF were not pro-Pakistan. In the words of Yasin Malik "dismemberment of JKLF was the main reason why the movement passed into Pakistani hands with Islamisation as its main thrust, the real militancy has started now" [25].

When the tide started turning in 1995 and the turmoil started hurting Kashmiris, over 10,000 were killed and 30,000 Muslims had to leave the valley due to brutal attacks by Pakistan mercenaries, the Kashmiris felt disillusioned and indigenous participation in militancy reduced to almost negligible. Burning of Sufi shrines brought home to Kashmiris that Islam was being used to further Pakistani political and strategic interests at the cost of Kashmiris.

The reestablishment of the political process and installation of an elected Govt. frustrated Pakistan Army and ISI efforts to precipitate the situation any longer in the Kashmir Valley. Pakistan sponsored terrorism with its Islamic motivation ventured into new areas in J & K and neighbouring states to target minority community. Massacres at Barshala, Parankot, Hinjan Gali, Surankot, Phagla, Chapnarir, Horna, Kalabam, Chandi and Sailan extended the conflict into Doda, Poonch, Rajouri and Udhampur areas. The aim was to create Muslim dominated areas and extended the Indian Security Forces. This did destabilize the situation for some time but it was brought under control during 1998. This also having been contained, Pakistan Army and ISI raised the anti in Kargil another Muslim dominated area by major intrusions in May '99. As discussed we must view Kargil as yet another episode in the Proxy war to open up further avenues in keeping with Pakistan's design of proxy war with Islamic and strategic objectives.

Unfortunately while the ground situation in the militancy field has been controlled but our failure to consolidate in the political and socio-economic field will continue to provide Pakistan the opportunity to do many more Kargils. Our success in the diplomatic field is only a part of it; the change in the internal environment still remains a key area, which we have failed to address fully.

The recent study by Rohan Gunaratna clearly brings out that Al Queda has effectively infiltrated Harkat, Jaish-e-Mohammed and Lashkar-e-Toiba and their cadres were trained and indoctrinated in Afghanistan before the 11 September 2001. Its ideology is to create universal Jehad; suicide bombings, attacks on core state institutions and killing of foreigners particularly westerners and Christians. We have had all these in Jammu and Kashmir and India. Suicide attacks against SF headquarters, attacks on the J & K assembly and Indian Parliament and capture and killing of 6 foreigners in 1995. Al Queda unites diverse Islamic terrorist groups by attacking high value targets like the World Trade Centre and USS Cole which act as an inspiration for Islamic groups like Hamas in Palestine, Kashmiri Jehadis in Jammu and Kashmir and India and Jaish in Pakistan. While Al Queda is under pressure but Osama bin Laden, Al Zawahiri and Mullah Omar are still at large. US war against Al Queda and Afghan Taliban has succeeded partially in disrupting their training camps but it is only a tactical set back. It will continue to operate through sympathetic organisations all over the world by funding these and infiltrating these. Their membership comes from 40 nationalities and has nucleus in 94 countries. It has decentralised operations till it fully re-establishes in the hilly region of Afghan/Pakistan border. Jammu and Kashmir will be their target for more than one reason as pressure there diminishes Pakistani establishment's ability to deal with them in the west and also it helps to diffuse domestic pressure in Pakistan. Towards this end Jehadis in Jammu and Kashmir will continue to be supported both by Al Queda and Pakistani government and their capability will increase.

The other facet of the Proxy War is the wide-spread subversion in different parts of India through fundamentalist Muslim organisations of which there is ample evidence which we can ill afford to ignore. Therefore the strategy for a fight against terrorism should be all inclusive and not confined to cross border terrorism in Jammu and Kashmir alone.

REFERENCES

1. *Seminar* 479, July 1999, p. 19.
2. *USI Journal*, July, September 1998.
3. *Indian Express*, 27 August 1999.
4. *Outlook*, 12 May 2003.
5. *Outlook*, 5 May 2003.
6. n4 above.
7. *India Today*,19 May 2003.
8. n4 above.
9. *India Today*,12 May 2003.
10. *India Today*, 19 January 2004.
11. *Outlook*, 19 January 2004.
12. *Indian Express*, 29 March 2004.
13. *Indian Express*, 17 April 2004.
14. *India Today*, 23-29 March 2004.
15. *Aakrosh*, January 2002, Vol 5, No. 14, p. 76.
16. *Indian Express*, 26 December 2003.
17. *Indian Express*, 26 February 2004.
18. *Indian Express*, 29 March 2004.
19. *Hindustan Times*, 15 March 2004.
20. *NZ Herald*, 14 July 2003.
21. *NZ Herald*, 21 July 2003.
22. *NZ Herald*, 18 July 2003.
23. *Hindustan Times*, 17 April 2004.
24. *India Today*, 21 April 2003.
25. Discussions with Yasin Malik on 23 July 1997.

8

The Way Ahead

While looking to the future and searching for a solution to the Jammu and Kashmir imbroglio, we cannot ignore the past history, happenings in the contemporary period and our experience of Indo-Pak relations. This is essential to put the current conflict in the correct perspective, help in identifying the parameters of the problem and defining our approach. In this regard we need to guard against the all prevailing tendency to examine the situation in Jammu and Kashmir primarily in Indo-Pak context as it distorts the problem and tends to equate the state of Jammu and Kashmir with the Kashmir valley and presents the conflict as Kashmiri Muslims struggle to Pakistan's advantage. It disregards the plurality of Jammu and Kashmir with multi-ethnic, multi-religious, and multi-lingual communities having different political and socio-economic perspectives. It also leads to ignoring the internal dynamics of the situation and efforts are mainly directed to resolve the conflict in the Indo-Pak context. While the external factors influencing the situation definitely need to be taken into account but equally and probably more important are the internal political and socio-economic dynamics of the situation, which affect the diverse communities of the state, who are equally seeking avenues for social and economic betterment. A solution disregarding these is unlikely to be lasting.

External Factors

The deep-seated Indo-Pak antagonism has elements of structural, political and security threats. Conflicting ideologies rooted in historical, geographical and cultural factors have created a situation which does not allow us to ignore each other or live in harmony. Pakistan was created on the basis of religion and India on secular and federal principles, the tension is rationalised on the dispute over Kashmir. Two nation theory has remained the ideology of the ruling establishments of Pakistan and the agenda of partition remains unfinished. This mindset compels Pakistan to project India as a permanent adversary and antagonism goes beyond the political arena in all fields of Indo-Pak interaction. It motivates Pakistan to strive for annexation of Kashmir and create opportunities to destabilise India. Kashmir will therefore continue to be centre piece of Pakistan's India policy, as both anti-India posture and Kashmir are essential for its self-perceived identity and rational for existence. Jammu and Kashmir's strategic location with its historic links to both central and south Asia gives the conflict strategic and economic dimensions.

The histories of Indo-Pak relations and efforts in the Track II diplomatic field have been dismal. The only confidence building measures or agreements are in the military field due to the harsh reality that in spite of confrontation and the ongoing proxy war, a war would be disastrous and must be avoided. With Pakistan's experience of failures in conventional wars with India, proxy war is the only option left to it in Kashmir. The opportunity for Pakistan to put its subversive designs in operation due to the disturbed internal situation in Jammu and Kashmir in the late 1980s coincided with it.

Islamisation of Pakistan and its pan-Islamic orientation has influenced its strategic thinking. In the words of Gen. Aslam Beg, it has provided Pakistan territorial depth and strategic opportunities. Talibisation of Afghanistan is proof of its success. Similarly, Pakistan's urge for nuclearisation was motivated by its desire to restrain India's conventional edge; it was Islamic and India centric, whereas India's was motivated by larger regional threats to its security. Nuclearisation of both India and Pakistan in 1998 may bring about a balance of deterrence and thus stability in the nuclear field but it has failed to deter Pakistan form escalating the proxy war, as was proved by the Kargil conflict during May/July 1999 and subsequent events. The only deterrence to proxy war is to make its cost prohibitive for Pakistan.

The external dimensions of the Kashmir problem have expanded beyond a bilateral confrontation due to nuclearisation of the sub-continent and expanding trans-national dimensions of terrorism. Any escalation of a conventional conflict to a sufficiently high intensity, where danger of a nuclear confrontation or exchange at any level is likely will draw strong international reaction as was found during the Kargil conflict. Nuclearisation had drawn the interest of the USA and China is proved by the reported close consultations between the US President Clinton and Chinese President Jiang Zamin during the Kargil conflict1, Bush administration's stand that South Asia is one of the most volatile areas of the world and the USA's deep involvement in the region after 9/11 will continue to influence events in the region.

There is a qualitative difference between the support that Pakistan was giving to the Kashmiri militants and the support being given to the present Jehadi militants. The main groups now operating in Jammu and Kashmir are Harkat-ul-Ansar (HUA) now called Harkat-ul-Mujahideen (HUM), Al Badr Mujahideen (ABM), Jaish-e-Mohammed (JEM) and the most prominent one being Lashkar-e-Toibe (LET); they are all Pakistan based Islamic Jehadis. While Pakistan has a compulsion to be cooperating with the USA in the war against terrorism but both its intensions and capability to control the trans-border Jehadis is a suspect. It is evident by its twin parallel strategy of helping USA in elimination of Al Qaeda and Taliban and adopting a benevolent attitude towards Pakistan based terrorists operating in Jammu and Kashmir. This is founded on the belief that Pakistan is indispensable in the fight against Al Qaeda and Taliban and that Pakistan's domestic compulsion to tolerate Jehadis operating in Jammu and Kashmir is well recognised and understood by the USA. The war against terrorism is seriously hampered by MMA's control of the border provinces with Afghanistan and its pan Islamic orientation and sympathy and support to Osama bin Laden, Taliban and Jehadis operating in Jammu and Kashmir. Jammu and Kashmir will continue to be target for more than one reason, as pressure in Jammu and Kashmir diminishes Pakistan's liability to deal with them in the West and it also suits Pakistan to diffuse domestic pressure. Towards this end support to Jehadis will continue both by Pakistan and Al Qaeda. Jehad in Jammu and Kashmir has clear political objectives; to rid the valley of Hindus and Sikhs, to drive out Hindus from Doda and Kishtwar, to coerce people to shun the option of independence and opt for Pakistan. In its wider theological ramifications Jehad has also been distorted to mean liberating of all Muslim pockets from non-Muslim rule and it frowns upon the Sufi culture of reverence to Peers and favors the establishment of Wahabi brand of Islam. It believes in the concept of Ummah, the objectives of Markaz Da'awat -ul-Irshad and its militant wing LET to establish the rule of Allah (whatever it may mean). The document prepared for the USA House of Representatives by the task force on terrorism and unconventional warfare titled, "The New Islamist International" dealing with Pakistan's sponsorship of terrorism gives penetrating analysis of not only the die hard Islamist objectives in fermenting terrorism in Kashmir and other parts of India but also export of fundamentalism to central Asian states. Within Jammu and Kashmir the emerging pattern is clearly to alter the mixed population pattern in the state from Kashmir valley to Kargil, Doda to Gulabgarh and Rajouri, Poonch-Nowshera to Akhnoor along the Chenab river and make it Islamic, the only Hindu areas left will be Jammu and Kathua. ISI's plan to foment exodus of Hindus and attention given to Doda, Kishtwar and

Baderwah since 1998 in particular is part of its plan of expansion of Muslim dominated areas within Jammu and Kashmir.

Seizure of over 100 kg of RDX from Assam, Bengal, Haryana and Delhi, explosions in trains in Assam in August 1999 and discovery of LET cells in Haryana, Andhra Pradesh and Mumbai during the same period are clear indicators of Pakistan's desire to destabilise India fermenting Islamic militancy[2]. We can defeat the Pakistani designs by dealing with Pakistani agents and collaborators firmly, some of whom may be Islamic zealots but it must not make 130 million Muslims in India suspects. In this regard we need to be equally firm with Hindu fundamentalist organisations, who have a tendency to exploit such incidents on the pretext of threat to national interest. Our strength lies in confronting Islamic or any other fundamentalism with our secular, pluralist and democratic ethos. Anything different will be disastrous.

Pakistan has also become the victim of Afghan drug peddling, while its efforts to control opium production have succeeded but Baluchistan has become the main gateway for drugs of Afghan origin to the rest of the world. Baluchistan offers access to land routes through West Asia and sea routes to Gulf and the West. The combination of Wahabi islamisation resulting in sectarian violence and drugs and proliferation of arms seems to be beyond Pakistan's control and poses a danger to its inner stability but our main concern is the danger it poses to the area.

The US lead war against terrorism is really aimed at countering danger to the USA from Islamic terrorism and guarding its national interests in the region. Pakistan is a key ally of the USA in the war against Al Qaeda and the Taliban and they cannot afford to let her down, therefore an Indo-Pak confrontation is viewed as an avoidable distraction. Similarly while cross-border terrorism is our main concern but is not a priority in the overall perception of war against terrorism. Therefore our strategy against terrorism has to operate on two planes, one domestic on cross-border terrorism and other at the strategic level against all inclusive terrorism world over.

In the context of Indo-Pak relations and the situation in Jammu and Kashmir, two key issues emerge. First one is the feeling of insecurity in Pakistan, which generally translates into anti-India rhetoric and at times to armed confrontation or action. Its two facets are the feeling itself and its fallout. We need to address both. We need to keep Pakistan assured that irrespective of past and present confrontations, its existence as a nation is not under threat from India and India is not interested in its dismemberment. Its stability and progress and peace will be to the mutual benefit of both countries. A viable and stable Pakistan is essential for peace and stability in South Asia. This is real politick and recognition of the post-cold war and Afghan imbroglio geo-strategic reality. It therefore follows that neither Pakistan's identity is threatened nor should she feel threatened on that account. This was made amply clear by our Prime Minister Shri Vajpayee by his visit to Minar-e-Pakistan during his historic bus ride to Lahore in 1999. Threat if any to Pakistan is from within due to its sectarian politics and internal dissensions.

Any effort on our part to interfere in the internal affairs of Pakistan will not only be counter-productive but would also not give us any permanent long term benefit. It will add to the turmoil and instability in the region. On its own Pakistan must accept that secession or self-determination as a basis of secession is unacceptable. She should learn from its own experience of East Pakistan and the threat that sectarian divisions, Islamic radicalisation of the society and violence is posing to its integrity. These are all indicators for negotiation, accommodation and respecting status of its neighbouring nations.

The second facet in the current context is the reality of proxy war which is a fall out of insecurity, tinged with a feeling of revenge for 1971 and Islamic fervour. This feeling of insecurity is India and particularly Kashmir centric— Kashmir both for identity and strategic reasons. Pakistan's motive for launching the proxy war is similar to the ones in the past, a perceived instability within India. Whenever India is strong and politically stable Pakistan has refrained from interfering in Kashmir. Maharaja's desire for independence at the time of partition brought Kabali raiders in 1947. In 1965 Pakistan sent raiders under a miscalculated notion of a weak India after the 1962 debacle against the Chinese. Again in late 1980s, Pakistan took advantage of the deteriorating internal situation in Jammu and Kashmir which questioned the legitimacy of Indian intentions and governance. This mindset compels Pakistan to exploit India's internal turmoils to strive for annexation of Kashmir and exploit opportunities to destabilise India. Conflict and confrontation are essential for Pakistani military to retain its power and position of eminence. As in the past, winning the proxy war is the most important single factor to resolve the current Indo-Pak confrontation. Victory will not be outright as in a conventional war. It will emerge slowly as Pakistan and Jehadis are made to pay increasing costs in terms of lives, material and moral values as it happened in Kargil.

Both the Kargil episode and its fallout of military take over in Pakistan are indicative of the continuation of the proxy war and Indo-Pak confrontation in the near future. It is a negative response situation and we must take into account the political, socio-economic and cultural threat that terrorism motivated by Islamic resurgence poses to the region and cooperation and interaction with affected countries in the near region should be part of our response. All the three major dimensions of the proxy war need to be addressed, external (requiring actions in the diplomatic and military field), internal (within Jammu and Kashmir), and the third, of subversive Pakistani designs in the rest of the country. All three are important for defeating Pakistani design of pan-Islamic expansion and terrorism. Efforts in the diplomatic field to contain and reduce the effect of cross-border terrorism sponsored by Pakistan have had a positive response from the world community. The quests in Afghanistan have highlighted the involvement of Pakistan in supporting terrorism, which has vindicated India's stand. These need to be sustained and reienforced, special effort to seek the cooperation of China, Russia and Central and South Asian countries is required.

Conflict resolution measures pertaining to the external factor of the Jammu and Kashmir situation limit themselves to preparing the ground for it and in the mean time emphasis has to be on better management of the conflict. The guiding principle for both should be real politick and political realism. On the other hand regional and international dimensions should be handled guided by a cooperative approach, its core being the common threat that terrorism poses to the world community.

To tackle the external dimensions of the problem, India needs to pursue a proactive policy rather than a reactive one. Adopting such a policy would have its political fallout and international ramifications. This would imply enlarging the area and scope of conflict beyond territorial limits of Jammu and Kashmir to punish the Jehadi militants and perpetrators of the proxy war. The LOC will no longer be sacrosanct and punitive actions will include destruction of militant camps in POK by missiles, raids on forward posts acting as launching pads and suspected hideouts. These actions must be planned within our tactical reach and will require full integration of agencies involved and government support for actions in the field. We should be prepared to go to war should the situation escalate. The pay off of a proactive policy would be positive in the long run. Simultaneously, we should attend to the internal dimensions of such a policy, which would require better management of the borders militarily, effective and responsive administration in the border areas and an effective village defense system. Such a proactive policy would have to be supported by aggressive diplomatic efforts to expose Pakistan's duplicity of while portraying as fighting terrorism on one hand she is supporting cross-border terrorism. As such Pakistan must face the consequences of a nation not only supporting but indulging in terrorism. Simultaneously, our stance of no role by a third party in Jammu and Kashmir in the changed international environment when influential nations are bypassing the UN when it suits them and are keen to play a role, needs a re-look. A dialogue with Pakistan to find a long term solution to the problem is essential, which at the bilateral level has greater chance of success with help from a facilitator, we should therefore not be averse to diplomatic moves by the USA and others to facilitate such a dialogue. We must remember that Tashkant Agreement in 1996 was facilitated through USSR efforts.

Internal

Internally, the situation in Jammu and Kashmir displayed changes in its orientation and configuration since the beginning of 1994 and these were fully evident in 1995. From a combination of pro-Azadi and pro-Pakistan militancy, it is mainly thriving as a Pakistani sponsored proxy war, with minimal Kashmiri participation. The key elements of the change were disillusionment of the Kashmiris both from militancy and Pakistani design. Instillation of a popular government in 1996 was the high point of this change. Unfortunately the period of Farooq Abdullah's National Conference government up to 2002 was marked by divergent trends. Initially there was genuine good will amongst the political and the community leaders to help the government in consolidation of the situation. However, the government failed to display willingness both at the political and the administrative level to utilise the opportunity and returned to its old ways of dispensations based on patronage and corruption. This resulted in despair amongst the people that neither militancy nor an elected government provided the basic dignity of life or mitigation of their hardships. The National Conference government paid for its failure during the elections in October 2002. In the fairest and bloodiest election peoples mandate was for a change discarding all segments of the old dispensation. The new government under Mufti Mohammed Sayeed's PDP-lead coalition with Congress has shown willingness to provide the healing touch and carry all segments of the Jammu and Kashmir society in seeking a solution. These are positive signs. Emotional fallout and wounds of militancy will take time to heal; there cannot be sudden shift of stances, patience and persistence with the approach is required.

The foremost requirement is to shed the past political inaptness of real politick and a confrontationist posture to meet the requirement of electoral politics. The need is for an open and transparent shift to ideal politick and a policy of accommodation and cooperation to consolidate the situation in the political, socio-economic and religious fields. First and foremost task is to remove the alienation of the people of Kashmir and the rest of the people in Jammu and Kashmir. The guiding principle for it should be restoration of self respect and trust of all segments of the society in Jammu and Kashmir. In the political field it will require accommodating the sentiment of autonomy and removal of interregional imbalances. The other facet of removal of alienation is revitalisation of states economy and the developmental process to mitigate people's hardships. In the social field the challenges of fundamentalism, revitalising the education system and reviving the spirit of Kashmiriyat will have to be met, while reestablishing the past kinship amongst communities of the state.

Alienation

Alienation is the cumulative effect of anger and frustration for what is perceived to be denied, it may be in any field political, socio-economic or religious or ethnic. It is also a dimension of the mistrust that exists within or with the outside world. In the case of Jammu and Kashmir it is a trilogy of mistrust; between people of different regions of the state, between people and their own leaders and suspicion or mistrust of the government of India. The feeling that Kashmiri's are a pawn in the Indo-Pak confrontation, a distrust of the democratic and developmental process based on past experience, non acceptance of genuine dissent by both Srinagar and Delhi, corruption, prolonged conflict, human rights violations and fundamentalism have all added to this feeling. At the social level the Kashmiri community which was closely interwoven was targeted. Those not supporting the militants were accused by them as traitors and un-Islamic. The security forces suspected them of connivance. Suppression and fear of social rejection left no space for dissent, resulting in ambivalence of Kashmiri mindset and depriving them of a clear vision. In the absence of opportunity to voice their feelings, suppressed and confused minds fell pray to Pakistani design and it created a crisis of identity and ideology. This confusion needs to be addressed seriously to win over support and confidence of the people.

Psychologically, dissidents (Pro-Azadi) and Pro-Pak elements and informers were dealt with the same harshness resulting in suspicion, anger and hostility in the Kashmiri Muslim community. The ghost of Pakistan and its ISI became larger than its reality. This helped Pakistan to successfully transfer, suspicions, hostility and anger from one generation to another. Any effort to relieve the Kashmiri community from the feeling of being watched is fundamental to its rejuvenation and removing alienation. Like elsewhere in such an environment, new class of young entrepreneurs who find the business of militancy lucrative have emerged. They lack the skills for alternate employment and weaning them away from militancy presents a serious challenge[3].

The issue of human rights remains potent in spite of the fact that it has failed to deliver for Pakistan. Elaborate plans were made by Pakistan to include Jammu and Kashmir in UN agenda on human rights. It has systematically focussed on the human rights situation in Kashmir with a clear communal stance in all international forums. Ironically, it made use of studies conducted by Indian activists and her attempts to introduce a resolution in the UN censoring India on human rights violations in 1995 did not succeed. International interest decreased as the emerging ground realities were different[4].

On the issue of autonomy, the Indian government should have been sensitive to the feelings of the people and not rejected the autonomy resolution passed by the state legislative assembly outright. The debate could have encapsulated the entire country and not only the state of Jammu and Kashmir. Some facets of autonomy have already been discussed in Chapter 6. This framework or any other acceptable one can form the basis of discussion and negotiations. Opinioned Sarkaria commission While deliberating on centre state relations that in any federal setup certain incidental and ancillary powers like currency and banking and matters connected with the functioning of the Union like parliament, the offices of the president and vice president, UPSC, audit and pensions rested with the Centre. Similarly subjects with national dimensions such as inter-state commerce, migration, census, insurance, weights and measures, standards, patents and survey of India and other surveys (geological, botanical and archaeological) fall into central domain. Finally commissioned detailed certain taxes, excises and other matters requiring uniform principles are best centrally administered and proceeds transferred to the states on the basis of tax sharing through the finance commission. Jammu and Kashmir has been a major beneficiary of these as a special category state, receiving grants and loans in the ratio of 70:30 and currently 90:10 respectively.

The major issues in contention are emergency powers, the role and powers of the governor, the central services, the jurisdiction of the election commission, Supreme Court and CAG and restoration of concurrent powers. These have been discussed in the Chapter 6. These must be viewed keeping in mind states financial dependence on the Centre and that the 1975 Indira-Abdullah accord restored residuary powers to the state and reaffirmed Article 370.

Article 370 of the Constitution provided a unique position to the state of Jammu and Kashmir and was a forerunner to the Article 371 providing various degrees of autonomy and safeguards to the North Eastern states. This has been discussed in detail in chapter 4 of Part I on the North-East. Due to the peculiar socio-economic structure and different political experience of the communities of the North-East, it will be futile to draw any parallel with the situation in Jammu and Kashmir. However, the debate therein indicates the need for greater regional autonomy for the three regions of Ladakh, Kashmir and Jammu as it only can lead to correcting the political, economic and development imbalance between the regions. Discussion on the North-East has also clearly brought out that real empowerment and economic and social well being of the people can best be ensured under the PRI institutional structure. Therefore, the urgent need not only for the enactment but implementation of the 73rd and 74th amendment in its full manifestation and spirit. To make PRIs effective, recommendations given in chapter IV of part I (North-East) should be incorporated.

At the root of political alienation is the total distrust of the electoral process and the feeling that honest dissent is not tolerated both by Srinagar and Delhi. It is a genuine feeling based on their experience over the years. The last elections held in October 2002 were largely accepted as fair, in spite of high levels of killings and violence perpetrated by Pakistan to disrupt these. This was verified and accepted by foreign observers. An overall participation of 44 per cent of the electorate, which included dissidents and hardliners, the results clearly reflected people's desire to seek a solution through political dispensation and a change in governance. This is a major turning point in the situation. While the rulers have lost, the people of Jammu and Kashmir and India have won. The new political dispensation of the state must be encouraged to function and local choices and honest dissent encouraged. We failed to make MUF a part of the constitutional and political process in 1987, let us learn from it. An inner turmoil within the democratic process should be preferred to disenchantment and alienation. The idea of trifurcation of the state has been rejected and the secular core of India and credentials of the people of Jammu and Kashmir have been reinforced. Accommodation, understanding and statesmanship are required to find a solution by consensus.

Reopen the Doors of Kashmiriyat

Discussion in the previous chapter has clearly brought out that Islamisation and spread of radical Wahabi culture is the outcome of the use of religion to achieve politico-strategic objectives initially by the USA against USSR and later by Pakistan to establish the Taliban regime in Afghanistan and to further her design in Jammu and Kashmir. Saudi Arabia used its alliance with the USA and mutual antagonism against Shiaite Iran as an opportunity to promote Wahabism and its rigid code. It found Pakistan as a willing partner for its own strategic and domestic reasons and it also legitimised its involvement in Afghanistan. While these strategic alliances of the cold war period achieved short term goals of containment of USSR and secured the USA and Western economic and military interests in the Middle East and Afghanistan (South Asia) but it let loose a pan-Islamic militant movement in the region in Afghanistan, Xinjiang and central and southeast Asia. It has spread from Chechniya to Philippines in the east. It is in contention with Shiaite orthodoxy in Iran and has its fall out in the domestic politics of Pakistan and to a lesser extent in other South Asian countries. In the Islamic and Arab world local dissent against authoritarian regimes found an outlet in radical Islam and lead to sectarian hardening of attitude and violence. The sentiment has also been exploited by local leaders in Islamic countries to legitimize militancy and authoritarian rule. It leaves the Islamic and Arab world divided both outwardly and domestically within, a sure recipe for instability.

Confining to Pakistan and its impact on Jammu and Kashmir, since the 1980s Islamic dimensions have been all prevailing in Pakistan and it has impacted on the Indo-Pak situation in all its political, diplomatic, economic, cultural and military dimensions. Turmoil in Afghanistan resulted in Islamic militant groups from outside and within Pakistan mushrooming with government and ISI connivance, and their coming into Jammu and Kashmir is well known. Pakistan was identified as sponsoring terrorism. To ward off Western criticism Pakistan privatised Jehad through the Islamic parties, who became central to the propagation of Jehad and achieved substantial political gains for the first time. The war against global terrorism post-9/11 has only resulted in Pakistani establishment outwardly distancing itself from USA identified militants but it has failed to curb Islamists and Jehadis. This is not only convenient but essential for Pakistan to achieve its political goals in Jammu and Kashmir and domestically. We therefore cannot ignore the strategic and political aims of Islamists and Pakistan against us in Jammu and Kashmir.

Within Jammu and Kashmir, it will be prudent to acknowledge that an Islamic fundamentalist streak has taken root amongst the valley Sunni Muslims. The JEI with its close links with Pakistani JEI has been its main propagator at the behest of Pakistan. While Islamisation of Pakistan was brought about by proliferation of madarassas, attempt at islamisation of Kashmir originated with the mushrooming of mosques. Beginning with insistence of attendance and harassment of the absentees, these mosques functioned as networking centres of militancy. Simultaneously, Hindu shrines were targeted by pro-Pakistani elements intimidating Hindus. However, JEI joining the political fray and later militants in 1990 was more due to the impetus provided by the intervention of Islamic groups based in Pakistan and to reclaim their political space against nationalists; opportunity for it was provided by the dismemberment of the JKLF. The JEI's propagation of Islamic agenda is entirely to suit Pakistani objectives and its own domestic political ends. This is borne out by the shift in the orientation and motivation of militancy, which is entirely Islamic. This fundamentalist streak will continue. However, we must not ignore the other aspect of polarisations of politics in Jammu and Kashmir on communal lines since 1980; these trends are likely to continue. Religion will also continue to provide an outlet for people to vent their grievances and it will continue to be exploited. The major content fueling fundamentalism will be alienation and deprivation along with its political exploitation.

Kashmiri composite identity has undergone a change due to militancy and communal politics into that of a Kashmiri Muslim with political goals of independence or greater autonomy to joining Pakistan. However, due to multi-ethnic nature of Muslim population in the state Kashmiri Muslims do not even represent other Muslim groups and these separate ethnic and religious groups need to be recognised. Demographic changes are closely linked to both militant's agenda and political agenda of the Kashmiri Muslim polity, which if ignored can give Islamists an edge. Both autonomy and self-determination are potent slogans to incite passions to achieve political goals. This will further lead to regional tensions in Ladakh and Jammu. The need is for a strong secular and democratic formulation in Jammu and Kashmir to fight these fundamentalist trends and maintain the multi-ethnic, multi-religious and multi-lingual nature of its society. Similarly, spread of Hindu nationalism unless controlled will only provide impetus to the Islamic streak spreading further.

In essence a combination of islamisation of the conflict, shift from Sufi Islamic culture and demographic changes manifested along religious lines threaten traditional ethnic identities of Jammu and Kashmir. The narrow parochial political advantage sought by Kashmiri leadership in presentation of their autonomy agenda and its acceptance by the Hindu leadership in the Jammu region is sure recipe for disaster. The creation of new provinces, division of Ladakh and the separation of Muslim areas from Udhampur district all will have the fallout of communal divide and will further add to the regional imbalances and tensions. The social tension that is likely to generate, signs of which are already visible will lead to fragmented ethnic conflicts as economic and social betterment urges and security of identity go beyond the bounds of religion and deprivation becomes the main issue. The sectarian violence in Pakistan and inner turmoils within India are realities which should not be wished away.

Nizam-e-Mustafa and Hindutva are both conflict oriented and tension prone. Secularism and religious and social harmony are the only viable options. A democratic and secular society is essential for the survival of democracy in Jammu and Kashmir as well as in India.

Fundamentalism is a multi dimensional phenomenon which has political, ethnic, social and cultural and religious fallout. The propagated islamisation of Wahabi orientation is alien to Kashmiri Muslim's social and cultural ethos. The main thrust of Pakistan Jehadis will be to exploit the feeling of alienation and isolation of Kashmiri's, particularly the younger generation. This must be prevented and Sufi culture and Kashmiriyat should be re-inforced.

From the above it should be clear that Islamic fundamentalism has a political agenda of strategic dimensions and its religious content is essentially exploitation of the Muslim sentiment to further it. Therefore the main effort to fight it will have to be in the political field with supportive action in the administrative and socio-economic fields. At the political level both Islamic fundamentalism and Hindutvta need to be tackled firmly and Gujrat like incidents must be prevented. Banning of fundamentalist parties like Jammait-i-Islami and Vishwa Hindu Prashid should be seriously considered.

In Jammu and Kashmir the main thrust has to be in reinforcing the ethos of Kashmiriyat and the Sufi Islamic traditions along with dismantling the fundamentalist structure of JEI and the use of mosques and madarassas for illegal and pro-militant activities. This can only be achieved by concerted political and social action plan backed by legal and administrative measures. The present coalition government has no agenda to defend and the healing touch approach over a period of time will revive the community responses, which are so essential for any social action plan to succeed. At the political level the fundamentalist and the harm that they have done to the Kashmir Muslim community and the Kashmiri society should be exposed. All religious activities need to be regulated irrespective of religion and a stricter control of madarassas and a uniform and unbiased curriculum needs to be introduced. If Maulvis have to come from India these should be the right ones—those who preach amity amongst religions and not hate. They should elaborate true meaning of Jehad. Bareilvis rather than Doebandis should be tapped. In this regard the Indian Muslim community need to take an active part and the Government of India should encourage it. In the administrative field a strict watch needs to be kept on the funding of JEI and other radical and militant organisations. Simultaneously, the education system in the state should be revamped and rejuvenated, the selection of teachers and curriculum needs special attention. For all this to succeed the body politick needs to shed its communal agenda and in this regard the Regional Autonomy Commission's report needs to be re-examined by a body with wider representations including the community leaders from all regions of Jammu and Kashmir.

Deprivation, the Core of Alienation

"It is argued that aggression is the main outcome of frustration. In the case of a system of individuals, it may take the form of crime; in a system of groups, the form of revolutions; and in a system of nations, the form of wars[5]." "The battle for the hearts and minds of the people is war by socio-economic, administrative and psychological measures (food, clothing, shelter, health care and civic services which affect all human beings). Insurgency/militancy thrives on deprivation. Only an administration which can fulfill these and provide security can succeed."

The truth of the above dictums was driven home to me during my meetings with three Kashmiri leaders in 1997, one a young political activist, second a militant and dissident leader and third an elderly community leader with a long political background. The young political activist is Mehbooba Mufti, who with her fire, sense of frustration and dedication left me fully impressed. But it was her sense of grave frustration which was disturbing. Her main lament was that the Farooq Abdullah Government had belied all hopes of the people by returning to its old ways of patronage and corruption. She as an elected representative was denied the opportunity to mitigate people's hardships and her efforts were frustrated at each step. The district plans were controlled by ministers and neither people's representative or the district administration had any part in it. Recruitment was entirely based on political patronage or bribes and State Public Service Commission was made defunct. These are all facts not difficult to verify. A clear case of democratic institutions failure to meet people's aspirations. Her main motivation was frustration and political aggression borne out of it. She is now the chairmen of the PDP and thus part of the present ruling coalition government. She is still motivated and very sincere, hope she is able to do now, what she could not do earlier.

The militant and dissident leader is Yasin Malik, he appeared to me an angry but genuine person. He believes in Azadi and has never changed his stance, he also believes in the entirety of the state of Jammu and Kashmir and has a totally secular outlook. Form our discussion two issues stand out in my memory. One concerned the militancy itself. He emphasised the changing face of militancy and its increasing Islamic and pro-Pakistan dimensions. He attributed it to a total lack of a politico-strategic perception of the Indian leaders, which resulted in taking over of the Kashmiri struggle by pro-Pakistani and communal elements. I have discussed it under militancy in the previous chapter. On the issue of talks and negotiation to resolve the issue, he was all for it but had a long tail of woes and said lack of trust was the main hurdle. He mentioned the denial of visas by the Government of India to him and his colleagues for a visit to PoK and Nepal to meet the Azad Kashmir leaders. He also narrated as to how the government of India having invited Kashmiri dissident leaders to Delhi, when asked by the press, Chavan the then home minister told them that they had come to Delhi as they have lost their political relevance. Yasin Malik called it an act of total mistrust and political one-up-manship. He was firm in his opinion that Kashmiris do not trust the Government of India and they do not trust Kashmiris. Mistrust is the bane of political dialogue. I agree with Yasin Malik, as trust begets trust. I hope that in the current changed environment the new political dispensation in Kashmir and Delhi can overcome the feeling of mistrust and get down to talking with each other and the dissidents with an open mind to resolve the issue.

The third community and political leader was the revered Gujjar leader Mian Basheer, whose son Mian Altaf was a minister in the Farooq Abdullah government. We had discussions on a wide range of subjects. Two things he mentioned are relevant to the present discussion. First that while the general standard of well being of the people of Kashmir and in the rest of the state is better since independence but the feeling of being deprived persists as the day to day life is not only upset by militancy but lack of essentials for existence like water, electricity, schools, roads and medical facilities. As an example to illustrate his point, he mentioned that Kashmiris no longer go as labourers to Punjab, Himachal Pradesh and the rest of northern India to work at bus stands, railway stations and in the saw mills but they are frustrated and feel deprived as life has become difficult. He also felt that in spite of all the money that has been pumped in Jammu and Kashmir, the life of the common man has become, more difficult as money is not being utilised for their benefit. Simply put but the core remains frustration and deprivation. The second issue he raised was the lack of knowledge and response and ultimately of governance. He put it simply and said that leaders from Delhi come and talk to ministers, bureaucrats and police and army officers but nobody talks to the community leaders or the people. He said this is a change since the days of the Nehru, Gandhi leadership. Nehru the father knew all of us, father passed it on to the daughter (Mrs Indira Gandhi) and mother passed it on to the son Rajiv Gandhi, so they knew us and the people. The present leaders do not know us and do not know what people want or feel. I am sure similar is the feeling of community leaders in the rest of the state. Similar feelings with and without dissident overtones were expressed by villagers in the north and south Kashmir which I have visited periodically. The core was deprivation with anger and frustration as its manifestation.

There has been a substantial improvement in the standard of living in the state of Jammu and Kashmir during the period 1977-84 preceding the 1987 elections and start of militancy. In 1977-78, 33.4 per cent of the population lived under the poverty line by 83-84 it declined to a mere 16.3 per cent 6. The per capita income in the state rose to Rs.3344 in 1986-87 from Rs.566 in 1971-72, the sixth highest in the country 7. While the average standard of living has gone up but in the perception of Kashmiri Muslims it did not benefit them in real terms. Free education resulted in higher aspirations for social and economic mobility and number of unemployed matriculates rose form 6875 in 1971 to 14374 by 1981 and to 26559 by 1986. The number of unemployed graduates rose form 1228 in 1971 to 6368 in 1981 and to 2866 in 1985. The number of unemployed engineering graduates increased from 166 in 1961 to 443 in 1986. It was observed that higher educational qualification resulted in higher level of unemployment in that category. The main source of employment for the Kashmiri Muslims was government services. In the state government their representation in non-gazetted posts and clerical services was high, but in gazetted post Hindus held 51 per cent of the posts against Muslims 42 per cent. In central government jobs as on 1 January 1989 Hindu monopolised the gazetted posts 83.66 per cent to 6.89 per cent of Muslims and their representation in clerical cadre was 79 per cent to Muslims 13 per cent[8]. From 1986-87 to 1989 there was an increase of 200 per cent in unemployed educated youth from 1,00,000 to 3,00,000[9]. Under the circumstances it was not difficult to mobilise the youth for militancy.

The Rajiv-Farooq accord was presented as an opportunity for progress, economic development and employment. But it proved a failure as neither commercial opportunities nor infrastructure for industrial development was improved. Out of the 19 public sector corporations with a total capital of Rs.74.16 crores, only 9 related to industrial sector. Except for DISCO, SICOP and SRTC, which showed marginal profits, other suffered losses of crores of rupees. Indian Telephone Industry and HMT are the only central public sector enterprises with annual production of 16 crores (1993), which is less than .01 per cent of the total public sector investment in the country. The state is industrially backward and the institutional finance made available is meager. Over 70 per cent of the population depends on agriculture and allied sectors, a major portion of land in Kashmir valley is irrigated but small holdings and mono-crop cultivation gives poor returns. Manufacturing and processing industries cater for only 11 per cent of the work force[10].

Power, the basic infrastructure requirement, is inadequately short. Jammu and Kashmir has one of the lowest power consumption in the country, it consumes 9.1 kw/hr per capita compared to 524 kw/hrs of Uttar Pradesh, Punjab 300.5 kw/hrs and Haryana 238 kw/hrs. The Jammu and Kashmir state has 9 per cent of the total hydel potential of the country, of which so far only 2 per cent has been tapped. The river basins of Chenab, Jhelum and Indus have a potential for 12, 000 MW. Against the total requirement of 700 MW, Mohra power station built in 1930 has a maximum capacity of 8 MW, Lower Jhelum project has a capacity of 100 MW during peak summer period which falls to 30 MW during winter. Salal and Chenani Hydroelectric projects located in the Jammu province produce 200-300 MW which feed the national grid for Delhi, only 80 MW from Salal phase one comes to Jammu and Kashmir. Uri Hydel project with a capacity of 500 MW was completed and energized some years ago. However, delivery of power to the valley has been delayed due to lack of resources for building of transmission lines and disturbed environment. Jammu – Srinagar power line is still to be taken up for construction. Rise in tariff and discontent against acute power shortage in June 1988 was ruthlessly suppressed and acted as a catalyst for the flare up[11].

Horticulture in Kashmir suffered after the boom of the 1960s due to competition from the fruit industry in Himachal, lack of cold storage facilities during transit/transportation, higher taxes compared to Himachal Pradesh, non-availability of pesticide due to privatisation and lack of chemicals and technology to combat infestations[12]. The problem is further compounded by resource crunch due to bank closures and disruption in banking owing to militancy. However it is on record that no fruits or dry fruits and other agriculture outputs failed to reach the markets during the period of militancy due to government assistance and profits from these were higher than in 1980s.

The above are the manifestations of deprivation inspite of general well being in economic terms. Rural Kashmir is the real ugly face of lack of development and deprivation, the state has failed to deliver in the fields of communications, Public Distribution System, education, health and civic amenities like water and electricity. While the same is true of other regions in the state but years of militancy has sharpened their sense of neglect and deprivation which needs to be satisfied.

Administrative Aspects

Jammu and Kashmir has had a very good record of land and administrative reforms, which compares favourably with some of the advanced states of the country. Notable amongst these are the Big Landed Estates Abolition Act of 1950, under which 396 Jagirs were abolished and 2,03,000 acres of land was distributed to the tillers free of cost. The holding of the erstwhile landlords was further reduced from 182 kanals to 100 kanals under the Jammu and Kashmir Agrarian Reforms Act 1976 and an additional 1,17,700 acres of land was further transferred to the tillers. On returning to power in 1975, Sheikh Abdullah ordered reorganisation of the administration, making district as the focal point and ensuring equitable development and participation by public representative in formulation and implementation of district plans, this was popularly known as 'Single Line Administration'. The concept was borrowed from the erstwhile NEFA (North Eastern Frontier Agency). Under this dispensation all departments at the district level came under administrative and financial control of the Deputy Commissioner and he was also designated as District Development Commissioner. The District Development Board functioned under him and had public elected members and official members representing major departments. Chief Minister presided over its meeting, so it carried the force of cabinet decisions. Some changes and amplifications were brought in the Single Line Administration in 1993 but the basic structure remained intact. During Farooq Abdullah's rule in 1996 government nominated ministers in charge of districts and district development officer now functioned as secretary or convener of the District Development Board. This completely politicised the development process and the ruling party functionaries both elected or non-elected interfered for parochial dispensation and gains. The worst affected were departments of Rural Development, PWD and PHE. As discussed earlier politicisation both during Bakshi Gulam Mohammed's period and later under Sheikh Abdullah resulted in corruption, politicisation of the bureaucracy and disillusionment of public from the administration. It returned with full vengeance under Farooq Abdullah in 1996. No Panchayat elections were held after 1976 till the recent ones held in January to June 2001. Effective functioning of Panchayats is essential for the democratic and development process to function and to restore the confidence of the people.

With the expansion of education facilities, while on one hand people's expectations have risen this is accompanied by a total lack of entrepreneurial initiative amongst the local population and reluctance of the youth to search for job opportunities outside, there is total dependence on government jobs. In a total population of one crore, there are over 3,75,000 government employees, 26,500 public sector job holders and over 60,000 daily wage earners/work charge employees. The government capacity to absorb is over-saturated. The level of satisfaction provided by the government services is dismal and it is a critical factor in people's disillusionment and resentment. There is an urgent need to formulate strategy for income generating activities and training of youth for self-employment. The emphasis on infrastructure and social services need a shift from expansion to consolidation as this will give better results and increase the level of satisfaction within the existing resources.

The need to make civil administration more responsive and efficient can hardly be over emphasised. This can only be achieved by providing effective leadership especially at the district level, which is the cutting edge. The mechanism for redress of public grievances can only function if officials visit areas of their responsibility. Unwilling and office bound officers need to be weeded out. Recourse must be taken to induct suitable officers from outside as was done in 1965 by GM Sadiq. The officers of the erstwhile Indian Frontier Administrative Service (IFAS) did extremely well, bulk of them were drawn from the Defense Services. Some officers of the IFAS are still remembered fondly by the local people and in way have become a legend in the remote areas in Ladakh.

The border areas, particularly the Pahari belt extending from Uri to Tilel adjoining PoK requires special attention. It is inhabited by communities of different ethnic and linguistic groups, who have been most loyal and even in the intense proxy war environment have not fully succumbed to the Pakistani and anti-India elements. The area has been neglected and relatively more deprived. This should be developed by special dispensation under the Border Areas Development Programme.

The seclusion and isolation of the Kashmiris has been broken as a fallout of militancy, where trade and commerce and disruption of education have driven people outside the state. The people in the valley thus saw the diversity and oneness of India over the length and breadth of the country. None was harassed due to his or her religion or being a Kashmiri. This has had a positive effect broken further by extending the railway both ways. These trends need to be strengthened. Along with this incidental opening, the physical isolation needs to be broken by extending the railway network up to Srinagar, which has been promised by the Prime Minister.

To rejuvenate the administration, restoration of the Single Line Administration in its entirety with District Development Commissioner as head of the District needs to be restored. This must be supervised and encouraged by the political leadership by visits to districts more as facilitators rather than as superiors. This can only be done if dedicated volunteers apart from the IAS from the other services are inducted. The present administrative set up is incapable of meeting the challenge, particularly after the 1990 subversion. Devolution of executive and financial powers to the Panchayats is essential to ensure proper utilisation of resources and to weed out corruption. To win the battle of hearts and minds this is vital.

As discussed earlier, education system requires reorientation both in the social and economic context. From the social point of view, it needs to move away from the fundamentalist madarssa education to a broad based one. From an economic point of view it requires scientific and technological orientation and vocational training infrastructure to tackle unemployment on a long term basis. Similarly, both to tackle unemployment and to help in bringing Kashmir into the Indian people should be provided job opportunities outside the state.

The infrastructure in Jammu and Kashmir needs special dispensation, particularly in communications, power, agriculture, horticulture and for industrial rejuvenation and expansion. Initially major infrastructure projects should be undertaken by national corporations and organisations like the Boarder Roads Organisation, Power Corporation, Bridging Corporation and other reputed private enterprises to ensure proper utilisation of funds and timely completion. This is essential till the state administrative machinery gears up. To rejuvenate the industry, government should examine the viability of all the public sector undertakings, both State and Centre owned and revive only those considered viable, of special mention and attention are the Indian Telephone Industry, HMT and the manufacturing and processing industries.

Conflict Management-How to Fight the Proxy War

As discussed earlier the proxy war has three major dimensions, one externally for containment and handling in the diplomatic field to reduce its overall capacity, internally within Jammu and Kashmir and thirdly equally important one to defeat Pakistan's subversive designs in the rest of the country. Our success in these areas will expose Pakistan's design of pan-Islamic expansion and terrorism and its sponsorship and would apprise the world of its dangerous dimensions. Internally, in Kashmir the proxy war must be defeated by making its cost prohibitive in terms of inflicting casualties and material losses on the Mujahideen and simultaneously removing the alienation of the people to separate them from the militants. People of Jammu and Kashmir have an equal stake in it and must participate in the struggle. To defeat Pakistani subversive designs in the rest of the country the responses have to be both in the political and administrative field. In the political field we must strengthen the ethos of secularism and democratic norms both psychologically and physically by correct political action. Any disruption of it must be dealt with severely. This will be possible only be making it an all party agenda for the next Lok Sabha and the coming elections in the states. In the administrative field our responses have to be in the intelligence and police operations field. For this a strategy has to be formulated by the central government and implemented jointly by the central and state intelligence and police forces. This will require coordination and monitoring by the central government.

Due to lack of a holistic approach to internal security, distortions have crept in the functioning of the administration and governance has become ineffective. The focus is primarily on law and order aspects and the civil face—political and administrative—tends to recede leaving the fight against proxy war entirely to the Security Forces. Counter insurgency includes measures to frustrate insurgency with minimum overt action, which is equally applicable to the proxy war in Jammu and Kashmir. The aim is to nullify elements on which insurgency and militancy thrives. It starts with a political structure, a responsive civil administration and cohesive security apparatus including police, intelligence, paramilitary forces, armed forces and a judicial system geared to meet the requirement. This must be supported by an economic infrastructure (material resources, finance, transport, communications, public distribution system and civic services), information and propaganda and diplomatic effort to gain recognition and support for such efforts. Counter insurgency also includes population and resource control, civic actions, psychological operations, political and administrative action and larger socio-economic reforms. It is a sum total of both preventive and remedial measures to control, contain and defeat the proxy war. Only a holistic policy incorporating all these aspects can provide the framework for a cohesive and potent action plan.

Both conflict resolution and efficient conflict management require a holistic approach incorporating political, socio-economic and law and other aspects. The overall policy framework at the apex level provides the long term strategic orientation and within these parameters conflict management deals with tactical aspects in all spheres at the ground level. Unless our approach encompasses both these aspects and all elements of the government and security forces function within such a framework, all our endeavours to resolve the situation will be inadequate and management of conflict inefficient. Unfortunately we have not fully succeeded in this respect and it requires greater attention. This also helps in creating synergy between the organs of the state, political leadership, bureaucracy and security forces at the central and state level, which is essential for efficient conflict management.

We have discussed Prime Minister Vajpayee's peace initiatives since April 2003 and events leading to the joint statement by him and President Musharraf of 5 January 2004 at Islamabad during the 12th SAARC summit in the previous chapter. Both events can be termed as historic but more important is the fact that these offer a chance for peace and therefore, need dispassionate discussion and analysis.

Peace Vision and Reality

The peace initiatives of 2004 and the agreed joint press statement have raised hopes in both countries and initial signs of cooperation and prosperity appeared on the South Asian horizon, with the signing of South Asia Free Trade Agreement (SAFTA) and the additional protocol on terrorism, which in reality only updates the SAARC convention of 1987 to make it compatible with UN Resolution 1373. President Musharraf's declared during his press conference on 6 January 2004 that history has been made and that there were no winners or losers; it was a victory for peace and prosperity for people on both sides. A few hours earlier Principal Secretary and National Security Advisor Brijesh Mishra had echoed similar feelings calling it a "win situation for both the countries."[13] World hailed resumption of talks between India and Pakistan and Colin Powell, US Secretary of State called it a historic beginning. Most noticeable was the absence of 'K' word throughout the summit and there was generally a consensus amongst the political parties in Pakistan for going ahead with the peace process and improving relations with India. Even from the religious parties who expressed dissidence and organised protests in 1999, there was no display of dissent. Most attended the reception for Prime Minister Vajpayee by the Indian High Commissioner and Murshid Hussain, former Information Minister, said, "No political party seeks confrontation with India[14].

Against an over whelming constituency for peace, there were rumblings of dissents from the Kashmiri fundamentalists and amongst a section of the powerful generals both retired and serving, who have a vested interest in continuation of the confrontation. Musharraf is under threat from the Jehadis, who feel he has betrayed them. HM Chief Syed Salahuddin, who is also head of the United Jehad Council is bitter about Kashmiri militants being sidelined and he sees peace ploy by India to gain time to complete the border fencing. Qazi Hussain Ahmed, JEI Chief and Chief Patron of HM, supports the HM's view that, "India should acknowledge that Kashmir is a disputed territory. If there is no dispute then why are we fighting? Jehad is the weapon of victims of injustice. Qazi is of the view that just because Musharraf is the Commander-in-Chief of the Pakistan Army, he cannot be allowed to put Kashmir on the back burner. Remember it was the Pakistan Army under Musharraf which sabotaged the 1999 peace proposal by the Kargil operations." The response of Profesor Hafiz Mohammad, the Ameer of Jamat-ul-Dawa the parent organisation of LET, is equally stringent: "Musharraf's priority may be peace but our priority is freedom from India. We do not need it at the cost of our freedom. If Musharraf and his men are also sincere, they will press India to resolve the core issue first." I A Rehman Director Human Rights Commission of Pakistan feels that "As national interest and those of Islamic extremists are no longer fully compatible with each other, the Jehadi's have closed ranks and are trying to eliminate the general. Under the circumstances Musharraf has no other option but to act against the Islamic extremists. Ironically those who want Musharraf dead have been traditionally the closest allies of the military establishment. It is a classic example of the monster (Jehadis) rising to consume its creater"[15]. President Musharraf repeatedly uttering 'K' word during his address to *India To-day* 2004 conclave in March and repeatedly emphasising it during the question-answer session can be attributed to his wanting to appease these elements.

The joint declaration embodied the vision of peace and dialogue, the key from India's point of view was the reassurance by President Musharraf that he won't allow terrorists to use Pakistani soil against India. Apart from the fact that he has finally conceded his country's role in Jehad, more important was his reassurance to put an end to it. It is important to understand it. It is widely believed that Washington's nudging Pakistan Military establishment undertaking measures which ultimately paved the way for Vajpayee going to Islamabad.

It was primarily due to international pressure on both the countries, possibly a lot more on Pakistan, which made the historic meeting possible. The key to it was change in Musharraf's and Pakistani Establishment's mindset. The twin attacks on Musharraf in December 2003, convinced New Delhi that the Jehadis are not only opposed to USA but also to Musharraf for pursuing the war against terrorism. This view is further reinforced by the killing/capture of Pakistani Army personnel during operations in Wana area of South Waziristan and the alleged Fatwa against Musharraf during March 2004. While he may not be able to completely halt cross border terrorism but he is the best option available for negotiation. The agreement provided Musharraf an opportunity to gain support of moderates by arguing that he has succeeded in managing India to negotiate on Kashmir and thus strengthen his hand against extremists. There is no denying the fact that there is a paradigm shift in Pakistani's policy after 9/11. The new realities demand a strategic shift in country's past position, relinquishing the extreme position and setting aside the

UN resolutions on Kashmir are its manifestations. Musharraf's new policy has support of Maulana Zafar-ul-Rehman who heads the Jamat-ul-Ulema-l-Islami an important component of MMA. While in 2001 terrorism was Musharraf's trump card by 2004 it has become a liability as space for the double game no longer exists or is getting severely restricted. The resurgence of Taliban generated greater pressure on Musharraf and attacks on him convinced him that the weapon of terrorism has boomeranged. Politically, Musharraf has strengthened his position by agreeing to give up his Army post by the end of the year in return of his being confirmed as President till 2007 by the parliament. It also helps MMA as he keeps out both Benazir Bhutto and Nawaz Sharief. Prime Minister of Azad Kashmir, Sardar Sikander Hayat Khan has said that "he has been kept in the loop relating to the Kashmir developments. Musharraf is a man of his word, He will not let the Kashmiris down[16]" The real implications of this will emerge only as negotiations proceed further in June 2004 and developments in Pakistan unfold.

The response in the Kashmir Valley was mostly positive, tinged with an element of hope smeared with blood as terrorist violence has not abated. The cynics show a sign of change of mind. Even Geelani changed his tune after January 6, "I must felicitate Vajpayee and Musharraf, it is a great moment". Professor Abdul Gani Bhat, former Chairman of All Party Hurriyat conference said, "I feel leaders in India and Pakistan have started seeing the hearts and minds of their people, instead of just geographical boundaries. Once there is sincerity and will to discuss issues, even the most difficult problems throw up solutions. I am confident that the defining moment in the history of the two countries has come. This in itself is a historic moment". Hurriyat chairman Moulvi Abbas Ansari is upbeat, "It has been our proclaimed stance that there can be no forward movement towards the resolution of the Kashmir problem unless India and Pakistan show fortitude and maturity. It is now clear that Vajpayee and Musharraf have agreed to jointly brave all odds and exhibit that crucial fortitude without which Kashmiris will continue to stew in their own soup". For Chief Minister Mufti, it was a moment to relish, he said, " For me it has been a matter of faith. I have always said there is no escaping from the fact that we must talk. I have said the road links must be opened so that divided hearts and minds are united. I have always said *Bandook se na Goli se, baat banegi boli se* (It shall be resolved by dialogue). I am happy every one has now started catching up on that line". It has also introduced an element of competitiveness between and amongst the main-stream and separatist politicians to occupy the middle space and claim credit for the dialogue process and opening up of communications. If there was change in the stance of Geelani, Jamat-e-

Islamic Master Habibullah's statement, "India has a stand on Kashmir, Pakistan has a stand on Kashmir and people of Kashmir have a stand on Kashmir as well. It is not impossible to find a (political) point where all the three apparently irreconciable stands must melt into an amicable solution". Such remarks by Jamat, who were most vocal advocates of Kashmir's merger with Pakistan[17] are astonishing. The underlying sentiment is the search for peace, years of violence and disruption and changed global realities, it is no longer a sentiment alone but a compelling human need and a question of life and death for the people of Jammu and Kashmir. The middle path has made the internal dialogue vital, can the Indian state and the Hurriyat and other political formations achieve the achievable.

Hurriyat spokesman and senior executive member of Hurriyat Prof. Abdul Gani Bhat announced in Srinagar on 11 April 2004 that Hurriyat has a road map for Kashmir to resolve the problem and that it will disclose it to the public along with the outcome of two rounds of talks with the Dy. Prime Minister on 21 May 2004 on the death anniversary of the Hurriyat leaders Maulvi Mohammad Farooq and Abdul Gani Lone. He also announced that Hurriyat will seek peoples' mandate for the talks[18]. Going public on the talks is a good sign and it will amount to a commitment which should be welcome as Hurriyat has been changing its stance when under pressure. This should equally draw a response from the Centre.

The Reality

Ever since the joint statement by Prime Minister Vajpayee and President Musharraf on 5 January 2004 during the 12th SAARC summit most experts on Indo-Pak relations and Kashmir have cited past history, particularly that of 1964 when a possible solution of the Kashmir problem was scuttled by the untimely and fateful death of Pandit Nehru (Ram Chander Guha-*Indian Express* 31 March 2004). While the precedent of the past may not be applicable due to the changed realities internationally and domestically but the criterion outlined by late Sheikh Abdulla for the solution that (i) it must strengthen and not weaken the position of the minorities in the subcontinent, (ii) it must not lead to a sense of defeat in either India or Pakistan and (iii) it must be consistent with the desire of the Kashmiri people themselves are largely still relevant and need to be pursued.

The external environment in South Asia has changed due to the presence of the core of the Islamic terrorism in Afghanistan and Pakistan-Afghan border areas and the American presence there to wage war against it. With the war in Iraq going against the Americans, new avenues have opened for terrorism which USA is unable to handle effectively. The fall out of Iraq is bound to be felt in the sub-continent and failure in Iraq will put greater pressure on the Bush administration to show results in Afghanistan. This has put pressure on president Musharraf domestically as was evident by the quick withdrawal of Pakistani Security Forces from the area after it suffered casualties in the operations during March 2004 and Pakistani officials had to be rescued by the tribal elders. Underlying these developments is the fact that while America with its military and economic power can subdue the so called rogue states but Islamic terrorists no longer draw their strength from the states but from the deprived societies and radical elements in the Muslim world, who see USA and states cooperating with it as their enemies. USA's war against terrorism in Afghanistan, Iraq and else where is driven by their self-interest. This is evident in their manner of dealing with terrorism and nuclear proliferation, which has different norms for different states as has been amply proved by USA's response to Dr. Abdul Qadeer Khan's confession on transfer of nuclear weapons technology to North Korea, Libya and Iran. Without global legitimacy and participation USA is bound to fail. The American failure with also be the failure of its allies like Pakistan. If peace process in South Asia has to succeed then USA must stop playing the spoiler, granting Pakistan the status of Major non-NATO ally even without informing India is the latest of such actions.

Where does this leave Indo-Pak negotiations for peace. First of all we must acknowledge and accept that war against global terrorism and Indo-Pak negotiations have to be tackled on two different plains keeping our national interest in mind. Pakistan will be a much closer strategic ally than us in USA's war against terrorism and we need not worry about it unduly but we should certainly be concerned with its fallout both in Pakistan and on our security environment. One of the issues likely to come up is India's involvement in Iraq as and when UN assumes the central role. Our stance of not militarily getting involved is correct and it should be maintained as even under UN guise USA will still be dictating the policy which will continue to be viewed as anti-Iraq.

Indo-Pak negotiations are a hopeful sign and need to be sustained irrespective of the past history, the situation alternating between crisis and cordiality. Before proceeding further we need to recognize certain facets of Indo-Pak antagonism. Over fifty years of confrontation and conflict has adversely affected both countries, more so Pakistan. Pakistan is fast losing the economic and even the military race against India. China is no longer a staunch ally of Pakistan, whom it views as the fountainhead of Islamic terrorism. USA as in the past is there as long as it suits its interests.

In Pakistan the real power is with the Army and we have to deal with it. Dealing with them when they are in power is better than when they wield power and manipulate from behind the politicians. While nuclearisation of Pakistan in its preception provides it security, at the same time the failure of the proxy war has dented its obsession that India must be kept busy in Kashmir and with other militancies. This in the changed geo-strategic environment and is fully realised by Musharraf and the Pakistani Army, therefore, the need to negotiate. Militarily, the chance of a limited war gets constrained due to likelihood of it going nuclear. Similarly, neither can we wrest POK, nor can Pakistan capture Indian Jammu and Kashmir. Corollary to it is that neither can Pakistan give up Kashmir ideologically, nor can India give it up as it will compromise its core values. A unified or independent Kashmir is beyond the realms of a possibility but people of the whole erstwhile state of Jammu and Kashmir need to be satisfied and permitted to interact and live across open borders. While a divided Jammu and Kashmir along the LoC with modifications is the only possibility both sides need to accept and sell to the people on their side, particularly in Pakistan. What was possible in 1971 under duress, now it needs to be negotiated. This is the real issue of Indo-Pak negotiations and will be possible over a long period of stability and sustained efforts in the Indo-Pak dialogue. Kashmir is one of the primary issues and not one of the eight issues. Realistically speaking Kashmiris on both sides are a party to dialogue with its own state and are not the third party to the dispute. This issue cannot be tackled initially at the very out set but will have to be faced as we progress. The key to resolving this is the satisfaction of Kashmiris and other elements of the society in Indian Jammu and Kashmir and POK in the political, socio-economic, ethnic and religious fields. Both sides have to have a different approach based on its core values. Internal dialogue and satisfaction is the key, this is also an area where no outsider can help.

The key to progress in the Indo-Pak negotiations and dialogue is the strategic vision of the leadership on both sides and confidence building measures in a sustained fashion over a long period to create the conducive environment. In the domestic field the key elements are mutual trust and sincerity and not political rhetorics. Both our foreign and domestic policy has been a slave to a bureaucratic stranglehold, which is wedded to confrontation and scoring tactical victories. Both the external and domestic process of negotiations and dialogue need a totally political orientation. This has been amply proved by the success of the process during the 12th SAARC submit resulting in joint declaration. We can only afford to go forward and not slide back. In the past even military agreement on Siachen have been doomed by bureaucrats trying to score points. Let us learn from the past.

The successful tour of the Indian cricket team to Pakistan and the public goodwill and camaraderie between players and officials unlike the past are clear indications of a change. The new generation on both sides is clearly looking ahead to a prosperous future in partnership with each other, the societies are changing, will our leaders read the winds.

Governance—the Key Factor

Policy implementation, rejuvenating the administration, implementation of economic development programmes and security management are all part of governance. Today governance is the prime requirement in our entire country, particularly in the disturbed areas. A critical analysis of our failures in various spheres point to failure of governance and more than anything else it is the absence of good governance which is bothering the people and is their main concern. Without effective and good governance neither will we be able to secure the environment nor implement our policies to remove people's deprivation. Special areas of concern for governance in Jammu and Kashmir are the establishment of the credibility and legitimacy of state and its institutions, implementation of developmental schemes to remove deprivation of the people, and management of varying and conflicting perceptions of the people of different areas of the state and security management. The credibility and legitimacy of the government can only be established by a pragmatic and implementable policy, institutionalised approach and a transparent and sincere implementation by credible people. While resolving or managing conflicting perceptions is primarily in the political field but implementation of solutions in a just and fair fashion is part of administration and thus governance.

We have been successful in addressing and propagating our cause with the international community and also to a fair degree with the political constituency and the elite in Jammu and Kashmir. However, our efforts to address the main constituency, the people of Jammu and Kashmir have not been very successful and leave much to be desired. The real and ultimate battle is for the hearts and minds of the people. Without winning this battle, all gains in the political, diplomatic and military fields will be nullified. This is where our major failures lie, whether in Jammu and Kashmir or the North-East. In the case of Jammu and Kashmir, it has two key elements, one – the healing touch to the hurt caused to the Kashmiris, which has been discussed earlier. Second is removing the deprivation of all segments of the society in Jammu and Kashmir. To remove peoples deprivation, you have to reach them and deliver what they want. To deliver, you have to be there; proxies, pronouncements and rhetorics will not do, they only turn people away and add to their alienation. This is where political will and governance is seen by the commonman.

To reach, you need to restore the disrupted communications, as without communications neither can you reach or deliver people requirements. VIPs reaching in helicopters only add to people frustration and anger as they don't deliver. Once communications are restored, supervision of delivery and administrative functioning at the grassroots level gives confidence to the people and wins them over. Public Distribution System (PDS) which has broken down should be restored, first in the villages then in towns and lastly in the cities. What PDS delivers is important, sugar, salt, rice, wheat and kerosene oil are a must. Also if people like coarse rice, deliver it. The stream once starts flowing gathers its own momentum.

The other areas of commonman's concern are water, electricity, shelter, health and education. Deliver potable water to people near their homes, without 'Ab' there is no Hayat. Restore light, else darkness will prevail. Only with light you can dispel fear. If government denies light then people cannot be well disposed towards it, it also shows the government in favourable light. Everyone needs shelter, Kashmiri Pandits, victims of shelling in Uri, Keren and Kargil. Return of migrants is not only a human issue but a challenge and test of political will of the governments at the State and Centre. Health care has been disrupted in the rural areas, where bulk of people live. Government is paying doctors to stay in towns. They should be in villages and go with adequate medical provisions and medicines.

Poverty of mind is worse than material poverty. It leads to ignorance and deprivation and provides ideal ground for disruptive and radical elements to exploit. Restore the education system and rejuvenate it with the right orientation. Education is also the key to employment, temper it with scientific blend and vocational training.

The question is that if the central and state governments are not aware of these basic requisites how can they govern? People must feel and see the government and not just hear of its existence. I have governed in an equally bad environment successfully through this dictum, and if you can reach beyond then you have created an ideal and healthy environment

Conclusion

The road ahead is pitted with obstacles which can only be overcome by a holistic policy based on recognition of the political, socio-economic and law and order dimensions of the problem in Jammu and Kashmir. Confining it to the proxy war will be courting a failure. The policy parameters must take into account the dangerous dimensions of the Islamic terrorism, the agony and deprivation of the people of Jammu and Kashmir and aim towards harmonizing the relationships and imbalances within the state in keeping with the federal structure under Article 370 of the constitution. The task may appear to be insurmountable but a good beginning will establish credibility of intentions and legitimacy of actions. The critical area is the inner core of sentiments in Jammu and Kashmir and their harmonisation with India's interest.

REFERENCES

1. *Hindustan Times*, 7 September 1999.
2. Prem Shankar Jha, A Dangerous Phase, *Hindustan Times*, 27 August 1999.
3. Prof. Riaz, Punjabi-Institute of Peace and Conflict Studies *Seminar*, 2 Feb 2001.
4. *Ibid.*
5. Galtung, John 1969. Structural Violence; 1964, 'Structural Theory of Aggression', Journal of Peace Research, 1:95-119, 1969, 'Peace, Violence and Peace Research, VI, p. 69.
6. Statistical Outline of India— 1989-90, Tata Services Ltd., 1989, p. 27.
7. *Ibid.*
8. M. L. Mishri and M.S. Bhat, Poverty, *Planning and Economic Changes in J and K*, Vikas Publishing House, New Delhi, p. 39 and Gul Mohammed Wani, *Kashmir Politics: Problem and Prospects*, Ashish Publishing House, Punjabi Bagh, Delhi, pp. 104-108.
9. Asgar Ali Engineer, *Secular Crown on Fire*, *The Kashmir problem*, Ajanta Publications Delhi, 1991, p. 263-266 and Nasir A Naqash and G.M. Shah Kashmir from Crisis to Crisis, p. 153
10. n8 Gul Mohammed Wani-*Kashmir Politics, Problems and Prospects*, pp. 101-103.
11. *Ibid*, p. 102 and *Kashmir Crisis to Crisis*, p. 152.
12. *Kashmir Crisis to Crisis*, p. 154.
13. *India To-day*, 19 January 2004.
14. *Ibid.*
15. *Outlook*, 19 January 2004.
16. *Frontline*, 30 January 2004.
17. *Outlook*, 19 January 2004.
18. *Indian Express*, 12 April 2004.

Part III

9

Drugs and Arms Linkages
Its Cross Border Nexus and Internal Security

The low level armed conflicts are aimed at the vulnerabilities of the states and the societies and low cost of pursuing such an option makes it attractive. Studies have also established the linkage between escalation of such conflicts and the easy availability of small arms and light weapons. These conflicts even if internal and indigenous develop external links over a period of time. This is the legacy of the cold war, wherein the contesting states and non-state actors and groups were supplied small arms and light weapons by the superpowers and China in the pursuit of their strategic interests. (Angola, Mozambique, Combodia and Afghanistan). Tara Kartha in her paper on "Southern Asia- The Narcotics and Weapons Linkage", presented at the first international Pugwash workshop on "Small Arms and Light Weapons, Implications for Global Security", in New Delhi in 1995 has clearly established the links between drug trafficking and spread of small arms. It is not possible to control the spread of arms without a tight control over drug trafficking and money laundering. The nexus is tripartite as will be argued later. The situation is made complex and intense by the exploitation of transnational, ethnic and religious links[1]. All these factors stand out in the study of the conflict in Afghanistan and the never ending intra-Afghan Civil War. In the words of Brigadier Mohammed Youssaf, who was incharge of Mujahideen operations in Pakistan's ISI, "the CIA supported the Mujahideen by spending American tax payers money, billions of dollars over the years on buying arms, ammunition and equipment"[2] China, SaudiArabia ,Egypt ,Israel, Turkey and UK amongst others cooperated in this enterprise. The involvement of governmental agencies, particularly the intelligence agencies always complicates the situation. The role played by CIA and Pakistan's ISI in Afghanistan and ISI role in arms supply and support to militancy in India is of special concern and interest to us. Capture of over 10,000 arms in Punjab and over 20,000 in Jammu and Kashmir are indications of the dimensions of the threat.

Crime, Drugs, Arms and Transnational Linkages

Organised crime operates within the legal economic system, seeking to gain a position of control and to produce income through the use of violence and the utilisation of illicitly acquired wealth[3]. Most profitable illicit activity is production and trafficking of drugs. The illicit drug industry is estimated to have an annual turn over of US$ 500 billion[4]. Drug profits have become by far the biggest source of revenue for organised crime. It is the biggest single element in Italian organised crime and of the cocaine cartels of Columbia. Columbian drug cartels have superseded the authority of the state, it has killed 12 Supreme Court and more than 50 other judges, 170 judicial employees, Narcotic Police Chief, over 300 policemen and soldiers, over 1000 public officials, three presidential candidates and dozens of journalists. They have infiltrated virtually every anti-drug agency in the country[5]. Attorney General Carlos Manro Hoyas in 1988 called them the super state. Two months after he made this statement he was assassinated.

Organised crime seeks political power, the clout wielded by the Italian Mafia on two of the country's political parties was clearly brought out during the recent investigations. Political terrorist groups like other terrorists also turn to criminal syndicates to utilise their ready made infrastructure. By aiding terrorism and insurgencies narco traffickers are able to expand their support base and network and they find terrorist movements useful allies. Drugs require patronage and protection from production to refining, during transit and till delivery to the consumer, the entire system has to be protected and no better agency to do it than organised terrorists. The interdependence of drugs and arms traffickers and terrorists is mutually beneficial and covers the entire area of their operations. Drug and arms trafficking, terrorism, organised crime and money laundering are the four ugly facets of the underworld crime activities which destabilises states and societies as it threatens political power.

While terrorism and insurgency relate to political violence, narco terrorism aims at evolution of criminal super states. It provides low cost option for internal destabilisation, without direct political and military interference. Indian mafia has also got involved in drugs and arms smuggling and a network of narco terrorism is emerging in the border states of J & K, Punjab, Rajasthan, Gujarat, Maharashtra and the North-Eastern States.

The trends in economic liberalisation and reduction of trade barriers has increased world trade and generated movement of big capital across international borders. Drug syndicates are unlikely to ignore such opportunities and acquisition of properties and firms and investment in second hand sales of high magnitude[6]. In Russia crime syndicates have already infiltrated the country's financial system. With the collapse of the centralised financial system, the banks have become both the target and vehicle for money laundering by mafia organisations to launder ill gotten gains[7]. In Afghanistan, the symbiosis between military conflict, arms trade, drug production, trafficking, production and addiction has resulted in total dependence on drug related revenues to maintain the armed forces. Warring groups continue to struggle for control over areas suitable for poppy cultivation and opium and poppy production, a fact that is fraught with implications for country's long term reconstruction. The political and economic development of the country, inevitably risks being stifled as long as drugs are seen and utilised as a source of power.

Most large scale drug trafficking operations are internationally based, the organisers of a criminal network may be in one country, the producers in second country and distributors in a third and proceeds of crime laundered in a fourth. Thus apprehending offenders involved in illicit distribution in one country is like cutting off some branches of a tree but leaving the roots in tact. As Ehrenfeld says it is time to stop pretending that drug trafficking is exclusively a criminal enterprise. The source is ultimately political and should be dealt as such. Failure to do so means the war will be fought on the wrong front, in the wrong way, with little or no chance for victory[8].

The international trafficking on narcotics and psychotropic substances has generated huge amount of capital for its initiators and organisers. The drug cartels and traffickers are organized and structured to function efficiently within national economies as well as at the international level. The profits derived from their illegal activities are either integrated into legal economy or are used in corrupt and criminal ways to enhance such activities[9]. These groups have influence on politicians, officials, judiciary, media and influential segments of the society to influence opinions and decisions of the Government.

Pakistan ever ready to exploit India's vulnerability has been supporting terrorist and separatist groups, with its ISI playing a leading role. Providing militants arms and drugs both of which can be sold at large profits is part of its plan to make militant movements in India self sufficient[10]. The clandestine working of smuggling groups easily meshed into terrorist activities. That additional incomes could be generated by combining narcotics with terrorism was not lost on the mercenaries nor on the sponsors of terrorism across the border. They found that this was a convenient means of self financing terrorism as it were. Since it is the drug traffickers who control and grant access to secure international smuggling routes. Terrorists are inevitably forced to act in collusion with the smugglers. Paramjit Singh Panjwar, the Chief of Khalistan Commando Force is an old smuggler who already had links with well known Pakistani smugglers like Khalid, Iqbal and Balal. For covert destabilisation of India, Pakistan has made use of religious fundamental organisations in conjunction with the underworld network as is evident from the March 1993 serial blasts in Mumbai and the role played by Dawood Ibrahim crime syndicate, communal riots in Ahmedabad and Surat and the Coimbatore blasts in February 1999 by muslim fundamentalist organisations.

Despite massive political, judicial, financial and military efforts, narcotics industry is the world's most successful illegal enterprise. It generates profits of $ 300 billion annually. The period 1991-2000 was declared as UN's decade against drug abuse. The world's largest drug growing regions are Latin America, the Golden Crescent (Afghanistan, Pakistan and Iran) and the Golden Triangle (Thailand, Myanmar and Laos). Our troubled areas in Jammu and Kashmir and Punjab in the west are located close to the Golden Crescent and the North-East to the Golden Triangle, narco terrorism is gradually and surely becoming a part of the disturbed environment of these areas. Its dangerous dimensions have already manifested in increased smuggling of arms and explosives, spread of subversive network and acts of sabotage. Of which, if the Bombay blasts of 1993 were the warning shots, the blasts in Coimbatore in February 1998 have clearly registered its grave threat both territorially and dimension-wise. Narcotic smuggling not only provided vast income and resources to the transborder nexus operating it, it also enlarged avenues for illegal transborder movement and provided our neighbours particularly Pakistan a viable infrastructure for subversive activities.

THE WEST

Narcotics

The tribes and sub-tribes of the Pashtuns straddling the vast areas around Afghanistan and Pakistan border had over the centuries carved out autonomous territories, which they defended against any intruder including the British and the governments in Kabul. They remained outside the British Control in spite of 42 military expeditions and two invasions of Afghanistan in 1838 and 1878.The British policy after the Second Afghan war settled on accepting internal autonomy of the country and keeping control over its external affairs to prevent it from entering into alliance with Russia. After partition and independence in 1947, Pakistan continued with the old regulations from the British time and the colonial administrative system of political agents supported by Tochi Scouts and Khyber Rifles, with little tinkering here and there. Trade in sophisticated weapons, manufacturing of small arms and narco trafficking take place without any control or interference from Govt. and criminals, murderers and terrorists take refuge in the area in return for working for the local chiefs, which may involve illegal activities.

Due to conducive climate and land opium has been grown traditionally by tribal chiefs for limited use, essentially to sell to caravans to Central Asia. At the time of independence these areas had limited opium output and Pakistan was dependent on import from India for its addicts and for pharmaceutical uses. With the opening of the tribal areas and its integration to whatsoever limited extent, within a decade the market forces played their own role in integrating opium growing areas of Pakistan and Afghanistan and a transnational network kept Iran and Pakistan well supplied. Drug production and trafficking gradually started playing a significant role in the political economy of the area. Drug trafficking in the Golden Crescent area got a boost in the last two decades due to various reasons. First was the Islamic revolution in Iran, which resulted in the banning of poppy cultivation, which was done at a large scale during the Shah's regime and execution of addicts and traffickers. Demand for opium from the area went up, when opium production declined in the Golden Triangle in late seventies due to climatic and political reasons leaving a big gap in supply as a result of which the focus of international drug mafia shifted to the Golden Crescent particularly to the poppy growing areas of Afghanistan and Pakistan. This resulted in the linking up of these areas to international trafficking network and introduction of chemicals and technology for processing opium into heroin. Soviet intervention further strengthened the hold of international drug traffickers. After the fall of the Najib Govt. and Soviet withdrawal the poppy growing areas got free of whatever little Govt. control was there. Mujahideen commanders who fought the war with Soviet forces, now indulged in profitable deals with drug traffickers, taxed the middlemen and some even indulged in its production.

The Golden Crescent is one of the major illicit drug supplying areas of the world. Afghanistan and Pakistan is the source of 75 per cent of the heroin seized in Europe, 25 per cent of the heroin seized in United States and 75 per cent of the heroin consignments intercepted in transit in Africa and Arabian Peninsula, as well as a large proportion of the cannabis resin seized in Europe[11]. According to the report of the officials of the Vienna based UN Drug Control Programme (UNDCP) the poppy production in Afghanistan, heart of the Golden Crescent during 1996/97, rose to an estimate of 2,800 metric tonnes (M.T.) almost a 25 per cent increase over the production in the last season. The estimated 2,800 MT also means that Afghanistan's opium production is 25 per cent more than the other production area of the Golden Triangle. The increased harvest should be seen in the light of stagnation in opium production during 1995-96 when total yield was about 2,300 MT. The total area of opium cultivation in Afghanistan and Pakistan stood at 36,450 hectares (ha) in 1994. The survey conducted annually found that between 1995-96 the total area under poppy cultivation was 58400 ha[12] and estimated to have gone up to approximately 64,000 ha yielding over 3200 M.T. during 1998. With the year (1999's) bumper crop Afghanistan has become the number one producer of opium in the world, accounting for three fourth of the output in 1999[13]. The latest reported figures of 4200 MT of poppy production indicate that the production of opium in Afghanistan continues to show an alarmingly upward trend. 96 per cent of the opium production of Afghanistanis from areas which were under the Taliban control and one of the biggest drug barons of Kandhar, Haji Bashar Mohammad is a friend of Taliban Chief Mullah Mohammad Omar, having fought side by side during the Jehad against Soviets.

By 1980, the drug cartels were pushed into Pakistan-Afghanistan border due to the Soviet invasion, advent of Khomeini Regime in Iran and a crack down in Turkey. Hundreds of Drug laboratories were set up (170 according to Gen Fazle Haq) [14] leading to massive operations in the Khyber region resulting in simultaneous recovery of 3,00,000 Kalashnikovs of Soviet and Chinese make[15], but there was no reduction in drugs, neither the weapons were heard of later. By 1984, forty drug cartels were operating in Pakistan and it was producing seventy per cent of the world's heroin. Opium production doubled between 1986 to 1988 (400 to 800 tons). In East Afghanistan, Hikmatyar had already undertaken opium cultivation in 1984, due to fear of cut off of weapons supply due to end of cold war and set up refining units in partnership with Pakistan drug syndicates. By 1992, 80 per cent of the arable land in Nangarhar was under opium cultivation. South under the mullah warlords undertook large scale cultivation of opium and virtually established a dictatorship over the peasants to impose opium cultivation. Kandhar under the traditionalists remained resistant to the mullahs. The opium produce went to refineries in Ribatal Ali, where Iran, Pakistan and Afghanistan borders meet. A drug centre also came up in Girdi jungles in Baluchistan and Landi Kotal became a major drug market[16]. The story of the drug in the Golden Crescent region will not be complete without mentioning that the drug cultivation went up by ten fold in the Central Asian Region between 1990 to 1993.[17]

Osama Bin Laden had himself gone in for large scale cultivation of opium in Afghanistan to produce heroin in the Eastern District of Shinwar. He had also promised to buy all the opium produced in the area. Waging the holy war and making money at the same time is an attractive option. Laden already had a wide network of international contacts to flood the west and USA with heroin, his new weapons in the war against the west[18].

The traditional route from Afghanistan and Pakistan leads to Iran, Turkey and then onto Europe. Another route from Afghanistan is from Khorog in Gorno – Badakhshan province, Tajikistan, through the only mountain road of 700 Kms to Osh in Kyrgystan. The heroin shipments are transported through different countries in Central Asia and Caucasus to Belarus, Estonia, Latvia, Lithuania, the Russian Federation and Ukraine to destinations in Central and Western Europe. Middle East and Arabian Peninsula are used as transit points for smuggling of heroin and cannabis resin to Europe.[19] Illicit traffickers take advantage of lack of border control along the roads from Afghanistan through CIS member states. Capture of Kabul by Taliban in September 1998, had turned the Afghan Tajik border as an unhindered border for drug smuggling by Afghan and Pakistani drug smugglers to former Soviet Central Asian republics and Russia. Official Russian Security Services say the volume of opium from Afghanistan and Pakistan through the corridor into Russia is hundreds of tons per year. While heroin in the border zones of former republics cost $ 7000 to 10,000 per Kg. by the time it reaches Moscow the price can go as high as $ 1,50,000 per kg. The bribes to Russian border military officials can reach up to $ 20,000 for narcotics to be given over or for a car to be passed through check posts is an indication of the million dollar narcotics business. In 1994, 260 kg of raw opium was seized at Tajik-Afghan border, in 1995 the figure reached 1,720 kg and in 1996 more than 2000 kg were confiscated[20]. Drug control officers also claim that 80 per cent of the heroin seized in Europe comes from Afghanistan. Importation and distribution of South-West Asian heroin is less concentrated than the South-East Asian heroin. In the United States a number of ethnic groups from South West Asia and the Middle East are active in the business, these include Turks, Pakistanis, Afghans, Iranians, Israelis and Lebanese. [21]

While bulk of the Afghan and Pakistani origin heroin is trafficked through Iran and Central Asian Republics to Europe but increasingly it is also pushed through from Pakistan to India and then to Africa, which has become a drug centre. From Africa it is either sent to Europe or North America.

Illicit drugs travel through Punjab and Sindh in Pakistan through hundreds of check posts and under the eyes of scores of law enforcement agencies to Karachi, which is the established and traditional outlet for international traffickers. Mehran coast of Baluchistan is the second route used for smuggling to Turkey and then to Europe. Indo-Pak border is also being developed as the third route. Pakistan probably carries the largest quantity of drugs to Gulf, Saudi Arabia and Western Countries.

After Iran imposed strict measures against drug trafficking, Afghan-Iran border has become the scene of pitched battles between Afghan traffickers and Iranian Security Forces. Iran claims that drug traffickers have killed 2,635 personnel of its law enforcement agencies. Iranian authorities have seized 194702 kgs of illicit drugs, which includes 1986 Kg of heroin, 11095 Kg hashish, 11,700 kg of cocaine and 255065 Kg of other drugs. [22]

Due to fragmented control of Afghanistan, pushing drugs through Salang route became difficult, alternative routes were created through Pakistan in NWFP, Baluchistan and Karachi and through Punjab and Kashmir in India with the involvement of the ISI and Pakistan military. India is a transit route for illicit, narcotics from Afghanistan, Pakistan and Myanmar bound for European markets. Nepal's open border with India and proximity to Pakistan and Myanmar makes it an alternative route both for the Golden Crescent and the Golden Triangle to Europe, Asia and USA While movement of drugs from and through Nepal so far discerned by our intelligence agencies is not significant but the Terai region of Nepal bordering UP and Bihar which has a growing Muslim population, has become the hub of ISI activities since 1993. Young Muslims have been recruited and trained in the use of explosives and the police has been able to link the explosions in 1993 in UP to the ISI. Nepalese government has also given intelligence and warned the Indian authorities of some Afghan students receiving training in Banke- Nabdian Jungles in 1994 [23]. The arrest of the prominent Sikh militant leader Sohan Singh and one of the Memon brothers confirm the spreading ISI subversive network. The open borders of Nepal pose a security threat which we need to take cognizance of.

Money laundering, which is an integral part of trafficking of narcotics poses a serious threat to the security and stability of states. In 1991, it was estimated that 750 billion dollars worth of drug money is laundered every year. Drug trafficking impinges on internal security in a number of ways. It creates tensions between consumer and producer states and leads to outside intervention as in Panama. Drugs have been the main source of funds for more than one armed conflict. Drugs and insurgent operations coexist and provide funds for the same. Columbia, Myanmar,

Tajikistan, Surinam, Afghanistan and Philippines are some of the examples. The drug cartels have made inroads into the corridors of power and controlled Pakistan's economy. Drug money was institutionalized as seen from the expanding activities of the Bank of Credit and Commerce International (BCCI) and Pakistan virtually became subsidiary of the bank. Apart from its money laundering operations, it was even involved in the actual operations of the arms pipeline helping Pakistan Army's National Logistic Cell (NLC) to move weapons and drugs into international markets. So close was the relationship that it became difficult to distinguish as to where BCCI operations ended and that of ISI began. Sixteen Army Officers were arrested in 1986 for involvement in the drug trade. Investigations of the BCCI affairs reveal that Gen Zia was paid Rs. 40 million by Cheque and President Ghulam Ishaq Khan was on the bank's pay roll as were prominent political and military families[24].

In Pakistan, the Govt. has made the task of legitimising drug money easier by allowing people to pay 10 to 15 per cent by way of legalising their ill gotten money, without going through complex process of money laundering. Most of these people had made their money either through kickbacks in Govt. contracts or by narcotics trafficking. Such people have been allowed to buy Govt. owned industrial units, hotels, choicest real estates and lands, without any questions being asked about the source of money[25]. Permission to maintain foreign currency accounts in Pakistan and foreign banks in the country provided the easiest and most profitable means of laundering money. No questions are asked about the source and no taxes are levied on earning from foreign currency accounts. When Govt. froze these accounts after the Nuclear tests in May 1998, the value of these accounts was $ 14 billion, late Dr. Mahbub-ul-Haq disclosed, which has been confirmed by foreign press, that Pakistani businessmen, bureaucrats and politicians had stashed immense stolen wealth away in foreign countries. The estimate of this wealth varies from $ 40 billion to $ 80 billion , more than double the entire foreign debt of Pakistan[26]. In May 1999, Finance Minister of Pakistan on the floor of the senate admitted that the size of black money was around Rs. 2,000 billion[27]. Geopolitical Drugwatch, a Paris based organisation in its annual report for the year 1998 claimed that many of Pakistan's most powerful people are known to be deeply involved in the production, transformation and trafficking of drugs. The drug trade in areas around Afghanistan, Pakistan and Iran generates around $ 5 billion a year, in which Pakistan's share in 1992 was $ 1.5 billion[28]. Acetic anhydride, the catalysing chemical used to convert opium to heroin is smuggled from India for onward use in Afghanistan.

Punjab province of Pakistan has been the centre of political and military power and it is also here that drugs and organised crime flourish under its patronage. The key figure was Haji Iqbal Beg and his closest political ally was none other than Malik Miraj Khalid later Chief Minister of Punjab , whose election campaign was funded by Beg. In 1990, when Beg was indicted on drug smuggling charges. Malik Miraj Khalid, negotiated his surrender and bail with the authorities and sent his car to fetch Beg. Beg was involved not only in smuggling drugs into India in 1980s but actively assisted the ISI in their programme to assist Punjab terrorists. Beg has close connections in Delhi and Bombay. Both Beg and, Khalid have close connections with Benazir Bhutto[29]. If Benazir Bhutto was close to drug operations, her successor Nawaz Sharif has been charged with close connections with drug cartels. Sohail Zia Butt a close relative, elected to Punjab Assembly in 1990, was a part of Haji Iqbal Beg's drug empire and when Beg went to jail he took over a part of his business. Both Nawaz Sharif and his brother Shahbaz Sharif are close to Sohail Butt, who was part of Sharif's entourage regularly. Nawaz Sharif's Ittefaq Industries given to him by mlitary showed phenomenal rise in a decade, largely attributed to drug money[30]. It is difficult to believe that Sharif was not involved or benefited from narcotics trade.

According to a report of the Sunday Times, John Banks, a confidential DEA informant taped five hours of conversation of Asif Zardari, husband of former Prime Minister Benazir Bhutto as to how he slips drugs through to America. British Intelligence knew of Zardari's role as financier of drug trafficking[31]. Some years back owner of Sheraton Hotel, Karachi, was convicted of drug trafficking by a German Court. In 1997, in a sting operation one Pakistan Air Force officer was caught red handed in New York selling heroin to an under-cover agent, which landed Ayaz Baloch, a Pakistani working for DEA, in trouble[32]. Manjur Manjh, a PPP parliamentarian and member of the anti-narcotics committee was arrested as his guards and vehicle were carrying a large quantity of heroin. Similarly, owner and publisher of Frontier Post was caught carrying drugs in Lahore for selling to an under-cover agent[33]. There was some controversy and he may have been framed by the authorities.

The CIA report on drug warlords in Pakistan asserts that the ISI not only has close rapport with big smugglers but also uses their money as payments for arms and ammunition and explosives supplied to terrorist groups in J & K. The key figures in the heroin trade not only sat on the inner political councils of the Prime Minister (Nawaz Sharif) but also married into the family. CIA report claims one of them is Nawaz Sharif's brother-in-law, Sohail Zia Butt, whose achievements in trade and business are in reality more of an unofficial record of Sharif family's direct involvement with the drug racket. Informally known as king of 'Hira Mandi', Sohail is crime boss of Lahore's underworld. Aslam Butt is another brother-in-law of Sharif's brother, who is a financial adviser and syndicate adviser to other drug mafia. The report also talks about Sharif family's efforts to cultivate the men in uniform, especially the Army[34]. This was proved by Nawaz Sharif's failed attempt to replace Gen Musharraf as Pakistani Army Chief by Lt. Gen. Ziauddin Head of ISI on 12 October, 1999 and the Army's coup under Gen Musharraf. The justification for involvement in drugs, prohibited by Islam is the plea of corrupting western and Indian markets. The policy has backfired and brought about a state of anarchy in Pakistan and ever increasing population of addicts. Pakistan has three million drug addicts of which half (1.5 million) are heroin addicts from an overall estimated number of eight million heroin addicts of which 75 per cent are less than 35 years of age, with the highest proportion in the 26-30 year age groups. [35, 36]

The Indian drug cartels are mostly dependent on Pakistan's protection. This is the direct result of Pakistan Government's patronage and sponsorship of organised crime and terrorism in India. This is well borne out by the established links of Dawood Ibrahim and interrogation reports of Pakistani ISI agents and unearthing of its links with Muslim Fundamentalist Organisations in the country and terrorists directly as well as through Bangladesh and Nepal. Pakistan support to such ventures has empowered drug syndicates to consolidate and expand their linkages in the region. Nearly over 75% of drugs seizures have their origin in Pakistan and Afghanistan. Both Punjab and Kashmiri militants are being incorporated into the drug and subversive network. Both the ISI reports and CIA reports are indicative of it. In 1992-93, Rs. 1584 crores were transferred through Foreign Contributors Regulation Act (FCRA), of which substantial amount was given to militants and fundamentalist organizations; Hawala and FERA are other channels. Hizb-ul-Mujahideen, Al Jihad Al Barq, Al Umar and Muslim Mujahideen received Rs. 56 lacs, 50 lacs, Rs. 44 lacs, Rs. 22 lacs and Rs. 40 lacs respectively[37]. Militant leaders like Wadhawa Singh Babbar and Wassan Singh Zaffarwal utilised Pakistani smugglers to induct arms and ammunition into Punjab. Young boys from border villages in Punjab were recruited to work as couriers, gradually they graduated to be militant leaders. Buta Singh a small time opium smuggler, graduated to smuggling of arms and later joined Babbar Khalsa. Even after joining insurgent organisations, these smugglers-terrorists continued the narcotics trade with benefit[38]. Arrest of Gurvinder Singh an associate of Paramjit Singh Panjwar, Chief of Khalistan Commando Force for trafficking of 24 Kg of heroin confirms the drug smuggling activities of Punjab terrorists and their links with Pakistani smugglers. For this even a cell was established in Nepal. Ali Bhatti, a former member of Pakistan Punjab Assembly has close links with Anis Ibrahim brother of Dawood Ibrahim, he controls all drug smuggling into India. Intelligence reports also indicate that Ali Bhatti brokered a $ 40,000 arms deal for Sikh terrorists with the arms dealers in Peshawar. The narcotic trade in the sub-continent is controlled from Karachi and UAE[39].

With the unearthing of a heroin manufacturing factory in Azadpur Mandi in Delhi on 30 November 1999 by the Narcotics Control Bureau and capture of 50 Kgs of heroin and 56 litres of Acetic Anhydride in simultaneous raids in Delhi and Bangalore confirms that drugs have reached the heart of the country and Delhi is not only a transit route but heroin capital of the country. The raid revealed that Sayyed Abul Ala, the owner of the unit in Azadpur, his son and other accomplices have an established set up for procurement of heroin, a medicine sales unit as a cover up and links in Bangalore where Ala was caught with 18 Kgs of heroin[40].

Pakistan has paid a heavy price for its support to the Afghan war as country's drug problem is linked to it. Drug mafia is operating in connivance with the ISI, who justify heroin trade to acquire weapons. Karachi city itself has 1.7 million drug addicts. UN drug agencies estimate that 30 billion dollars worth of heroin is manufactured in Pakistan. The drug mafia controls Pakistan's political structure. Seizure of Kabul had opened a new corridor for Pakistan and Afghan drug traffickers to Central Asian Republics and Russia. The volume of opium pushed through has gone up to hundreds of tons per year. A kilogram of heroin costing $ 7000 to $ 10,000 is sold at as high as $ 1,50,000. The seizures of raw opium had gone up from 260kg on Afghan-Tajikistan border in 1994 to 2,000 Kg in 1996. The profits were used both by the Taliban and the Tajikistan opponents to purchase arms[41]. The smuggling operations do not cease at Pakistan's borders; it flows and flourishes right into India. Apart from smuggling arms to Punjab and Kashmir Militants as a sequel to the Bombay blasts in 1993, 7,700 kg of RDX and a sizeable catch of Kalashnikovs rifles were recovered.

ARMS

There is truth in the claim that over 140 terrorist bands in nearly 50 countries of disputed territories were connected in some way or the other in 1976[42]. The financial dimensions of the world's arms trade are even higher than the drug trade. Erstwhile Warsaw Pact countries reeling under a post-cold war economic down slide are reaping a bonanza with the supply of Kalashnikov rifles and related ammunition. The AK 47 and its variants are being manufactured in Hungary, Romania, Germany (Old GDR) and Poland. In addition China, Finland, North Korea and the Serb portion in Bosnia, South Africa, Egypt and Pakistan have also cloned the weapons to derive benefit from its world wide demand, .55 millions copies of these weapons have already been made so far[43].

The UZI sub machine gun produced in Israel is essentially supplied in Europe and 20,000 weapons per year are produced. Strella, the favourite of terrorist groups is again manufactured in all the old Warsaw Pact countries. The weapon has also been produced in Egypt and China by reverse engineering. The disintegration of the Soviet Union and dissolution of Warsaw Pact countries has resulted in proliferation of small arms in the former Soviet Union and Europe due to economic and social pressure. Scrapping of arms in the erstwhile East Germany has become a problem. It will require a work force of 4,000 strong for 40 years to dispose off the surplus ammunition. Lithuania has bought 10,000 of the latest. AK 47 rifles at the rock bottom price of $ 150 to 200. The world wide trade in illegal arms can be visualized by the fact that a cargo ship carrying 1,500 missiles and anti-tank weapons of Russian and Chinese manufacture to Bosnia was reported by Italian TV network. Supply of arms to LTTE through sources in the Far East and West and Pakistan's supply of arms to Bosnia militants has often been reported.

The proliferation of small arms in South Asia commenced during the Afghan war (1974-1988) but it really escalated after its culmination. USSR on one hand and USA on the other hand pumped in millions of weapons into the region. The resentment of the devout Muslims towards pro-communist khalq encouraged Pakistan indoctrinated Islamic militants with US connivance entering the fray. The American support to Mujahideen through CIA's covert operations was managed by Pakistan's ISI, who were made responsible to identify the beneficiaries. Kalashnikov assault rifles and Strella missiles reached Afghans through the double supply routes and it is confirmed that at least 40 per cent of these arms never reached the target groups. Six million dollars worth of arms were assessed to have been pumped in by the USA and Saudi Arabia[44].

According to Christopher Smith, a senior research fellow at the centre for Defence Studies at Kings College, London, since the early 1980s CIA had been buying hardware from such disparate sources as Turkey and China to feed the Mujahideen. In 1983, 10,000 tonnes of weapons were supplied to Afghan fighters through Pakistan and supply rose to staggering 65,000 tonnes in 1987. An estimated $ 9 billion were spent by United State National Security Council and the CIA to arm the Mujahideen. The arms were mainly routed through the ISI and massive amount of weaponry of war pilfered by the ISI functionaries. According to one estimate ISI had access to nearly 3 million Kalashnikovs in the year 1993, the rest of the arsenal ended up in arms bazars in NWFP[45].

Senior Pakistan police officers have admitted that there are half a million Kalashinkov rifles in NWEP which enables drug mafia to maintain ethnic armies. Add to it the arms reported to have been siphoned off by ISI meant for Afghanistan (the details of which have been covered in the Part on Kashmir), one has a complete picture of the drug menace, illegal arms availability and the nexus operating under ISI patronage. According to Brigadier Youssaf, the ISI was handling 65,000 tons of weapons per year. The former director of Fulbright Foundation observed that the Mujahideen had no where the amount of weaponry credited to them, the Mujahideen signed false receipts and arms were sold to private arms dealers, with both parties sharing the profit. The money thus made was piled into drug trade. The arms pipe line to Afghanistan leaked due to its distance requiring trans-shipments (loading and unloading), which made it prone to pilferage. The contracted transport operators made money both from drugs and arms. Mohammed Ayub Khan Afridi who began as a transporter became a drug baron[46]. Armed convoys passing through restricted areas in NWFP were taxed by the local chieftains. Weapons influx increased as Soviet pull out became inevitable, both sides pushed in large quantities of weapons and equipment, Soviet from Central Europe and USA directly to the Mujahideen. Failure at Jalalabad resulted in demoralisation of the Mujahideen and they started dumping their weapons at Karachi, the main drug center, which also became the arms centre with 1,00,000 Kalashnikovs as did Baluchistan.

The Fallout

The increase in drugs and arms resulted in increase in covert operations and advocacy of Islamic Jihad came in as a handy cover-up. Benazir Bhutto failed to curb the activities of ISI and drug barons inspite of the arrest of Gen. Haq and removing Gen. Gul. The disclosures made by Prime Minister Nawaz Sharif that the then Army Chief Gen. Aslam Beg had approached him with the proposal that the drug money be used to fund covert operations next door[47]. This was a masterpiece of doublespeak as by then the ISI involvement in the proxy war in Kashmir was well established. The BCCI bank scandal, donations to Pakistan Army and elections of IJI MPAs with deep drug connections clearly brings out the links of the drug barons, ISI and later Army in sponsoring terrorism in Punjab and Jammu and Kashmir and their links with the fundamentalist organisations.

This is also the main reason for violence in Pakistan as sectarian groups like Sipah-e-Sahaba and Sipah-e-Mohammed both are linked to crime syndicates. The weapons seized up to 1994 in Army operations in Karachi (888)) is only a drop in the ocean. It is estimated that 4000 weapons entered Karachi every day. The drug barons in NWFP, Lahore and Karachi are pushing drugs into India. Dera Baba Nanak, Run of Kutch and Bombay are the main areas.

The propagation of struggle in Kashmir was a front for drug operations, in addition, it helped in recruiting foreign mercenaries from Libya, Egypt and other Middle East countries apart from Afghanistan. According to sources in Pakistan, 5000 of Afghan volunteers are held by the three fundamentalist parties (Jamait-I-Islami, Jamait-e-Ulema-e-Islam, Fazlur Rehman) and Jamait-e-Ahle-Hadees[48]. The sidelining of JKLF and reduction in the number of militant groups is motivated by ISI desire to have an Afghan type control over the militant organisations and give it a fundamentalistic outlook as is evident in the names of the groups like Harkat-Ul-Ansar and Harkat-Ul-Mujahideen. The drug seizures in India escalated from worth 21.74 crore rupees in 1992 to 539 crores in first half of 1995. The drug seizures have also spread territory wise to cover Rajasthan and Gujarat (Sir Creek) [49] apart from J & K and Punjab.

Statistics and analysis clearly indicate that density of small arms and intensity of violence in the areas of conflict is correlated and is the highest in areas in close proximity to the international borders. In Punjab over 90 per cent of militancy related killings and activities took place in the border districts of Gurdaspur, Amritsar and Ferozepur adjoining to indo-Pak border. In Jammu and Kashmir at the height of insurgency upto 1994, the major incidents of violence were in Kupwara, Baramula, Srinagar and Anantnag. Similarly insurgency in the North-East has been more intensive and active and over longer periods in areas bordering Myanmar, Bangladesh (earlier East Pakistan) and recently Bhutan. This is also related to sanctuaries, procurement of arms and training facilities. As was the case in Afghanistan, bulk of the fighting took place in Kandhar, Ghost and Jalalabad areas adjoining Pakistan. In Myanmar the insurgency has remained active in its border areas inhabited by non-Burman ethnic groups. Tamil militancy has been most intensive in the Jaffna peninsula.[50]

THE NORTH-EAST

To complete the picture in the North-East, apart form the Chinese involvement, Bangladesh Intelligence and ISI Nexus and the happening in Myanmar are relevant. In Myanmar, the break-up of the CPB in 1988 resulted in country's most powerful insurgent army fragmenting into small ethnic groups with vast arsenal supplied by Chinese in sixties and seventies. To prevent a link up of armed ethnic insurgent groups with pro-democracy forces, the Military Junta negotiated cease-fire agreements with them and permitted them to retain their weapons. There are at least 30,000 armed members of these ethnic groups beyond government control. This was followed by the Eastern Shan drug lord Khun Sa, surrendering with 15000 of his followers of the Mong Tai Army (MTA). The Myanmar Government struck a deal with him, permitting him to continue his drug operations, if he stops guerilla operations against the government. Khun Sa forged an alliance with the former CPB warlords for drug operations into Yunnan[51]. Agreements with 15 of the 16 ethnic groups during the period 1989 to 1996 is an achievement for SLORC but it has long tem implications for Myanmar and its neighbours in the security field. Retention of arms by ethnic insurgents, retaining of administrative control over their areas, with freedom to engage in business activities (mostly illegal) to support themselves, in real term means business arrangements with drug syndicates and smugglers, resulting in gangsterism, crime and subversion of the economy. Drugs have had its fall out in Yunnan, other neighbouring area and in Manipur and Mizoram in our North-East.

Drugs

Impetus to drug manufacturing and trafficking was provided by the economic decline in the 1980s and Ne Win's socialist policies, which have been further enhanced after the agreement with ethnic insurgent groups from 1989 to 1996. The incentives for ethnic warlords to control the trade is high as most of the trade passes through the border areas of the CPB. The CPB's official policy was to collect 20 per cent of the opium harvested in the area and sell it to traders from Tang Yan, Lashio and other trading centres in the North. The CPB also collected a 10 per cent tax on opium sold in the local markets and a five per cent tax on any quantity leaving the area. With such incentives the opium cultivation of 92,300 ha in 1987 grew to 1,65,800 ha in 1993, heroin production went up from 53 MT to 190 MT and heroin exports from 51 MT to 186.5 MT, with seizures remaining a meagre .2 per cent.[52]. The Burmese blamed the Americans particularly the CIA for sowing the seeds of the narcotics, who had ferried weapons and drugs in support of the KMT 12000 troops in the areas between Salween and the Chinese border[53]. The opium production in the Shan area jumped from 30 tons to 6000 tons by mid 1950, mainly drugs being lifted to Taiwan. U NU's appeal to the United Nations remained unheard. This encouraged other ethnic groups to establish their drug set up to support their insurgent groups and for procurement of weaponry for them.

In 1995, world wide opium production was 4,157 MT an increase of 748 MT over the 1994 production of 3,409 MT. Opium production in South East Asia, estimated to be 2,158 MT in 1994, increased to 2,561 MT in 1995.

Myanmar alone supplies 60 per cent of the US heroin market and its production of 2575 MT of opium grown in 1993 accounted for nearly 50 per cent of the opium production of the world. It is also the biggest opium refinery centre of the Golden Triangle. Acetic anhydride used in the process is mainly smuggled from India, with a small quantity coming from Thailand and Malaysia. The morphine base is refined into two types of heroin, heroin #3 which is smokable and heroin #4, which is 95 per cent refined, is intravenously injected. The former is popular locally in Asia and later variety in the west particularly in USA. Illicit heroin factories were mainly concentrated in the border areas with China, Laos and Thailand. Consequent to the surrender of Mong Tai Armies and challenge posed by new drug armies to Khun Sa has resulted in refining factories shifting to distant places, some close to Indo-Myanmar border. The biggest threat to Khun Sa comes from Wa tribe and the bands of Kokang Chinese.

Drug trafficking into China from the Golden Triangle has picked up as has the density of small arms. The boost to drug trafficking has been provided by the opening up of the Chinese economy and setting up of free trade zones. Over the four years from 1991 to 1993, 14 tons of heroin, 9.7 tons of opium and 3.1 tons of marijuana were seized in China. Pingyan in Yunnan has become a major drug trafficking centre and a semi-open arms bazaar[54]. At first drug runners needed arms to protect themselves and soon the arms trade itself became more attractive. There is substantive arms movement across borders of Myanmar, Thailand, China and other South-Eastern States. The Chinese authorities are worried due to the social disorder as a result of arms trafficking into the South-Western provinces from its borders with Myanmar and leakages of arms from PLA. An arms market is coming up at the border town of Ralli, where weapons like Type 54 Army Automatic pistol can be bought for 1,500 yuan ($ 180) and the price doubles by the time it reaches Kunming. A crack down by Public Security Bureau (PSB) resulted in the recovery of 120,000 illegal weapons, which according to an official of the PSB is just the tip of the iceberg. Most of the weapons used in criminal activities across 24 of China's 31 provinces come from the city of Pingyan, which are mostly smuggled from Myanmar and partly from China. One of the factors aiding and abetting drug and gun running through China is the good transport infra-structure.

The induction of Chinese military weapons and equipment into the Burmese army encouraged them to launch attacks against Mong Tai Army to cut off its base at Homang from its drug growing areas, along with attacks against other insurgents groups like Karens, Kachins and Mons. While it established Rangoon's writ to a limited extent, but it disturbed the established drug routes and resulted in diversifying these into India in the North-West and into Laos, Cambodia and Vietnam in the South. It also led to inter group clashes to control the drug routes. Ethnic groups in CPB's old areas control the Northern areas and others are pushing South. But with large scale availability of weapons, it is an uphill task. Weapons are leaking through China and Thailand. The Thai Army's involvement in arms trading is well established and confirmed by a large cache of 1500 tons of weapons at Chantaburi. Cambodia is a haven for drug smuggling and 600 kg of heroin moves through it every day[55]. Americans supplied the Thai military worth 1 billion dollars of arms, some of which were passed onto the Khmer[56]. The glut of arms in Thai arms bazaars has reduced costs of AK 56 rifle to $ 20 and in Combodia $ 8[57]. Thai starving soldiers sell every thing to feed their families. Thailand's central location amongst the ongoing insurgencies in the region has added to its involvement in drugs and illegal arms trading. Rangoon has benefited economically due to money laundering essentially through real estate transactions. The chances of redemption are bleak as 3,00,000 farmers in Shan state depend on drug cultivation for living[58].

Consequent to the break up of CPB and Chinese throwing open its borders to Myanmar as a part of its economic offensive, Chinese had to pay a heavy price for it. It has 2,50,000 drug addicts and over 1000 HIV positive cases. Chinese have taken stringent action and a massive search in 1992 yielded 16000 illegal weapons, followed by similar action in 1994. In Guangdong, Chinese authorities executed 51 traders, arrested 1,200 drug dealers and rounded up 10,000 addicts[59]. In China gun running is as profitable as drug running with the Far East arsenal of weapons. Basically there are two overland routes converging onto Kunming, Northern-Kohang-Mongko-Via-Mangshi to Kunming and Southern-Kengtung (near the Laos border) to Kunming. Ethnic Chinese in Hong Kong, Myanmar, Thailand are integrated into the network. From the above routes, subsidiary smuggling axes have been established through Thailand and India. The hub of Western India axis is Mandalay, from where smuggling through Manipur, Mizoram and Bangladesh originates. Indian axis is also the main source of Acetic Anhydride used in the production of heroin. There has been cooperation between Rangoon and New Delhi, with regular meetings between nodal agencies. In 1994, the meeting at Tamu decided to dismantle heroin factories on the chidwin R. Burmese claim to tackle drug menace through sub-regional arrangements with China, Thailand, Laos and India and later on incorporating Bangladesh has met with limited success due to involvement of the members of the Junta and the Burmese Army in smuggling and lack of control and infrastructure in the border areas. Indian insurgents have become a part of the conduit for drug smuggling in connivance with local police and officials for monetary benefits and the access that it gives to the foreign arms markets. This is also a factor in Naga-Kuki strife to control NH 39.

With the shifting of drug routes North in Myanmar and drug refineries based on Chindwin R, Kaleymo is emerging as a drug centre. It is also being developed as a communication centre with roads from China and India coverging there. Mokokchung in Nagaland in the North may emerge as a drug route with drugs coming in from Pangsha and other areas at the border in Mon and Tuensang districts. Moreh in the south has always been on the smuggling route and with new drug routes emanating from Kaleymo towards Bangladesh and India, the North-East is bound to feel its sway.

Golden Triangle has been historically the main supplier of drugs to India, through its 1650 km border with Myanmar and approximately 20 Kg of heroin is smuggled daily through this border. Some 70 odd refining factories have come up near Indo-Myanmar border in the last ten years, most of them are mobile[60]. Drug trafficking across Indo-Myanmar border is facilitated due to the barter trade agreement between both the countries as common ethnic groups straddle the border. Smuggling is also facilitated due to hilly jungles with thick forestation, which is also the domain of insurgent groups in both countries. Burmese insurgents protect and push drugs up to the border on their side, which are then picked up and delivered by the North-East insurgents, particularly both factions of NSCN and the Kuki Chin groups. Smuggling activities have increased across the border right from Tirap in Arunachal Pradesh, Nagaland, Manipur and Mizoram. Unlike the west the main channels are through insurgents rather than drug syndicates. Beyond the Border States in the North-East the drugs are sent both by land and air to Bangladesh, Bombay, Calcutta and right up to Delhi.

Arms

Consequent to the meeting at Tamu in 1994, regular meetings with Myanmar authorities resulted in the success of operation Golden Bird, resulting in capture of Chinese AK 56, M 26 and G3 Rifles and over 10,000 rounds of ammunition[61]. Interrogation revealed that weapons were picked from Wyakaung beach on Myanmar-Bangladesh border and source was the Thai arms Bazaar. The consignment consisted of 775 AK 56 Rifles, 65 guns, 10 Grenade Launchers, anti-tank and anti-personnel mines, 50 pistols and 2,00,000 rounds of assorted ammunition[62]. Bulk of the arms were meant for ULFA. Intelligence agencies have confirmed beyond doubt that Bangladesh Intelligence and ISI are continuing their policy of arming the Indian insurgent groups. The Bangladesh Intelligence is acting as a conduit for insurgents and drug money is being passed to bank accounts in Bangkok for purchase of weapons in Thailand. Weapons are moved by sea to Teknaf and other areas near Cox Bazar and then moved by land through Chittagon Hill Tracts (CHT), then along Indo-Myanmar border and into the North Cachar (NC) Hills. A well established set up (Atlee Command) has been created under the overall control of NSCN (IM) for training and coordination of movement of arms for the North-East insurgents. The help of Burmese and Bangladesh insurgents in the movement of weapons has also been confirmed.

In the North-East unlike in the west, drug trafficking and arms trafficking are not co-terminus so far essentially due to aversion to drugs by the North-Eastern insurgent groups. The interest of insurgent groups in drug trafficking is limited to control of routes of their interest and as a source of funds for arms procurement. This is also helped by the difficult terrain on the Indo-Myanamr border and absence of roads. Coxs Bazar in Bangladesh has emerged as a major arms and drug centre. We need to keep an eye on it, as powerful drug runners/syndicates may make assistance in arms procurement conditional to assistance/help in drug smuggling. The fact that the NC Hills corridor is linked with Sylhet in Bangladesh and is the corridor for main avenues of insurgent movements into Nagaland, Manipur and Assam, clearly points to a nexus between insurgent groups and the Bangladesh Intelligence.

The Chinese supported the Naga and other insurgents of the North-East for over twenty years up to the seventies through the CPB, with arms supplied by them. Similar arrangements through the ethnic insurgent groups of Myanmar via the newly established drug and arms smuggling syndicates has high possibilities. The task is made easier by the Bangladesh Intelligence and ISI nexus with its well established network in the North-East.

It is a well established fact that most of the arms in the North-East come from the Far-East as has been amply proved by operation "Golden Bird" in 1995 and operation "Leech" in February 1998. Subsequent seizures or arms and 50 Kg of heroin in May 1998 near Narcodom Island also proves beyond doubt the well established arms and drug trade that flourishes in the Far-East, whose main beneficiaries are the insurgent groups in Myanmar and South Asia, of these NSCN (IM) and ATTF in the North-East and CNA of Myanmar were identified in operation "Leech". While the cooperation between the Indian Army and the Burmese Army has been largely responsible for these successes, the intelligence agencies particularly RAW have been playing their own game (apparently arms consignment captured during operation Leech was initiated by RAW). The MOD directive of 27 July 1998 asking the Services not to undertake joint operations due to objections likely to be raised by Myanmar and Thai authorities is all too confusing, specially when the military intelligence and the Indian Ambassador had definite intelligence of arms consignments being routed through the sea off the Andamans in later half of 1998. This has upset the Myanmar authorities and confused our own security forces in the North-East[63]. One of the main beneficiaries of this stand off policy will be the LTTE as most of the arms in the North-East come from the Far-East markets and via LTTE, which has exploited the sea routes both for narcotic smuggling and for arms.

The LTTE has been exploiting the open seas East of Andamans for shipping gold and narcotics to the west and weapons from the East. According to a well informed Sri Lankan spokesman, "The LTTE is the Suez Canal". It provides a short route to link the East and the West. The LTTE links the narcotic barons and gun runners of the East and the West. It has created a new route. Cambodia to Myanmar to Mullatiou (in Sri Lanka) via the uninhabited Islands of Andaman and Nicobar group, from where the trail leads to the Cape of Good Hope, then to the Mediterranean and Latin America. The blowing up of MV Ahath by Kittu, when intercepted by the Indian Navy in 1993 which was carrying arms collected from Thai and Cambodian sources mid sea proves the established nexus. LTTE's arms purchases included SAM missiles from Cambodia. The Russian made SAM 7 were sold (1 million a piece) by corrupt Royal Cambodian Army Officials to LTTE and Khun Sa. The purchases have been confirmed by Robert Karnoil, Regional editor of Jane's Asia Pacific Region. According to Thai intelligence, the SAM contingents were moved from South West of Cambodia to Thailand then across Kra Isthumus to Phuket. LTTE invests money in legitimate ventures, making it difficult to trace its origin, the methodology of money laundering is similar to that of Latin America drug cartels. 80 per cent of the drugs in America are shipped from the Golden Triangle through the LTTE network. LTTE is in business for themselves and others, the North-East insurgents find the arrangement handy.[64]

ISI of Pakistan has exploited its links with Indian drug smugglers to incorporate LTTE's drug links to mutual benefit as most of the drugs smuggled to Europe from Sri Lanka enters from India. Sri Lankan drug traffickers have established close links with Indian and Pakistani drug traffickers as it gives them access to drugs from the Golden Crescent and Sri Lanka has become a major transit country. In may 1993, 66. Kg of heroin was seized at Salem, the consignment was meant for Sri Lanka. Tamil refugees from Sri Lanka settled in Tamil Nadu are increasingly involved in drug trafficking. For ISI it serves the dual purpose of propagating fundamentalism and terrorism and drug trafficking to finance it. Chennai, Bangalore, Salem and Tuticorin are emerging as bases for the same. It also provides opportunity for money laundering, which helps both LTTE and ISI. Dawood Ibrahim is reported to have established links with LTTE, which has helped him in drug trafficking and establishing bases for subversive activities. LTTE has travel agencies in Mumbai and LTTE sympathisers (known as Capt. David) own shipping companies provides a network for smuggling drugs, arms and explosives to Sri Lankan and on to Europe and UK, where both Dawood and LTTE have establishments Umarji Moosa Patel, a Dawood ally in UK, coordinates operations with Surai Kumar Selvadurai, an LTTE agent based in Dusseldorf in Germany.[65]

Smuggling on India-Sri Lanka route is reaching alarming proportions as much as 123 kg of heroine is seized in the south, of a total of 766 kg in rest of India in the year 2001. During 2002 up to June 160 kg were intercepted in the south zone compared to 134 kg in the rest of India. Drugs reach Tamil Nad by road and then sent to Sri Lanka by boat from Tuticorn or by air from Chennai. It is suspected that a portion of it lands in the hands of LTTE before it is sent to destinations in Western Europe and North Africa. LTTE is helped in this by its close connections with the underworld in Chennai and Bangalore. LTTE supporters have made specials inroads into both the Dawood Ibrahim and Chota Rajan camps in Bangalore where Tamilians are in large numbers. LTTE has an iron grip on the Chennai underworld which has helped it to smuggle heroine to Sri Lanka and then to Europe and Africa.[66]

Nepal in recent years has not only come up as a safe haven for criminals and terrorists but has also attracted drug traffickers due to its conducive banking facilities for money laundering. Its open borders with India (800 Km) and proximity to Pakistan and Myanmar makes it attractive for drug trafficking. Criminals and terrorists from Northern India have always found sanctuaries in Nepal and Terai area of Indo-Nepal border has always been a criminal's arena[67]. Late Mirza Dilshad Beg an underworld lord of the Terai region operated both from Khatmandu and Baharaich in UP controlling illegal trade in the area. He exercised influence both as a member of Nepalese Parliament and an underworld don and is reported to have links with Dawood Ibrahim. Narcotic smuggling to Nepal started at a small scale due to presence of illicit opium cultivation in the adjoining hill areas of UP but with drugs network expanding, Nepal has become a major transit country for drugs both from the Golden Crescent and the Golden Triangle. Heroin is funneled into Nepal from India and from Pakistan through India and from Myanmar, Thailand and Hong Kong for onward despatch to Europe and USA[68]. There are reports that apart from narcotics, gold is also smuggled from Hong Kong, Thailand and Dubai through Nepal by the Indian smugglers[69]. It is emerging as a base for organised crime, drug trafficking and terrorist activities. ISI has developed an effective network in Nepal and used it as a sanctuary for its operatives and terrorists.

RDX's Deadly Trail

RDX has become the explosive elixir of the Kashmir Militants and Punjab Terrorists to revive their movements. Inspired by their example the North-East insurgents have started using RDX based IEDs to target Security Forces. In recent times a police unit was attacked on 19 December 1998 in Dhubri Distt. Of Assam killing 10 people and a Car Bomb near Assam Tea Centre in Guwahati killed 6 and injured 46[70]. The North-East insurgents displayed their expertise in the use of RDX explosive during the attack on Nagaland Chief Minister SC Jamir near Piphema on 29 November 1999 when they engineered fourteen blasts during the attack. The arrest by Delhi Police of Bangladeshi national Sayed Abu Nasir with 2 KGs of RDX and his links with ISI and Osama bin Laden's group points to both the source and links of induction of RDX into India. Similarly, in November 1998, Nepal Police had recovered 18.75 KG of RDX from a room in a hotel in Khatmandu suburb. The room's occupant later captured was Lakhbir Singh of the Khalistan Zindabad Force. On 18 October 1998, Army recovered 800 kg of high grade explosive in Baramula sector. The haul of RDX in 1998 was 1,200 kg, the highest ever so far. The Home Minister LK Advani in a statement in the Rajya Sabha on 1 December, 1999 said that the central and state Govts. have recovered over 4,000 Kg of RDX during raids in the year 1998-1999. The explosive is being pumped in through Nepal and Bangladesh[71]. The entire seizures trail leads to Pakistan. While the brunt of RDX attack is faced by the Security Forces, its terror dimensions in urban civil areas are amply brought out by seizures in Delhi, Bombay, Gujarat, Punjab and Rajasthan and the capture of ISI operatives tasked to target such areas. It is part of the urban terrorist tactics, which the ISI is exploiting through various insurgent groups.

Conclusion

With the induction of RDX, light weapons like SAMs and ever increasing availability of financial resources through laundering of drug money, the weaponry of insurgents has attained a high degree of technological sophistication, which has in certain cases given the insurgents and militants an edge over the Security Forces. The Chinese had agreed to supply SAM 7 and RPG anti-tank rockets to Mujahideen in Afghanistan in 1980. In 1986, the US supplied 900 stinger missiles, resulting in 296 soviet aircrafts being shot down at the cost of 340 stringer missiles fired. Soviet Strella 2 downed 47 aircraft at the cost of 510 missiles fired[72]. Today, a large number of terrorist/insurgent groups are in the possession of man-portable SAM's, LTTE has shot down five Sri Lankan Airforce aircraft in the last few years. According to reports 560 Stinger missiles out of stocks supplied to Afghan Mujahideen were missing; of these some appeared in Iran and 312 were sold in the open market at Landi Kotal in Pakistan in 1993.[73] This technological upgrade in the weaponry of the insurgents has increased their range, lethality and accuracy for destruction with minimum cost in terms of casualties to them.

The above discussion should put the threat posed by the proliferation of weapons and drug trafficking in our neighborhood both in the North-West and the North-East in the correct perspective. It is not possible to control the spread of small arms without an effective control over drug trafficking and money laundering. The propagating countries, Pakistan in the North-West and Pakistan and Bangladesh in the North-East must realise that the cost that they themselves have to pay for it will be prohibitive, the signs of which have already fermented in Pakistan. Similarly, Bangladesh must realise that unless spread of small arms and light weapons though its territory is controlled, it will fall prey to the evil. The Rohingiya insurgents should be a cause of worry for Bangladesh as they have reportedly been trained by the Hekmatyar group of Afghan Mujahideen, with funds provided by Rohingyas settled in Saudi Arabia, Dubai, Kuwait, Malaysia and Bangladesh. There are 3000 Bangladeshi mercenaries involved in the Afghan war. Without controlling the spread of arms, cooperating in the control of insurgent groups, these will turn inwards and escalate violence within as terrorists, drug traffickers, and arms dealers do not recognise countries and their boundaries.

REFERENCES

1. Bruce Hoffman, Holy Terror: The implications of Terrorism motivated by a Religious Imperative, RAND Paper, p. 7834, (RAND, Santa Monica, 1993).
2. Mohamad Youssaf and Adkin, *The Bear Trap, Afghanistan—untold Story*, Jang Publications, Lahore, 1992, p. 81.

3. The Anti-Mafia Joint Committee Proposals for a Crime Free Economy, Document presented to the presidents of the House of Parliament of Italy on 29 July 1993, p. 2.
4. United Nations Drug Control Programme (UNDCP), Drugs and Development – UNDCP Technical Series No.1 Discussion paper by UNDCP for the world summit for Social Development, p. 2.
5. Ehrenfeld, Rachel, Narco Terrorism, 1990, pp. 86-88.
6. UNDCP n4 above, p. 9.
7. US Department of State, 93 International Narcotics Control Strategy Report (INCSR), p. 219.
8. United Nations, 'Report of International Narcotic Central Board (INCB) for 1995 and Ehrenfeld, p. 186.
9. *Ibid.*
10. Special Report on arms smuggling, "A Lethal Invasion", in India Today, 15 February 1996.
11. Bureau of Narcotics Matters, US Dept. of State 1994, International Narcotics Control Strategy Report (INCSR), p. 3.
12. *Hindustan Times*, 14 July 1997, Kabul Opium output worries UN officials.
13. *Indian Express*, 2 December 1999, Heroin gives Taliban its dangerous high.
14. Robert G Wirsing, *Pakistan Security under Zia*, Houndmills Macmillion, 1991, p. 220.
15. Tara Kartha, Spread of arms and instability in Pakistan, *Strategic Analysis* Vol XVI No.8, November 1993.
16. Tara Kartha, "South Asia – The Narcotics and Weapons Linkage-Light Weapons and International Security", Published by Pugwash Conference on Science and World Affairs and IDSA, 1995, p. 74.
17. *International Journal* Vol XLIX No.1, Winter 1993-94, p. 28 as quoted in *ibid*, p. 80.
18. *Indian Express*, 7 December 1998 (Observer News Services).
19. United Nations Report of the International Narcotics Control Board (INCB) for 1995, p. 42.
20. *Indian Express*, 9 December 1998; Golden Triangle Expands by Dadan Upadhyay.
21. NNICC 1996, pp. VII-IX, 2.
22. *The Nation*, 5 May 1999.
23. *India Today*, 15 May 1994, p. 46.
24. n16 above, p. 72.
25. *Dawn*, Karachi, 14 March 1999.
26. Coping with Forex crunch, *Dawn*, 24 October 1998.
27. *Dawn*, Karachi, 13 May 1999.
28. UN International Drug control programme, *World Drug Report*, Oxford University Press 1997, p. 287.
29. INCSR 1995, p. 230.
30. *Ibid.*
31. *The Sunday Times*, 14 September 1997.
32. *The News*, 18 May 1997.

33. *The Nation*, 2 May 1999.
34. *Hindustan Times*, 7 July 1999, ' Many Faces of Nawaz Sharif' by OP Saberwal and PN Jalali.
35. *The Nation*, 14 April 1999.
36. CIA Report on "Heroin in Pakistan Sowing the Wind", The Friday Times, Lahore.
37. Westrate David 1 'Role of Law Enforcement', 1994, p. 96.
38. Ministry of Home Affairs, Govt. of India, 1995, Vora Committee Report, p. 4.
39. Stockly David, UNDCP Law Enforcement Consultant Report, Review of Drug Enforcement Agencies in India and Recommendations for Future Structure and Development, p. 92.
40. *Indian Express* 2 December 1999 and Hindustan Times 2 December 1999.
41. *India Express*, 9 December 1998.
42. *India Today*, 1 February 1999.
43. *Dawn*, 1 March 1993.
44. Bakhtiar News Agency report dated 5 January 1992 as quoted in *Asian Strategic Review*, 1992-93, p. 215.
45. INCSR 1995, p. 231.
46. *Friday Times*, September 3, 1993 as quoted in n 6 above.
47. *Washington Post*, 12 September 1994.
48. *Herald*, November 1994, p. 29.
49. *Statesman*, 31 August 1995.
50. Light weapons and International Security, IDSA Paper 1995, pp. 56-58.
51. Current History Asia, December 1996, p. 437, Narco Politics in Burma, Bertil Lintener.
52. Asia, February 1994, Janes Intelligence Review, p. 85.
53. Bertil Lintener, Cross Border Trade in Golden Triangle Boundry Research Press, 1991, p. 13.
54. *Asia Week*, 25 August 1995, p. 42.
55. *Asian Age*-(Interpole), 17 August 1995.
56. *Asian Wall Street Journal* in the Asian Recorder, July 23-29, 1994, p. 24126 as quoted in n16.
57. *Asian Age*, 12 May 1995.
58. *Asian Age*, New Delhi, May 10 and 17, 1995.
59. *Asian Age*, New Delhi, 16 May 1995.
60. Vora Committee Report, p. 5.
61. *Asian Age*, 14 August 1995.
62. *Outlook*, 1 February 1999.
63. *Ibid.*
64. *Asian Strategic Review* 1992-1993, IDSA, p. 210.
65. *Out look*, p. 15, 1997.
66. *Hindustan Times*, 2 June 2002 .
67. Westrate David 1, The Role of Law Enforcement, 1994, p. 81.
68. Vora Committee Report, p. 4.
69. n67.

70. Prashant Dixit, "Proliferation of Small Arms and Minor Weapons", *Asian Strtegic Review* 1992-93, p. 219.
71. *Hindustan Times*, 2 December 1999.
72. *Jang*, 10 January 1993.
73. *Ibid.*

Index